SLOW TRAVEL

Dorset

Local, characterful guides to Britain's special places

T0203404

Alexandra Richards

EDITION 4
Bradt Guides Ltd, UK
The Globe Pequot Press Inc, USA

Fourth edition published August 2024
First published 2012
Bradt Guides Ltd
31a High Street, Chesham, Buckinghamshire, HP5 1BW, England
www.bradtguides.com
Print edition published in the USA by The Globe Pequot Press Inc,
PO Box 480, Guilford, Connecticut 06437-0480

Text copyright © 2024 Alexandra Richards
Maps copyright © 2024 Bradt Travel Guides Ltd; includes map data ©
OpenStreetMap contributors
Photographs copyright © 2024 Individual photographers (see below)
Project Manager: Emma Gibbs
Cover research: Pepi Bluck, Perfect Picture

ISBN: 9781804691687

British Library Cataloguing in Publication Data
A catalogue record for this book is available from the British Library

Photographs © individual photographers and organisations credited beside images & also
from picture libraries credited as follows: Alamy.com (A); Dreamstime.com (DT); Hampshire
Cultural Trust (HTC); Shutterstock.com (S); Superstock.com (SS)

Front cover Pulpit Rock, Portland Bill (Stephen Emerson/A)
Back cover Sunset over Eggardon Hill (Andrew Martin/DT)
Title page The much-photographed Gold Hill in Shaftesbury (chrisdorney/S)

Maps David McCutcheon FBCart.S. FRGS

Typeset by Ian Spick, Bradt Guides
Production managed by Gutenberg Press Ltd, printed in Malta
Digital conversion by www.dataworks.co.in

Paper used for this product comes from sustainably managed forests, recycled and
controlled sources.

AUTHOR

Alexandra Richards (⌀ alexandrarichards.net) grew up in Dorset, where she developed a love of rural life, the natural world and outdoor pursuits. Following a degree in Modern European Languages at the University of Durham, Alex became a freelance travel writer and photographer. Based Australia for many years, Alex has now returned to live in Dorset and is loving being back in the place she has always referred to as 'home'.

FEEDBACK REQUEST

At Bradt Guides we're aware that guidebooks start to go out of date on the day they're published – and that you, our readers, are out there in the field doing research of your own. You'll find out before us when a fine new family-run hotel opens or a favourite restaurant changes hands and goes downhill. So why not tell us about your experiences? Contact us on ⌀ 01753 893444 or ✉ info@bradtguides.com. We will forward emails to the author who may post updates on the Bradt website at ⌀ bradtguides.com/updates. Alternatively, you can add a review of the book to Amazon, or share your adventures with us on Facebook, Twitter or Instagram (@BradtGuides).

ACKNOWLEDGEMENTS

I would like to thank all those who took the time to show me around their businesses, among them farm shops, museums, bed and breakfasts, hotels, campsites, restaurants, and nature reserves. I would also like to thank all of the experts who contributed to this edition. My sincere thanks to John Wright, who showed me the delights of foraging and home-brewed alcohols, and who took time out of his busy schedule to contribute to this book.

My thanks also to the Dorset Wildlife Trust, National Trust and English Heritage for helping me to update the sections relating to the places in their care.

I would like to thank all of my Dorset friends for their anecdotes, advice and practical support, especially during the past few very challenging years since Archie's leukaemia diagnosis. In particular, Kate Whyte, Jane Williams, the entire White family, Vicky Todd, and Lou and Dave Stone. As well as sharing his knowledge of Dorset with us, Steve Broughton is instrumental to us keeping our little smallholding going. My thanks also to the Harwood-Foxes for their support of this project and my family.

Without the help of Young Lives vs Cancer (younglivesvscancer.org. uk) and Dorset children's cancer charities like Teddy20 (teddy20.org) and Amelia's Rainbow (ameliasrainbow.com), I would have found it far harder to write this book while caring for Archie.

I am grateful to Neal Sullivan for assisting me with my research and for his help with the maps for this book. But most importantly I am grateful to him for being willing to make Dorset his home.

DEDICATION

I would like to dedicate this book to my sons Archie and Humphrey. Archie is battling leukaemia as I write this edition, and his bravery inspires me every day. Humphrey was born while I was researching this edition, and it was lovely to share my travels around Dorset with both boys.

AUTHOR'S STORY

I was fortunate enough to grow up in the tiny North Dorset village of Stour Provost, in the Blackmore Vale. It was a magical place for a childhood – I spent hours making camps, picking blackberries, riding ponies and fishing in the River Stour, always accompanied by an assortment of pets, including a sheep named Perky. In those days the village was the domain of dairy farmers and farm workers, and the odd self-appointed squire; it was all rather *Vicar of Dibley*. The school run had to be timed with military precision to avoid being stuck behind the cows crossing the lane for milking; village cricket and the church flower rota were serious business; and the pub was where all the big decisions were made.

When I moved back to Dorset with my family in 2019, after 15 years living overseas, I moved close to where I grew up. People warned me about trying to go back and recapture the past because places and people change. Certainly, things have altered: there are fewer farms, more second homes, more new residents who've escaped to the country, and far more houses and cars. Dorset's profile has been raised by TV programmes and Covid brought a new wave of 'incomers' or 'DFLs' (Down From Londons). Urban trends and tastes have reached us: cafés have vegan menus and at agricultural shows you'll find stalls selling kimchi, kombucha and kefir, alongside the more traditional producers selling Dorset cheese, meat and cream teas.

But I'm frequently reminded that the county's identity, built on centuries of tradition and a special way of life, remains strong. We live opposite one of the Blackmore Vale's few remaining small dairy farms, so we still have the pleasure of seeing cows sauntering down the road at milking time. Recently, I was driving through our village and saw a trailer full of freshly shot pheasants parked on the pavement outside the pub, while members of the shoot were inside having a drink. You see, there's still an authenticity and a simplicity to life here. I love that our existence is tightly linked to the seasons and nature, as it has been for generations. In summer we, and our neighbours, are busy with haymaking. In autumn we gather blackberries and sloes from the hedgerows, and villagers leave their excess apple crop on the roadside for others to share. In winter we watch the leaves fall from the woodland and see the local beagle pack trail hunting over the adjoining fields. In spring we giggle at the cows leaping for joy as they're let out into the fields for the first time in months.

So, while some things have changed, it was the right decision to come back. I now have the pleasure of sharing my love of Dorset with my two sons. I'm endeavouring to give them the same outdoor childhood I enjoyed, which gives me a great excuse to once again build camps, pick blackberries, ride ponies and go fishing in the same valley where I did those things as a child.

I must confess I was once one of the protective Dorset folk who referred to visitors as 'grockles', lamented the summer influx of 'townies' and bemoaned ramblers trampling over our land, but having returned home with fresh eyes and written four editions of this book, I now love sharing the county with anyone who wants to experience Slow Dorset.

SUGGESTED PLACES TO BASE YOURSELF

These bases make ideal starting points for exploring localities the Slow way.

Somerset

SHERBORNE page 108
Huddled at the edge of the Blackmore Vale, this delightful town offers two castles, an abbey and an historic centre with plenty of independent shops.

CERNE ABBAS page 143
A small village showcasing a jumble of architectural styles, best known for its 180-foot chalk carving of a giant, standing naked and proud on a hillside.

LYME REGIS page 178
An ancient seaside town at the heart of the Jurassic Coast and prime fossil-hunting territory. Lyme gets busy in summer but there are quiet spots to stay a few miles inland.

Sherborne

A37

A356

A352

Cerne Abbas

CHAPTER 3
page 174

CHAPTER
page 120

Dorset National Landscape

Dorse

Symondsbury

A3066

Bridport

Burton
Bradstock

A35

DORCHESTER

Bride Valley

Lyme Regis

LYME BAY

A354

A353

SYMONDSBURY page 199
An unspoilt village close to Bridport, and the verdant Bride Valley. Go crabbing at West Bay harbour and walk stretches of the South West Coast Path.

CHAPTER 4
page 226

WEYMO
BAY

WEYMOUTH

DORCHESTER page 124
Dorset's historic county town lies at the heart of Thomas Hardy country. Nearby Maiden Castle is England's largest Iron Age hillfort.

Isle of Portland

KEY

Dorset National Landscape

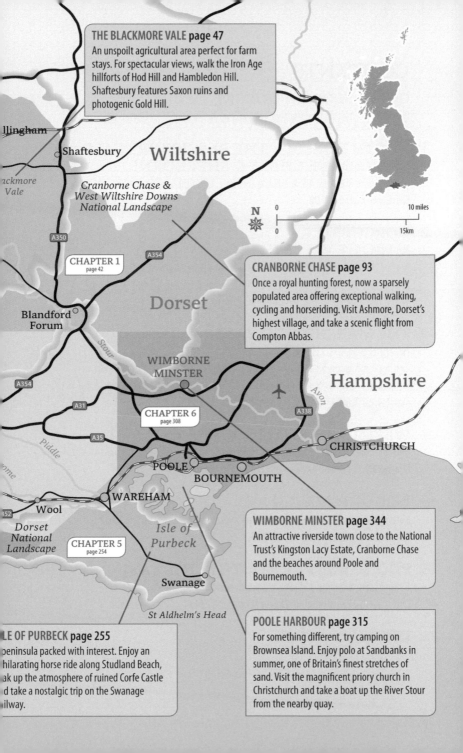

THE BLACKMORE VALE page 47

An unspoilt agricultural area perfect for farm stays. For spectacular views, walk the Iron Age hillforts of Hod Hill and Hambledon Hill. Shaftesbury features Saxon ruins and photogenic Gold Hill.

CRANBORNE CHASE page 93

Once a royal hunting forest, now a sparsely populated area offering exceptional walking, cycling and horseriding. Visit Ashmore, Dorset's highest village, and take a scenic flight from Compton Abbas.

WIMBORNE MINSTER page 344

An attractive riverside town close to the National Trust's Kingston Lacy Estate, Cranborne Chase and the beaches around Poole and Bournemouth.

POOLE HARBOUR page 315

For something different, try camping on Brownsea Island. Enjoy polo at Sandbanks in summer, one of Britain's finest stretches of sand. Visit the magnificent priory church in Christchurch and take a boat up the River Stour from the nearby quay.

LE OF PURBECK page 255

peninsula packed with interest. Enjoy an hilarating horse ride along Studland Beach, ak up the atmosphere of ruined Corfe Castle d take a nostalgic trip on the Swanage ilway.

CHAPTER 1
page 42

CHAPTER 6
page 308

CHAPTER 5
page 254

N

0   10 miles
0   15km

Shaftesbury

Wiltshire

Cranborne Chase & West Wiltshire Downs National Landscape

Dorset

Hampshire

Blandford Forum

WIMBORNE MINSTER

CHRISTCHURCH

POOLE

BOURNEMOUTH

WAREHAM

Wool

Dorset National Landscape

Isle of Purbeck

Swanage

St Aldhelm's Head

llingham

ackmore Vale

Stour

Piddle

Avon

A350

A354

A354

A31

A35

A338

52

ome

CONTENTS

DORSET

I should mention from the outset that this is not your typical travel guidebook. It doesn't attempt to cover every aspect of the county and analyse all the accommodation and eateries. Instead, it is a personal look at what I love about Dorset, highlighting the elements that I believe encapsulate Dorset-ness and the Slow approach. There are, of course, many more places that fit the bill than I could squeeze into this book, so I must apologise to those that don't get a mention. I am always open to suggestions and you can send me your ideas via Bradt Travel Guides (page 3).

In our fast-paced lives, where multi-tasking and time-saving devices are key to survival, the notion of travelling slowly and mindfully may seem unnatural but it is the perfect antidote to a hectic existence. This is one of a series of guides that builds on the Slow Tourism and Slow Food movements and encourages readers to take the time to explore an area thoroughly and at a relaxed pace, finding out what really makes it distinctive, rather than racing around and ticking off attractions from a glossy brochure. Slow Tourism involves seeking out special landscapes, engaging with local people, savouring the area's produce and discovering local culture and heritage; this book invites you to do just that.

Dorset does Slow very well indeed – its quintessentially English rural landscapes, bountiful local produce, even the lilting Dorset accent has an unhurried, lullaby quality. As I was wandering the county explaining that I was writing a book called *Slow Travel Dorset*, the response was frequently, 'Hmmm, I suppose we are pretty slow around here', accompanied by an enigmatic smile.

It occurs to me that my family, like many Dorset folk, lived in accordance with the Slow ethos but without giving it a label. We bought our meat fresh from a farm in the village, our milk from the local dairy

and our Christmas turkey from Mr Cox in Stour Row; collecting sloes, elderflowers, blackberries and mushrooms was an annual ritual, and homemade sloe gin in time for Christmas was one of the resulting treats. One of the great joys for me in moving back to Dorset is that I have been able to do all of those things again. There is something wonderful about following the rhythm of the seasons in the countryside. Autumn is one of my favourite times of year, when we gather elderberries to make elderberry vinegar, and our hedges and apple trees provide the key ingredients for blackberry and apple crumble.

One of the silver linings of the Covid lockdown was that people began to source their produce locally, and many of us tried to avoid supermarkets altogether. This meant that village shops, farm shops, and local butchers, bakers and grocers really came into their own, and milk vending machines at farms saw a huge rise in popularity. There was a greater connection between producer and consumer, a return to 'Slow' living and 'Slow' food. When travelling through Dorset, there are still plenty of opportunities to buy direct from producers, and I encourage you to do so.

You may also like to consider staying on a working farm, where you chat to the farmer and see for yourself the effort that goes into producing our food and into looking after our environment.

A wise Dorset countryman, one of nature's gentlemen, once said to me in his broad West Country accent, 'I like cities, I do.' I had known him for many years and had barely heard of him setting foot outside his native Blackmore Vale, so I was shocked by this pronouncement. He continued, 'I've never been to one but I like them because they keep all the idiots in one place.' Without wanting to insult the majority of the population, I concede he has a point – a lack of large cities is one of the intrinsic qualities that makes Dorset distinctive and ideal for Slow Travel.

As I chatted with Dorset friends about the places I had seen and things I had done in my quest for suitable material for this book, many of them said, 'I've never been there' or 'I never knew that.' I hope that locals as much as visitors will find this book helps them to become better acquainted with the county and encourages them to view it with the enquiring mind of an amateur sleuth, seeking out what makes Dorset Dorset.

◀ A rural idyll: Cranborne Chase (page 93).

DORSET

The county of Dorset is small, but is yet so varied in its configuration as to present an epitome of the scenery of Southern England. It is a land of moods and changes that knows no monotony, and is indeed so full of hills and dales that there is scarcely a level road within its confines, save by the banks of streams.

Sir Frederick Treves, *Highways and Byways in Dorset*, 1906

Treves's words still hold true – Dorset's geological diversity crammed into a small area has produced varied and intimate landscapes, from fertile vales and chalk downland to pristine heathland and a rugged coastline. Visitors need not fear monotony around these parts.

Dorset lends itself to Slow Travel, and its status as one of only seven counties in England without a motorway seems to emphasise that fact. It has no large cities and its only heavily populated area (Poole and Bournemouth) is discreetly tucked into the southeastern corner. Slow Travel conjures up images of pottering about in unspoilt rural areas and Dorset is one of the most rural counties in England, with the highest proportion of conservation areas in the country, including a National Landscape (formerly Area of Outstanding Natural Beauty) covering 44% of it. Idyllic, bucolic scenes are all around – rolling hills, carefully tended farmland and quaint villages. Visitors are often struck by the number of thatched buildings. In fact, 10% of all the thatch in England is found in Dorset.

North Dorset is largely taken up by the **Blackmore Vale**, a landscape of lush fields defined by ancient hedgerows and dotted with tiny thatched villages. This is traditionally a dairy-farming area, although since the decline in that industry there are far fewer cows than there were when Treves wrote in 1906:

> **Everywhere are there cows, for the smell of cows is the incense of North Dorset.**

The Iron Age hillforts of **Hambledon Hill** and **Hod Hill** provide memorable walks, almost aerial views of the Blackmore Vale and archaeological interest. To the east of the vale is **Cranborne Chase**, once a royal hunting forest and now a sparsely populated area offering exceptional walking, cycling and horseriding. Gentle, rolling chalk downland dominates the centre of the county, which is where the county town, **Dorchester**, is found. The west is more hilly, while the east

THE SLOW MINDSET
Hilary Bradt, Founder, Bradt Guides

**We shall not cease from exploration
And the end of all our exploring
Will be to arrive where we started
And know the place for the first time.**
T S Eliot, 'Little Gidding', *Four Quartets*

This series evolved, slowly, from a Bradt editorial meeting when we started to explore ideas for guides to our favourite part of the world – Great Britain. We wanted to get away from the usual 'top sights' formula and encourage our authors to bring out the nuances and local differences that make up a sense of place – such things as food, building styles, nature, geology, or local people and what makes them tick. Our aim was to create a series that celebrates the present, focusing on sustainable tourism, rather than taking a nostalgic wallow in the past.

So without our realising it at the time, we had defined 'Slow Travel', or at least our concept of it. For the beauty of the Slow movement is that there is no fixed definition; we adapt the philosophy to fit our individual needs and aspirations. Thus Carl Honoré, author of *In Praise of Slow*, writes: 'The Slow Movement is a cultural revolution against the notion that faster is always better. It's not about doing everything at a snail's pace, it's about seeking to do everything at the right speed. Savouring the hours and minutes rather than just counting them. Doing everything as well as possible, instead of as fast as possible. It's about quality over quantity in everything from work to food to parenting.' And travel.

So take time to explore. Don't rush it, get to know an area – and the people who live there – and you'll be as delighted as the authors by what you find.

features heathland and the county's major conurbation incorporating **Poole** and **Bournemouth**. The coastline in the east has fine sandy beaches but as you head west it becomes gradually more dramatic and culminates in the ancient cliffs of the Jurassic Coast.

The **Jurassic Coast** is England's first natural World Heritage Site, joining the likes of the Great Barrier Reef and the Grand Canyon as one of the wonders of the natural world. It was granted its status for its outstandingly diverse geology, capturing 190 million years of the earth's history in just 95 miles, making walking, cycling or sailing along this stretch of coast an exhilarating experience in time travel. It begins with the oldest red stone Triassic rock around Orcombe Point in east

Devon, before it enters Dorset and the Jurassic period, then leads on to the younger Cretaceous period seen in the white chalk stacks at Old Harry Rocks, where the Jurassic Coast reaches its official eastern limit. The grey cliffs around Lyme Regis and Charmouth are rich in the fossils of creatures that swam in Jurassic seas some 190 million years ago. They are constantly eroded by the sea, releasing their fossils on to the beaches, where they are eagerly scooped up by delighted fossil hunters. You don't need to be a geologist to be blown away by the Jurassic Coast and get bitten by the fossil-hunting bug.

Another striking feature on the Jurassic Coast is **Chesil Beach**, a shingle bank stretching for 18 miles between West Bay and Portland and reaching around 40ft at its highest point. Formed by rising seas at the end of the last Ice Age, it protects a large lagoon known as The Fleet, home to a diverse population of resident and migrating birds.

As you wander around Dorset, ancient manmade additions to the landscape stand as reminders that you are walking in the footsteps of much earlier inhabitants. It seems just about every hill you climb has a Neolithic site lying beneath your feet and the countryside is dotted with the telltale lumps and bumps of ancient burial grounds. **Maiden Castle** is the largest Iron Age hillfort in Britain and lies just outside Dorchester, which is laid out along the lines of its Roman antecedent and has the best-preserved Roman townhouse in the country. The Saxons left their mark all over the Kingdom of Wessex, visible in towns like **Shaftesbury**, where King Alfred built an abbey in AD888. **Sherborne** has some delightful medieval buildings and a fine abbey dating from the 15th century. The origin of one of Dorset's most famous landmarks, the **Cerne Abbas Giant** or 'Rude Man', is still much debated. Recent investigations concluded that the 180ft-high figure of a naked man wielding a club, incised into the chalk of the hillside, is most likely Saxon in origin.

Perhaps one factor that has helped to preserve Dorset's character is that significant portions of it have remained in the hands of the same few families for centuries – it is one of the last bastions of feudalism. Numerous large estates still exist and their villages are carefully maintained – the areas around Lulworth Cove (Lulworth Estate) and Abbotsbury (Ilchester Estates) fall into this category. In 1981, Ralph Bankes bequeathed his family's 8,500-acre estate to the National Trust. At its heart is one of Dorset's finest houses, Kingston Lacy (page 351), and it extends all the way to the coast at Studland, with its beautifully unspoilt beach and nature reserve.

Most custodians of the land are making every effort to preserve and protect the very special Dorset landscape. Landowners and conservation organisations across the county are undertaking ambitious rewilding and regeneration projects; in 2023, Dorset became the first county to hold its own COP climate conference. Those who produce food are very conscious of the need to protect the land for future generations and many are employing regenerative and environmentally friendly farming practices like those used at the Symondsbury (page 199) and Chettle (page 97) estates. The old ways of doing things are enjoying a comeback because they tend to be gentler on the environment. While researching this book, I met Toby Hoad of Dorset Horse Logging (⊘ dorsethorselogging.co.uk). He and his French comtois horses were thinning out an overgrown woodland, with the horses able to get into places that machinery just wouldn't reach without causing significant damage. Not only are people like Toby helping to look after our countryside, they are helping to preserve skills and heritage breeds of animal that could otherwise have died out.

One thing that strikes me about Dorset is how happy and proud people are to live here; they consider themselves lucky to dwell in this serene corner of England and are keen to preserve its landscapes and way of life. On your travels you are likely to see the Dorset flag – a white cross with a red border on a gold background – flying outside homes and businesses. Often referred to as St Wite's Cross, it recognises the female Anglo-Saxon saint buried at Whitchurch Canonicorum.

Any Dorset journey is inevitably enhanced by the implausibly delightful place names you encounter along the way; some of my favourites are Whitchurch Canonicorum, Toller Porcorum, Tincleton and Sixpenny Handley. The River Wriggle is found in the northwest of the county and the River Piddle winds through its centre, lined by a string of villages which take their amusing names from it: Piddlehinton, Piddletrenthide, Tolpuddle, Puddletown, Affpuddle and Briants Puddle. While we are on the subject of toilet humour, the town of Shitterton, near Bere Regis, is the butt of its fair share of jokes. I must also give a mention to the village of Fishpond Bottom in the Marshwood Vale, the uncomfortably named Scratchy Bottom near Durdle Door, and its more contented counterpart Happy Bottom in Corfe Mullen near Wimborne Minster.

SOME PRACTICAL MATTERS

HOW THIS BOOK IS ARRANGED

Please note: no charge has been made for the inclusion in the main text of any business in this guide.

Maps

The map at the front of this book shows the area covered in each of the six chapters. In turn, each chapter begins with a sketch map of the area, highlighting the places mentioned in the text. The numbers on the map correspond to the descriptions in the text, helping you to find your way around. The ♥ symbol on these maps indicates that there is a walk in that area. There are also sketch maps for these featured walks.

Accommodation

Dorset is overflowing with special places to stay, from smart hotels to seasonal campsites on fields overlooking the sea.

Special stays

The places to stay listed within this book are a personal selection of bed and breakfasts, campsites, self-catering cottages and one or two very special hotels – places that struck me for their location, friendliness or character, or a mixture of all three.

The hotels, bed and breakfasts and hostels are indicated by the symbol 🏠 under the heading for the nearest town or village in which they are located; self-catering options by 🏡. Camping options, which cover everything from full-on glamping to no-frills pitches, are indicated with a ⛺ symbol.

Food & drink

I have included a cross-section of food and drink options, including farm shops, food producers, cafés, pubs and restaurants. They were selected because they use local produce, serve homemade goodies, have a special character or follow sustainable principles – or a mixture of all four.

Attractions

For attractions, activities and eateries I have listed contact details and, in some cases, opening hours but it is worth checking websites for any changes. I have not listed admission fees as these change regularly, although I have mentioned if admission is free. If a description does not say admission is free, you should expect to be charged.

Getting to & around Dorset

I've given some suggestions for getting to and around each area, including car-free options wherever possible and ideas for cycling and walking. For some parts of Dorset, car-free is not feasible as public transport is limited and the little-known, distinctive places I have tried to highlight are often, by their nature, out of the way and harder to reach than the usual tourist haunts.

General travel information is available at ⊘ visit-dorset.com, and ⊘ traveline.info is useful for journey planning. **Bournemouth International Airport** links Dorset to other domestic and European airports, while **ferries** operate between Poole and Cherbourg. Coaches and trains connect Dorset to other English cities. The main rail operator servicing the area is **South Western Railway** (⊘ southwesternrailway. com), with regular trains from London Waterloo to Gillingham, Sherborne, Dorchester, Axminster (for Lyme Regis), Weymouth, Poole and Bournemouth.

Local buses can be helpful, although services are limited in rural areas and may only operate on certain days of the week. The **Jurassic Coaster** bus is handy; it runs regularly along the coastline between Axminster and Poole, and stops at all the key places en route.

Tourist information & additional resources

I have listed the tourist-information centres for each area at the start of the relevant chapter, along with any websites on specific areas. For general information see ⊘ visit-dorset.com.

For information on the region's arts and food scenes, including a calendar of events and reviews of theatre and film, the *Fine Times Recorder* (⊘ theftr.co.uk) is a handy resource.

MAKING THE MOST OF SLOW DORSET

Dorset's variety means it has a wide appeal – it has much to offer the lover of the natural world, the history buff, gastronome, archaeologist, hiker and adventure-sports enthusiast, just to name a few. I had countless memorable experiences while pottering around Dorset researching this book, and I hope you will be able to enjoy some of them too.

WALKING

Dorset's varied countryside and coastline provide excellent opportunities for walking and you will find some suggestions for short and medium-length walks in each chapter.

Information on walking is available at tourist-information centres and online at ⬧ visit-dorset.com and ⬧ dorsetcouncil.gov.uk, from where you can download guides to some of the most popular trails, including the Wessex Ridgeway and the Stour Valley Way. The Tess of the Vale website (⬧ tessofthevale.com) is packed with suggested walks, some of which are free to access, while others require you to subscribe.

Waymarked with a dragon symbol, the **Wessex Ridgeway** is a ridge-top trail from Marlborough in Wiltshire to Lyme Regis, part of the Great Ridgeway, an ancient trading route between the Devon and Norfolk coasts. The Dorset section begins at Ashmore in Cranborne Chase and runs along a chalk ridge across the centre of the county, providing strikingly unhindered views of the surrounding countryside. Further information is available at ⬧ dorset-nl.org.uk. In contrast, the **Stour Valley Way** takes the low road, following the River Stour for 64 miles from Stourhead to Christchurch, where the river flows into the sea. The Stour Valley Way is waymarked with a kingfisher symbol.

Dorset walks are often packed with history. The county's ancient hillfort settlements make for excellent walks with stunning views. In North Dorset, head to Hambledon and Hod hills, or in the southwest visit magnificent Eggardon Hillfort. In the county's centre you can walk around the Cerne Abbas Giant and the beautiful valley in which he sits, while walking at the Dorset Gap means travelling along ancient rights of way that have seen millions of feet and hooves pass through over the centuries.

The South West Coast Path

The standout piece in Dorset's repertoire of walks is the hugely popular South West Coast Path, which combines heritage, flora, fauna, geology and spectacular coastal scenery. The UK's longest national trail, it runs for 630 miles from Minehead in Somerset to Poole in Dorset's east, tracing the coastlines of Cornwall, Devon and Dorset on the way.

The South West Coast Path website (⊘ southwestcoastpath.org.uk) is extremely helpful for planning and its walk-finder tool can help you choose the right route for you. You can download a range of themed walks of varying lengths and levels of difficulty, including information about where to eat and drink en route. The path is easy to find from most coastal towns and villages or from beaches, and is waymarked by an acorn symbol.

The Dorset section offers some of the most spectacular seaside scenery and the path provides access to the entire length of the Jurassic Coast World Heritage Site, which runs from east Devon to Old Harry Rocks, off Studland. It passes through **Lyme Regis** and **Charmouth**, popular for fossil hunting. Between Charmouth and Seatown is **Golden Cap** (page 193), the highest point on England's south coast; it is a steep walk up from Seatown but the reward is expansive views along the coast, and on a clear day you can see as far as Dartmoor National Park.

One of the most rewarding and popular walks is the short section of the path between **Lulworth Cove** and **Durdle Door**, two of the most spectacular features within the Jurassic Coast World Heritage Site. Durdle Door, a near-perfect coastal arch of limestone rock, lies half a mile to the west of Lulworth Cove. The walk involves some moderately steep climbs along a remarkably well-preserved and photogenic section of coast. A less busy and similarly stunning section of coast is that heading westwards from Durdle Door to Bowleaze Cove on the edge of Weymouth.

A gentle four-mile walk leads from Studland along the cliffs to the dramatic chalk stacks of **Old Harry Rocks** (page 279), from where you can see across to another chalk formation: The Needles, off the Isle of Wight. Early morning is the best time for this walk, when the sun casts its first gentle rays on the crisp, white rock.

The South West Coast Path provides plenty of opportunity for wildlife watching; on a clear day you may be lucky enough to spot basking sharks, seals or dolphins, particularly around **Durlston Country Park** near Swanage. **Portland** and **Poole Harbour** are good for watching resident and migrating seabirds, and you may catch a glimpse of rare butterflies on the Isle of Purbeck's chalk downland.

The South West Coast Path works well in combination with the **Jurassic Coaster bus service** (page 176). Luggage Transfers (✆ 0800 043 7927 ⊘ luggagetransfers.co.uk) is a very clever idea for walkers and cyclists – the company will transport your bags between your stop-off points along the Southwest Coast Path and around the southwest.

HORSERIDING & CYCLING

Horseriders and cyclists can feel vulnerable on Dorset's narrow hedge-lined lanes but there are usually plenty of passing places to pull into out of anyone's way. A network of **bridleways** provides interesting off-road options and is complemented by the Wessex Ridgeway (page 18), the North Dorset Trailway (page 45) and the Castleman Trailway (page 312) in the east of the county. Suggestions for cycling routes and cycle hire are given in each chapter, and there are two detailed cycle rides with maps provided, one in North Dorset (page 80) and one in the Isle of Purbeck (page 259).

Suggested horserides and stables are mentioned where applicable. The British Horse Society (BHS ⊘ bhs.org.uk) is the best resource for horseriders and provides a list of riding establishments offering trekking and instruction. The BHS and ⊘ bedandbreakfastforhorses.co.uk provide lists of accommodation where both you and your horse can stay. There are surprisingly few places in Dorset that offer accommodation for owners and their horses, but one of those is Fishmore Hill Farm at Milton Abbas (⊘ fishmorehillfarm.com). On a second BHS website (⊘ bhsaccess.org.uk) you will find suggested rides and more lists of equestrian establishments.

Some Dorset **beaches** are ideal for memorable horserides along the sand, in particular Studland (page 275), and also certain beaches around Christchurch (page 314). From the east of the county you can ride into the **New Forest**, while North Dorset offers excellent riding through woodland and open countryside, including in remarkable spots like the Iron Age hillfort on **Hod Hill**, **Bulbarrow Hill**, **Okeford Hill** and **Cranborne Chase**.

◀ 1 Walking the SWCP near Durdle Door (page 302). 2 Cycling in Moors Valley Country Park & Forest (page 107). 3 Birdwatching cruise along the Purbeck coast. 4 Learning to sail with Lyme Regis Sea School (page 189). 5 The Jurassic Coast is rich with fossils.

FREE ACTIVITIES WITH CHILDREN IN DORSET

The cost of attractions and activities soon adds up, but there are plenty of free options. The most obvious is a walk and this book suggests some family-friendly routes.

If you're a National Trust member you will have free entry to Corfe Castle, Kingston Lacy and Brownsea Island (ferry costs apply), all of which are fantastic for children. Similarly, English Heritage properties, like Portland Castle, have plenty to entertain and educate.

FORAGING AND PICK YOUR OWN

Can be done on a pick-your-own farm (page 31) or in the countryside with the landowner's permission.

BY THE SEA

You can't beat time spent rock pooling and crabbing. West Bay Harbour and Mudeford Quay are top crabbing spots. The best baits are bacon and squid.

DINOSAURS

Fossil-hunting (page 184) on the Jurassic Coast is fun for all ages. At Spyway (page 290) you can walk in the footsteps of dinosaurs.

FARM ANIMALS

Madjeston Milk Station (page 52), Kingston Maurward Animal Park and Gardens (page 141) and The Walled Garden in Moreton (page 157) all have farm animals, play areas and cafés.

Margaret Green Animal Rescue Centre (page 274) welcomes visitors for a donation.

OUTDOOR SPACES

Durlston Country Park (page 287) has wonderful coastal walks and information on Jurassic Coast geology and wildlife.

Moors Valley Country Park (page 107) has walking trails, bike hire, lakes and a miniature railway. Avon Heath (page 343) is similar. Upton Country Park (page 321) has large gardens, birdwatching and picnic spots.

The RSPB sites at Radipole Lake (page 237) and Lodmoor (page 236) are free, as are the Dorset Wildlife Trust reserves.

Portland's Tout Quarry (page 245) has quirky sculptures and views of the coast. Take care with children as it's on top of a cliff.

At Lulworth Castle (page 301) and Mapperton House and Gardens (page 220) you can visit the café and play area without paying admission for the main attraction.

MUSEUMS

Many museums offer school-holiday activities; some are free entry, including Wareham Town (page 265), Red House (page 337), Tolpuddle Martyrs (page 152), Gold Hill (page 59), West Bay Discovery Centre (page 201) and Bournemouth Natural Science Society (page 332).

Hengistbury Head's visitor centre (page 334) has information on the area's wildlife and prehistory. Combine the visitor centre with a walk, bike or land-train ride to Mudeford Beach.

If you're keen to instil an interest in history in your children, the deserted village at Tyneham (page 300) is likely to make an impression.

BOAT TRIPS

One of the best ways to appreciate the magnificence of the Dorset coastline is by boat. My family thoroughly enjoyed a birdwatching cruise along the coast from Poole, the highlight of which was seeing puffins near Swanage (page 292).

You can hire a boat to potter along a river at Christchurch, Wareham or West Bay, or take a fishing trip out of one of the coastal towns.

SAVOURING THE TASTES OF DORSET

Dorset is ideally suited to the growing and savouring of seasonal, traditional and local food; its fertile soils, long farming history and food heritage combine to provide a rich variety of tasty treats, from fish caught off its coast, to artisan cheeses, breads and ciders. A visit to Dorset would not be complete without sampling Dorset Blue Vinny cheese (page 84), Dorset apple cake (page 24) and Moores Dorset Knob biscuits (page 196). And remember, Devon does not have a monopoly on cream teas – the Dorset version is just as delicious. And if you crave them after you leave Dorset, you can order cream teas online from ⊘ thedorsethandmadefoodcompany.co.uk. You will find many of the county's artisan food producers and suppliers mentioned in this book. You may also like to head along to one of the growing number of food festivals, such as the Dorset Seafood Festival, Sturminster Newton Cheese Festival, and Dorset Food and Arts Festival at Poundbury.

Self-caterers are spoilt for choice when it comes to stocking the pantry, and a picnic is a great way to enjoy the Dorset countryside. In fact, I've made it a family rule that we never leave home without a picnic basket and rug in the car. Rather than trudging around the supermarket, you can make gathering your ingredients into a treasure hunt by calling into local bakeries, markets and farm shops. As you are exploring the country lanes, look out for handwritten signs promising free-range eggs, homemade jams, honey, gooseberries and the like, which usually sit on a wonky table next to an honesty box. In autumn, you'll see piles of apples left outside houses for passers-by to collect. For dessert you can pick up one of the local farmhouse ice creams, such as those made by Madjeston Dairy (page 52) and Purbeck Ice Cream (page 306).

There's no better way to buy milk than from a vending machine at a dairy farm. All you need is a glass one-litre bottle, and most of the dairies sell those. Milk stations became very popular during the pandemic but many are still thriving and offer a range of fresh local produce alongside the milk. I caught up with Abi Williamson, who runs the excellent Madjeston Milk Station near Gillingham (page 52). Abi's business has gone from strength to strength and now includes a café, farm park, playground and more. She explained to me that many of the milk vending machines that closed when people returned en masse to the supermarkets were those that weren't clearly linked to farms. The ones that have survived are those on farms, where people can physically see the link between the dairy herd and the milk, ice cream and yoghurt they produce, and where they can meet (and thank!) the cows.

Drinking Dorset

To wash down your Dorset meal, you could try a locally made cider. In early October, apple-pressing days are held around the county, and many places invite you to bring your own apples for pressing.

My late friend, Alf Wallis, remembered the days when badger leg was eaten in Dorset pubs; happily, these days when you hear someone ordering a half a Badger in the pub they are after a beer from the Hall & Woodhouse Brewery. The brewery's badger logo is a familiar sight around Dorset, as are its quirkily named beers, among them Fursty

DORSET APPLE CAKE: A RECIPE

On every tea-shop menu you will see Dorset apple cake, a truly local treat. Countless different recipes exist, each subtly different, but I really enjoy this slightly lemony one.

Ingredients

8 oz self-raising flour
4 oz butter
4 oz caster sugar
8 oz cooking apples – peeled, cored and diced

Grated zest of 1 lemon
1 medium egg, beaten
2 oz sultanas (optional)

Method

Preheat the oven to 375°F/190°C. In a large mixing bowl, rub the butter into the flour until the mixture resembles fine breadcrumbs. Stir in the sugar, apples, lemon zest and egg, and mix well. If you want to add the sultanas, you can do so now. Put the mixture into a well-greased 8-inch cake tin and bake for 30–40 minutes, or until golden in colour. Serve warm or cold, with or without custard or ice cream.

Ferret, Pickled Partridge and Poacher's Choice (sold under the name Badger rather than Hall & Woodhouse). Hall & Woodhouse is run by the fifth generation of the Woodhouse family and has a formidable history. A Dorset farmer, Charles Hall, founded a brewery at Ansty in 1777, providing beer to the troops during the Napoleonic Wars. In 1847, Robert Hall, the founder's son, went into partnership with George Woodhouse, and the badger was adopted as the brewery's trademark in 1875. It is now a successful independent brewery with a network of over 250 pubs across the south of England. Dorset is well stocked with other established breweries, such as the Piddle Brewery (page 149) and Palmers (page 196).

The county produces its own wine, thanks in no small part to its temperate climate. Furleigh Estate (Salway Ash DT6 5JF furleighestate.co.uk) near Bridport is a dairy farm that has been transformed into a winery producing white, red, rosé and sparkling wines. Cellar-door sales are available (09.30–16.00 Tue–Sat) and winery tours take place from March to October. Wines and gin from the Sherborne Castle Vineyard (sherbornecastle.com) are available at the castle shop (page 116), other local outlets and online. Melbury Vale Vineyard (Redmans Lane, Melbury SP7 0DB mvwinery.co.uk) sells its wines and liqueurs in shops and restaurants in the Shaftesbury area, online, and at their winery shop (10.00–16.00 Fri & Sat). Also near Shaftesbury, Breezy Ridge Vineyard (breezyridgevineyard.com) produces sparkling wines.

With 30 acres of land and 38,000 vines, Langham Wine Estate (Crawthorne, Dorchester DT2 7NG langhamwine.co.uk) is the largest vineyard in the southwest of England. Winery tours can be booked online, and a tasting room and café operate in August and September (10.00–16.00 Wed–Sun). Lyme Bay Winery (lymebaywinery. co.uk) produces delicious fruit wines and fruit liqueurs, as well as cider and mead.

As we all know, dairy farmers have had to diversify. A creative diversification is Black Cow vodka (blackcow.co.uk), a smooth vodka made from milk and with a distinctly creamy quality.

Conker Gin (conkerspirit.co.uk) uses locally foraged botanicals to give its gin a Dorset identity. The company is based near Bournemouth and offers distillery tours. Fordington Gin (fordingtongin.co.uk) is created near Dorchester, and Shroton Fair Gin (shrotonfairgin), launched in 2021, is gathering a loyal following. They have a small store on their farm (The Old Glass House, Ash Farm Courtyard, Stourpaine DT11 8PW ⊙ 09.00–noon Fri & Sat).

DORSET FARMERS' MARKETS

See also ⚭ dorsetfoodanddrink.org and ⚭ visit-dorset.com.

Blandford second Friday of the month (Market Place)
Bridport second Saturday of the month (Barrack Street)
Dorchester fourth Saturday of the month (South Street)
Poundbury first Saturday of the month (Queen Mother Square)
Shaftesbury first Saturday of the month (Town Hall)
Sherborne third Friday of the month (Cheap Street)
Sturminster Newton Tuesday mornings (The Exchange)
Wareham Saturday
Westbourne first Saturday of the month (Landseer Road)
Wimborne Minster third Saturday of the month (Market Square)
Wool every Thursday (D'Urbeville Hall)

GENERAL MARKETS

In addition to the farmers' markets, there are the following general markets.

Blandford Forum Thursday and Saturday
Bournemouth (Boscombe) Thursday and Saturday
Bridport Wednesday and Saturday
Christchurch Monday
Dorchester Wednesday
Poole Thursday and Saturday
Shaftesbury Thursday
Sherborne Thursday and Saturday
Swanage Friday
Verwood Friday
Wareham Saturday

FORAGING

Foraging is nothing new – until around 10,000 years ago all modern humans were hunter-gatherers – but in more recent times interest in foraging has waxed and waned and it is currently enjoying one of its periodic heydays. Foraging was encouraged during World War II, flourished during the hippy years and is now trendy again in our era of environmental awareness. Television shows are devoted to it, celebrity chefs espouse its virtues, and restaurant menus tempt diners with foraged delicacies, such as nettle soup, fish dishes topped with seaweed and just about anything accompanied by wild garlic.

Foraging is the ultimate rebellion against convenience food – there is nothing convenient about scrabbling through brambles, getting plastered in mud and being chased by an irate bull in the pursuit of a few morsels that have already been chewed and rejected by a grub of some description. Yet somehow it appeals to the hunter-gatherer in many of us, including me.

While researching this book I was lucky enough to spend a day foraging at the Kingcombe Centre with the charming and entertaining John Wright (page 223), who regularly appeared on Hugh Fearnley-Whittingstall's *River Cottage* television series. He was kind enough to provide some words for this book on the subject of foraging.

Tips for happy foraging
John Wright ⅋ ediblebush.com

I gave up growing my own fruit and vegetables years ago. Although it was fun and ultimately rewarding it was also unreliable and rather hard work. But my main objection to gardening is that it all takes too long. This book celebrates the concept of Slow Food but gardening, I think, is far too slow. For me, instant gratification is everything. With gardening one needs to prepare the ground, sow the seed, weed, water and worry, and one day, all being well (and sometimes it isn't) you pick. Foraging however is quite a different matter – you just pick.

My foraging career began over 30 years ago when I moved to Dorset (in my village I am described as a 'relative newcomer'). An early passion for wild fungi found full expression in the fields and woods around the farmhouse I rented. 'Top field' would keep me for hours picking field mushrooms – 120 pounds one year – and 'eight-acre field' would supply a magnificently large form of the delicious shaggy parasol. St George's mushrooms in spring, puffballs in summer, field blewits and the riotously colourful wax caps in autumn, and jelly ears and velvet shanks in winter would fill my mushrooming year. Of course everyone thought I was mad and sure to poison myself.

But, mad or not, I am also extremely careful and never, ever eat anything unless I am sure of its name. My best advice to anyone embarking on a mushroom hunt is to do the same. Get a couple (you really need at least two), of field guides and study them carefully. Collect just a few different species at first – no more than one or two specimens of each in case you have picked something rare – and carefully identify them by examining all their characteristics and using the advice in your books. Never jump to conclusions but always match all of the characteristics of your find to the description given. If the book says a species should have a ring on the stem or turns yellow when bruised it really means it – if any characteristic is missing then it must be something else and maybe a deadly something at that.

Identifying fungi is quite a tricky business but once you have a few species committed to memory you are set for life – you do not need to become an expert mycological taxonomist. My magnificent seven edible fungi are easy to identify, common and delicious: the parasol, giant puffball, horse mushroom, jelly ear, cep, charcoal burner and the hedgehog mushroom. If you only choose one then I suggest the last of these. It is the mushroom with everything – delicious, nutty texture, very common, never gets maggots and completely unmistakable. It grows in woodland, often in substantial rings, and has a 'chamois leather' cap with little spines hanging down underneath. Nothing else looks remotely like it, making it the safest of all the wild mushrooms.

It would be remiss of me not to warn you of the species that causes 99% of all poisonings. The yellow stainer looks almost exactly like the field mushroom except the edge of the cap and the base of the stem turn a remarkable chromium yellow when bruised. This fades to brown after about 15 minutes. If you eat a yellow stainer you will have to cancel all engagements for a day or two before recovering completely, sadder but wiser.

Of course there are times when mushrooms are not to be found and, caught by the foraging bug, I determined to explore other wild sources of food. My Dorset farm yielded the familiar blackberries and

---

1 Blackmore Vale dairy cows. **2** Visitors can take a brewery tour of Dorset institution Hall & Woodhouse. **3** Be sure to sample Dorset apple cake. **4** Taking a foraging course in Dorset can be richly rewarding. **5** Volunteer millers at Town Mill in Lyme Regis still produce stoneground flour (page 183). ▶

ALEXANDRA RICHARDS

VISIT DORSET

MSHEV/S

ALEXANDRA RICHARDS

MATT AUSTIN IMAGES/THE TOWN MILL TRUST, LYME REGIS

sloes but I wondered what else might be found and bought several guides to expand my repertoire. Most edible wild plants are easy to recognise. Everyone knows, usually to his or her cost, what a stinging nettle looks like and no-one hesitates when deciding whether the nut they are looking at is a hazelnut or some deadly impostor. Wild plants are, generally, much safer than wild mushrooms. However, some very common and excellent species can be a little more challenging: fat hen, red goosefoot, sea beet and even cherry plums may have the novice forager sensibly consulting a field guide. Incidentally, and I trust I am not putting you off the whole idea entirely, the most deadly of all plant and fungal toxins is found in a very common native plant. Its leaves look like that of flat-leaved parsley and it has substantial and tasty-looking roots. It is called hemlock waterdropwort, and a plateful will have you dead in three hours.

While most people will have picked wild plants at sometime or other, even if it is just blackberries, and mushroom hunting has become quite fashionable, few venture on to our rocky shores to collect that least likely addition to a dinner party – seaweed. When I started investigating seaweeds it was not with any expectation that I would actually enjoy eating any of them – their appearance, not to mention their smell, does not encourage the gourmet; and the evangelical zeal expressed in the few books I had on the subject I rejected as the misguided rantings of eccentrics. Well, I seem to have taken up ranting myself and proclaim the virtues of seaweed at every opportunity.

Seaweeds are eaten the world over, with Japan being the most accepting of this unusual food. The main problem for the British, apart from a disinclination to eat anything that doesn't come in a packet, is that they just do not know how to cook it. With one exception there is no point collecting a basket of seaweed and trying to cook it like, say, cabbage – you end up with a smelly, slimy mess. Most of the half-dozen or so good, edible seaweeds found around these islands require special treatment. Laver – a membranous, brown seaweed found, mostly, attached to rocks – must be boiled for ten hours (no less!) to form the sticky paste that is laverbread. This is used, notably in south Wales, to make oatmeal cakes or as a (rather sticky) sauce for lamb. The slightly fishy flavour is of the 'umami' kind found in other delights such as Marmite and Parmesan cheese. Laver, put through a papermaking process, will be familiar to many as 'nori', the stuff that little bits of fish and rice are wrapped in to make sushi. With carragheen – a small, bushy seaweed found attached to rocks or in rock pools at low tide – you do not eat the seaweed at all; it is simply boiled for half an hour to extract the incredibly slippery/slimy substance called 'carragheenan' that is used to set such things as panna cotta. Gutweed – a bright green, hairlike seaweed of upper shores – can be deep fried to form genuine (the stuff you get in Chinese restaurants is actually cabbage) crispy seaweed. Sugar kelp is dried and fried to make seaweed crisps and the other kelps are used for their flavour-enhancing glutamates and removed from the dish prior to serving. The exception I mentioned earlier is dulse. The deep red, flat, fingered fronds can be cooked like any other vegetable and make an excellent 'seaweed bubble and squeak'. I do recommend you give seaweed a try. So much of it is wasted for want of knowledge and courage.

Food collected from the wild is, of course, free and I hope I have been able to convince you that it is also delicious. But collecting wild food can feed the soul as well as the body. The forager comes to truly appreciate food. Food from the supermarket is just a commodity, the origin of which we neither know nor care. When you eat food you have gathered yourself you understand it in a way not open to others. You know where it came from, how it lived, what problems it faced, how fresh it is and how jolly hard it may have been to come by in the first place. So, I entreat you, go foraging – it will be good for your karma.

PICK-YOUR-OWN FARMS

In summer, an outing to a pick-your-own farm to harvest fruit and vegetables can be a fun way to spend a few hours.

Blagdon Fruit Farm Coldharbour, Chickerell, Weymouth DT3 4BG ✆ 07557 337679

Cat and Fiddle Farm Lyndhurst Rd, Hinton BH23 7DS ✆ 01425 672451

Lenctenbury Farm Soldiers Rd, Norden BH20 5DU ⌂ purbeckfood.co.uk

Puddletown Blueberries Puddletown DT2 8QL ✆ 07568 099065 ⌂ puddletownblueberries.com

Sopley Farm Sopley, Christchurch BH23 7AZ ✆ 01425 672451 ⌂ dantanners.co.uk

Trehane Nursery Staplehill Rd, Wimborne BH21 7ND ⌂ trehaneblueberrypyo.co.uk

DORSET WILDLIFE TRUST

Dorset is one of the richest counties in England in terms of biodiversity, with some precious habitats and wildlife. To assist in preserving this great asset, Dorset Wildlife Trust (DWT) works to champion wildlife and natural places, engage and inspire people and promote sustainable living. Its 44 reserves cover many of the most important wildlife havens, including ancient woodlands, wetlands, wildflower meadows and some of Britain's rare surviving lowland heaths. DWT has scored many notable achievements, for example in restoring coppiced woodlands by careful management and by grazing neglected grasslands so that wildlife can flourish, and in campaigning for protection of marine habitats.

Most of DWT's reserves are open daily and free to visit. Visitor centres provide a wealth of wildlife information at Brooklands Farm, Chesil Beach, Lorton Meadows, Kingcombe Meadows and Brownsea Island nature reserves, the voluntary Purbeck Marine Wildlife Reserve and the Urban Wildlife Centre at Upton Heath Nature Reserve. More information about DWT, its reserves and opportunities to volunteer is available at ⊘ dorsetwildlifetrust.org.uk.

A SLOW LEARNING CURVE

If you find the Slow way of life in Dorset appealing, there are various short courses on offer with a Slow theme.

At Dorset Wildlife Trust's Kingcombe Centre (page 223) you can improve your knowledge of **local flora and fauna** with courses on tracking wildlife, identifying butterflies and getting to know the area's wildflowers. They also teach rural skills and crafts, including beekeeping and willow-weaving, and for hobby farmers there are sessions on livestock management.

Bere Marsh Farm (⊘ thecrt.co.uk) near Shillingstone in North Dorset runs a limited number of nature-based events during the year, which usually involve a guided walk around the farm with an expert focusing on a particular species. Previous events have looked at bats, butterflies and fungi, and there have been guided walks along the River Stour. The Ancient Technology Centre (⊘ ancienttechnologycentre.com) near Wimborne is open to the public a handful of times a year. Their

---

1 Kingcombe Meadows is managed by the DWT. **2** At Bere Marsh Farm, visitors can participate in courses on countryside crafts and wildlife. ▶

site has replica ancient buildings, including an Iron Age roundhouse, a Viking longhouse and a Neolithic log cabin. The centre hosts courses aimed at school-age children, exploring traditional building methods and ancient ways of life.

At the Burngate Stone Centre (⊘ burngatestonecentre.co.uk) in the Isle of Purbeck you can have a go at stone carving. If wood is more your thing, the Dorset Coppice Group (⊘ dorsetcoppicegroup.co.uk) runs courses throughout the year at its base not far from Blandford. Past courses have included hurdle making, hedge laying and willow basket weaving.

Toby Hoad of Dorset Horse Logging (⊘ dorsethorselogging.co.uk) offers experience days in woodland close to Corfe Castle, where you can learn about sustainable woodland management and even take the reins behind his handsome, hardworking equines.

TALKING DORSET

Although the local dialect is less spoken than it once was, I hope that as you explore Dorset you will hear traces of it and the distinctive lilting regional accent. Although I grew up in Dorset I don't speak the dialect, nor do I have a West Country accent, but I know plenty of people around the Blackmore Vale who do, particularly among the older generation and the farming community. Friends will often chat to me about 'diddicoys' or 'diddies', meaning gypsies, and when asking the whereabouts of something or someone, they will add 'to' to the end of their question, 'Where is Harry to?'. The reply might be 'He's goen on', meaning he has left. 'Mind' is often added to statements, as in, ''Tis a nice day, mind', and 's' is often pronounced as 'z' and 'f' pronounced 'v'.

No-one has done more for the Dorset dialect than the poet William Barnes, whose *Poems of Rural Life in the Dorset Dialect* (1844) celebrated the lives, customs and language of the people among whom he was raised. It included a glossary of Dorset terms so that more genteel readers could understand it. Barnes was also a philologist, and in his *Glossary of the Dorset Dialect with Grammar* (1863) he recorded hundreds of words and expressions that he felt were in danger of dying out. Middle-class Victorians tended to look upon the dialect as a corruption of standard English; Barnes disagreed and maintained that the dialect of the southwest was the closest form of speech to the Old English spoken in Wessex at the time of King Alfred, that it was purer and closer to

AN ARCHAEOLOGIST'S PERSPECTIVE ON DORSET

Dr Tim Clayden, Wolfson College, Oxford

Dorset's outstanding contribution to our understanding of ancient Britain is its Jurassic coastline, and the many prehistoric burial mounds (nearly 500) and hillforts (27 in all) that dot the landscape. After the AD43 conquest by the Romans of the local Celtic tribe, the Durotriges, Dorset never had a period of such riches again.

Websites and textbooks can tell you where the best sites or remains are, but Dorset is a county made for walking. Being in the landscape is a chance to touch the face of time, whether that be on one of the beaches that offers an endless treasure hunt for fossils, or on the Wessex Ridgeway about whose ancient track burial mounds cluster and hillforts shape the skyline.

If you do nothing else in Dorset, fossicking for ammonites on **Charmouth Beach** (page 190) and walking Maiden Castle hillfort should not be missed (page 136).

The cliffs around Charmouth and Lyme Regis are being worn away by the sea. As they collapse, the sea washes and shifts the soil, causing bullet-like belemnites and ammonites made gold by the local soil to gather in rock pools or on the tideline, waiting to be found. Local experts offer fossil-hunting tours, or you can have a go yourself (page 184). It is difficult to comprehend the aeons that have passed since those fossilised creatures lived, and yet it is possible to take home in your pocket evidence of life millions of years ago.

Walking to the summit of **Maiden Castle**, you pass through a maze of banks and ditches, which formed part of the settlement's defences and were ultimately breached by the Romans in AD43. The Romans buried the dead in large pits, excavated by Mortimer Wheeler in the 1930s, and built a small temple inside the fort. A walk around the fort reveals social cohesion on a considerable scale. In the surrounding fields burial mounds of men and women can be seen, which were ancient even when Maiden Castle was built. Keep an ear open for the skylarks that rise out of the scrub and ascend on a song.

Abbotsbury hillfort (page 209) is a bit battered and less visited than Maiden Castle, but the views along the coast, including of Chesil Beach, are wonderful. Being Dorset, there is more archaeology: in this little parish alone are 22 round barrows. Many are visible on the ridgeway that runs parallel to the sea.

The **Cerne Abbas Giant** (page 143) is hard to ignore. The huge figure of a naked man holding a club in his right hand, with his erect penis and ballooning testicles, has understandably attracted archaeological investigation and much ribaldry. Theories as to its origin used to centre on it being prehistoric or Roman, depicting Hercules or a fertility deity, but more recent research suggests it is likely Saxon. Either way it is a striking and memorable sight, better seen from a distance than close up.

Perhaps the best introduction to Dorset's archaeology and history is a visit to the **County Museum** in Dorchester (page 129).

the lives of those who spoke it than standard English. Subsequent publications on the dialect draw heavily on Barnes's pioneering work.

At the time of Barnes and Thomas Hardy, dialect had already begun to decline: Hardy noted that shortly after the railway arrived in Dorchester, London music-hall songs had started to replace the old folk tunes of the area. The teaching of standard English in schools, increased travel, the migration of people from other areas and pervasive mass media have all contributed to the loss of England's dialects. However, some Dorset words have been reincarnated and found new modern usages; for instance, dumbledore, the Dorset word for bumblebee, is now the name of a character in J K Rowling's *Harry Potter* books.

Dorset dialect words are often far more fun and descriptive than their standard English cousins, for example:

betwattled – confused
biggity – conceited
chattermag – magpie or a woman who talks a lot
gallybagger – scarecrow
gurt lummock – big, clumsy person
tinklebobs – icicles
wops – wasp
zennit – seven nights (a week)
zull – plough
zummit – something

LITERARY DORSET

Dorset's scenery and its people have long inspired writers of prose and poetry, most notably the county's favourite literary son, **Thomas Hardy** (see opposite). However, Dorset has many other lesser-known literary connections, which you are likely to stumble upon as you explore the county.

A friend of Hardy's, and the son of a Blackmore Vale farmer, **William Barnes** (page 47) wrote pastoral poetry in Dorset dialect, giving a voice to the county's humble farming folk and immortalising their lives and the county's landscapes in his emotive descriptions. He is buried at St Peter's Church in Winterborne Came near Dorchester, where he served as rector for 24 years.

Novelist **Henry Fielding** (1707–54) was also from the Blackmore Vale, more precisely the village of East Stour, and some of his characters are based on people he knew while living in Dorset.

William Wordsworth (1770–1850) is commonly associated with the Lake District but he and his sister, Dorothy, spent two years in the 1790s

THOMAS HARDY

Thomas Hardy was born on 2 June 1840 in a small, thatched cottage at Higher Bockhampton, a hamlet east of Dorchester; his father was a master mason and his mother a servant and cook. The eldest of four children, Thomas was initially pronounced stillborn but an observant nurse realised the newborn was breathing.

Hardy's mother encouraged him to read and study beyond the usual level for local children. He went to school in Bockhampton and then Dorchester and at the age of 16 was apprenticed to architect John Hicks in Dorchester. He practised as an architect at Hicks's London office for five years but returned to Dorset to write fiction, living first in Sturminster Newton and then at Max Gate, the house he had built in Dorchester. Hardy's first novel was rejected but in 1871 *Desperate Remedies*, set at Kingston Maurward, was published anonymously, followed by *Under the Greenwood Tree*. Over the next 25 years he wrote 12 novels, over 50 short stories and a significant amount of poetry, including *Wessex Poems*, an anthology written over 30 years and published in 1898.

When Hardy began writing about Dorset it was a little-known county beyond its seaside resorts. The Dorset countryside was immortalised in his writings as Hardy's Wessex, and although he slightly altered the place names it was easy to guess their true identities from the descriptions. Dorchester was the inspiration for the eponymous town in *The Mayor of Casterbridge* (1886), set in the county town in the 1850s, when Hardy was at school and starting his apprenticeship there. *Tess of the d'Urbervilles* (1891) was set in the Blackmore Vale, Hardy's 'vale of little dairies', and Tess was born in the village of Marlott, actually Marnhull. The publication of *Tess* and *Jude the Obscure* (1895) cemented Hardy's fame but not perhaps in the way he would have liked – many Victorians found the books' mildly racy content immoral and offensive.

Hardy married Emma Gifford in 1874 and although he later became estranged from his wife, her death in 1912 greatly affected him and was the subject of some of his finest poetry. In 1914, Hardy married his secretary, Florence Dugdale. He died in 1928 and his heart is buried alongside Emma in the churchyard at Stinsford, while his ashes are in Westminster Abbey.

Hardy aficionados can visit his birthplace at Higher Bockhampton (page 138), his home in Dorchester, Max Gate (page 133), and Stinsford (page 138). A reconstruction of his study is on display at the Dorset County Museum in Dorchester (page 129).

in west Dorset near Pilsdon. It was here that he started to write seriously and Pilsdon Pen is said to have soothed his sister's longing for the hills of the Lake District. Poet **Samuel Taylor Coleridge** (1775–1834), who lived in neighbouring Somerset, visited them frequently.

Robert Louis Stevenson (1850–94) wrote *Kidnapped* while living in Bournemouth; he suffered from a weak chest and was one of many at the time who came to the seaside town for its healing air.

T E Lawrence (Lawrence of Arabia) lived at Clouds Hill, a cottage between Dorchester and Wareham, when he was stationed at Bovington Camp and he finished *Seven Pillars of Wisdom* and *The Mint* while living there. He died in 1935 in a motorcycle accident and is buried at Moreton. Clouds Hill is now run by the National Trust and open to the public, and a walking trail links Bovington, Moreton and Clouds Hill, all being points associated with Lawrence (page 160).

Lyme Regis became a literary-tourism destination as early as the 1820s, after **Jane Austen** described Louisa Musgrove falling from the steps on the Cobb in her novel *Persuasion* (1818). Austen loved Lyme Regis and the surrounding area and spent a good deal of time there. The Cobb later featured in **John Fowles**'s well-known novel *The French Lieutenant's Woman* (1969); Fowles (1926–2005) had moved to Lyme Regis in 1968. He was a fan of Thomas Hardy's work and Tess is reputed to have been the inspiration for his own scandalised woman.

Children's writer **Enid Blyton** made regular visits to Dorset, in particular the Isle of Purbeck, where she and her husband bought a golf club in 1950. In 1958, Blyton bought Manor Farm in Stourton Caundle, between Sturminster Newton and Sherborne. She didn't live there but used to visit when she was in the area, while a manager took care of the day-to-day running of the farm. Lifelong Blackmore Vale resident Brenda Broughton remembers those days at Manor Farm well. Her father, Jimmy Gray, worked on the farm during Blyton's ownership. The author used to send handwritten draft manuscripts down to the farm for the children of the farmworkers to read and critique. Brenda remembers her mother reading the stories to her and some of her eleven siblings. She also remembers meeting the author at the farm. Blyton told her fans that Manor Farm was the setting and inspiration for her book *Five on Finniston Farm*. In the book, one of the five, Julian, says 'I somehow feel more English for having seen those Dorset fields, surrounded by hedges basking in the sun'. I feel the same way – we are so lucky to see those views every day. Dorset places and landscapes were the inspiration for many other locations in her *Famous Five* and *Secret Seven* books. The golf club featured in *Five Have a Mystery to Solve*, and Corfe Castle is said to have been the inspiration for Kirrin Castle. Blyton's Whispering Island, also known as 'Keep-away island', was based on Brownsea Island in Poole Harbour, which during Blyton's day was owned by the reclusive Mrs Bonham-Christie who shunned visitors and let the island return to nature.

Author of the James Bond novels, Ian Fleming, went to prep school at Langton Matravers near Swanage. The nearby Moigne Combe Estate was owned by Dorset's Bond family. A member of the family, John Bond, was an Elizabethan spy and is said to have been the inspiration for Fleming's famous character. The family's motto is *non sufficit orbis* ('the world is not enough'), which appears in *On Her Majesty's Secret Service* and became the title of the 21st Bond film in 1999. Fleming used another old Dorset name, Drax, for his villain Sir Hugo Drax. By all accounts the prep school was brutal towards its boys and Fleming was pretty miserable there, so it is easy to imagine that his mind may have wandered and perhaps begun to create his well-known hero, taking inspiration from that local family's name and their motto.

A handy resource for me in writing this book has been *Highways and Byways in Dorset* (1906) by **Sir Frederick Treves** (1853–1923), who managed to combine a successful career as a surgeon with travel writing, and in the former capacity famously rescued Joseph Merrick, the 'Elephant Man', who had been displayed as a circus freak. He was born in Dorchester and his forthright account of his tour of Dorset makes interesting and, in parts, amusing reading.

Today Bridport is the heart of the Dorset literary community: a literary festival is held there annually and incorporates the Bridport Prize for poetry and short stories (⌀ bridportprize.org.uk).

ARTY DORSET

It is easy to see why generations of artists have been moved to paint Dorset's beautiful landscapes. John Constable spent a good deal of time in Dorset, including in the house in which I grew up (page 66). Going further back, 17th-century painter Sir James Thornhill was a Dorset man. Sculptor Elizabeth Fink lived at Woolland near Sturminster Newton from 1976 until her death in 1993; her work is celebrated at the Dorset County Museum (page 129).

DORSET UGLIES

07760 431009 ✉ hello@dorset-uglies.com 🖉 dorset-uglies.com

Ceramics have always stirred emotions for Emma Mauger, the creator of Dorset Uglies, and she delights in the range of reactions she sees when exhibiting the Uglies. She has been making Dorset Uglies since around 2017, after leaving a career behind a desk, and is having a great time sculpting, with the aim of 'Bringing a wonky smile to your home and garden'.

Emma makes a range of creatures, from wildlife and monsters to Ugly versions of family pets – dogs being a particular favourite. Emma is also interested in expanding her range of bespoke Ugly busts of people – who could resist having an eternal Ugly version of themselves poking out of a flowerbed?! She recounts her amusement when a tradesman uttered a profanity at spotting an Ugly bust in her flowerbed, and proclaiming she was the spitting image of his wife!

Each Ugly is individually hand-built, so they are all one-off pieces, using crank (grogged) clay, painted with either oxides or stains, and then fired up to 1,230^{0}C (stoneware). This means that the Uglies are frost-proof and tend to find their homes in people's gardens.

In keeping with the Slow Dorset ethos, each Ugly commission takes around a day to make, followed by around a month of drying, then oxide application, before the 24-hour firing. Commissions, and suggestions, are always welcome.

Today there are plenty of artists and potters inspired by Dorset. You'll find their work in small galleries and collective shops. And there are memorable experiences to be had – Sculpture by the Lakes (page 159) invites you to walk around a beautiful series of lakes with sculptures displayed against this natural backdrop. The highlight of the county's artistic calendar is Dorset Art Weeks (🖉 dorsetartweeks.co.uk), one of the UK's largest open-studio events.

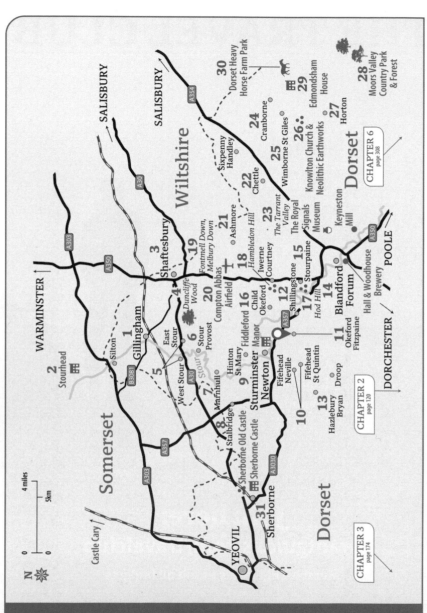

1
NORTH DORSET – THE BLACKMORE VALE, CRANBORNE CHASE & SHERBORNE

I admit to being biased when it comes to this part of Dorset, for this is where I grew up. I have travelled to many countries around the world but there is no landscape that makes my heart sing like the glorious **Blackmore Vale**, with its tapestry of verdant fields divided by neat hedges and sprinkled with beguiling villages.

The best way to appreciate the beauty of the vale is to look down on it from above, whether by taking a flight from Compton Abbas Airfield or by viewing it from the top of Hambledon Hill, Bulbarrow Hill, Okeford Hill or the Saxon town of Shaftesbury. Alternatively, you can see it up close with a walk along the Stour Valley Way, which follows the River Stour.

The sparsely populated **Cranborne Chase**, which reaches into Hampshire and Wiltshire, offers a very different, but equally exquisite, landscape of chalk hills and vast fields of arable crops. This National Landscape (formerly Area of Outstanding Natural Beauty) has exceptional walking, cycling and horseriding. At Knowlton is a rare and intriguing sight, the ruins of a medieval church perched in the centre of a Neolithic henge.

Nestled in the wooded Yeo Valley in the northwest of the county, **Sherborne** is one of Dorset's, and perhaps England's, most appealing towns. It enchants the visitor with its blend of historic buildings, two impressive castles and imposing abbey.

North Dorset has historically been great farming country, in particular dairy farming. With the decline of the agricultural industry, many farmers have had to diversify but the area's farming heritage is obvious – in its landscapes and its first-rate local produce.

Tourists tend to bypass North Dorset and head straight for the coast, which means the area is largely unspoilt and you can expect genuine Dorset hospitality and real Dorset characters. The delightful singsong of Dorset accents still hangs thick in the air around these parts.

GETTING THERE & AROUND

The areas within this chapter are easily reached from the A30 and the A303. Driving is a good option because public transport services are scant.

PUBLIC TRANSPORT

The towns of Gillingham (pronounced with a hard 'g' at the start), not to be confused with Gillingham in Kent (with a soft 'g'), and Sherborne are on the Exeter to London Waterloo **train** line (⊘ southwesternrailway. com). Trains are frequent (roughly every hour), catering for those prepared to suffer a commute of two hours. Most trains divide at Salisbury, with only a few carriages continuing further south into Dorset and Devon, so choose your carriage carefully.

Reaching the Dorset coast from Gillingham by train is not as straightforward as you may think. Getting to Bournemouth involves heading up to Salisbury, changing trains, then going across to Southampton, and changing again to hop on a train to Bournemouth. The journey time is something over two hours. Similarly, travel to Wareham involves changing at Salisbury and Southampton, with a journey time of almost three hours.

Public transport is limited in the Blackmore Vale and Cranborne Chase. However, on weekdays there are regular buses between Gillingham and Shaftesbury and between Shaftesbury and Blandford Forum. There are hourly buses between Blandford and Poole and the journey takes about 45 minutes.

CYCLING

The quiet **rural roads** and **bridleways** of the Blackmore Vale and Cranborne Chase have excellent scope for cycling.

You can download a leaflet on cycling in North Dorset (⊘ dorsetcouncil. gov.uk) featuring suggested routes that largely focus on the Blackmore Vale, although one ventures into Cranborne Chase. The cycling section of the **Wessex Ridgeway** begins in Tollard Royal and cuts diagonally across Dorset through changing scenery: across the Blackmore Vale, through the chalk downland around Cerne Abbas to the Marshwood Vale in the southwest.

The **North Dorset Cycleway** (regional route 41 gps-routes.co.uk) is a 73-mile circular on-road route linking Gillingham, Sturminster Newton, Blandford Forum and Shaftesbury. It wends its way along country lanes through classic Blackmore Vale landscapes with sections that run beside the River Stour, and skirts into Cranborne Chase.

The **North Dorset Trailway** (northdorsettrailway.org.uk) is a 14-mile route for walkers, cyclists and horseriders along the old Somerset and Dorset railway line, which closed in 1966. Suggested routes can be downloaded from the website. The longest and most popular portion is between Stourpaine and Sturminster Newton, a six-mile route linking up with the Wessex Ridgeway.

On page 80 you will find a suggested circular cycle route starting in Okeford Fitzpaine. Okeford Hill Bike Park (okefordhillbikepark.com) has downhill trails for intermediate to experienced mountain bikers.

CYCLE HIRE

Dorset Cycles High St, Stalbridge DT10 2LL 01963 362476. Small cycle shop established in 1993 that also does cycle hire.

WALKING

The Blackmore Vale and Cranborne Chase are criss-crossed by a dense web of footpaths and bridleways. A walk up one of the hills surrounding the Blackmore Vale, especially Hambledon, Okeford or Bulbarrow, provides breathtaking views. All are easily accessible with car parking nearby. The Iron Age hillforts of **Hambledon** and **Hod Hill** combine superb scenery with archaeological interest, while **Duncliffe Hill** offers the opportunity for an easy walk in one of the vale's few remaining wooded areas. The **Stour Valley Way** (stourvalleyway.

i TOURIST INFORMATION

Blandford Riverside House, West St, DT11 7HW 01258 454770
Shaftesbury has a tourist-information hub within the supermarket at the top of town (Morrisons Daily, Bell St, Shaftesbury SP7 8AR).

co.uk) follows almost all of the 64-mile course of the river, passing through the Blackmore Vale from its source at Stourhead. It passes the remains of the many mills that once operated on this stretch of river, and it is worth taking a detour to visit some of them, such as the ones at Sturminster Newton and Stour Provost. The paths through the vale are far less used than those around Christchurch, making for some peaceful riverside walks.

The walking section of the **Wessex Ridgeway** (⌂ dorsetcouncil.gov. uk) begins in the village of Ashmore in Cranborne Chase and drops down through the Blackmore Vale before continuing across the county to Lyme Regis on the coast.

You don't have to stray far from Shaftesbury for some superb walks high on **Cranborne Chase**, at Fontmell and Melbury Downs, and at Win Green, just over the Wiltshire border.

The café at Compton Abbas Airfield (page 95) is perfectly positioned for replenishing the energy stores.

HORSERIDING

North Dorset lends itself to being explored on horseback, as it has been for centuries. Bridleways are plentiful in the Blackmore Vale and Cranborne Chase, and the Wessex Ridgeway (⌂ dorset-nl.org.uk) and the North Dorset Trailway (⌂ northdorsettrailway.org.uk) are both open to riders. Some farm-based accommodation may allow you to bring your own horse by prior arrangement.

Unfortunately, there are now few places that offer hacking on their own horses.

⌂ RIDING STABLES

Bushes Equestrian Centre Bushes Rd, Stourpaine DT11 8SU ⌂ 07974 001936
⌂ bushesec.com. Riding for all ages and abilities near Blandford Forum.
Equestrian Escapes Rose Cottage, Duddon, Cheshire CW6 0HG ⌂ 01829 781123
⌂ equestrian-escapes.com. An equestrian travel company that offers a two-night riding break at the Rushmore Estate, adjacent to Cranborne Chase.
Hill View Stables Sunnyside Farm, Cathole Bridge Rd, Crewkerne, Somerset TA18 8PA
⌂ 01460 72731 ⌂ hillviewridingstab.wixsite.com/hvstables. Hacks in the Dorset and Somerset countryside, plus an indoor school and cross-country course.
Pevlings Farm Cabbage Ln, Horsington, Somerset BA8 0DA ⌂ 01963 370990
⌂ pevlingsfarm.co.uk. Hacking just over the Somerset border.

THE BLACKMORE VALE

Most visitors to the West Country whizz down the A303, overlooking the Blackmore Vale just beneath it and, as a result, the area remains remarkably unspoilt. It lies in North Dorset and stretches just over the border into southwest Wiltshire, a wide, sheltered valley of fertile agricultural land dotted with charming, quintessentially English villages, many of which are built from warm, golden stone. The **Dorset Downs** and **Cranborne Chase** border it, with the towns of Shaftesbury (in the north) and Blandford Forum (in the south) being natural boundary markers. Hills such as Hambledon and Bulbarrow encircle the vale, and provide fine vantage points over its neat fields lined by hedges, its woodland and its villages. Those views would once have been quite different as the vale was densely wooded and the area around **Gillingham** a royal hunting forest. Few pockets of woodland remain, the most notable being on **Duncliffe Hill**, which rises like a beacon from the flat base of the vale.

WILLIAM BARNES

William Barnes (1801–86) was born at Bagber, near Sturminster Newton, the son of a yeoman farmer. Although best known as a poet who wrote mostly in dialect, Barnes was also a philologist. He was fluent in Greek, Latin and several modern European languages and studied the close relationship between Dorset dialect and Old English. He authored a comprehensive English grammar and called for the removal of foreign-derived words from the English language, so that it might be better understood by those lacking a classical education.

There is not a language Barnes loved more than that of the Dorset folk around him. His pastoral poetry written in Dorset dialect brought to life the voices of the county's ploughmen, milkmaids and farmers. His fondness for Dorset's landscapes, as well as its local people, shines through in his poetry.

From 1835 until 1862, Barnes ran a school in Dorchester and in 1844 he published *Poems of Rural Life in the Dorset Dialect*. From 1862 until his death, he was rector of St Peter's Church, Winterborne Came, and is buried in the churchyard.

Although younger than Barnes, Thomas Hardy was a fan of Barnes's work and the two became friends. Not everyone was impressed by Barnes's use of the Dorset dialect, but Hardy defended it: 'The veil of a dialect, through which except in a few cases readers have to discern whatever of real poetry there may be in William Barnes, is disconcerting to many, and to some distasteful, chiefly, one thinks, for a superficial reason which has more to do with spelling than with the dialect itself.'

From its source at Stourhead, just over the Wiltshire border, the River Stour meanders through the vale on its way to the sea at Christchurch. A series of mills used to punctuate the water's journey, and several of them are named in the Domesday Book. Of some 50 mills that used to operate on the River Stour, many are now derelict but some have been lovingly restored. **Sturminster Newton Mill** (page 72) is a beautiful example; it's still in working order and is open to visitors in the summer months.

Dairy farming used to be the lifeblood of the Blackmore Vale, prompting Thomas Hardy to use it as the inspiration for his 'vale of little dairies'. Sadly, prolonged troubled times have meant many of the dairy farms have now shut up their milking parlours. I live opposite one of the vale's last remaining small dairies and I see on a daily basis what a difficult way it is to earn a living. Rather than sell up farms that have been in their family for generations, many dairy farmers have diversified into other activities. The silver lining for the visitor is that those resilient farming folk have built some fantastic rural businesses, including accommodation, farm shops, niche food production and recreational fishing lakes. Some of those that have continued milking have installed milk vending machines, which has to be the best way to buy milk. Two of the best I have found in the county are in North Dorset, one at Madjeston Milk Station (page 52) near Gillingham and one at Woodbridge Farm (page 84) at Stock Gaylard.

The vale's towns, in particular **Shaftesbury** and **Sturminster Newton**, draw visitors for their history and beauty, but perhaps the best way to appreciate the Blackmore Vale is to get out and walk its pristine countryside and hike the surrounding hills for a bird's-eye view. For generations the scenery has inspired artists, such as John Constable; writers, such as Thomas Hardy; and poets, such as William Barnes. Hardy's description of the view from the hills in *Tess of the d'Ubervilles* still holds true today:

> Here, in the valley, the world seems to be constructed upon a smaller and more delicate scale; the fields are mere paddocks, so reduced that from this height their hedgerows appear a network of dark green threads overspreading the paler green of the grass.

1 GILLINGHAM & SURROUNDS

Being on the main train line to London, Gillingham is the gateway to the Blackmore Vale. Today the trains are used by suit-clad commuters travelling to Salisbury, London or one of the cities in between but farmers June and Alf Wallis, now sadly both passed on, told me that the trains' cargo used to be quite different. June and Alf farmed in Dorset all their lives and in nearby Stour Provost from 1963. They recalled the days when cattle from nearby farms were loaded directly on to trains at Gillingham and the farmers' supplies of fertiliser arrived by train and they collected it from the station in their tractors. The station, and the town, must have had quite a different character in those days.

At that time, Gillingham's small-scale industries would have been very much alive, including its glove makers, once a significant employer in the area. Sadly, the last glove maker, Chester Jefferies, closed its factory in 2022.

Gillingham gets a bit of a bad rap, partly because its neighbour, Shaftesbury, is considered more attractive. Like many across the

MERE DOWN FALCONRY

Manor Farm, Mere BA12 6HR ✆ 01747 824913 ⊗ meredownfalconry.co.uk

Just over the border into Wiltshire, at the base of the Mere Downs, falconer Allan Gates carefully tends to his much-loved birds of prey: hawks, owls and falcons. He is a regular sight at local country shows, flying his birds over the heads of delighted spectators. For a truly memorable experience, you can have a go at flying Allan's birds under his expert supervision.

I accompanied Allan, his German short-haired pointer and two of his Harris hawks onto the downs, where we flew the birds over the bowl created by the crescent-shaped hills. The views back towards the Blackmore Vale provided a suitably impressive backdrop for these marvellous birds. The hawks and dog hunted as a team, the dog flushing out prey and the birds watching keenly from above, and although we didn't catch anything that day that didn't seem to dull their enthusiasm.

The majesty and power of these birds in flight is something to behold, but just as fascinating is Allan's relationship with them: they are clearly bonded to him but maintain that wild, instinctive spirit. Allan told me each bird very much has its own personality and he gives them the jobs to which they are best suited and, from what I saw, they enjoy their work.

Falconry is an ancient tradition believed to date back to at least 3500bc in the Middle East. The equipment used has barely changed since falconry began; you feel like you are stepping back in time as the birds soar on the thermals over the valley then swoop back to land on your glove with pinpoint accuracy.

As well as half- and full-day flying experiences, Allan offers two-hour family handling sessions and occasionally runs special events such as owl night flights.

country, Gillingham's high street has declined in recent years. Many of the shops lie empty, almost all the banks have closed their branches and all that remains are charity shops and estate agents. Both Shaftesbury and Gillingham have seen a great deal of new housing development, but Shaftesbury has done a better job of maintaining its charm. Gillingham wasn't always the ugly sister, however, as in the 19th century John Constable felt it a worthy artistic subject and painted the bridge, the mill and the entrance to the town. Of these, the most recognisable scene today is **Gillingham Bridge**, which lies three-quarters of the way down the High Street; Constable's depiction of it is in the Tate Britain in London. When he visited the town in 1823, Constable described the area as 'beautiful, full of little bridges, rivulets, mills and cottages – and the most beautiful trees and verdure I ever saw'. Sadly, the mill buildings that were once at the centre of the town, and that housed a corn mill and silk mill until 1895, were destroyed by fire in 1981.

Before you rush off to Shaftesbury, the **Gillingham Museum** (✆ 01747 823234 ⌾ gillinghammuseum.co.uk ⊙ mornings Mon, Tue & Thu–Sat) is worth a look. It is next to Gillingham library, opposite Waitrose supermarket on the Wyke Road. The museum tells the story of the area's inhabitants, from Neolithic times to the present. The 1790 manual fire engine on display is the only surviving one of its kind. Also on show are reproductions of John Constable's paintings of the area.

The museum reminds us that the area east of Gillingham was once a royal hunting forest that contained a deer park. In 1210, King John is said to have rewarded two huntsmen for killing wolves here. He was a regular visitor and the hunting lodge in which he stayed, and to which he made substantial alterations, became known as King's Court. In 1369 King Edward III had the lodge destroyed and in 1628 the area was deforested. Today locals walk their dogs where the lodge once was. All that remains are the tell-tale earthworks, but you can make out the banks and the moat. It can be reached from Kings Court Road, off the Gillingham to Shaftesbury road.

There are some pleasing villages around Gillingham, notably Silton and **Milton-on-Stour**, where there are sturdy stone farmhouses and a bridge over the river, which rises in nearby Stourhead.

◀ **1** Views across the Blackmore Vale. **2** The Wyndham Oak at Silton – one of England's oldest trees. **3** Autumn at Stourhead House & Gardens.

Silton

The village of Silton is worth visiting for its 15th-century church and a very special ancient oak. The handsome **church of St Nicholas** is thought to stand on Saxon foundations. The interior walls carry a distinctive, dainty, stencilled decoration but the church's most striking feature is a highly theatrical 17th-century memorial to Sir Hugh Wyndham (1602–84), who is flanked by his two weeping wives. Wyndham was a judge of the court of common pleas and was one of 22 judges who sat in the Fire Court, set up in 1667 to hear cases relating to property damaged in the Great Fire of London. Wyndham bought the Manor of Silton in 1641, on the site of the present Manor Farm, just south of the churchyard.

In a field behind the church is the **Wyndham Oak**, one of Britain's oldest trees, thought to be around a thousand years old. It is said Sir Hugh Wyndham used to rest under the oak and admire the view, so it must have been a substantial size by the 17th century. It is thought that the tree may have been used for hangings following the Monmouth Rebellion, although this has not been confirmed. To visit the oak today is to be in the presence of plant majesty: its gnarly, split trunk and branches like witches' fingers attest to its momentous age. Personally, I wouldn't sit Wyndham-like beneath it as it doesn't look as robust as

MADJESTON MILK STATION

Newhouse Farm, Cole Street Ln, Madjeston SP8 5J ✆ 07584 029454
🖰 madjestonmilkstation.co.uk

What started as a milk vending machine on this dairy farm back in March 2018 has evolved into a hugely popular local attraction with an array of local produce on sale, delicious ice cream, a café and a petting farm. Abi Williamson and Dave Pike have created something really special. For many families, including mine, the vending machines selling milk, ice cream and local goodies were a lifeline during the Covid-19 lockdowns. The milk is produced from the farm's pedigree Ayrshire herd. It is pasteurised but not homogenised, making it unbelievably creamy and delicious. The ice cream is made on site and is superb. If you value knowing where your food comes from, there is nothing better than meeting the cows who produce your milk as you're buying it.

The vending machines are open 24/7. The petting farm (check website for opening hours) has all the usual favourites – pygmy goats, ponies, pigs and giant rabbits – and there is even a guinea-pig village. Children can feed and cuddle the animals (for a fee), and there's a great play area, making it a fantastic place to take the family.

it must once have been. Should it finally give up the ghost, it will not be lost altogether because in the 1970s the residents of Manor Farm planted an acorn from the ancient oak in the same field as its ancestor so that it can one day take over the mantle.

¶¶ FOOD & DRINK

In addition to the below, don't miss Madjeston Milk Station (see opposite).

The Old Brewery Café and Kitchen Wyke Rd, SP8 4NW ✆ 01747 442164. On the B3081 towards Wincanton, this café serves freshly cooked meals or lighter bites. There's a courtyard garden, and a display of classic motorcycles.

Secret Garden Café Thorngrove Garden Centre, Common Mead Ln, SP8 4RE ✆ 01747 822242. This well-stocked and reasonably priced garden centre has been much-loved by locals since it opened over 50 years ago. It provides training for young people with special educational needs. Expect reasonably priced light lunches and excellent homemade cakes.

2 STOURHEAD HOUSE & GARDENS

Stourton BA12 6QD ✆ 01747 841152 ☺ garden: 09.00–18.00; house: opening times vary; National Trust

Just over the Wiltshire border, the 2,650-acre Stourhead Estate is one of the area's key attractions. As the name indicates, it is here that Dorset's longest river, the Stour, rises. The house is a Palladian mansion brimming with antique furniture and artwork, and evokes the lives of its former residents, the Hoare family, who made their fortune in banking. When you're exploring the house, don't miss the Pope's cabinet, one of the most elaborate items of furniture in the National Trust's collections. The cabinet is thought to have been commissioned by Felice Peretti, Pope Sixtus V, around 1585. The 153 drawers would have kept items hidden. It's an ostentatious piece, modelled on the shape of a church façade, and decorated with gilt bronze, ebony, alabaster and semi-precious stones. Henry Hoare II bought the cabinet from a Roman convent during a grand tour of Europe around 1740.

The sprawling 18th-century gardens are magical, inspired by the great landscape painters of the 17th century and grand tours of Europe. A magnificent lake constitutes the centrepiece, fed by the infant River Stour, which shimmers with the reflections of autumn colours as the leaves change hue. Classical temples, a romantic bridge and a mysterious cobbled grotto create a dreamy atmosphere. The European influence is

THE GILLINGHAM & SHAFTESBURY SHOW

Turnpike Showground, Motcombe SP7 9LP 🔍 gillshaftshow.co.uk

A highlight of the Blackmore Vale calendar is the annual agricultural show, held in August, between Gillingham and Shaftesbury. It has all the best features of an agricultural show: livestock, equestrian classes, heavy horses, parades by the local hunts, food producers and handicrafts. Locals spend months preparing their entries for the fiercely contested jam, cake, vegetable, embroidery and art classes.

clear, with a mini Pantheon and a Temple of Apollo among the features. Nearby is King Alfred's Tower, a 160ft folly built in 1772 in honour of the Saxon king by Stourhead's then owner, Henry Hoare II. The woods around the tower offer memorable walks and when the tower is open in summer you can walk to the top for superlative views of the surrounding countryside. The tower is typically open on weekends and bank holidays in summer but it is best to contact the Stourhead office (☎ 01747 841152) to check.

One of my family's favourite walks starts just opposite King Alfred's Tower and heads down through the Six Wells Valley towards Stourhead's gardens. On the way you pass St Peter's Pump, which marks the start of the River Stour. This ancient 14th-century pumping house was moved here in 1786 by Henry Hoare; prior to that it stood in Bristol for 300 years. It is clear the stone was heavily decorated although some of the detail has now eroded.

3 SHAFTESBURY

🏠 **Grosvenor Arms**

Shaftesbury is best known for its much-photographed Gold Hill (see opposite), which is undoubtedly worth seeing, but there is much more to discover. A rich history, fascinating architecture and beautiful rural views combine to make Shaftesbury a charming town. Its centre is compact, packed with enticing, independent shops and easy to explore on foot.

Shaftesbury was founded by King Alfred the Great around AD880 and is one of four Dorset towns named in the Burghal Hidage, which recorded Alfred's plan to provide fortified safe havens for local people at times of invasion (page 56). Although many of the town's buildings are

Georgian and Victorian, constructed from distinctive local greensand stone, traces of its Saxon origins can be seen around the site of the abbey.

Thomas Hardy referred to Shaftesbury as 'Shaston' in his writings and it appeared in both *Jude the Obscure* and *Tess of the d'Urbervilles*. He described it as 'one of the queerest and quaintest spots in England', 'breezy and whimsical' and said that 'beer was more plentiful than water'. It is certainly quaint and, thanks to its hilltop position at 700ft, has a tendency to be very breezy and chilly. Mercifully, the water supply is now far more reliable than it once was and although there is a healthy population of pubs serving local ales, I doubt beer is more plentiful than water. On a dull day, the town is often shrouded in cloud and this, combined with its cold greensand stone, has given it a reputation as a rather dreary, melancholy place. Catch it on a fine day, however, and you will be amply rewarded by this queer, quaint, whimsical town that so fascinated Hardy.

"Catch it on a fine day, however, and you will be amply rewarded by this queer, quaint, whimsical town."

The town centre is an easy walk from the car parks at the top and bottom of the High Street, and buses stop outside the Town Hall, in the town centre. The **Town Hall** is a Georgian building whose battlements seem designed to project a serious, castle-like image; the weekly **street market** takes place here on Thursdays. Next to the Town Hall is the diminutive **St Peter's Church**; built in the late 15th century, it is the oldest church in Shaftesbury.

Just behind the Town Hall is the instantly recognisable **Gold Hill**. This impossibly steep, cobbled street with its row of attractive cottages and pastoral Blackmore Vale backdrop is a local celebrity. The highlight of its career was appearing in the 1973 Hovis bread commercial directed by Ridley Scott, which featured a boy pushing a bicycle up the hill. A statue of a Hovis loaf sits next to the Town Hall, a reminder of that pinnacle of Gold Hill's fame. Along one side of Gold Hill a formidable stone wall is all that remains of the walls that once encircled Shaftesbury Abbey. At the top of Gold Hill is a café, where you can sit and pity the poor folk walking up the steep incline. Nearby is the **Gold Hill Museum** (page 59). Gold Hill is the site of an annual cheese race, where contestants power up the hill carrying replica wheels of cheese. The event is a tribute to the Blackmore Vale's long history of milk and cheese production.

A narrow alleyway (Park Lane) leads from the top of Gold Hill to **Park Walk**, which has peaceful public gardens and is home to the **Abbey Museum and Garden** (page 58). With the abbey ruins behind and the mesmerising countryside in front, the gardens are an ideal place to sit and ponder the history of the place and how it might have been when King Alfred ruled the roost around these parts.

Shaftesbury Abbey was built by King Alfred around AD888 on the site of a pagan temple; it was the first religious house solely for women and Alfred's daughter, Aethelgifu, was the inaugural abbess. The remains

KING ALFRED THE GREAT

Alfred is the only English king to be known as 'The Great', an epithet bestowed for his valiant defence of his kingdom against a formidable enemy, for securing peace with the Vikings, and for his educational and legal reforms.

He was born in AD849 in what is now Wantage, Oxfordshire, the fifth son of Aethelwulf, king of the West Saxons. In AD871, at the age of 21, he succeeded his brother Aethelred as King of Wessex.

Viking armies had been raiding England since around AD790 and had taken much of the north; in AD870 they attacked the last remaining independent Anglo-Saxon kingdom, Wessex. After turning to guerrilla tactics to defeat the Danes in several protracted battles, Alfred negotiated a partition treaty with them in AD886, whereby the areas between the rivers Thames and Tees became Danish territory and Alfred took charge of an extended Wessex, which now included West Mercia and Kent.

To protect his kingdom, Alfred established a navy and built a series of well-defended settlements across southern England, fortified marketplaces or 'burhs', where residents could seek shelter. Settlers received plots in return for manning the defences in times of war. The programme was recorded in the Burghal Hidage, a document detailing the building and operation of Wessex and Mercian burhs according to their size, the length of their ramparts and the number of men needed to garrison them. This network of burhs, with strong points on the main river routes, ensured that no part of Wessex was more than 20 miles from the refuge of one of the settlements.

Alfred believed strongly in education, learnt Latin in his late thirties and was patron of the Anglo-Saxon Chronicle, a patriotic history of the Anglo-Saxons. He lamented that much of the population could not understand Latin and so arranged the translation into Anglo-Saxon of a series of important books he thought 'most needful for men to know'. He also advocated justice and order and significantly reformed Anglo-Saxon law. Alfred reigned until his death in AD899 and was buried in Winchester, capital of Wessex.

of Saxon king Edward the Martyr were brought to the abbey after his murder at Corfe Castle in AD978 (page 271); his shrine and the promise of associated miracles attracted streams of pilgrims. The abbey thrived and became one of the largest in the country, with around 350 inhabitants and large tracts of land in Dorset, Wiltshire and beyond. It attracted royal visitors, including King Canute who died here in 1035. In 1491 Henry VII stayed at the abbey, as did Catherine of Aragon in 1501 on her way to marry Prince Arthur, elder brother of Henry VIII. After 650 years of continuous worship, the abbey closed in 1539 as part of Henry VIII's Dissolution of the Monasteries and soon fell into disrepair. The ruins are visible within the Abbey Museum and Garden, while the ramparts on Gold Hill are all that remain of the outer walls.

"Some of the best-preserved greensand cottages, with tiny doors and thatched roofs, are found at the top of town."

The views from Park Walk are rivalled by those from **Castle Hill**, which is within walking distance of the abbey ruins. Head along Abbey Walk then turn left when you reach Bimport; after a short distance, a lane on your right leads to Castle Hill, once the site of a Saxon fort. The views across the Blackmore Vale to the Somerset and Wiltshire border are topped off by King Alfred's Tower in the distance. Thomas Hardy described the scene as:

As sudden a surprise to the unexpected traveller's eyes as the medicinal air is to his lungs.

Aside from Gold Hill, some of the best-preserved greensand cottages, with tiny doors and thatched roofs, are found at the top of town on Bell Street and at the bottom of town in **St James**, an area at the base of Gold Hill. In St James look out for a U-shaped collection of workers' cottages set back from the road, known as Pump Court and still with the pump at its centre.

You will see plenty of references to the Grosvenor family in and around Shaftesbury, for they owned much of the town until just over a hundred years ago. In 1820, Earl Grosvenor (later Marquis of Westminster) bought the 'Property of Shaftesbury' (the 400 premises large enough to have voting rights) in order to control elections in the borough. The Grosvenors grew very wealthy and were responsible for much of the development in the town, and it is for that reason that it has an estate village character; the keen-eyed will spot many cast-iron windows of similar design and uniform rows of workers' cottages. The family also alleviated one of the town's greatest problems, a lack of water, when in the mid-1800s the marquis provided a well and a steam engine to pump free water to the residents. In 1918, Robert Grosvenor's great-grandson sold his Dorset estates, and Shaftesbury was again put up for sale. It was bought by a Londoner and then re-sold to a consortium of three men of the town: the doctor, the innkeeper at the Grosvenor Arms and the manager of a grocer's shop. They subsequently held the 'sale of Shaftesbury' in which, over three days, most tenants bought their own houses and shops.

There are some thriving independent shops in Shaftesbury. The area known as Swan's Yard (⚘ swansyard.co.uk), off the High Street, is owned by Swans Trust (a community-development charity) and the retail units here are used for local, small, start-up businesses. Currently, they include the Cygnet Gallery, which gives local artists and makers a place to exhibit and sell their wares, Forget-me-not Eco Shop, The Potting Shed plant shop and the Ugly Duckling Cafe. The town has some good bookshops too. Foodies will enjoy The Kitchen Table (59a High St, SP7 8JE ✆ 01747 855769 ⚘ thekitchentabledorset.co.uk), a shop specialising in cookery books and unusual ingredients. Folde Bookshop on Gold Hill (1 Goldhill House, 21 High St, SP7 8JE ✆ 01747 852181 ⚘ foldedorset. com) focuses on nature-inspired writing. At the top of town, opposite the Bell Street car park, Farm Soap Co (1A Bell St, SP7 8AR ⚘ farmsoapco. com) creates handmade botanical skincare products.

"In the mid-1800s the marquis provided a well and a steam engine to pump free water to the residents."

Shaftesbury Abbey Museum & Garden

Park Walk, SP7 8JR ✆ 01747 852910 ⚘ shaftesburyabbey.org.uk ☉ Apr–Oct daily

This small museum on the site of the abbey gives a feel for what life would have been like for the women who lived there. It is best visited in decent weather, as you can explore the excavated foundations of the abbey in the walled garden. The foundations are all that remain of the abbey, as much of the stone was taken for building elsewhere, and a small herb garden commemorates the nuns' extensive use of herbs; the commanding statue of King Alfred was made as recently as 1989.

DORSET BUTTONS

Dorset buttons, with their characteristic wheel appearance, used to be handmade in households around the county. Their manufacture was at a peak between 1622 and 1850. Originally, they were made on a disc cut from the horn of a Dorset Horn sheep, which was covered with needle-worked thread; in around 1720, the horn was replaced with a metal ring.

In 1622 Abraham Case set up a commercial button-making enterprise in Shaftesbury. He had a workshop there but as the business grew Case paid people to make buttons in their own homes and buttony became an important cottage industry. For many, especially those who could not work in the fields, it was their main source of income.

Abraham's descendants carried on the business and by the late 18th century employed over 4,000 people.

A button-making machine displayed at the 1851 Great Exhibition in Crystal Palace spelt the beginning of the end of buttony as a cottage industry. Handmade buttons were gradually replaced by those made by these machines in factories in England's growing cities. The decline hit Dorset hard as many households had relied on the industry to survive. Some people were forced into the workhouse, others emigrated to Australia, Canada or the USA, including 350 people from Shaftesbury.

The Blandford Fashion Museum (page 86) tells the story of Dorset buttons.

Indoor exhibits include a model of the abbey church as it would have been in the 11th century.

Gold Hill Museum

Gold Hill, SP7 8JW ☏ 01747 852157 ⊘ goldhillmuseum.org.uk ☺ Apr–Oct 10.30–16.30 daily; free admission

This well-run museum in a cottage at the top of Gold Hill was once a dosshouse (cheap lodging) for the drovers, jugglers and traders who came to Shaftesbury's markets and fairs. Exhibitions cover archaeology and local history. The industries on which the town was built are given due attention: agriculture, lace-making and the production of Dorset buttons. Murals by local artist, Janet Swiss, help bring the history to life.

The most extraordinary object on display is the Byzant, an exotic gilded totem embellished with peacock feathers. While it may look like the product of a school project, the Byzant was central to securing the town's water supply. Shaftesbury had no water supply of its own, so the Byzant was paraded annually to nearby Enmore Green, along

STOATE & SONS STONEGROUND FLOUR

Cann Mills, Shaftesbury SP7 0BL ✆ 01747 852475 🖱 stoatesflour.co.uk ⏰ 08.30–13.00 & 14.00–17.00 Mon–Fri

The Stoate family began milling in the West Country in 1832, and in 1947 took over this mill about a mile south of Shaftesbury. Today it is in the hands of Michael Stoate, fifth-generation miller.

The mill is powered largely by the River Sturkel, a tributary of the Stour, and the flour is ground using French burr stones. It produces organic and non-organic flours, including spelt, rye, wholemeal and maltstar (its own version of granary).

You can buy Stoates flour direct from the mill, the website or farm shops across the South West.

Paul Merry runs artisan bread- and pastry-making courses at the mill, which include a mill tour (✆ 01747 823711 🖱 panary. co.uk).

with gifts of ale, bread, a calf's head and gloves, to secure the town's right to water from that area. The Byzant is recorded as early as 1364 and the ceremony continued until 1830, when Shaftesbury acquired its own water.

 ## SPECIAL STAYS

The Grosvenor Arms High St, SP7 8JA ✆ 01747 850580 🖱 grosvenorarms.co.uk. With its elegant Georgian front, the exterior has a sense of history but this small hotel sports an up-to-date interior. Flanking the central courtyard are a country-style bar (picture tweed and leather furniture around an open fire) and a popular restaurant, where the food is carefully presented and the choice of wines is impressive.

Rooms vary in size and are individually decorated with playful modern touches. The Cranborne Suite is spacious, overlooks the courtyard and has a decadent bathroom with free-standing bath and vast walk-in shower. Being in the town centre, the hotel is within easy walking distance to all of Shaftesbury's best bits, including Gold Hill.

 ## FOOD & DRINK

Nest 51 High St, SP7 8JE ✆ 01747 854172. Serves carefully prepared Asian fusion dishes.
Pamplemousse 9 Bell St, SP7 8AR ✆ 01747 228439. This gorgeous florist shop has a small café serving delicious cakes and light bites.
Salt Cellar Gold Hill Parade, SP7 8JW ✆ 01747 851838. This café's greatest asset is its location, right at the top of Gold Hill. If you have climbed the hill, you will have earned tea and cake here.

The Shaftesbury Deli 37 High St, SP7 8JE ✆ 01747 685063 ⌂ theshaftesburydeli.co.uk.
This deli and tea room is crammed with delicious local produce.
Sorelle Bittles Brook Farm, Motcombe SP7 9NX ✆ 07811 346212 ⌂ sorelledorset.com.
On a farm in Motcombe, just outside Shaftesbury, this quirky café is run by hard-working
sisters, Natalie and Tilly. Expect tasty, homecooked Italian-inspired food and friendly
service. The café is in a stretch tent so dress warmly if it's chilly. Natalie has also
created an organic flower farm here and arrangements are created without
single-use plastics.

4 DUNCLIFFE WOOD

A visit to Duncliffe is perhaps the best way to gain an impression of what
Blackmore and Gillingham would have been like when they were royal
hunting forests. As the many farms grew up in the area, the land was
cleared but on the twin summits of Duncliffe
Hill a pocket of well-preserved woodland
remains, cared for by the Woodland Trust.
The Domesday Book records a wood here,
which was traditionally coppiced, and is
said to have been the inspiration for Thomas
Hardy's *The Woodlanders*. Although some
huge, ancient trees remain, much of the
ancient oak, ash and hazel was felled in the 1950s and replanted with
Norway spruce, oak, larch and beech. Today, the Woodland Trust
manages this Site of Nature Conservation Interest (SNCI) in such a way
as to encourage a greater mix of native broadleaf species.

"Whenever I walk through the wood, I always half expect to encounter the wildlife characters from a children's book – it has that magical feel."

Footpaths and a bridleway lead through the 228-acre wood to the top
of the hill (690ft), which provides far-reaching views of the surrounding
farmland. Some of the tracks are gravel, so can be walked even when the
ground is wet, and the other paths are deep in mud.

Whenever I walk through the wood, I always half expect to encounter
the wildlife characters from a children's book – it has that magical feel
– and if you walk there on a summer's evening you are likely to catch
a glimpse of many of them – the local roe deer, badgers, pheasants
and foxes. Butterflies are also abundant, including silver-washed
fritillary, white admiral and purple hairstreak. Six species of bat call
Duncliffe home. In spring the woodland floor is carpeted with bluebells
and wild garlic, and in summer there is a mass of wildflowers in the
surrounding meadows.

Duncliffe Wood lies off the A30 between Shaftesbury and East Stour; from the A30 take the turning signed Stour Row. There is a car park and a sign showing the various paths you can follow through the wood.

5 EAST STOUR & WEST STOUR

The importance of the River Stour is evident in this area, with a string of villages named after it. This is an area of small farms, watched over by Duncliffe Hill. East Stour and West Stour lie on the A30 between Shaftesbury and Sherborne; both villages were mentioned in the Domesday Book but now have a noticeable amount of modern development, East Stour in particular. Thankfully it also has handsome original farms and the short, squat **church**, which was rebuilt in 1842 on the site of an earlier one. Henry Fielding, author of *Tom Jones*, lived in the old rectory, which has now been demolished; Church Farm now stands on the site. As you enter East Stour from Shaftesbury you pass the marvellous **Udder Farm Shop** (see below), which has breathed new life into the area.

From East Stour the A30 continues through West Stour, providing views back across the fields towards Stour Provost, where the River Stour flows. The **Ship Inn**, a handsome coaching inn built in 1750, is a good starting point for walks across the fields to Stour Provost.

¶¶ FOOD & DRINK

Crown Inn East Stour SP8 5JS ✆ 01747 838866. Enthusiastic new management took over in 2023 and quickly earned a reputation for excellent food and sensible pricing. The menu is largely pub classics with enough variety to suit most people and specific menus for children and seniors. The weekend all-you-can-eat breakfasts and Sunday carvery are popular.

Ship Inn West Stour SP8 5RP ✆ 01747 838640. A traditional coaching inn; the menu is diverse and uses local ingredients wherever possible. The bulk of the parking is across the road, so take care when crossing as visibility is poor.

The Udder Farm Shop Manor Farm, East Stour SP8 5LQ ✆ 01747 838899 ⌂ theudderfarmshop.co.uk. This fabulous farm shop is the brainchild of local farming personalities Brian and Jane Down. Brian's family has farmed here since his grandfather bought the farm in 1938. Since it opened in 2005, the farm shop and restaurant have grown and grown. They stock a great range of their own meat, lots of local food and drink, and gifts. The restaurant serves the farm's own produce and sources as much as it can locally. Keep an eye out for its themed evening meals. There are now other businesses on the site too, including a gym and hairdresser.

6 STOUR PROVOST

I grew up in this tiny village, whose centre is little more than a single street lined with conspicuously picturesque golden limestone houses, some of them thatched.

As is the case with many rural villages, Stour Provost's character has changed enormously in the last 40 years. When I was growing up at Riversdale Farm, Stour Provost still had a village shop and a pub but they are long gone. There were several working dairy farms and it was not uncommon to see herds of cows, including our own small family of beef cattle, being walked through the village to pastures new.

These days most of the farms are farms in name only, bought by Londoners escaping to the country, or using them as weekend pads. A few diehard locals remain and the village still has that small community feel but it is a smarter, more sophisticated version of its former self, without a single cowpat on the street. For the visitor it offers unabashed architectural beauty, an ancient church and tranquil walks along the River Stour. The stretch of river here has also become popular for **wild swimming**.

Stour Provost's history has helped to preserve its character because until less than a hundred years ago the village as a whole was owned by one entity. From the 11th century until 1467 it was owned by the nuns of the Saint Léger de Préaux Abbey in Normandy, and was known as Stour Préaux. During the wars with France, Henry V rescinded the title of various French-held lands in England, including the village, and Henry VI gave

"For the visitor it offers unabashed architectural beauty, an ancient church and tranquil walks along the River Stour."

it to Eton College. Edward IV subsequently gave it to King's College, Cambridge, which owned much of the village until 1925, when it began to sell the houses to individuals.

St Michael and All Angels Church was largely built in 1302, probably on the site of an earlier Saxon church, but has undergone alterations over the centuries. An avenue of pollarded lime trees leads to the small church; sadly it is not usually left open but you can get the key from one of the church wardens. The interior is modest but with some elaborate stained glass, while the font is Purbeck stone and dates from the 15th century. Adjacent is **Church House**, a fine 16th-century building. The incredibly romantic thatched cottage known as **Mundy's**, which lies

towards the bottom of the main street, was a house for 'poor orphan children and other poor of the parish' in the 18th century.

The River Stour runs at the base of the gardens of the houses on the west side of the street. At Riversdale Farm (my childhood home) is an oxbow that was used as the local swimming pool until the 1960s, and known as Lucky Dip. At the opposite end of the village, at the end of Mill Lane, is the **Mill House**. A footpath runs through here so the mill, its waterwheel and the millpond can be seen close up. The Domesday Book of 1086 records a mill here; the present waterwheel was made in 1886, fell into disuse and was restored in 1988 by the then owners of the house, the Llewellyn family, and run to provide electricity to the house. A **circular walk** takes you from the mill across fields to the village of **Fifehead Magdalen** and from there to **West Stour**, where you can pause at the Ship Inn (page 62). From the Ship Inn a footpath leads directly back to the other end of Stour Provost, taking you through fields and over a footbridge (ideal for Pooh sticks), arriving in Stour Provost near Riversdale Farm. From there you can simply walk up The Street back to the centre of the village. It's a lovely walk and one of the best routes in North Dorset for getting close to the River Stour.

Stour Provost enjoyed a brief stint as the fictional village of Upper Drake's Bottom. Steve Broughton, whose family has lived in the village for generations, remembers sitting in the garden of his grandmother's cottage at the top of The Street one Sunday morning when two familiar faces arrived. He watched, fascinated, as The Two Ronnies filmed their long-running sketch, Charlie Farley and Piggy Malone. Many of their countryside sketches were filmed in North Dorset and Ronnie Barker and Ronnie Corbett lived in King's Stag near Sturminster Newton during filming. A farm in King's Stag was rearing turkeys and Ronnie Corbett told the farmer he'd like to buy one at Christmas. Apparently, it was so good that for years after that Corbett would send a car and driver to the farm to collect his Christmas turkey.

◀ **1 & 2** Much photographed, Gold Hill in Shaftesbury hosts an annual cheese race. **3** Stour Provost as seen from West Stour. **4** A stained-glass window in Shaftesbury Abbey depicting Edward the Martyr. **5** The annual Oak fair near Sturminster Newton is a chance to see local craftspeople at work. **6** Family-friendly walks in Duncliffe Wood.

Hawkers Farm (⌂ hawkersfarm.org), adjacent to Duncliffe Wood, is the home of Hawkers Re-Creatives, a sustainable sewing hub set up by Jennifer Morisetti. A former milking parlour provides a space in which to learn to mend, sew and redesign, allowing people to rework existing clothing rather than discard it. A clothing library 'Wear me Out' offers special-occasion outfits that can be borrowed f ree of charge. There is also a clothing swap shop, and natural-fibre clothing for sale. The farm has fantastic views and there is a shepherd's hut and bell tent for visitors. If you're in the area in May/June look

JOHN CONSTABLE & THE LAWYER'S WIFE

The late K J Richards (this is adapted from an article written by my father for a Canadian newspaper, *Farm and Country*, in which he wrote a regular column on European rural affairs; he was an author, farmer, film director and entrepreneur).

When we first moved to Riversdale Farm in Stour Provost some of the more ancient locals referred to the place as 'Tinney's', yet none of them knew quite why. They were right: a man called John Pern Tinney did once own the farm and John Constable's painting of *Stratford Mill* used to hang above the fireplace. The story I stumbled across played out in a Dorset village tucked away in the Blackmore Vale, and combined the agony and the ecstasy of an artist, the stubborn possessiveness of a house-proud wife and the intermediacy of a wise friend.

Stour Provost consists of a village street, almost unchanged since Constable's time, and a lane leading down to the farm. Tinney, a small-town lawyer, had become the proud owner of *Stratford Mill*, now more commonly known as *The Young Waltonians*, in part payment for a law suit that he had successfully undertaken on behalf of John Fisher, Dean of Salisbury Cathedral.

Fisher was Constable's closest friend and perhaps the first to realise the genius of the temperamental painter. Many in the Establishment had little time for Constable's landscapes and his canvases regularly returned unsold from exhibitions. With a family to support he was approaching middle age increasingly riven and in despair.

The picture must have reached the farm in early summer 1821, for on 19 July Dean Fisher wrote: 'King George IV crowned this day! My dear Constable, your picture is hanging up in a temporary way at Tinney's till his new room is finished. It excites great interest and attention.' For Mrs Tinney, probably no great *connoisseuse* of the arts, it quickly became the most treasured possession in her home.

Slowly but surely, and in no small measure due to Fisher's patronage, Constable's work began to find recognition and in its exhibition of 1825 the Royal Academy agreed to find a space for one of his larger canvases. The out for Defashion Dorset and Dorset Art Weeks at Hawkers Farm. Defashion Dorset brings together local fibre producers and makers. Workshops and demonstrations provide an opportunity to gain new skills.

In nearby Stour Row, at Jolliffe's Cottage, potter Johnathan Garratt makes beautiful creations from Cranborne clay, fired with wood. He takes a truly traditional, slow approach to his craft, and to his marketing too. He has no online presence but welcomes passers-by dropping in to browse.

picture Constable chose to show was *Stratford Mill*, and he wrote to Tinney requesting its loan for the period of the exhibition. Tinney, who had begun to fancy himself as a patron of the arts and had already made offers for further works by the painter, readily agreed, although it can be assumed that Mrs T was more than a little vexed to see her best room denuded of its much-admired decoration. Nevertheless, *Stratford Mill* took the stage to London.

Later that year Constable was approached to give his support to the first exhibition of the newly formed Scottish Academy and again wrote to Tinney asking him to lend the painting for the purpose. This was too much for Mrs T. Quite a few angry words must have been exchanged between the lawyer and his wife in front of the fireplace and this time she prevailed. Sharpening his quill and with his wife's shadow cast from spluttering candles above his shoulders, Tinney penned a letter to Constable, 'With respect to the beautiful picture which is the principal ornament of our house, Mrs Tinney says she will not consent to its being again removed as it was last year

for so long a time ... I hope you will not think her unreasonable.'

Constable did think the lady unreasonable and exploded into an artistic fury that must have shaken his studio to its foundations. His reply to Tinney marked the end of a friendship and the end of the lawyer's brief sway as a collector of contemporary art; Constable cancelled the arrangements under which he had agreed to sell further canvasses to Tinney.

Dean Fisher acted as intermediary and with a series of wise letters calmed the fiery Constable, who eventually accepted, 'My name (though looked for) will not appear at the opening of the noble institution in Edinburgh – I should have liked to have struck a blow in that quarter – but I must submit to circumstances'. Without the calming influence of the dean, Constable would surely have severed an ear, as well as disposed of his reason.

Stratford Mill remained with Tinney for his lifetime and was doubtless the object of minute adjustments and daily dustings by the obstinate Mrs T.

7 MARNHULL

Thomas Hardy enthusiasts seek out Marnhull, which Hardy referred to as Marlott, for it was here that the eponymous heroine of *Tess of the d'Urbervilles* was born and raised. The historic, partly thatched Crown Inn on the edge of the village was the Pure Drop Inn in the novel.

I fear that visitors expecting a village barely changed since Hardy's day will be disappointed; it is a large scattered community with much new development. There are, however, some attractive, old buildings in the local, creamy limestone, quarried at nearby Todber. Particularly handsome are the village's stone farmhouses, such as **Senior's Farm**, adjacent to the church, which dates from 1500, and **Chantry Farmhouse** (formerly Pope's Farm) on the road to Stalbridge. The appealing **church of St Gregory** is largely 15th century and its tall tower can be seen from miles around. Treves (and other writers) recorded a memorial to parish clerk John Warren, who died in 1752, which is sadly no longer visible:

> Here under this stone lie Ruth and old John,
> Who smoked all his life and so did his wife,
> And now there's no doubt,
> But their pipes are both out
> Be it said without joke
> That life is but smoke
> Though you live to fourscore,
> 'Tis a wiff and no more.

John's case does the anti-smoking cause no good at all, as he lived to the age of 94.

Marnhull was reportedly famous for bull-baiting until 1763, when it was banned because of the hooligan behaviour of fans. The annual contest, held on 3 May, saw bulls brought from the surrounding area but rivalry was so intense it often led to violence, which spread to outlying villages.

¶¶ FOOD & DRINK

Blackmore Vale Inn Burton St, DT10 1JJ ✐ 01258 820701. Simple, home-cooked pub food and pizzas served in a building dating from the 16th century.

Crown Inn Crown Rd, DT10 1LN ✐ 01258 820224. This thatched, 16th-century pub appeared in Thomas Hardy's writings as the 'Pure Drop Inn'; it oozes history with its chunky beams, wonky walls and flagstone floor. The menu offers plenty of choice with modern 'small plates', pub classics and Sunday roasts with all the trimmings.

8 STALBRIDGE

Dorset's smallest town sits close to the Somerset border. The long main street lined with historic buildings runs from St Mary's Church to the 32ft-tall 15th-century market cross, said to be one of England's finest. The cross head has a carving of the crucifixion but is a modern copy as the original fell off in 1950.

Guggleton Farm Arts AKA The Gugg (⊘ guggletonfarmarts.com) occupies the outbuildings of a 16th-century farm on Station Road. It supports artists, providing them with studio and exhibition space. It offers courses, such as painting, pottery, stone carving and textile design.

Artist Sir James Thornhill lived south of the town in Thornhill Park, which he bought in 1725; Sir Walter Raleigh is believed to have owned the house in the 16th century. Thornhill was best known as a painter of grand interiors, including the dome of St Paul's Cathedral. In 1727, he erected an obelisk in the grounds to honour the accession of Kind George II. You can see the obelisk from the road (Cook's Lane) near Spire Hill Farm.

¶¶ FOOD & DRINK

Dike & Sons Ring St, DT10 2NB ⊘ 01963 362204 ⊘ dikes-direct.co.uk. Stalbridge has something you don't see very often: a family-run, independent supermarket. The Dike family has had a shop in Stalbridge since 1851. Dikes is a firm favourite with locals and supports local farmers and businesses by stocking their products. It has over a hundred local suppliers, meaning food miles are kept to a minimum, and makes its own sandwiches, pizzas and salads. There is a café on site.

Thyme after Time Units 3 & 4, The Sidings, Station Rd, DT10 2SG ⊘ 01963 362202 ⊘ thymeaftertimecafe.com. Entrepreneur and force of nature, Margot Foot, has put her all into this super little café, where she also operates a catering business and a cream-tea hamper business (page 23). Margot's slogan is 'Dorset born, Dorset fed', a twist on the saying 'Dorset born, Dorset bred, strong in the arm, thick in the head'. And Margot loves feeding people well. The café uses top-quality local ingredients to make favourites like breakfast baps, quiches, Scotch eggs, cream teas and cakes. Its location at the end of the North Dorset Trailway makes it a perfect pit-stop for walkers and riders.

The Trooper Inn Golden Hill, Stourton Caundle DT10 2JW ⊘ 01963 362405. This cosy, independent, family-run pub is the heart of this small community. It lies opposite Manor Farm, once owned by author Enid Blyton (page 38). The menu is traditional pub food done well and reasonably priced. Sunday roast lunch draws people from miles around. There is a pleasant courtyard and the pub hosts regular events and live music.

9 STURMINSTER NEWTON

Sturminster Newton, known to locals as Stur, has been the nucleus of life in the Blackmore Vale for centuries. The town's livestock market, dairy farming, and button- and candle-making brought great prosperity to the area, particularly from 1863 when the Somerset and Dorset Railway opened and the area's milk, cheese and other produce could be sold further afield. The railway closed in 1966 but parts of it now form the **North Dorset Trailway**, a cycle- and footpath that links Sturminster Newton to surrounding villages (page 45).

Sturminster Newton is justifiably proud of its literary connections and celebrates them each year with a literary festival (page 74). Thomas Hardy lived in the town with his wife Emma while writing *The Return of the Native* (1876–78). Dorset poet and author William Barnes (page 47) was born on the outskirts of the town, christened in the church of St Mary and went to school in Sturminster Newton. Robert Young (1811–1908) was born and raised in Sturminster Newton and was an admirer of Barnes, who was ten years his senior. Like Barnes he wrote poems in Dorset dialect.

Although there is much new development on the outskirts of Stur, the town centre, and the marketplace in particular, is overflowing with a variety of historic buildings and architectural styles, including 17th- and 18th-century thatched cottages, Georgian stone houses and 19th-century brick buildings. **Church Street** and **Tanyard Lane** have some particularly pretty houses.

"Around the market square you'll find a refreshingly large number of independent shops."

Prominent in the marketplace are the well-worn stone remains of a 15th-century **market cross**, which was reportedly shaped like a mushroom until 1540 when it was smashed by thieves. A Monday market is held in the town centre. On Tuesday mornings there is a country market in The Exchange, where you'll find fantastic local food and handicrafts.

The town centre has fared better than most, in part because there is no large supermarket in the town but also because the community has fought hard to keep Stur's identity. Around the market square you'll find a refreshingly large number of independent shops, including an excellent butcher, a bakery and a greengrocer. In a former bank building is The Emporium, a community-run second-hand shop where the funds raised benefit the town. Under the same community-benefit umbrella is a second-hand clothing shop, The Boutique. These community projects benefit the town in many ways, including investing funds in keeping the town tidy, clean and attractive through floral displays – all to encourage locals to shop in the town and visitors to come and enjoy its attractions.

A little further down, past the market cross, is 1855, another community-run shop where over 70 local small businesses sell their wares. Expect to find art, cosmetics, food and drink.

In a quaint 16th-century thatched building in the town centre is **Sturminster Museum** (Old Market Cross House ✒ 01258 471878 ⊘ sturminsternewton-museum.co.uk ☉ Easter–Dec 10.00–16.00 Mon & Fri, 10.00–13.00 Thu, 10.00–12.30 Sat; Feb & Mar 10.00–12.30 Mon, Fri & Sat; free admission). The history of the livestock market and local dairy farming features strongly. There are fascinating displays on the local Roman settlements, including the very large, almost complete mosaic found at nearby Hinton St Mary. The original mosaic was discovered in 1963 and the central motif is thought to be the earliest depiction of Christ found in Roman Britain and dates from the fourth century. In 2022, the British Museum commissioned a second round of excavations and a second mosaic was found.

St Mary's Church on Church Lane has a beautiful, intricate 15th-century wagon roof with 14 angels along it. During a 1910–11 restoration, lead shot was removed from the roof that is believed to have been the legacy of Cromwell's soldiers when they were here during the Civil War of 1642–51.

The Station Road livestock market, once the largest in Britain, was central to the vale's important agricultural industry until it closed in 1997. As I grew up in nearby Stour Provost, the Stur Monday market was very much part of my childhood and I recall the sadness that swept the area when it was announced it would close. The historic market had originated from a royal charter of 1219 and there was a fear that Stur would lose its identity when the market was demolished and a seven-acre gaping hole left in the town. However, ten years after the market closed, and thanks to a committed band of locals, **The Exchange** (✒ 01258 475137 ⊘ stur-exchange.co.uk) opened on the site and its art exhibitions, theatre, cinema and community activities now draw crowds from around the vale, just as the market once did. It is an impressive facility for a small country town and the complex in which it stands also houses a much-needed medical centre and some shops. Just as the concept of the new community centre was a local one, so was the building of it. The committee engaged an architect from Shaftesbury and a local builder, while local blacksmith, Ian Ring, created the wrought-iron balustrade on the staircase. The design was inspired by the River Stour, with the supports representing bull rushes and lilies.

Near the exchange is the Railway Garden. The Somerset and Dorset Railway ran through here until 1966 and a section of the original track remains on display.

At the southern end of town an incredibly handsome six-arched 16th-century stone **bridge** spans the River Stour. It is one of the finest medieval bridges in Dorset. A 19th-century plaque warns would-be graffiti artists, 'Any person wilfully injuring any part of this county bridge will be guilty of felony and upon conviction liable to be transported for life'. You have been warned.

From the bridge you catch your first glimpses of **Sturminster Newton Mill** (see below), 250yds upstream.

Locals are used to watching out for **deer** along the A3030 about four miles southwest of Sturminster Newton because the road runs through the **Stock Gaylard Estate** (DT10 2BG ⬥ stockgaylard.com) and alongside its 80-acre **deer park**. Although the common deer and menil fallow have been there for generations, they always seem surprised and a little indignant to see cars pass by. The estate's Georgian house is visible from the road and is occasionally open to the public (see website). Near the house is a tiny 12th-century church, where services are held monthly. In August the estate hosts an **Oak Fair** (⬥ theoakfair.com), which celebrates all things woody and is a chance to meet and buy from local hedgelayers, coppicers and woodturners.

Close to the Stock Gaylard Estate is the village of **Holwell**, which boasts the oldest Royal Mail **pillar box** in use in Britain. Made between 1853 and 1856, it is cast with Queen Victoria's cipher and has a tiny, vertical letter slot. The box is outside Barnes Cross Cottage, not far from the turning to the church.

Sturminster Newton Mill

DT10 2DQ ✐ 01747 473760 ⬥ sturminsternewton-museum.co.uk ◷ Apr–Sep 11.00–17.00 Mon, Thu, Sat & Sun

As you cross the bridge to the south of the town you'll see the picturesque, historic, red-brick mill overlooking a lily-filled meander in the River

Stour. When the mill is open, volunteers are on hand to show you around, explain its workings and recount its history. There is evidence that a mill existed here in 1016 and the Domesday Book of 1086 records a mill on this site. For many years it was thought the present mill dated from the 17th and 19th centuries, but some parts are much older. There is a section of the attic where the beams are particularly old and the construction method is believed to date from the 1400s. In 2013, lime plaster began to peel off one of the mill's interior walls and revealed new evidence that cast doubt on earlier assessments of its age: a stone bearing the date 1566 and other fascinating carvings. Millers had carved their initials into the stone over the centuries, creating a sort of milling wall of fame. Volunteer Pete Loosmore, whose grandfather worked at the mill, explained to me the meaning behind a more magical-looking carving on the same stone: the date 1610 inside a rectangle with a shark's-teeth pattern around the edge. Experts believe the shark's teeth depict VM (Virgin Mary) and ask for her help to protect the mill against witchcraft. The curious carving is a forerunner of the many horseshoes that have been hanging from the building's beams for centuries to bring the mill good luck.

"Millers had carved their initials into the stone over the centuries, creating a sort of milling wall of fame."

The mill has a long and well-documented history of grinding grain to produce flour, but lesser-known is the role it played in the production of swanskin fabric prior to the industrial revolution. Swanskin was an undyed woollen cloth that was hammered and treated to make it waterproof. The fabric was favoured by the fishermen who worked in the freezing waters of the Atlantic, which led Sturminster to establish strong trading links with cod fisheries in Newfoundland, Canada. From the 1600s to the 1800s many local people migrated to Newfoundland and there are still many Dorset surnames recorded in Newfoundland today.

This was a working mill until 1991, but it now only grinds into action when open for visitors, producing flour on the second weekend of each month between April and September. The flour is sold on site and at the Sturminster Museum.

The River Stour is wide here and it is easy to see why generations of artists have been inspired to paint the mill. On a summer's day the water seems to drift unhurriedly towards its destination, lilies provide

STURMINSTER NEWTON LITERARY FESTIVAL

⌂ sturlitfest.com
Rachael Rowe

When Sturminster Newton decided to create a literary festival in 2019, the organisers wanted it to include the community, raise the profile of the town and be somewhat different to the usual circuit of high-profile writers and celebrity ghostwritten biographies. We focused on the three writers associated with the town (Thomas Hardy, William Barnes and Robert Young), contemporary authors and poets with a Dorset or Wessex connection, and aspiring writers. The talent on our own doorstep is inspirational and continues to fill the programme each year.

For ten days, starting in the second week of June, the town is filled with events celebrating Dorset and Wessex literary heritage. We love integrating parts of the community with literary events. For example, a pre-loved fashion show complemented a talk by a writer who set her book in a vintage clothes shop. When we heard about a book on local cider orchards, tastings from local producers were the natural thing to include.

Our walking programme always sells out. You can walk around the village that inspired Hardy's *Tess of the D'Urbervilles* and hear the poetry of William Barnes recited by a Dorset dialect expert close to where the poet was born. As a team of volunteer organisers, we are constantly looking at innovative ways to celebrate and share Dorset's literary heritage and make the festival fun.

colourful decoration and cows graze nonchalantly in the adjacent fields. The scene is best appreciated from the fields opposite the mill, which you can reach across the bridge over the weir, and where a footpath leads along the river towards Hinton St Mary in one direction and Fiddleford in the other. Both are beautiful walks. The picnic benches around the mill make a pleasant lunch spot, and it's also a popular area for fishing. The Hinton St Mary Estate owns this section of the river and if you wish to fish here you will need to obtain a licence from the Sturminster and Hinton Angling Association (⌂ s-haa.co.uk).

Fiddleford Manor

DT10 2BX ℰ 0117 9750700 ⊙ Apr–Oct 10.00–18.00 daily; Nov–Mar 10.00–16.00 daily; free admission; English Heritage

This atmospheric medieval manor a mile east of Sturminster Newton on the A357 is one of the oldest buildings in Dorset and is absolutely worth the small detour. In 1355, the land passed through marriage to William Latimer, later sheriff of Somerset and Dorset. The main parts of the house, which was grand for its time, are thought to have been built for Latimer around 1370. The arched timber braces of the Great Hall and Solar are spectacular and, combined with the low ceilings, wood panelling and hefty fireplaces, give an impression of what a medieval Dorset house may have been like. Upstairs, in what was the family's quarters, is a 14th-century wall painting of the Angel Gabriel announcing that Mary would give birth to the son of God. It was discovered in 1990 under layers of whitewash and is remarkably well preserved. It is a privilege to admire the 14th-century craftsmanship and the 16th- and 17th-century additions. As you look out of the upstairs window at the River Stour, it is humbling and exciting to think of the characters that have stood there over the centuries, enjoying a view that has barely changed.

From the car park at the manor it is a short walk along the lane to pick up the footpath along the river. Turn left and it will take you past Fiddleford Mill, across the weir and along the river towards Sturminster. In summer you will often see people swimming at the weir, but it can be very dangerous. Turn right and you can walk along the North Dorset Trailway (page 45), where the Fiddleford Inn (see below) makes a good rest stop.

¶¶ FOOD & DRINK

From 1913 until its closure in 2000, the Sturminster Creamery was a major employer in the town. It was founded by a co-operative of local farmers, who sought to supply fresh milk and Cheddar cheese to the area. Today, Stur's cheese-making history is celebrated via the town's annual **Cheese Festival**, one of the largest in England (⌂ cheesefestival.co.uk).

Fiddleford Inn Fiddleford DT10 2BX ✆ 01258 472886. A traditional pub with a good-sized beer garden, which is a popular stop for walkers, horseriders and cyclists on the trailway. Serves real ales and pub fare.
Holebrooks 6 Market Pl, DT10 1AR ✆ 01258 472077 ⌂ holebrooks.co.uk. In the centre of town, this butcher was taken over by The Udder Farm Shop (page 62) in 2023. It stocks a good range of meat, locally made ice cream and deli items.
Olives et al 1 North Dorset Business Park, DT10 2GA ✆ 01258 474300 ⌂ olivesetal.co.uk. There is far more than just delicious, marinated olives at this fabulous deli on the outskirts of Stur, making it a great place to pick up self-catering or picnic fare. The flavoured kiln-roasted nuts and salad dressings are superb. You will see their products in farm shops and delis throughout the West Country.

Oxford's Bakery 1 Market Cross, DT10 1BB ✆ 01258 472834. Fresh bread, quiches and pastry baked locally.

The Stur of the Moment Bath Rd, DT10 1AS ✆ 01258 473182. Tracy Young and her team run a super café in this handsome, characterful, Grade II-listed building. The building was formerly the offices of the auctioneers that ran the livestock market and still has the original walk-in safe. The hearty breakfasts are very popular, the cakes are made in house and the afternoon tea served on a pretty, tiered cake stand is a real treat. On a sunny day, you may like to take your tea in the courtyard. Good value for money.

Sweet Pea Market Cross, DT10 1AN ✆ 01258 473006 . It is clear a lot of love has gone into creating this popular option in the town centre. The menu includes vegan and gluten-free dishes.

The White Horse Hinton St Mary DT10 1NA ✆ 01258 915001. A delightful country pub just outside Sturminster Newton. Expect good-quality pub favourites plus more upmarket dishes.

10 THE FIFEHEADS

⌂ **Plumber Manor**

About three miles southwest of Sturminster Newton are the attractive and historic hamlets of **Fifehead Neville** and **Fifehead St Quintin**, both of which are listed in the Domesday Book. The dainty River Divelish runs between them, and at the entrance to Fifehead Neville is a ford and a photogenic medieval stone packhorse bridge across the water. The bridge is thought to have been built around 1200 and has two distinctive pointed arches. It's typical of a packhorse bridge – around one horse wide and with low parapets to allow the animals and their panniers to pass unhindered. It would have been essential before the days when transporting goods by horse and cart became the norm. It is one of only a handful of packhorse bridges surviving in Dorset. In the centre of the hamlet, behind a towering yew tree, is the small but beautiful All Saints Church. In the churchyard is a huge table tomb, the mausoleum of the Brune family, whose descendants still live in the area at Plumber Manor (see below).

🧳 SPECIAL STAYS

Plumber Manor DT10 2AF ✆ 01258 472507 ⌂ plumbermanor.co.uk. It's hard to imagine a hotel where guests are made to feel more welcome, which is perhaps why Plumber Manor

1 Sturminster Newton Mill. **2** The interior of medieval Fiddleford Manor. **3** The photogenic stone bridge in Fifehead Neville. ▶

HONEYBUNS BAKERY

Naish Farm, Holwell DT9 5LJ 📞 01963 23597 🔗 honeybuns.co.uk

Naish Farm in Holwell is the headquarters of the wonderful Honeybuns, which makes exquisite cakes and traybakes that just happen to be gluten-free; there are also dairy-free and vegan options. Emma Goss-Custard started Honeybuns 20 years ago, making cakes in her student digs and delivering them by bike to local businesses. On the first Saturday morning of the month (except January and February) there is a pop-up shop at the bakery, where you can find not-quite-perfect cakes at perfect prices. You can also order their delicious treats online or pick them up in local retailers. Emma and her team take sustainability seriously and have impressive green credentials.

I have done some extensive taste testing and I can tell you their flapjacks are superb. My other personal favourites are the cinnamon slice and the raspberry bakewell.

enjoys such a high rate of repeat guests. Key to the warm atmosphere are the charismatic Richard Prideaux-Brune, whose ancestors built the house in the 17th century, and his hard-working wife Alison. This is their home, and it feels like you're being welcomed as an old friend rather than a hotel guest. The Jacobean manor sits in beautiful, peaceful gardens crossed by the River Divelish and surrounded by farmland. Accommodation is in the main house, packed with family history, or a converted courtyard of buildings in the grounds. The atmosphere is delightfully old school as befits the historic building – antiques and ancestral portraits abound. The hotel is popular with shooting parties in winter so welcomes dogs. There are plenty of dog walks straight from the grounds. The fine-dining restaurant serves tasty, traditional fare in elegant surroundings and is excellent value for money – bookings essential.

11 OKEFORD FITZPAINE

If you can ignore the extensive new development on the outskirts of this large village, the centre of Okeford Fitzpaine is charming and well worth exploring on foot. There are some lovely, wonky, old cottages, a thriving village shop and the handsome church of St Andrew. Unlike many, the church is open during the day. Visitors will notice the lack of pews; the Victorian-era pews were sold off by the church in 2020. The move caused outrage among many of the villagers but it was deemed necessary to create more space in the church. One of the reasons cited was that the pews were 'not suited to the human form of today'; apparently during some weddings the happy couple had been too wide to fit down the aisle side by side!

Next to the well-stocked village shop is a tiny museum containing firefighting equipment from 1809, an ancient funeral bier and a government-issued, hand-cranked siren from 1993 designed to warn of impending disaster. Opposite it are the remains of the market cross, thought to date from the 14th century. Nearby, in a row of cottages, a pointed arch oak door with a grille looks rather out of place. The building dates from the 1700s and served as the village lock-up. These small gaols were common in villages and used for holding troublemakers before they went before a justice of the peace. The lock-up's former cells have now been incorporated into a cottage, with the door and grille preserved as a reminder of its former use. It is said that cider was piped through the grille to refresh the unfortunate occupants.

To the south of the village is a historic pound, where travellers could leave their stock overnight and where stray cattle wandering the streets could be kept safely until their owners could collect them. Just beyond the pound is the left turning up to Okeford Hill. It is a steep climb and a parking area at the top gives superb views over the Blackmore Vale with Hambledon Hill, Duncliffe Hill and Shaftesbury standing out as landmarks. Okeford Hill offers wonderful walking and bridleways through open fields and woodland, which in spring is carpeted with bluebells and wild garlic. The paths link up with the Wessex Ridgeway, which leads all the way to the coast at Lyme Regis. The hill is very popular with paragliders when the conditions suit and there is also a downhill mountain-biking track (⊘ okefordhillbikepark.com) for experienced riders.

> *"It is said that cider was piped through the grille to refresh the unfortunate occupants."*

¶¶ FOOD & DRINK

The Royal Oak DT11 0RN ⊘ 01258 861561. There were once five pubs in the village, but now there's just one. It's an unassuming country pub with a menu of traditional pub grub.

12 SHILLINGSTONE

As you enter this large village, a sign proudly announces it as the bravest village in Britain. This is because of the high proportion of villagers who volunteered to enlist in World War I. During the first six months of the war, there was a prize for the village that sent the highest proportion of its men to join the services. It was initially won by a village in Kent,

Cycle ride: Wessex Ridgeway & Winterborne Valley circular

Dilys Gartside – cycling instructor, Cyclewise Dorset & cyclewisedorset.co.uk

※ OS Explorer maps 117 and 129; start: Okeford Fitzpaine; ♥ ST 80649 10938; 18 miles; moderate

In springtime, your senses will be delighted by bluebells and wild garlic but first you must climb from the village nestled in its foothills to the Wessex Ridgeway. Your return up through the Winterborne Valley has a magic of its own and the view from Okeford Hill is breathtaking. The ride demands a good level of fitness, or you could use an e-bike. For refreshments, try Milton Abbas (half-mile detour) for Steepletonbill Farm Shop or The Hambro Arms; The Crown in Winterborne Stickland; or the Village Stores or The Royal Oak in Okeford Fitzpaine.

1 From Okeford Fitzpaine, take the road south uphill through Fippenny Hollow and keep straight ahead, ignoring the left turn to Turnworth.

2 On reaching The Cross at Belchalwell, turn left for the big climb up Bell Hill and along the route of the Wessex Ridgeway towards the tall masts in the distance.

3 Just past the viewpoint car park, at the junction take the sharp turn back to your left and after 875yds turn right towards Milton Abbas. In spring basketfuls of garlic may be collected along here.

4 Stop at the junction of High Lodge; on a clear day you'll spy Poole Harbour glistening in the sun. Turn right downhill (ignore the right turn to Milton Abbas except as a detour for refreshments) and continue straight on to Winterborne Whitechurch.

5 Turn left for around 30yds on the A354 before turning left again to start your return journey up the lovely Winterborne Valley, passing through Winterborne Clenston, with its

with Shillingstone as runner-up. However, Shillingstone's vicar objected on the grounds that the winner had only six houses and was therefore a hamlet. After reconsideration, Shillingstone was awarded the title of 'The Bravest Village in England' and received a letter of praise from King George V. Out of a total population of 565, 99 men volunteered; 25 of them did not return.

The village's main attraction is the lovingly restored Shillingstone Station, which survives on the former Somerset and Dorset Railway line, now part of the North Dorset Trailway (page 45). Shillingstone is one of the best starting points for a walk along the trailway. Parking is pretty church and tithe barn. As you reach Winterborne Stickland, the climb starts gently towards the Ridgeway once more, but not until Hedge End (it really is at the end of a long hedge) and Turnworth Church (attended by Thomas Hardy and rebuilt in the late 19th century with his architectural input) have been reached does the climb require concentration.

6 When you reach the top of Okeford Hill, stop to admire one of England's best views, over the Blackmore Vale. Negotiate the 25% descent with care and fork right at the bottom to Okeford Fitzpaine, where the Royal Oak awaits.

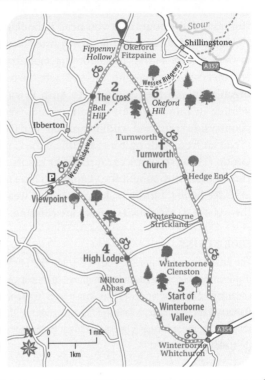

available at the station or in the parking area at the junction of the A357 and Bere Marsh. The restored railway station is full of vintage charm and has a small museum and café (page 82).

On the outskirts of the village, heading towards Blandford, is the Big Yellow Bus Project (🖰 bigyellowbus.co.uk). This four-acre community garden run by volunteers is designed to provide a wellbeing space for local people. It was founded by Paul Williams to offer gardening to young people as a therapeutic activity. Since then the garden has evolved into a resource for the whole community. Some people come simply to relax, others want to be given a job to do. The garden has an acre of orchard, a wildlife pond, a bird hide, seating areas, and flower and vegetable gardens. It is relatively flat and there is a gravel path through most of the garden, so it is accessible to all. It runs alongside the North Dorset Trailway so you can easily pop in and have a look around if you're walking the trailway. Bikes are available to borrow free of charge (for up to three hours) but you need to book in advance.

Along the trailway on the Sturminster Newton side of Shillingstone is Bere Marsh Farm. In 2020, the Countryside Regeneration Trust (⌖ thecrt.co.uk) bought this 92-acre farm that had been farmed organically and they continue to farm it with conservation and local wildlife in mind. There is a café on site (see below) and courses on countryside crafts and wildlife are run here (see website).

Not far from Shillingstone, at Hillcombe Coppice, the Dorset Coppice Group (⌖ dorsetcoppicegroup.co.uk) has its living classroom where it runs courses throughout the year. If you have always wanted to have a go at hedge laying, hurdle making or basket weaving, it is worth checking the website to see which courses are running.

¶¶ FOOD & DRINK

The Buzz Bere Marsh Farm, DT11 0QY ⌖ 07944 790514 ⌖ thebuzzcafe.co.uk. A handy, dog-friendly stopping-off point for hot drinks, cakes and sausage rolls on the trailway at the Countryside Regeneration Trust's Bere Marsh Farm (see above).

Railway Café Shillingstone Railway Station, Station Rd, DT11 0SA. It's basic (sandwiches, soup etc) but the attraction is being able to eat in a vintage railway carriage and walk along the trailway.

13 HAZLEBURY BRYAN

This scattered, confusing village consists of seven tiny hamlets, each with its own name. Hazlebury Bryan is one of those deliciously descriptive Dorset village names, so it is rather deflating to learn that the older part of the village lies in the area known as Droop. The **church of St Mary and St James** is charming, a simple golden stone building by a large pond. It is of mainly 15th-century construction; the well-preserved wooden door and wagon roof date from that period.

On the road from Hazlebury Bryan to Kings Stag is **Alners Gorse Butterfly Reserve**. This 35-acre reserve is one of Dorset's few remaining areas of common land and open to visitors on foot. The wet grassland, scrub and woodland is being restored, and is grazed by Dartmoor ponies as part of the management programme. It supports an important population of butterflies and moths, and is managed specifically to encourage the marsh fritillary butterfly, which was once abundant in the area. The Blackmore Vale is the only area of Dorset where the brown hairstreak is found (usually seen in July and August); other species you may see here include grizzled skipper, silver-washed fritillary and white admiral. Around one fifth of the UK's moth species have been spotted here, including rare species such as dingy mocha and ruddy carpet. Birds have cottoned on that this is a great place to live, and there are good numbers of nightingale, green warber, and green and greater spotted woodpeckers here.

14 BLANDFORD FORUM

Blandford is hailed as one of the finest Georgian rural market towns in England, and occupies an enviable position in a wooded valley on the banks of the River Stour. Much of the original town was destroyed by a devastating fire in 1731, which began in a tallow chandler's (candle maker's) shop on the site now occupied by the Kings Arms. Over 450 people lost their homes and at least 14 townsfolk died; the town museum (page 85) has a model showing the extent of the damage. Memorably named local architects and builders John and William Bastard were engaged to design and rebuild the town: the elegant, coherent Georgian town centre is the result. Its uniformity gives it a very different feel to other Dorset towns.

The **church of St Peter and St Paul** (☉ 09.30–noon Mon–Fri) dominates the town centre, a simple, classical building built on the site of its medieval predecessor. Its most recognisable feature, the wooden cupola on its tower, was not part of the original design. The Bastard brothers intended a steeple to be built but apparently the money ran out and they had to make do with the cupola, which was added in 1758. (By all accounts, the Bastard brothers were not impressed with this deviation from their plan.) The interior is unashamedly grand, with Portland stone columns supporting a vaulted ceiling.

In front of the church is the **Fire Monument** designed by John Bastard and dated 1760, known as the Bastard's Pump. It was intended to provide water for firefighting in the event of a further fire. The inscription acknowledges, with just a touch of hyperbole, 'the divine mercy that has since raised this town, like the Phoenix from its ashes to

DORSET BLUE VINNY CHEESE

Woodbridge Farm, Stock Gaylard DT10 2BD ☎ 01963 23133 ✆ dorsetblue.co.uk

Dorset has many fine food traditions and one of the best known is Dorset Blue Vinny cheese. The Davies family makes this pasteurised farmhouse cheese at their farm just outside Sturminster Newton, along with a range of fresh soups and chutneys.

There was a time when the manufacture of Dorset Blue Vinny cheese was virtually ubiquitous throughout the county's farmhouses. It was a by-product of butter-making, using the milk after the cream had been skimmed off.

However, the production of Dorset Blue Vinny ceased following the establishment of the government's Milk Marketing Board in 1933. The board purchased all of the milk produced by a farm, which meant the farmer's wife was no longer able to set aside milk for making cheese. Michael Davies revived the tradition in the 1980s. During the time of milk lakes and butter mountains, Michael began to question his commitment to early mornings and milking; he had originally trained as a cheese maker and thought it might be time to put those skills to use. According to his daughter Emily, 'he was truly one of the first to diversify and value-add – the buzzwords of today'. The family produced its first Dorset Blue Vinny in 1982, matured in the farmhouse pantry; it turned the walls, cornflakes and marmalade blue

The process of making this cheese begins with the milk from their herd of Holstein Friesian cows, which graze the lush pastures of the Blackmore Vale. Once the milk has been brought up to temperature they hand-skim the cream from the milk. A penicillin promotes the blueing of the cheese. Once the milk has coagulated, it is cut into small pieces and left overnight. The resulting whey is drained off and the curd cut into blocks, ground, salted and packed into moulds. After a few days, the moulds are transferred to the ripening room where they stay for between three and five months, and are turned and spiked according to whether the blue needs to develop.

As you drive from Sturminster Newton towards Sherborne along the A3030 you pass Woodbridge Farm. In the mornings and afternoons you'll see the herd patiently waiting in the yard for milking. You can buy their excellent, unhomogenised fresh milk from a vending machine in the farmyard, where other local produce is also on sale, including the farm's famous Dorset Blue Vinny. My husband was at the milk station recently and met a man from Birmingham who had stopped in especially to buy Dorset Blue Vinny cheese – it really is that good!

its present beautiful and flourishing state'. John Bastard signs himself off as 'a considerable sharer in the great calamity'.

Opposite the church, marked with a plaque, is the house that was built for John and William Bastard following the fire. Along with the

Town Hall and the former Greyhound Inn (with a hare and a hound painted above the entrance), it is one of the town's finest buildings. A few buildings survived the fire, including the Ryves Almshouses of 1682 in Salisbury Street and the Old House of 1660 in The Close. Most of East Street escaped unscathed as it had been rebuilt in brick after an earlier fire in 1713.

Today's Blandfordians can see the lighter side of the 'calamity': a paving stone in front of the Town Hall bears the inscription, 'Recipe for regeneration: take one careless tallow chandler and two ingenious Bastards', words drafted by the Blandford poetry group for the Millennium project.

The Georgian marketplace comes into its own on Thursdays and Saturdays, when it hosts a bustling food and bric-a-brac **market**. Blandford is justifiably proud of its Georgian heritage and a **Georgian Fayre** is held on the May Day Bank Holiday in the town centre, when people dress in period costume and enjoy market stalls and a funfair.

"The Bastard brothers intended a steeple to be built but apparently the money ran out and they had to make do with the cupola."

It is said that in 1788 a band of smugglers was apprehended near Sixpenny Handley and their loot taken to Blandford and put into an excise store. The following night some unsavoury characters broke into the store, grabbed the tea and liquor and rode through the town handing it out to the townspeople. As you stand in the centre of Blandford it is easy to imagine the event – and the townspeople's delight.

On the edge of town, bordering the River Stour, is the Milldown Nature Reserve, pleasant for walking and wildlife spotting. If you are lucky you may even see a kingfisher or otters. It is close to the North Dorset Trailway, so the two can be combined for a longer walk. Blandford also has strong military links, with Blandford Camp lying just outside the town, and the Signals Museum within it (page 87).

Blandford Town Museum

Beres Yard, Market Pl, DT11 7H   ✆ 01258 450388   ⟁ blandfordtownmuseum.org.uk
◷ Apr–Oct 10.00–16.00 Tue, Thu–Sat

This museum opposite the church of St Peter and St Paul gives a glimpse of life in the town as it used to be. Detailed reconstructions bring the history to life and include a 19th-century forge used to service the local

Portman Hunt horses, a Victorian kitchen and Blandford market in the 18th century. Particularly interesting is the model of the town following the fire of 1731, showing the devastation caused and the few areas that survived.

Behind the museum is a small Victorian garden; the shop sells plants grown there, along with honey products from local bees. A dedicated team of volunteers ensures the museum keeps running.

The Blandford Fashion Museum

Lime Tree House, 11 The Plocks, DT11 7AA ✐ 01258 453006 ✐ blandfordfashionmuseum. co.uk ☉ 10.00–16.00 Mon & Thu–Sat (Apr–Sep till 17.00), closed Dec–mid-Feb

Within an attractive red-brick house built by the Bastard brothers just after the fire that destroyed Blandford, this costume collection dates from the 1730s to the 1970s and was begun by the late Betty Penny MBE after World War II. For 35 years Mrs Penny toured the country with her historical fashion show, *Cavalcade of Costume*, raising money for charity. A benefactor bought Lime Tree House for Mrs Penny in 1996 to house her collection. Enthusiastic volunteers are on hand to show you around and will even help you try on a corset, and in one of the rooms mannequins are dressed in clothing from the era in which the house was built. For me, the highlights were the Victorian wedding collection and crinolines, and the display of Dorset buttons (page 59). There is a resources room for students and a very good tea room (see opposite).

Hall & Woodhouse Brewery

The Brewery, Blandford St Mary DT11 9LS ✐ 01258 486004 ✐ hall-woodhousebrewerytap. co.uk ☉ tours Jan–Nov 10.30 Mon–Fri, 10.30 & 13.30 Sat; booking essential

The badger logo of the Hall & Woodhouse Brewery is a familiar sight around Dorset, as are its quirkily named beers, among them Fursty Ferret, Pickled Partridge and Poacher's Choice (all sold under the name Badger rather than Hall & Woodhouse).

Hall & Woodhouse is run by the fifth generation of the Woodhouse family and has a formidable history. A Dorset farmer, Charles Hall, founded a brewery at Ansty in 1777, providing beer to the troops during the Napoleonic Wars. In 1847, Robert Hall, the founder's son, went into partnership with George Woodhouse. The badger was adopted as the brewery's trademark in 1875. It has developed into a successful independent brewery with 240 pubs across the south of England.

The visitor centre tells the story of the brewery and guided tours are available, ending with a tasting.

The Royal Signals Museum

Blandford Camp DT11 8RH ✆ 01258 482248 ⌖ royalsignalsmuseum.co.uk ◷ 10.00–16.30 Mon–Thu, 10.00–noon Fri, plus Feb–Oct 10.00–16.00 Sat

This museum tells the story of military communications through the ages. It lies within Blandford Camp Military Base, two miles northeast of Blandford Forum. As it is on base, visitors need to sign in; you will need photo identification and you will have your photograph taken. Fascinating displays on codes and code-breaking include the story of the Special Operations Executive (SOE) in World War II and the ENIGMA cipher machine. Motorcycle enthusiasts may enjoy the collection of military motorcycles from 1914 to the present.

¶¶ FOOD & DRINK

Cafés and restaurants seem to come and go regularly in Blandford, but there are always plenty of them.

Crown Hotel West St, DT11 7AJ ✆ 01258 456626. A former coaching inn in the centre of town, owned by Blandford brewery Hall & Woodhouse. Georgian architecture and antiques give an elegant feel to the restaurant, while the oak-panelled bar has more of a country-boozer vibe. The menu is made up of pub classics.

Fashion Museum Tea Rooms Lime Tree House, The Plocks, DT11 7AA ✆ 01258 453006. Very reasonably priced cream teas and homemade cakes are served by cheerful volunteers. Has a vintage feel and the tea is served in pretty blue and white Poole Pottery teaware. You don't need to pay the museum entry fee to enjoy the tearoom and there is a courtyard for sunny days, where dogs are welcome.

Hall and Woodhouse Brewery Tap Blandford St Mary DT11 9LS ✆ 01258 486005 ⌖ hall-woodhousebrewerytap.co.uk. A pub at the home of the Hall & Woodhouse Brewery (see opposite). It's popular for breakfast, lunch and dinner, or just coffee and cake. Expect a traditional pub menu and the use of their own beers wherever possible, for instance in the steak and Tangle Foot pie. Brewery tours must be booked in advance.

Lo's Coffee Shop R Lukins Fitness, Stud Farm, Pimperne DT11 8XA ✆ 07810 433501. Just outside Blandford, at a gym in the village of Pimperne. A very dog-friendly café with a map of suggested dog walks starting from the cafe, and doggy ice cream. Owner Laurie Griffin has clearly got something right – within months of opening in 2023 the café had trebled in size. Look out for themed evenings and events.

Yellow Bicycle Café 30a Salisbury St, DT11 7AR ✆ 01258 480356. Owner Steve takes pride in the café's homemade food. and he takes care to source produce locally. Even the dough for the flatbreads is made on site. This is far more than a café, serving sophisticated restaurant-quality dishes like partridge in a creamy mushroom sauce.

15 STOURPAINE

The busy A350 runs through the village but there are some attractive, quiet spots away from the road, in particular near the Holy Trinity Church. Here you will find dainty cottages, some thatched, with flower-filled gardens; the smell of roses and other flowers hangs in the air on a summer's day. Just north of the church is a crossroads; the turning to the left leads to the **North Dorset Trailway**, a foot-, cycle- and bridle path that runs to Shillingstone (2½ miles) and Sturminster Newton (5½ miles). To the right of the Trailway is a track leading to a footpath running through woodland beside the River Stour and up on to Hod Hill.

"Here you will find dainty cottages, some thatched, with flower-filled gardens; the smell of roses and other flowers hangs in the air."

In 2010, Stourpaine suffered a loss that has been felt by many villages around the country – its post office and village shop closed. A year later, thanks to village spirit and 'The Pub is the Hub', they reopened at the White Horse pub on the main road (see below). The Pub is the Hub (⊘ pubisthehub.org.uk) is a scheme initiated in 2001 by King Charles III when he was Prince of Wales, champion of preserving rural ways of life; his venture encourages local people, breweries and pub owners to provide essential services, like a village shop, within rural pubs.

Stourpaine did just that and villagers now have access to a well-stocked little shop adjoining the pub. A letter from the Prince of Wales's office in support of the move has pride of place on the wall of the shop, and in May 2011 Prince Charles and the Duchess of Cornwall visited the White Horse to see the changes for themselves. The pub has also provided regular 'surgeries' for residents with the local vicar and police, a prescription collection point and a book exchange.

⅋⅃ FOOD & DRINK

White Horse Shaston Rd, DT11 8TA ✆ 01258 453535. A popular pub with village shop (see above) on the main A350, which serves traditional food and local beers. Each summer, London theatre company Shooting Stars puts on a Shakespeare play in the car park.

16 CHILD OKEFORD

Child Okeford is a large village with some appealing 18th- and 19th-century houses and farm buildings, and several modern housing developments on the outskirts. Its principal attraction is that it lies in the shadow of Hambledon Hill and is a good starting point for walks up it to view the Iron Age hillfort on the summit and the Blackmore Vale stretching out beneath it.

In the 1560s the village vicar, William Kethe, composed the well-known hymn, The Old Hundredth ('All People That on Earth do Dwell'). A Bible from his era (1568) is on display in the church, although the church would have looked rather different in his day; while the tower is 15th century, the rest dates from the mid-1800s.

Gold Hill Organic Farm (DT11 8HB ✐ 01258 861916 ✆ goldhillorganicfarm.com ○ 10.00–18.00 Thu & Fri, 10.00–16.00 Sat) was one of the first organic farms in Dorset, started over 30 years ago. The shop sells organic meat, dairy products and vegetables. Some of the farm buildings have been converted and it has developed into a small complex with arty shops and a café.

⅞ FOOD & DRINK

Gold Hill Farm Kitchen DT11 8HB ✐ 07443 893135 ✆ goldhillfarmkitchen.co.uk. Located at Gold Hill Organic Farm, the menu uses as much of the farm's produce as possible. The menu is predominantly vegetarian and each dish is prepared from scratch with great care. The courgette fritters are excellent.

Meggy Moo's Dairy Park Farm, Iwerne Courtney DT11 8TP ✐ 07908 267410. Vending machines selling dairy products courtesy of the farm's Holstein herd. Also locally made cakes, cheese, ice cream and take-away coffee made with the farm's milk. There are a couple of picnic tables where you can enjoy your purchases with a view of Hambledon Hill.

17 HOD HILL

National Trust; free access

Hod Hill stands unassumingly beside its more celebrated neighbour, Hambledon Hill, yet Hod's hillfort is larger: 54 acres versus Hambledon's 30. Its multiple ramparts protected an Iron Age village of over 250 roundhouses, the footprints of many of which are still visible as depressions in the ground. The Romans, led by Vespasian, captured the Celtic settlement of the Durotriges tribe around AD44 and built their own camp in the northwest corner. By that stage, they had already taken Maiden Castle, near Dorchester.

There is a small car-parking area at the base of Hod Hill; to reach it take the Child Okeford and Hanford turning from the A350. Several paths begin here; one leads through woodland and along the River Stour to Stourpaine, while a bridleway leads to the top of Hod Hill. A steep walk up rewards you with glorious views of the surrounding countryside and a fabulous archaeological juxtaposition: the rigid lines of the Roman fort and the softer, more organic ones of the earlier settlement. This is a fine place to contemplate life for the original inhabitants and what must have gone through their minds when they saw the mighty Roman army advancing across the countryside. These days it is remarkably peaceful on top of the hill: the only sound is the breeze and the occasional shriek of a buzzard circling over the vale, while livestock graze nonchalantly, oblivious of the many layers of history beneath them.

"A steep walk up rewards you with glorious views of the surrounding countryside and a fabulous archaeological juxtaposition."

Hod Hill is a rich chalk grassland site with a colourful carpet of wildflowers. Cowslips are prolific in spring, followed by milkwort, horseshoe vetch, rock rose and common spotted orchids. It is a popular butterfly-watching spot thanks to its populations of Adonis blue, chalkhill blue, marsh fritillary and grizzled skipper.

18 HAMBLEDON HILL

National Trust; free access

The view from Hambledon Hill is one to soothe the soul and replenish the energy stores, which is just as well as the walk to the summit is one to tire the legs. The hill juts out into the Blackmore Vale, providing a natural viewing platform over the tapestry of small fields and villages.

Archaeologists flock to Hambledon Hill and although its earliest occupation was Neolithic, it is best known as an Iron Age hillfort. The site seems to have been abandoned around 300BC, possibly in favour of nearby Hod Hill. One summer when I was walking on Hambledon Hill, photographing the view towards Shaftesbury, a group of archaeologists

---

1 Hambledon Hill. 2 The Blandford Fire Monument. 3 Vintage trains at the restored Shillingstone Station. 4 & 5 Look out for grizzled skippers on Hod Hill. ▶

A walk around Hambledon Hill & Hod Hill

✺ OS Explorer map 118; start: Cricketers Pub, Iwerne Courtney ♀ SY859127; approximately 5½ miles; medium (some steep hills). Refreshments at The Cricketers pub (see opposite). To walk Hod Hill only, start at the car park at the base of Hod Hill ♀ SY853112.

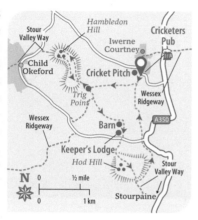

This walk is mostly well signed, and uses parts of the Stour Valley Way and the Wessex Ridgeway. The hillforts are natural vantage points for fabulous views over North Dorset's enchanting farmland. The footpath is signed from behind The Cricketers pub. Keep the cricket pitch on your right and head for the chalk path up the hill, then bear right through the fields, which are often lined with poppies. At the top of the hill is a trig point, from where you get your first sight of the hillfort on your right. You are free to wander the hilltop and the impressive ramparts, which are owned by the National Trust, but be aware that Hambledon Hill is grazed by livestock.

Return to the trig point and take the path signed Steepleton Iwerne. When you reach the large barn you will need to head through the gate and turn right down the hill, following the hedgerow. Hod Hill is visible in front of you. At the bottom you will cross the road near Keeper's Lodge and start the climb up Hod Hill. The path takes you diagonally across the hillfort, where signs of its ancient settlements are visible. A gate at the other side leads to Stourpaine, where there is a pub if you fancy a detour, but for this route turn left before the gate and follow the path below the ramparts. Go through the next gate on your right and turn left then follow the path to the bottom of the hill. You will need to cross the road again then head up the bridleway, which takes you back to The Cricketers pub. Doing this walk in late summer offers the chance to fuel yourself on blackberries on the way.

on a guided tour came up beside me and I heard several shrieks of excitement. It was the end of a particularly hot and dry spell and the weather had exposed the outline of a Neolithic enclosure, which even the tour leader had never seen before.

Hambledon Hill is where the Dorset Clubmen were routed by Cromwell in 1645 during the Civil War. Armed only with clubs, 2,000 to

4,000 farmers and yeomen banded together to protest at the plundering by the armies traversing Dorset. They were not in favour of either the king or the parliament, they had simply lost patience with troops from both sides trampling their crops, stealing their livestock and ransacking their barns. Their motto made their grievance clear:

If ye offer to plunder or take our cattle, be assured we'll give you battle.

Cromwell attacked with a thousand men; a dozen farmers were killed and some 300 taken prisoner in Iwerne Courtney Church, where Cromwell rebuked them before releasing them.

Of various starting points for walks up Hambledon Hill, a particularly good one is from just behind The Cricketers pub in **Iwerne Courtney** (also known as Shroton) because of the promise of a hearty meal on your return (see below).

FOOD & DRINK

The Cricketers Main St, Iwerne Courtney (Shroton), Blandford Forum DT11 8QD ⌀ 01258 860421 ⌀ thecricketersshroton.co.uk. A family-friendly pub opposite the village green and backing on to Hambledon Hill – the perfect spot from which to explore this huge prehistoric hillfort. The menu features pub classics done well, and a traditional roast on Sunday.

CRANBORNE CHASE

The B3081 from Shaftesbury takes you up on to the hills of Cranborne Chase for sweeping panoramas of the Dorset and Wiltshire countryside. **Win Green** (National Trust) lies just over the Wiltshire border; it is the highest point in Cranborne Chase and draws an assortment of walkers, model-aircraft enthusiasts and kite-flyers. The hill is crowned by a clump of trees growing on a Bronze Age bowl barrow.

Cranborne Chase was once a royal hunting ground, hence the 'Chase' part of the name, and originally covered the area between Shaftesbury, Salisbury, Ringwood, Wimborne and Blandford Forum. An impressive line-up of monarchs hunted here, including King John, Henry VIII and James I. In those days much of the area would have been wooded but today it is characterised by open downland with pockets of woodland. The land remained in royal ownership until James I handed the estate to Robert Cecil, First Earl of Salisbury, and the royal hunting lodge became Cranborne Manor, which remains at the heart of the estate. In the 18th and 19th centuries, the chase's remoteness made it a favourite haunt of smugglers, who hid contraband here.

Unblemished Cranborne Chase draws walkers, cyclists and horseriders, as well as archaeologists, who come in search of the **Dorset Cursus**, a Neolithic cursus monument spanning 6¼ miles of chalk downland. A cursus consists of large, parallel linear banks with external ditches, perhaps used as a processional route or as part of ceremonial competitions. The Dorset Cursus, the longest known example of its kind, crosses a river and three valleys, and runs close to Knowlton and its Neolithic henge topped with the ruins of a medieval church (page 106).

In 2019, the whole Cranborne Chase was designated an international dark-sky reserve. The status is awarded to areas that have exceptional starry skies with minimal light pollution and a commitment to protect them. Cranborne Chase National Landscape (⊘ cranbornechase.org. uk) is very active and organises regular events – check the website for details.

En route to the village of Cranborne from Shaftesbury, the road sneaks briefly into Wiltshire again around Tollard Royal and the Rushmore Estate. This well-managed estate incorporates a popular golf course, preparatory school and the **Larmer Tree Gardens** and café (Tollard Royal, Wiltshire SP5 5PT ⊘ 01725 516971 ⊘ larmertree.co.uk ⊙ Apr– Oct 11.00–16.00 Sun–Thu; check website for closures due to events).

19 FONTMELL & MELBURY DOWNS

The unclassified upper Blandford road from Shaftesbury takes you through the village of **Melbury Abbas** and up on to Fontmell and Melbury Downs, which open up before you in a burst of bucolic beauty. The quintessentially English rolling hills with patches of woodland provide inspiring views and walks on the western edge of Cranborne Chase. Many locals escape here to walk the dog, or just admire the scenery.

At 720 acres, Fontmell and Melbury Downs is the National Trust's largest chalk-downland site, and in summer the area is awash with wildflowers, birdlife and butterflies, including the Adonis blue and chalkhill blue. Access to the walks above Melbury Abbas is from small car parks on Spread Eagle Hill; take care along this road as visibility is poor and traffic moves at high speeds. It is an easy, mostly level walk of three miles along the hilltop to **Melbury Beacon**, erected in 1588 to warn of the invading Spanish Armada. The walk skirts around the edge of the Blackmore Vale, providing far-reaching views across the fields and villages. Buzzards can often be seen drifting on the currents that swirl around the bowl formed by the hills, and skylarks provide a tuneful accompaniment to a walk. On the opposite side of the road, another walk leads along the base of Melbury Down, with Compton Abbas Airfield on the hilltop above.

Dorset Wildlife Trust manages 148 acres on **Fontmell Down**, above the village of Fontmell Magna. A variety of wildflower species grow here, including nine different orchids and the rare early gentian, while 35 species of butterfly have been recorded on the reserve. Glow worms are plentiful in summer and winged residents include sparrowhawks, green woodpeckers and yellowhammers. Evidence of Bronze Age habitation is visible in the form of two cross dykes, which were probably used as territorial boundary markers. On the flatter land on top of Fontmell Down are traces of a Bronze Age field system, most easily seen when the sun is low in the evening.

20 COMPTON ABBAS AIRFIELD

Ashmore SP5 5AP ✐ 01747 811767 ⬧ comptonairfield.com ◷ 09.30-17.00 Tue-Sat, 09.30-16.00 Sun

For over 30 years, this grass airfield near Ashmore was run by the Hughes family but in 2023 it was bought by film director Guy Ritchie, who lives nearby. The airfield sits high on Spread Eagle Hill, overlooking Shaftesbury. It was first utilised as an airfield in 1960 by the farmer who owned the land; he used it to fly his Tiger Moth and then opened the runway up to others.

You can visit the airfield by plane (prior permission required), or simply walk or drive there, sit in the café and enjoy the view of the runway. There's an unfussy menu offering American-inspired meals (burgers etc).

Vintage aircraft experience flights offer the chance to take to the skies in classic aircraft such as the Spitfire or Tiger Moth. The airfield also holds regular events. See website for details.

21 ASHMORE

As you enter Ashmore, the highest village in Dorset, you might feel transported back to an earlier era. It is a tiny village, with 17th- and 18th-century stone houses huddled around a village pond, which some believe is of Roman origin.

One of the major problems for hilltop settlements like Ashmore was that of water supply. The chalk drained the water away, so to preserve water the hilltop settlers dug 'dew ponds' and lined them with clay to retain water. Ashmore's **dew pond** is one of the few remaining in the local area.

The pond is the venue for the village's annual **Filly Loo** festival, held to celebrate the summer solstice. This is rural tradition at its best: a Green Man kicks off the dancing to folk music, which continues throughout the evening. At dusk the celebrations reach their climax with the 700-year-old Abbots Bromley Horn Dance. This is a torchlit procession with six men wearing antlers and four other colourfully costumed characters: Maid Marian, a bowman, a hobbyhorse and a fool. It is accompanied by a haunting solo flute melody. The celebration finishes with everyone joining hands around the pond for a final torchlit dance. If you happen to be in the area at the right time, it is a magical and uniquely British experience.

Ashmore is worth a visit at any time of year, and being so high the area around the village offers uninterrupted views towards the Dorset coast. On a clear day you can even see the Isle of Wight.

On the way from Ashmore to Cranborne, travelling along the B3081, you pass through the curiously named village of **Sixpenny Handley**, whose name is derived from two medieval 'hundreds', 'Sexpena' and 'Hanlega'. Over the years, local folk and the highways authority have reduced it to the memorable 6d Handley, and it sometimes appears on signposts as that.

22 CHETTLE
🏠 Chettle Lodge

Chettle is a remarkable place. It is the very essence of an English rural idyll, with lovingly maintained thatched cottages, the obligatory manor house and church, and a population of only about a hundred. It is something of a rarity; up until 2015 it was the only entire village (encompassing the entire parish boundary) still owned by one family, the Bourkes, and that is what has helped to preserve it. Sadly, **Chettle House**, an elegant Queen Anne manor (not open to the public) that

◀ **1** Ashmore is the highest village in Dorset. **2** Cranborne Manor Garden. **3** Listen out for skylarks on Fontmell and Melbury Downs. **4** The rolling countryside of the Cranborne Chase.

you may glimpse across the fields as you enter the village, was lost in a court case in 2015, along with some woodland, parkland and fields surrounding the house. The rest of the estate is still owned by the family and is currently in the hands of Alice Favre.

Chettle has avoided the sad fate of many small villages, where outsiders buy up the houses as second homes, thereby driving up property prices and leaving the village empty except at weekends, and where the village shop and post office close and the young local people can't afford to buy in their own area. Chettle doesn't have that problem because outsiders can't buy houses here. Today 32 houses are still owned by the Chettle Estate and are rented out to people who live and work in the village, at well below market value. As a result the village has a distinctly old-world flavour – people walk down the middle of the road, everyone knows everyone, residents support the village shop and there is a tremendous sense of community. The village's history (pre-World War II) is the subject of a book entitled *Enduring Village*, published in 2008.

In the centre of the village is a playground that reflects Chettle's identity. Much of the equipment is upcycled and a bit quirky – half a round hay feeder turned on its side and painted red, an old boat, two trampolines, and a tractor made from tree trunks. The playground is maintained by village residents so new things are always being added. Alice told me that it's a favourite playpark with local under-tens.

SPECIAL STAYS

Chettle Lodge DT11 8DB ✆ 07774 353010 ⌂ chettlelodge.co.uk. This handsome 18th-century dower house in the centre of the village, formerly the much-loved Castleman Hotel, is now available as a whole-house rental. The estate has taken care to preserve the building's eccentric character; it has two drawing rooms with woodburners, a snug and a hot tub for stargazing. It can sleep up to 24: there are eight beautiful en-suite rooms in the main house and a two-bedroom flat above the old stables. Chettle is a wonderfully friendly and relaxing place to stay and perfectly located for walks in Cranborne Chase. Activities such as yoga and foraging can be arranged and there is massage, reike and gong baths in a beautiful old barn near the church. It is hard to imagine a more elegant, yet homely, self-catering property.

FOOD & DRINK

Chettle Village Store DT11 8DB ✆ 01258 830223. In 2023, Chettle's famous village shop moved to converted farm buildings, having outgrown its humble but much-loved World War II Nissan hut. It aims to be the equivalent of a mini supermarket so locals don't have to

CHETTLE – AN OVERVIEW FROM THE CUSTODIAN

Alice Favre

I am the 42-year-old woman who owns Chettle Estate. Some days that is a blessing and some days it's a curse. I could be an out-of-town or greedy landlord, charge rents at market value and do the bare minimum to people's houses, but my mother instilled in me how important community is. She rarely put herself first (standard female trait) and was a very hard worker. My grandmother was the same. Most days I feel that I barely match what they achieved and how effortless they made it look. But we are living in different times. My grandmother had a war to grapple with, my mother had a difficult time with various family issues and I take over with the very real threat of climate change, biodiversity loss, total chemical overload in our soils, sea and air, and an uncertain future ahead. The place where we meet is that we have all had to run this estate with no big salary or pot of family money to help us along. When my mother died in 2017, I had had only three years warning that I would be the next owner of Chettle Estate, and my previous career had been running big festivals and events in London. I had been coming back to Chettle weekly for nearly 6 years when she died, so I wasn't totally blind to the challenge. In around 2015 I had my eyes opened to the realities of the world and now, nine years later, I am well read on all of the topics I mentioned before and I use this knowledge to guide my decisions on the estate – whether that's for the buildings, the land, nature, the residents or just those who visit Chettle as passers-by.

In 2020, I held an event called Hooray Day for the whole village, quite a few of whom I had known since birth or my childhood, to tell them who I was now and what my aims were for the estate. I based everything around nature, as everyone has a love of nature. My ultimate aim would be for Chettle to be a regenerative village, putting back more than it extracts; this is where the world needs to get to. This feels achievable when you relate this to food, trees, soil, insects and worms, but is more challenging when you think about the wealth of 'stuff' we buy and use without thinking because it is created across the world in a place we can't see, and which ends up in giant landfills that we also can't see.

One of the greatest things Chettle is doing is regenerating the people who live, work or pass through the village and you hope that in turn, that regeneration of souls leads to people realising their part in the wider world. We hold many events that connect people to nature (like tree-planting and apple day), the changing seasons (May day, wassail), food (venison-butchery lessons in Auntie B's kitchen), the dark (Women of the Dark Skies), and held spaces that allow people to speak their truth (women's circles). But the one thing I am very aware of is that first and foremost this is a community and people's homes – we are not a spectacle to be gawped at, and that is a hard balance to strike.

shop anywhere else. It also endeavours to sell something cheap and something organic, so there is something for everyone, and to try and tempt you into shopping more ethically and environmentally with an extensive range of eco-friendly products. There is a surprisingly large range of gluten-free goodies. In line with the estate's emphasis on sustainability, most of the shop was built with timber felled on the estate, the insulation is wood fibre (rather than synthetic foam), and as much as possible was upcycled. One of the old cattle troughs in the courtyard is a community tree bank with Chettle residents invited to collect and plant tree seeds in its soil. If you're passing Chettle, the shop really is worth a visit.

Museum Inn Farnham DT11 8DE ✒ 01725 516261 ⌖ museuminn.co.uk. This gastropub a few miles from Chettle offers an extensive menu of creative dishes. Now owned by the Butcombe group, the food is good, the cocktail list is better than most and the staff are friendly.

23 THE TARRANT VALLEY

Lying on the southern edge of Cranborne Chase, the valley's eight Tarrant villages bear the name of a tributary of the River Stour. They are thriving communities, proud of their agricultural roots. The open landscape of rolling chalk hills is largely given over to arable crops and offers invigorating walks with expansive views.

"The open landscape of rolling chalk hills is largely given over to arable crops and offers invigorating walks."

In 2023, to mark the coronation of King Charles III, three walks were launched. Skylark Loop (4 miles), Drover's Way (6 miles) and Hancock's Bottom Hike (7 miles) all start and end at Tarrant Gunville Village Hall. Free maps of each are available from the hall, where there is also an information board showing the routes. **Tarrant Monkton** lies about four miles northeast of Blandford, an idyllic village, whose name derives from the abbey that was once in the area. The village's standout feature is a ford across the river next to a 17th-century packhorse bridge. It makes for a beautiful scene and links Tarrant Monkton to the hamlet of **Tarrant Launceston**.

South of Tarrant Monkton, **Tarrant Rushton** has a former World War II airfield that played an important role in D-Day. The gliders that landed at Pegasus Bridge took off from here, and it was also used for clandestine flights to drop supplies to the French resistance. It is now farmed, but the runways and some of the old buildings remain. The concrete perimeter road is now a bridleway.

▌¶ FOOD & DRINK

Home Farm Shop Tarrant Gunville DT11 8JW ✆ 01258 830083 ⬙ homefarmshop.co.uk.
A fabulous farm shop and café on a working farm. Owners Abi and Paul Dunnseigh run the
business with the help of a professional young team, including their own children. Abi's
mum started the farm shop years ago – it was one of the very first. The café serves excellent,
homemade food with ample options for vegetarians. In summer, Friday night pizza nights draw
a big crowd. It's a treat for children to visit, thanks to an entertaining assortment of pygmy
goats, chickens and ducks. Hampers showcasing local produce are also on sale. Camping,
glamping and a self-catering cottage are available and there are fantastic walks from here.
The Langton Arms Tarrant Monkton DT11 8RX ✆ 01258 830225 ⬙ thelangtonarms.co.uk.
The Cossins family has farmed in the valley for six generations and in 1993 Barbara and Dave
bought this attractive thatched pub. They serve a traditional menu featuring meat, fish and
game, and take great care to ensure the local provenance of their ingredients. Some of the
chef's specials are available as ready meals from the family's **Rawston Farm Butchery and
Shop** (Tarrant Rawston DT11 8SF ✆ 07796 801525 ⬙ rawstonfarmbutchery.co.uk).

24 CRANBORNE ESTATE & CRANBORNE VILLAGE

The seemingly endless acres of fertile farmland and woodland that you
see in this area have been the property of just one family since 1604,
when King James I granted Cranborne Manor and the lordship of the
Chase to Sir Robert Cecil, the First Earl of Salisbury. King John built
the original house at Cranborne as a hunting lodge and the first earl
enlarged it and modernised it. Cranborne Manor is the home of the
current Viscount Cranborne, the eldest son of the Seventh Marquess
of Salisbury.

Adjacent to the manor is the village of Cranborne, where (unusually
for Dorset) most of the buildings are brick. The village is centred on an
attractive square; in 1748, a fire destroyed many of the older buildings
– the north side is 18th century and the south side Edwardian. Cottages
with doors painted in the ubiquitous Cranborne blue belong to the
estate. At the superb **Cranborne Stores** (1 The Square, BH21 5PR
✆ 01725 517210 ⊙ 07.00–17.30 Mon–Fri, 08.00–16.00 Sat, 08.30–13.00
Sun) you can buy game and other meat from the surrounding area,
while locals catch up on gossip.

The predominance of red brick belies Cranborne's true age. The village,
which lies on a winterborne (a stream which flows only in winter) called
the Crane, dates from Saxon times. There was a Benedictine Abbey here
from circa AD980 until the Dissolution of the Monasteries in 1539.

Until the 18th century Cranborne was a thriving market town on the main route from Salisbury to Poole but in the 1750s the Great Western Turnpike from Salisbury to Blandford was built, bypassing Cranborne, and its trade declined. Thomas Hardy described it as 'a decayed market town' but it has a pleasant feel today and is unmistakably an estate village. The excellent Cranborne Garden Centre draws a lot of visitors to the village.

The **church of St Mary and St Bartholomew** dates from the 12th century; the faded wall-paintings are 14th century and the tower 15th century. On the wall a memorial commissioned by Lady Norton for her grandson, John Elliot, features a statue of a boy with a skull on his knee. According to the inscription he was a very promising boy who had made 'an almost supernatural progress' in his studies, and who died suddenly at school on 2 February 1641, reputedly from choking on a fish bone.

Cranborne Manor Garden

BH21 5PP ✐ 01725 517289 ⟁ cranborne.co.uk ☉ Mar–Oct 09.00–17.00 Wed and a few other dates (see website)

Although the manor house is not open to the public, visitors are able to wander through its quintessentially English garden during opening hours. One of Dorset's finest, the garden was partly laid out by 17th-century gardener John Tradescant, and more recently owes its splendour to the Dowager Marchioness of Salisbury, a noted garden designer. The walled gardens, herbaceous borders, espaliered apple trees and yew hedges are particularly fine. In the rather fun Sundial Garden a sundial stands sentinel on a mound surrounded by raised parterres. Various statues and sculptures catch the eye as you wander, and the garden runs down to the River Crane, where a mass of spring bulbs flower in April and May. Although it has a formal layout, parts of the garden are left wild and it is used by the family, making it feel very much like you have wandered into a much-loved private garden. The garden appeared in the 2020 Netflix film of *Rebecca* by Daphne Du Maurier, as Manderley, Maxim de Winter's estate.

Cranborne Garden Centre

Cranborne BH21 5PP ✐ 01725 517248 ⟁ cranbornegardencentre.co.uk

Within the beautiful walled garden of Cranborne Manor lies this independent, boutique garden centre specialising in old-fashioned and modern roses, of which it stocks several hundred varieties each year. Other unusual plants and garden items are beautifully laid out within the walled garden. The garden centre has been created by the incredibly hardworking and visionary Claire Whitehead. Claire has a real eye for beautiful things and the shop is filled with carefully selected gifts, homewares and local food. A building known as the vintage barn is packed with second-hand treasures, and there is an excellent café (see below). Check the website for details of events at the garden centre, which hosts talks, workshops, yoga, and even weddings in its purpose-built garden room.

¶¶ FOOD & DRINK

Café at Cranborne Garden Centre BH21 5PP ✆ 01725 517248. A delightful, informal café within the attractive walled garden that houses the garden centre. The food is freshly prepared and locally sourced wherever possible. A very relaxing setting with the bonus of plenty of parking and the chance to browse through the plants and gifts.

La Fosse London House, The Square, BH21 5PR ✆ 01725 517604. A small restaurant that punches above its weight. Owner-chef Mark Hartstone has impressive credentials, having worked at some top restaurants. He conjures delicate dishes using the best fresh, local, seasonal ingredients. There are also a few very comfortable rooms.

25 WIMBORNE ST GILES

⌂ St Giles Estate

This small, peaceful community is the estate village at the centre of the Earl of Shaftesbury's 5,500-acre landholding. The ancestors of the Ashley-Cooper family arrived here in the 15th century and reminders of them can be seen all around. Facing the village green is a row of **almshouses** and **St Giles Church**. The almshouses were built in 1624 by Sir Anthony Ashley and were intended to house 11 poor people; an inscription above the door reads, 'he hath delivered me out of all trouble'.

The church has been through several incarnations. In 1732, the Dorset architects responsible for rebuilding Blandford Forum (page 83) after the 1731 fire, John and William Bastard, were commissioned to build a church on the site of an earlier, disused one. In 1908 it burnt down in a fire accidentally started by workmen repairing the lead roof and the Shaftesburys called in renowned architect Ninian Comper to conduct the restoration. The result is a magnificent and colourful interior, far more elaborate than that of most village churches. An ornate rood

screen carved in dark wood separates the altar from the nave. Prevalent are impressive tombs of various members of the Ashley-Cooper family, including Sir Anthony Ashley who has the unglamorous claim to fame of being the first person to grow cabbages in England. The seventh earl (1801–85) was a philanthropist and social reformer, who improved the lot of working children through a series of reforms; he was offered burial in Westminster Abbey but declined and is buried here.

The current (12th) earl is young and energetic. Nick Ashley-Cooper was not expecting to inherit the peerage, but did so in 2005 in his mid-twenties, after the tragic deaths of his father and later his elder brother. Nick had been travelling down a different path, following a passion for music and working as a DJ in New York, when his life suddenly changed direction. After taking stock of the situation, he returned to Wimborne St Giles to better manage his responsibilities. In 2011, he and his wife embarked on a massive restoration of the family home, **St Giles House**, which had been empty since 1961, when his antecedents, who were struggling to maintain the big house, moved into the dower house. Nick told me he realised that it was important not only for his family, but also for the community, that he would do everything in his power to preserve the history of the Shaftesburys. He was spurred on in his challenge by the loyalty and support of the estate workers and the wider community. The handsome building sits in 400 acres of classic 18th-century parkland and regular events are held there, including bar nights at the Forestry Bar. Details of the various activities and events at the estate, including information on hiring it as a wedding venue, self-catering accommodation and fishing, are available on the website (⊘ stgilesdorset.com).

🧳 SPECIAL STAYS

St Giles Estate Wimborne St Giles BH21 5ND ✆ 01725 517214 ⊘ stgilesdorset.com. You can experience the tranquillity and beauty of the St Giles Estate by staying in luxurious converted outbuildings or glamping in bell tents. When the 12th Earl and Countess of Shaftesbury decided to turn some of their stables and groom's cottage into holiday accommodation, they were keen to preserve the buildings' character. They have certainly succeeded. The 17th-century stables have been converted into eight-bedroom, self-catering

◀ **1** Moors Valley Country Park & Forest. **2** Dorset Heavy Horse Farm Park. **3** The 140ft-high Horton Tower. **4** Knowlton Church and Neolithic earthworks.

accommodation that celebrates its equestrian origins. The original stalls have been cleverly preserved and incorporated into the rooms – some have even kept their hay racks. Exposed brick, beams, antique furniture, bold colours and clawfoot baths all add to the atmosphere. The Groom's Cottage has a similar style and two maisonettes each with two bedrooms, luxurious bathroom and kitchenette. The two converted Pepperpot Lodges are cosy and homely, ideal for couples. The location on the estate, the sense of history and the blend of the rustic and luxurious makes the accommodation unusual and thoroughly memorable. There are beautiful walks around the parkland and beyond, across Cranborne Chase.

26 KNOWLTON CHURCH & NEOLITHIC EARTHWORKS

BH21 5AE; free admission; English Heritage

At Knowlton, on the B3078 south of Cranborne, you can visit two monuments in one: a ruined medieval church stands in the middle of a Neolithic henge. It is a magical, almost eerie, sight, and is said to be haunted by a ghostly horse and rider galloping through the rings, a nun, who kneels within the church, and the ringing of a non-existent bell. In the snow, the site resembles a decoration on top of a tiered Christmas cake. On a deeper level, it represents the transition from pagan to Christian worship – it is thought the church was built to symbolically destroy the power of the Neolithic rings.

The henge is circular with a substantial ditch around it and is just one part of a complex of **Neolithic earthworks** in the area. The clump of trees 200ft to the east of the henge stands on the Great Barrow, the largest individual barrow in Dorset. The church is 12th century with a 15th-century tower; it was abandoned after the roof collapsed in the 18th century. Not many people visit Knowlton, so you may well have the site to yourself, making it all the more atmospheric. It's always on my list of places to take visitors, especially those from overseas, because it is such a fascinating and unusual place. The fact that it's free to visit is a bonus.

27 HORTON

On a hill on the edge of the scattered, low-lying village of Horton is **Horton Tower**, a triangular, turreted brick structure 140ft high. Local landowner Humphrey Sturt built this folly in 1750, possibly as a vantage point from which to watch the hunt when he became too old to ride to hounds. Although it can be seen from miles around and a bridleway runs nearby, the tower stands on private land and is not open to the public. It was the location for the cockfight in the 1966 film *Far from the Madding Crowd*; in recent years it has found a new purpose, as a discreet mobile-phone tower.

The Duke of Monmouth was reportedly captured in Horton in 1685 after his failed rebellion. Following his defeat at the Battle of Sedgemoor, Monmouth disguised himself as a shepherd and headed towards Poole, where he planned to catch a boat to Holland. Monmouth was crossing Cranborne Chase when he was recognised by an old woman, who reported him to the authorities. A search ensued and he was discovered hiding in a ditch under an ash tree, now known as Monmouth's ash (although it's unlikely to be the same tree).

28 MOORS VALLEY COUNTRY PARK & FOREST

Horton Rd, Ashley Heath BH24 2ET ✆ 01425 470721 ⌗ moors-valley.co.uk ⏱ 08.00–dusk daily; free admission but car parking is charged

The 1,000 acres of woodland, grassland, heath and lakes here are run as a countryside recreation facility, a joint venture between East Dorset District Council and the Forestry Commission. The emphasis is on family fun: you can walk, cycle or catch a narrow-gauge steam train around the park; there are high-ropes courses, adventure play areas, orienteering, segways and an 18-hole golf course. You can hire mountain bikes, along with trailers, tag-a-longs and child seats. No advanced booking is needed and bikes are an ideal way to explore. Coarse fishing is available from June to March; you can buy a day ticket or season ticket from the visitor centre, but anyone over 12 years of age will need to show a valid Environment Agency rod licence. Wheelchair access is good, and dogs are allowed. There are lots of activities for families, such as themed activity trails searching for children's book characters. My family had fun hunting for the Gruffalo and friends. You can bring a picnic or take advantage of the restaurant. Some of the activities are only available at certain times of the year; check website for details.

29 EDMONDSHAM HOUSE

Edmondsham BH21 5RE ✆ 01725 517207 ⏱ house: Apr & Oct Wed; garden: Apr–Oct Wed & Sun

Owner, Julia Smith, gives guided tours of her home, an Elizabethan building with Georgian extensions, which has been in the family since it was built in 1589. It is a family home and the tours are very personal with plenty of anecdotes and family history. The six acres of attractive grounds are typical of a country house of this size, with colourful herbaceous borders and a pleasant walled garden. A circular grass hollow is believed to have been the site of a **medieval cock-fighting pit**. The Victorian stable block will be the envy of most horse owners and the octagonal Victorian dairy is built over an underground stream, with louvered windows in order to keep it cool.

30 DORSET HEAVY HORSE FARM PARK

Edmondsham, near Verwood BH21 5RJ 01202 824040 dorset-heavy-horse-centre. co.uk Apr–Sep daily, closed Mon outside school holidays; Oct Thu–Sun, opening varies & is weather dependent so check ahead

This centre is home to gentle giants of various breeds, including rare breeds such as the Suffolk Punch. At the other end of the scale, there are miniature ponies, pigs, sheep and goats. Before you visit, check the daily schedule on the website; there is plenty to entertain the children, including wagon rides, pony rides, pony grooming, feeding the farm animals, play areas, fairground rides and a café. There are presentations daily, including on the Romany people and the resident heavy horses.

SHERBORNE & AROUND

This ancient town marking the boundary of the Blackmore Vale has much to offer the visitor, including two castles, a splendid abbey and a charming town centre. Allow at least one full day to explore.

31 SHERBORNE

 Eastbury Hotel

Sherborne has an impressive aristocratic pedigree spanning hundreds of years and still exudes a refined sense of style. In most towns and villages in the Blackmore Vale you will see a farmer fresh from his tractor (which may be parked around the corner) or a woman in well-worn jodhpurs and wellies popping into the bank or the grocer, but this doesn't seem to happen here. Sherborne is the sort of place where you get dressed up and slap on some make-up to go shopping.

Sherborne's aristocratic pedigree is embodied in its finest buildings, Sherborne Abbey, Sherborne Old Castle and Sherborne Castle (built by

Sir Walter Raleigh), which are all open to the public. A stroll around the town centre with its medieval buildings is enough to gain an appreciation for the town's history; it dates back to the Saxons, who named the town 'scir burne', meaning the place of the clear stream, and made it the capital of Wessex. Today it is a vibrant market town and a centre of learning, thanks to its three private schools: Sherborne Boys, Sherborne Girls and Leweston.

With its compact centre and abundance of buildings of architectural interest, the town is best explored on foot.

Cheap Street

The name of Sherborne's main shopping street is misleading, for it is crammed with upmarket shops, art galleries, antique shops and eateries. Refreshingly, many of them are small independents. Be sure to look above the tempting shop windows to appreciate the blend of architectural styles, with many buildings dating from the 16th century. Some 19th-century shopfronts survive, as do some of the grand houses that were built

"Sherborne is the sort of place where you get dressed up and slap on some make-up to go shopping."

for merchants made wealthy by the silk-throwing and cloth-, glove-, button- and lace-making industries that existed in Sherborne until the 19th century.

Just above the junction with Long Street is **The Conduit**, a hexagonal stone structure that was originally the monk's *lavatorium* or washhouse; it was moved here in 1539 following the closure of the monastery for use by the local community. It is mentioned in Thomas Hardy's *The Woodlanders* as the place where Giles Winterborne, who was seeking work, stood in the marketplace 'as he always did at this season of the year, with his specimen apple tree'. The Conduit has been used variously as a police station, a bank and a reading room. At Christmas it houses a nativity scene, one of many festive features that draw visitors from miles around at that time of year. Sherborne is particularly beautiful at Christmas.

Near The Conduit, an alleyway leads to the abbey, with the 15th-century **Bow Arch** spanning the gap above. It was once the gateway between the abbey precincts and the commercial parts of the town. It is said that 12 local Monmouth followers were hanged from the arch in

1685 following their unsuccessful rebellion. It is along here that you will find the **Sherborne Museum** (page 114).

Henry Willis Antique Silver (38 Cheap St, DT9 3PX ✆ 01935 816828) is within a wooden, jettied building dating from around 1490, the Shoemaker's House. It is worth popping in to browse the lovely, shiny items inside and to see the preserved square of wattle and daub in the wall, which is now visible behind glass. The large stone fireplace was rediscovered in 1992, and according to Henry it would have been built before the wooden frame of the building, giving it stability. Today the fireplace provides a characterful backdrop for an ever-changing display of antique silver.

"It is said that 12 local Monmouth followers were hanged from the arch in 1685 following their unsuccessful rebellion."

The small, **independent shops** along Cheap Street contribute to the town's bygone-era flavour. The Sherborne Antiques Market (71 Cheap St, DT9 3BA ✆ 01935 713760 🖉 sherborneantiquesmarket. com ⊙ 10.00-17.00 Mon-Sat, 11.00-16.00 Sun) is eminently browsable, with antiques and curious vintage items crammed into every inch of space. Over 40 traders share the building, so there is plenty of variety. The **Swan Gallery** (51 Cheap St, DT9 3AX ✆ 01935 814465) is a family-run business selling fine watercolours, oil paintings, antique maps and prints, and it has a section devoted to antique prints and maps of Dorset. It stands at the entrance to **Swan Yard**, a small pedestrianised shopping area converted from stables.

At the top of the hill Cheap Street leads into **The Green**. On the corner stands **Julian House**, a 16th-century stone-built hospice with mullioned windows, which now contains shops. Beside it is the 16th-century **George Inn**, Sherborne's oldest surviving inn.

Markets are held in Cheap Street on Thursday and Saturday, and there's a farmers' market on the third Friday of each month (⊙ 09.00–13.00).

Sherborne Abbey
(Abbey Church of St Mary the Virgin) & around
✆ 01935 812452 🖉 sherborneabbey.com ⊙ daily; free guided tours Apr–Oct, 10.30 Tue & 14.30 Fri

The centrepiece of Sherborne is undoubtedly its abbey, a glorious spectacle of architecture and history. Resplendent in its golden hamstone, it stands proudly on a perfectly groomed lawn platform, surveying the goings-on of the town. In front a memorial commemorates George Winfield Digby of Sherborne Castle, one of the principal financiers of the abbey's Victorian restoration.

The land on which the abbey stands has been consecrated for over 1,300 years. In AD705 King Ine divided the Diocese of Winchester in two, created a new seat at Sherborne and appointed Aldhelm, Abbot of Malmesbury, as the first bishop of the West Saxons. The Cathedral of Sherborne served Aldhelm and 26 succeeding Saxon bishops until the bishop's seat was moved to Old Sarum (near Salisbury) shortly after the Norman Conquest.

The abbey became the church of a Benedictine monastery from AD998 until 1539, when it was dissolved as part of King Henry VIII's Reformation. The building as it stands today was largely the work of Abbot Ramsam (1475–1504).

The people of Sherborne were not thrilled to have lost their church to the Benedictine monks. They were relegated to the smaller church of All Hallows, which used to adjoin the abbey. On the exterior walls of the abbey, to the left and right of the West End, the 'joins' can still be seen. There was no font at All Hallows so the townspeople had to hold their baptisms at the abbey. Tensions between the monks and the town came to a head in 1437 when the people decided they had had enough of having to ask the Abbot's permission every time they wanted to hold a baptism. They decided to erect a font of their own in All Hallows. The Abbot

"Resplendent in its golden hamstone, it stands proudly on a perfectly groomed lawn platform, surveying the goings-on of the town."

was furious and reportedly sent a 'stout butcher' armed with a hammer to break the font. This caused a riot, during which a burning arrow was shot into the east end of the abbey. The resulting fire permanently reddened the walls of the quire and the crossing, and you can still see the red marks if you look carefully. It took the Pope himself to settle the conflict – and the people had to pay for the repairs. No wonder that at the Reformation they were delighted to regain possession of what has ever since been their parish church, and they immediately pulled down All Hallows. As you enter the abbey today, there is a large Victorian font just inside the door, but if you look straight down the south aisle you will see a second font, in the Bow Chapel. The bowl of this is medieval, and is possibly all that remains of the broken font from All Hallows.

Perhaps the abbey's most striking architectural feature is its superb **fan-vaulted stone roof**, the earliest in England. In his book, *England's Thousand Best Churches*, Simon Jenkins proclaims, 'I would pit Sherborne's roof against any contemporary work of the Italian Renaissance.' Another highlight is the **engraved glass reredos** (1968) by Lawrence Whistler in the Lady Chapel.

St Katherine's Chapel contains most of the abbey's surviving medieval glass and is where Sir Walter Raleigh attended services, while the rear choir stalls feature ornate 15th-century misericords.

Fascinating tombs and monuments are dotted about the abbey, vestiges of various periods in its history. The north choir aisle contains Saxon tombs believed to be those of two kings of Wessex, Ethelbald and Ethelbert, elder brothers of Alfred the Great. In the south transept is an impressive marble monument to John Digby, Third and Last Earl of Bristol, dated 1698 and featuring a rather troubling skull and crossbones. In the north transept, within the Wykeham Chapel, a monument of 1564 honours Sir John Horsey, who bought the abbey estates from the Crown during the Reformation and then sold the abbey back to the people of Sherborne as their parish church. Life-sized effigies of Horsey and his son lie next to each other, both of them wearing armour dating from around 1470,

"Horses' heads, looking like chess pieces with enigmatic expressions, adorn the top of the monument."

presumably to emphasise the fact they were from an old family. Horses' heads, looking like chess pieces with enigmatic expressions, adorn the top of the monument.

Today, the abbey holds regular classical music concerts and performances, in particular during the annual Sherborne Abbey Festival, held over five to six days in early May (sherborneabbeyfestival.org). It is also a memorable and extremely popular venue for its atmospheric Christmas services.

Behind the abbey, occupying some of the former monastic buildings, is **Sherborne Boys' School**, which was founded in 1550 as King Edward's School. The handsome stone buildings may look familiar, as the school

---

SHERBORNE: **1** The interior of the abbey. **2** The atmospheric ruins of the Old Castle. **3** The Almshouse of St John the Baptist & St John the Evangelist. **4** The green drawing room in the Elizabethan castle. ▶

has been used as a location for various films, including *The Browning Version*, *Goodbye Mr Chips* and *Far from the Madding Crowd*.

The Almshouse of St John the Baptist & St John the Evangelist

Half Moon St, DT9 3LJ ℘ 01935 813245 ⚇ stjohnshouse.org ⊙ chapel tours May–Sep 14.00–16.00 Wed, Thu & Sat

In front of the abbey is this monastic-looking almshouse, built between 1440 and 1445 and extended in 1864, when additions included the cloister and the Victorian railings. Now a residential home for the elderly, it has been providing assistance to local people for over 500 years. In 1437, Henry VI granted a licence for a home for 'twelve pore feeble and ympotent old men and four old women' to be cared for by a housewife whose duty was to 'feeche in and dyght to the victaill wash wrying make beddys and al other things do'. When new residents first arrived they had to bring their few possessions with them and surrender them to the house on their death. They also swore to obey the rules of the house and could be evicted for serious misdemeanours; daily religious services were compulsory. Residents were required to wear uniform; for women in Victorian times this was a red cape and black bonnet, while the men were dressed in black.

"When new residents first arrived they had to bring their few possessions with them and surrender them to the house on their death."

Inside, a chapel features fine medieval stained-glass windows and a vivid triptych (c1480), a three-panelled altarpiece of oil on wood depicting five of the miracles of Christ. For a small fee and by prior arrangement, you can take a guided tour of the chapel and antechapel. Items on display include the uniforms worn by earlier residents, copies of the royal licence and foundation deed, a solid wooden chest requiring five separate keys, and a letter from Sir Walter Raleigh to the Almshouse Master.

Sherborne Museum

Church Ln, DT9 3BP ℘ 01935 812252 ⚇ sherbornemuseum.com ⊙ Apr–mid-Dec 10.30–16.30 Tue–Sat; free admission

Between Cheap Street and the abbey, this museum is dedicated to the history of the town and the surrounding area. It covers prominent buildings, such as Sherborne Castle and the abbey, as well as giving an insight into the life of local agricultural workers and tradesmen. A scale model of the old castle before it was seized puts the ruins visible today into perspective.

In the early 1400s the monks of Sherborne Abbey wrote and illuminated the **Sherborne Missal**, the largest and most ornately decorated English medieval service book to survive from the Middle Ages. The original is held in the British Library but a digital copy can be viewed here.

Sherborne Old Castle

Castleton DT9 3SA ℘ 01935 812730 ⊙ Apr–Nov 10.00–17.00 daily; English Heritage

This atmospheric ruin, which once belonged to Sir Walter Raleigh, lies to the east of the town, adjoining the grounds of the new Sherborne Castle, and is all that remains of the original, which was destroyed by Cromwell's troops during the Civil War. It reportedly took 16 days for Cromwell's men to bring the castle down in 1645; only the imposing gatehouse, parts of the keep and the outer walls survive.

The entrance passes over a modern bridge with the piers of the medieval one beneath it. It is a serene spot with fine mature beech trees, whose rustling leaves provide musical accompaniment to your visit. It sits on a natural knoll and has views of the surrounding countryside and the town. Built of local yellow hamstone, the ruins have a golden glow. It oozes history and mystery, conjuring up images of medieval banquets and battles.

The castle was built in the 12th century by Roger de Caen, Bishop of Salisbury and Chancellor of England as a bishop's palace. When passing through Sherborne en route to Plymouth, Sir Walter Raleigh fell in love

SHERBORNE CASTLE COUNTRY FAIR

⌀ sherbornecountryfair.com

Sherborne Castle plays host to an annual country fair, usually held in May or early June, which incorporates one of the biggest rare-breeds shows in the country.

A great day out, the fair showcases country pursuits and crafts, including Morris dancing, heavy horses, gun-dog trials, falconry and local hunts and their hounds. A more unusual inclusion is the dragon-boat racing on Sherborne Castle lake. The food hall, crammed with local produce, is another highlight, and cookery demonstrations are held.

with the castle and Queen Elizabeth I leased it to him from 1592. The castle was already deteriorating. Raleigh initially tried to modernise it but gave up and built a home (Sherborne Castle) in the deer park opposite; he kept the old castle for ceremonial use.

Sherborne Castle

New Rd, DT9 5NR ✐ 01935 812072 ⊘ sherbornecastle.com ☉ Apr–Oct 11.00–16.15 Tue–Thu, Sat & Sun

Having decided that Sherborne Old Castle was not fit for habitation, Sir Walter Raleigh built this Elizabethan mansion on the other side of the River Yeo in 1594. Raleigh and his wife enjoyed their new home for less than nine years before his execution during the reign of James I. In 1617 the estate, with its two castles, was purchased by Sir John Digby and has remained in the family ever since. At its core is the house built by Raleigh with polygonal turrets in each corner. It was extended in a similar style (more turrets) by various Digbys through the generations, giving it its rather unusual shape. During World War I the house was used by the Red Cross as a hospital, and in World War II as the headquarters for the commandos involved in the D-Day landings.

The interior presents a parade of styles from different eras: Tudor, Jacobean, Georgian and Victorian. The furniture, art and family memorabilia give it a very human touch. There is a lot to take in, so it is just as well that there are guides on hand to explain each room. The slightly comical ostrich with a horseshoe in its beak, which you can see depicted all around the building, has been the heraldic symbol of the Digby family since 1350. The symbol is said to originate from around 100BC when the king of Numidia (now Tunisia) put warriors on ostriches to fight the Roman cavalry; the speedy ostriches outflanked the Romans and they fled. The ostrich and horseshoe crest was later used in Hungary but it is not clear why it was adopted by the Digbys. The 18th-century library is striking, with formidable-looking busts tucked into recesses between the highly decorative bookcases. The green drawing room has Raleigh's arms on the ceiling and three beautiful 17th-century fireplaces.

The spectacular gardens were created in 1753 by Capability Brown with a 50-acre lake fed by the River Yeo as their centrepiece. Around the lake are sweeping lawns, majestic old trees and colourful flower borders, while the remains of Old Sherborne Castle in the distance

MY ORCHA'D IN LINDEN LEA

The following poem by Dorset dialect poet William Barnes is considered to be an unofficial Dorset anthem. It was set to music by Ralph Vaughan Williams.

'Ithin the woodlands, flow'ry gleaded,
By the woak tree's mossy moot,
The sheenen grass bleades, timber-sheaded,
Now do quiver under voot;
An' birds do whissle auver head,
An' water's bubblen in its bed,
An' ther vor me the apple tree
Do lean down low in Linden Lea.

When leaves that leately wer a-springen
Now do feade 'ithin the copse,
An' painted birds do hush ther zingen
Up upon the timber's tops;

An' brown-leav'd fruit's a-turnen red,
In cloudless zunsheen, auver head,
Wi' fruit vor me the apple tree
Do lean down low in Linden Lea.

Let other vo'k meake money vaster
In the air o' dark-room'd towns,
I don't dread a peevish measter;
Though noo man do heed my frowns,
I be free to goo abrode,
Or teake agean my hwomeward road
To where vor me the apple tree
Do lean down low in Linden Lea.

provide a romantic backdrop. Exploring the grounds is like being lost in a Jane Austen adaptation. As you walk around the lake in the direction of Sherborne Old Castle you come to **Raleigh's seat**, a large stone seat where the adventurer reportedly used to sit to survey the estate and keep an eye on the road below, the main route to Dorchester. Raleigh's role in popularising tobacco in England is well documented and legend has it that a servant happened upon Sir Walter smoking his pipe at the stone seat and, thinking his master was on fire, threw a pitcher of beer over him to extinguish the flames. Raleigh's ghost reportedly walks the castle grounds and sits on the stone seat gazing longingly across the estate.

Both the castle and its gardens are open to visitors; you can visit both or just the gardens. The gardens provide a beautiful, peaceful spot to enjoy a picnic or to walk the dogs around the lake.

Adjacent to the entrance is the Castle Gardens plant nursery and café. It has a spectacular Christmas display in the winter months, which draws visitors from miles around.

 SPECIAL STAYS

The Eastbury Hotel & Spa Long St, DT9 3BY ✆ 01935 581035 ✎ theeastburyhotel.co.uk. You can easily explore Sherborne on foot from The Eastbury, which occupies a Georgian townhouse close to the town centre. Rooms in the main house vary greatly in size but all feel homely. The pick of the accommodation is the new garden suites. Inspired by Victorian potting sheds, they have modern interiors with masses of natural light, wet rooms and small private terraces. A characterful 17th-century, three-bedroom cottage will appeal to families wanting to self-cater.

It's far more peaceful than you'd expect for a town-centre hotel, with a tranquil walled garden at the rear. A hobbit house in the grounds contains a tiny spa. Little touches like sloe gin and homemade treats in the room on arrival make you feel spoilt. Children and dogs are made extremely welcome in both the hotel and the restaurant. The fine-dining restaurant is a highlight and uses home-grown and local produce to create beautifully presented dishes. The seven-course tasting menu is memorable for a special occasion.

¶¶ FOOD & DRINK

Eastbury Hotel Page 117.

Kafe Fontana 82 Cheap St, DT9 3BJ ✆ 01935 812180. This small, casual café serves tasty quiches, pastries and cakes. Plenty of gluten-free options.

Olivers 19 Cheap St, DT9 3PU ✆ 01935 815005. Casual, counter-service café with long tables and a back room with unusual two-person booths. Serves homemade cakes and light lunches. Uses as much local produce as possible, including coffee roasted by Reads of Sherborne.

Oxford's 34 Cheap St, DT9 3PX ✆ 01935 812642. A wonderful, traditional bakery, established in 1911 and now run by the fourth generation of the family, Steve Oxford. The preservative-free bread is baked daily at Steve's farmhouse in the nearby village of Alweston, in the same ovens his great grandfather used over a hundred years ago. It is then delivered to their shops around Dorset. They use untreated, unbleached flour, sourced locally whenever possible, such as that from Stoate & Sons near Shaftesbury (page 60).

Three Wishes 78 Cheap St, DT9 3BJ ✆ 01935 817777. A popular café/bistro that prides itself on using local ingredients in its carefully presented dishes. On the menu is the 'Sherborne Stodger', a bun containing dried fruit and spices.

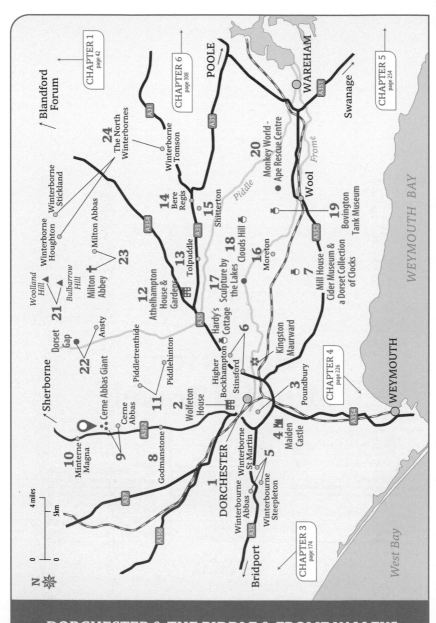

DORCHESTER & THE PIDDLE & FROME VALLEYS

2
DORCHESTER & THE PIDDLE & FROME VALLEYS

At the heart of Dorset is a captivating landscape of rolling chalk downland, wooded hills and river valleys. The area is sparsely populated, its chalk hills with their short springy grass being relatively inhospitable farmland.

Villages huddle in clusters along the river valleys, like those along the **River Frome** and the evocatively named **River Piddle**. In the east the Frome and Piddle valleys lead into water meadows and from there to an area of heathland, which spreads towards the Isle of Purbeck and Poole Harbour. The chalk hills hold a large water table, which means there are many seasonal rivers. The area has 15 villages with names prefixed by 'Winterborne', indicating that they lie on a stream that only runs in winter.

Dorchester, the county town, and the surrounding area have a strong sense of history, having been settled since around 4000BC. Dorchester still bears the imprint of Roman occupation, including the only fully exposed and best-preserved Roman townhouse in Britain. It also has arguably the most comprehensive museum in Dorset, the Dorset County Museum.

Just outside Dorchester is **Maiden Castle**, the largest Iron Age hillfort in Britain. It is one of several prehistoric sites in this area, along with Maumbury Rings and Badbury Rings. Dorset's past inhabitants have left their mark all over this part of the county – at **Cerne Abbas** a hillside chalk carving of a naked, club-wielding, 180ft giant famously dominates the landscape.

Dorchester and the surrounding countryside inspired one of Dorset's most famous sons, author Thomas Hardy, who was born in a tiny hamlet near Dorchester in 1840 and later moved into the town. In this part of the county are innumerable reminders of Hardy's work and thankfully much of the landscape has changed little since his day. The various sites for aficionados to visit include the cottage where he was born.

GETTING THERE & AROUND

Unless you have all the time in the world, a car really is the best way to reach the delightful hidden places in this area. The main roads are good (the A35 running east to west and the A352 running north to south) but getting away from them and exploring is where the real fun is.

PUBLIC TRANSPORT

London Waterloo to Weymouth **train** services (South Western Railway) call at Dorchester South station (journey time is around two hours 40 minutes), while Bristol to Weymouth services (Great Western Railway) call at Dorchester West. A **National Express bus** from London Victoria to Dorchester via Bournemouth takes just under four hours.

Getting out into the villages and more remote points of interest is less straightforward. However, **buses** run between Dorchester and some of the main attractions, including Maiden Castle, Cerne Abbas, Milton Abbas and Bovington Tank Museum.

Hardy's Cottage at Higher Bockhampton is not well served by public transport: the closest bus stop is on the A35, but you need to walk across the busy road and then on to the cottage. A simpler solution is a **taxi** from Dorchester.

CYCLING

The charming countryside and relatively quiet roads make cycling a pleasure. National Cycle Network (NCN) **Route 2** covers 30 miles between Lyme Regis and Dorchester, taking you through the Marshwood Vale and Bride Valley. It runs close to the Hardy Monument and Maiden Castle. NCN **Route 26** starts in Somerset and

---

𝑖 TOURIST INFORMATION

General information ⊘ dorchesterdorset.com and discoverdorchester.co.uk
Dorchester There is no tourist-information office in Dorchester, but there is an information point (leaflets) within the Shire Hall Museum (page 132).

runs from Sherborne to Dorchester, continuing south to Weymouth and Portland Bill. A circular cycle route goes from Dorchester to Cerne Abbas via the Piddle Valley, returning to Dorchester via Sydling St Nicholas. Suggested routes are available on ⊘ dorsetcouncil.gov.uk and ⊘ discoverdorchester.co.uk.

There is no cycle hire in the Dorchester area; the nearest is in Weymouth (page 229).

WALKING

The town of **Dorchester** lends itself to being explored on foot and The Walks, following the Roman town walls, are a good place to start.

Prehistoric **Maiden Castle** offers a memorable short stroll, as well as the chance to soak up thousands of years of history and some breathtaking views of the countryside.

The **Cerne Valley** is criss-crossed by footpaths and bridleways that can tie in with a walk up Giant Hill to get a closer look at the chalk carving.

For those with an interest in **Lawrence of Arabia**, a themed trail starts at the Bovington Tank Museum and takes in Clouds Hill and Moreton. A leaflet is available at (⊘ dorsetcouncil.gov.uk).

If you want to walk in quintessential **Hardy country**, the obvious starting point is Hardy's Cottage, and the walk into Thorncombe Wood and Duddle Heath ('Egdon Heath' in Hardy's writings), or perhaps along the river from Lower Bockhampton to the church at Stinsford. The 212-mile trail known as the **Hardy Way** links together many of the key sites. A leaflet can be downloaded from ⊘ visit-dorset.com.

Bulbarrow Hill lies on a section of the Wessex Ridgeway and has superb views of the Blackmore Vale. You can easily reach it from car parks on the hilltop or you can combine it with a longer walk, such as starting from Ibberton beneath the escarpment, climbing steeply to the top, then from Bulbarrow dropping down through Woolland.

The **Dorset Jubilee Trail** runs 90 miles from Forde Abbey on the Somerset border across Dorset to Bokerley Dyke on the Hampshire border and takes in several places mentioned in this chapter, including Moreton, Bere Regis and Milton Abbas.

There's a beautiful stroll from Milton Abbas to historic Milton Abbey Church (page 169). The best longer walks around the village lie to the north, including Hilton and Winterborne Houghton.

HORSERIDING

The area is rich in bridleways, including around the Cerne Abbas Giant where you can enjoy superb views of the Cerne Valley. The **Wessex Ridgeway** crosses the centre of the county and you can download a trail guide from ⬧ dorsetcouncil.gov.uk.

♘ RIDING STABLES

Kingston Maurward Equestrian Centre Dorchester DT2 8PY ✆ 01305 215063 ⬧ kmc. ac.uk. Riding lessons and longer courses in equine studies.

DORCHESTER & AROUND

You may be tempted to assume that **Dorchester**, being Dorset's county town, is large, crowded and surrounded by new, soulless housing developments. That is not the case. Dorchester is full of old-world charm and, with around 20,000 inhabitants, is a manageable size. The countryside and villages around it are alluring and it only takes a brief look at a road atlas to see that many of Dorset's archaeological and historical attractions are in this area, including the hillfort at Maiden Castle. As for new housing developments, they don't come any more remarkable than Poundbury, the community designed in the 1990s by the then Prince of Wales.

Dorchester is the heart of **Hardy country**: devotees come to the area to pay homage to the author. High on the list of Hardy haunts to visit are his birthplace at **Higher Bockhampton** and his former home at **Max Gate** in Dorchester.

1 DORCHESTER

♠ The King's Arms

> The town is populous, tho' not large, the streets broad, but the buildings old, and low; however, there is good company and a good deal of it; and a man that coveted a retreat in this world might as agreeably spend his time, and as well in Dorchester, as in any town I know in England.

I am inclined to agree with Daniel Defoe's description in his *A tour thro' the whole island of Great Britain* (1724–26).

Dorchester as you see it today has been forged over a long and fascinating history. One of the great pleasures of wandering around the town is the chance to trace portions of that history by visiting sites of Neolithic, Roman, medieval and more recent importance. The area has been inhabited since Neolithic times, circa 4000BC, with settlements based around what later became the Iron Age hillfort of Maiden Castle (page 136). When the Romans arrived in AD70 they laid out what is now the town of Dorchester, which they called Durnovaria, in their usual cruciform manner, surrounded by a wall.

The basic structure of the town remains unchanged. Today, pleasant avenues lined with lime, chestnut and sycamore trees trace the town walls. Known as **The Walks**, the avenues were laid down in the 18th century and to wander along them is

"Today, pleasant avenues lined with lime, chestnut and sycamore trees trace the town walls."

an enjoyable way to get a feel for the town. It may strike you that the buildings do not look as ancient as you may expect. That's because much of medieval Dorchester was lost in five devastating fires between 1613 and 1775 – though thankfully the rebuilding left streets of handsome 18th-century houses.

Dorchester has a surprisingly long and varied list of museums, some devoted to themes that have little to do with the area, such as the Tutankhamun Exhibition on West Street (⊘ tutankhamun-exhibition. co.uk), a recreation of the treasures, and the Terracotta Warriors Museum on High East Street (⊘ terracottawarriors.co.uk). Of the town's museums, two really stand out as worth visiting: the **Dorset County Museum** (page 129) and the **Keep Military Museum of Devon and Dorset** (page 131). Children may enjoy the Dinosaur Museum (⊘ thedinosaurmuseum.com); it's small but has plenty of information on the county's prehistoric residents and those from further afield. And it if leaves you feeling inspired to go fossil hunting, the Jurassic Coast is just seven miles away.

The clues pointing to Dorchester's Roman origins were certainly not lost on Thomas Hardy. In his novel *The Mayor of Casterbridge*, Hardy based the fictional town on Dorchester, which he knew well, being born and raised in the area. His description of Casterbridge may as easily have been a description of Dorchester: 'Casterbridge announced old Rome in every street, alley and precinct. It looked Roman, bespoke the art of Rome, concealed the dead men of Rome.' Dorchester's Roman origins are even more evident today than they were in Hardy's time, for Hardy

JUDGE JEFFREYS & THE BLOODY ASSIZES

In May 1685, the Duke of Monmouth set sail from Holland, where he had been in exile, bound for Lyme Regis. Monmouth, the Protestant son of Charles II, intended to overthrow the Roman Catholic King James II. Lyme Regis was strongly Protestant; Monmouth gathered over 3,000 supporters and marched towards Somerset. When Monmouth was defeated on 6 July at the Battle of Sedgemoor, around 1,200 men were taken prisoner and Monmouth was executed. Judge Jeffreys held his infamous 'Bloody Assizes', a series of trials which began in Winchester and then moved through Salisbury, Dorchester, Taunton and Wells.

While presiding over the trials in Dorchester, Judge Jeffreys lodged at 6 High West Street and on 5 September, 312 trials were held in the Oak Room of the Antelope Hotel. The 'hanging judge' sentenced 292 Monmouth supporters to death and around 800 to be transported to the West Indies. After the hangings, the heads of some of the executed were impaled on church railings, and left there for several years as a warning of the penalty for treason.

In 1688, when King James II was overthrown by William of Orange, Judge Jeffreys was imprisoned in the Tower of London. He died a year later, aged 44, of kidney disease.

would not have seen the most striking proof of Roman occupation, the **Roman Town House** (∂ dorsetmuseum.org). The house, which dates from the 4th century, was found in 1937 during the building of a new county hall and is the only fully exposed Roman townhouse in the country. It is perhaps surprising (and certainly refreshing) that you are able to walk freely around the ruins and that no entry fee is charged. Most of the ruins are protected by roofs and glass walls but the basic structure, mosaic floors and underfloor heating are clearly visible. An audioguide is available through your mobile phone, or there are display panels for the less technically minded. The items found during the excavation are on display in the Dorset County Museum (page 129). The only disappointing aspect of the ruins is their location, backing on to the county council's rather unlovely offices.

Not far from the Roman Town House, on the banks of the River Frome, is **Hangman's Cottage**. This pretty thatched building in the traditional Dorset style is believed to have been home to the town's executioner. Thomas Hardy's short story *The Withered Arm* features the hangman's cottage on this site and the association has remained to this day, reinforced by stories of hangman's ropes being found in the roof in the late 19th century.

Nearby is **John's Pond**, part of the intricate drainage system of the water meadows that enabled low-lying areas to be flooded in winter to stop the ground freezing and allow fertile silt to settle. The name is reportedly in memory of a hapless prisoner, who, having managed to escape the nearby jail on a dark night, fell into the pond and was drowned.

Dorchester's **High Street** is brimming with character, points of interest and some decent shops. On the south side of High West Street are the only timber-framed buildings surviving in anything like their original state. The black-and-white building at 6 High West Street is where **Judge Jeffreys** lodged during the trials of those who took part in the Monmouth Rebellion of 1685 (see opposite). The trials, known as the **Bloody Assizes**, were held in the Oak Room of the **Antelope Hotel**. 'The Hanging Judge', whose deadly zero-tolerance policy made him highly unpopular, is said to have had a secret passage leading there from his lodgings.

The sturdy-looking **Shire Hall** on High West Street is built of Portland stone and opened in 1797, serving for over 200 years as Dorset's county hall and centre of law, order and government. Inscribed on the outside of the building, at a level for stagecoach passengers to read, are the distances to the nearest towns. It was here that the Tolpuddle Martyrs were tried in 1834 (page 150), and Thomas Hardy was a magistrate here between 1884 and 1919. Today the building contains a museum (page 152).

One of the accused who passed through Shire Hall was Martha Brown, the last woman to be publicly hanged in Dorset. She was found guilty of murdering her husband with an axe after he beat her with a whip during an argument. She was hanged in 1856 from the north-facing main entrance to Dorchester prison, only 150yds downstream from Hangman's Cottage (see opposite). One of the 4,000-strong crowd present at the hanging was the 16-year-old Thomas Hardy. It is said the memory stayed with Hardy and that Martha inspired the ultimate fate of Tess of the d'Urbervilles.

"Inscribed on the outside of the building, at a level for stagecoach passengers to read, are the distances to the nearest towns."

Martha Brown was one of many people buried at Dorchester Prison. When the prison closed in 2013, the site was sold for development. There were plans to build over 200 houses on it, without removing the bodies buried there, but Dorset resident, actor and screenwriter Lord Julian Fellowes intervened and wrote to the Bishop of Salisbury urging the church to take care of the remains. In March 2018 authorities agreed the bodies would be exhumed and given a Christian burial in a common grave at Poundbury Cemetery.

St Peter's, at the junction of South Street and High Street, is the town's only surviving medieval church. It makes a lovely peaceful retreat from the bustling town centre. The church was restored by the Dorchester architect John Hicks in 1856, along with his 16-year-old assistant, Thomas Hardy, who trained as an architect. The plans Hardy drew for the church are on display in the south chapel. Outside the church is a statue erected in 1888 to the Dorset dialect poet **William Barnes** (page 47), who lived in Dorchester from 1837 until 1886. Barnes was a rector of nearby Winterborne Came and a great friend of Thomas Hardy. Dorchester couldn't possibly have a statue of Barnes without one of Hardy too; the Hardy one is at the western end of High West Street, near the top-of-town roundabout. Opposite St Peter's Church is the **Corn Exchange** of 1848. The playful clock tower was added in 1864.

Another peaceful spot within the town is the flower-filled **Borough Gardens** on Cornwall Road, where the colourful bandstand and clock provide a Victorian feel. On the southern side of town, opposite where the market is held, is the **Brewery Square** development. The site of the former Eldridge Pope brewery is now home to modern shops, a cinema and pleasant public spaces. The centrepiece is the stunning and gigantic bronze sculpture of a dray horse by Shirley Pace, who came out of retirement in 2013 at the age of 81 to complete the work. The horse is Drummer, the last dray horse to work at the brewery. The sculpture was paraded through the town on a horse-drawn dray cart before being placed in its present position in 2014.

"During the Middle Ages it was a venue for bear-baiting and, when the Civil War came, it became an artillery fort."

Nearby **Maumbury Rings** (⌂ maumburyrings.co.uk; free access) acts almost as a physical representation of a timeline charting the area's history. The rings began life as a Neolithic henge around 2500BC. Just over 2,500 years later the Romans turned the site into an amphitheatre and held gladiatorial conquests here. During the Middle Ages it was a venue for bear-baiting and, when the Civil War came, it became an artillery fort.

In the 17th and 18th centuries Maumbury Rings was again used as an amphitheatre, drawing excited crowds to its public executions or 'Hanging Fairs'. The site continues to host public entertainment today, although the violent displays of the past have been replaced by more genteel activities, such as choral recitals and food festivals. You can visit and walk along the steep banks, although busy roads run around it and the views are very urban.

Grey's Bridge on London Road leads over the River Frome and towards Poole and Bournemouth. The bridge is one of several in Dorset bearing a sign that warns any person damaging it is liable to be transported for life. During World War II fear of invasion resulted in Royal Engineers drilling holes in the stonework, ready for explosives. No invasion took place but in 1942 several bombs fell on the water meadows and riverbank, killing ten cows and a horse, injuring several people and damaging nearby houses.

Dorset County Museum

High West St, DT1 1XA ✆ 01305 262735 ⬙ dorsetmuseum.org

The fetching mock-medieval-style building (1884), with high ceilings and fine cast-iron work inspired by the Great Exhibition of 1851, provides a suitably impressive backdrop for the exhibits here. They encapsulate what makes Dorset special: its natural history, landscapes, half a million years of human habitation, and its art and literature. The first room you come to is the magnificent Victorian Hall. Look up and you'll see intricate metalwork and a delightful rose window, while beneath your feet are mosaics collected from Roman town

"Beneath your feet are mosaics collected from Roman town houses excavated in and around Dorchester and inlaid into the floor."

houses excavated in and around Dorchester and inlaid into the floor. In fact, this is one of few places in England where you can walk on a Roman mosaic floor (if you can bring yourself to do so, that is—I couldn't).

The Jurassic Coast exhibit with its fossilised dinosaur remains and footprints is bound to be a hit with children. The People's Dorset area looks at the county's inhabitants from the Palaeolithic era to the 20th century. It includes some fascinating displays from the Bronze and Iron ages, including skeletons of members of the Durotriges tribe of Iron Age Britons found at nearby Maiden Castle.

NIGEL JARVIS/S

THE KEEP MILITARY MUSEUM

SS

ALEXANDRA RICHARDS

ROBERT HURWORTH/S

A large area is devoted to Thomas Hardy, and includes a reconstruction of his study. The top floor focuses on the county's art and includes work by sculptor Elizabeth Frink, who lived near Blandford.

The Keep Military Museum of Devon & Dorset

Barrack Rd, DT1 1RN ℘ 07586 161872 ⟁ keepmilitarymuseum.org

The museum occupies the imposing former gatehouse of the Dorsetshire Regiment barracks, built in 1879 from Portland stone. The regiments of Devon and Dorset have a history spanning over 300 years. Here you can follow their story right up to 2007, when the Devon and Dorset Light Infantry was disbanded and absorbed into The Rifles.

I found this a highly emotive museum, dedicated to the many West Country folk who have left their beloved towns, villages and farms to serve their country in a faraway land. During World War I they were joined by many of the area's finest horses. The **Queen's Own Dorset Yeomanry Horses** are best known for their 26 February 1916 charge of the Senussi forces at Agagia in Egypt. Despite being outnumbered almost three to one, the Yeomanry charged across the desert in the face of rifle and machine-gun fire. They lost half their horses and a third of their men but won the ensuing battle and captured General Jaafa Pasha. On the ground floor of the museum is a life-size model of Second Lieutenant Blaksley on horseback, carrying the original sword he used in the battle. On 3 March 1916 he wrote to his mother: 'I was within 30 yards of the enemy when my horse came down, shot through the heart. He was, I think, the nicest horse I have ever ridden, a well-known hunter in the Blackmore Vale.' For me, this was perhaps the starkest illustration of what a shock it must have been for both soldier and horse to be plucked from the tranquillity of Dorset and sent to a battlefield in northern Africa.

The museum is brilliantly laid out and has some gems that you may not expect to see tucked away in Dorset, such as Hitler's desk. The Dorsetshire Regiment recovered the desk from the ruins of the Chancellery in Berlin in 1945. From the roof there are breathtaking 360° views of Dorchester and the surrounding countryside.

◀ DORCHESTER: **1** Brewery Square: the old building is now home to shops. **2** The Keep Military Museum of Devon & Dorset. **3** An exhibit at the Shire Hall Museum. **4** The Roman Town House. **5** Thomas Hardy statue.

Shire Hall Museum

58–60 High West St, DT1 1UY ✆ 01305 261849 ⊘ shirehalldorset.org

🕐 10.00–16.00 Mon–Sat

Dorset's former centre of justice has been transformed into a moving museum of law and order. This is not a museum with masses of objects on display, rather the building itself is the attraction. The cells and courtroom are virtually unchanged since Georgian times and are hugely evocative. With the help of an audio guide, you can experience them as one of the people tried here would have done, including walking from the cells up into the dock. Listening to one of a selection of four trials as you follow in the footsteps of one of the unfortunate law-breakers is chilling.

For me, the most thought-provoking part is the handful of tiny Victorian cells. Look carefully at the wall of the last cell and you will see some graffiti that conjures images of the very homesick American man who etched it into the bricks. You can just make out the buildings of a ranch, complete with cactus plant, and the word 'home'. It was created by L Cox, a merchant navy sailor on trial here in 1948. He was originally a cowboy from Arizona and clearly longed for life back on the ranch.

The stories of individuals who passed through the courtroom are fascinating. Elijah Upjohn was brought to Shire Hall in 1834, aged 11, for stealing a pair of trousers in Shaftesbury. He was imprisoned for three months and whipped. It wasn't the deterrent it was intended to be and Elijah continued to get into trouble; he ended up being transported to Australia and spent time in Melbourne Jail. While there, the bailiffs asked for a prisoner to volunteer to execute the notorious bush ranger, Ned Kelly. No one stepped forward for fear of what the Kelly gang may do to them or their family, except Elijah. So, on 11 November 1880, Elijah executed Ned Kelly. Throughout the remainder of his time in jail, Elijah earned money whipping and executing fellow prisoners. He made a lot of enemies and after his release spent the rest of his life trying to steer clear of the Kelly Gang and the other enemies he had made dishing out punishment in prison.

Also popular with visitors is the single room where the Tolpuddle Martyrs (page 150) were held. Museum staff told me that every year descendants of members of the group from around the world visit the museum to see where their ancestors were held while on trial.

The museum is designed with families in mind, with plenty of activities for children, including dressing up in period costume. For one weekend in December, the cells are transformed for an atmospheric Christmas market.

Max Gate

Alington Av, DT1 2FN ✆ 0344 2491895 ⊙ Mar–Oct pre-booked guided tours; National Trust

Max Gate, on the eastern peripheries of town near the A35, was the home of Thomas Hardy from 1885, when he was aged 45, until he died in 1928. Construction of the house was a family affair – it was designed by Hardy and built by his brother. It was here that the author wrote *Tess of the d'Urbervilles*, *Jude the Obscure*, *The Woodlanders* and much of his poetry, and entertained other literary figures of the day, including Robert Louis Stevenson, Rudyard Kipling and T E Lawrence. Hardy had no children with either of his wives (Emma and Florence) but had a number of pets, including a dog called Wessex, who are buried in the garden. Max Gate provides a rare glimpse into Hardy's personal life, as many of his letters were destroyed upon his death, in accordance with his will.

 SPECIAL STAYS

The King's Arms 30 High East St, DT1 1HF ✆ 01305 238238 ⌂ thekingsarmsdorchester. com. If you're after accommodation in the centre of Dorset's county town, this historic former coaching inn is a good option. The Stay Original Company bought The King's Arms in 2015 when it was in a sorry state and spent four years sympathetically refurbishing it. They uncovered original features and decorated it with rich paint colours, vibrant wallpaper, antiques and modern pieces. Thomas Hardy spent time here and described it in *The Mayor of Casterbridge* as having a 'spacious bow-window, projected into the street over the main portico', just as it does now. There are 28 stylishly decorated rooms of varying sizes that successfully blend traditional and modern. The ground floor is taken up by a large restaurant and bar, popular with locals. The menu is a blend of traditional dishes and more modern offerings, all prepared to a high standard using fresh, seasonal ingredients. The hotel and restaurant are child- and dog-friendly.

 FOOD & DRINK

A market is held opposite the Brewery Square development (Weymouth Avenue) every Wednesday and Sunday. The Sunday market includes a car-boot sale. There's also a **farmers' market** on the fourth Saturday of each month in South Street (⊙ 09.00–16.00).

The Fridge 17 Tudor Arcade, DT1 1BN ✆ 01305 269088 ⌕ thefridge.biz. This shop has been supplying desirable deli items and local produce to the area since 1995.

The Horse with the Red Umbrella 10 High West St, DT1 1UJ ✆ 01305 262019. A popular, casual café in the former Loyalty Theatre building. Serves sandwiches, jacket potatoes and a good range of cakes.

The King's Arms Page 133.

Posh Partridge 29 High East St, DT1 1HF ✆ 01305 342024. Father and daughter, Murray and Emily Pulman, make a superb team running this cafe close to The County Museum. Murray prepares all the food, from delicious pâtisseries to bacon that he cures and smokes on site. A deservedly popular option, it can get busy at lunchtime. Don't think that because the ground floor is full there is nowhere to sit – there is more seating upstairs. Dog friendly.

Potter's Café 19 Durngate St, DT1 1JP ✆ 01305 260312. Centrally located and with a courtyard garden for sunny days. On offer is a variety of lunch dishes, delicious cakes, and homemade smoothies. Generous portions, reasonably priced.

Yalbury Café Brewery Sq, DT1 1GA ✆ 01305 260185 ⌕ ycscafe.com. An outpost of fine-dining restaurant Yalbury Cottage at Lower Bockhampton (page 141). You can expect a similar level of attention to detail here. Serves an excellent full English breakfast. See the website for special events.

2 WOLFETON HOUSE

Wolfeton DT2 9QN ✆ 01305 263500 ⌕ historichouses.org ⊙ Jun–Sep 14.00–17.00 Mon, Wed & Thu

This fine medieval and Elizabethan manor to the north of Dorchester is the home of the Thimbleby family, and was the home of the Lady Penelope in Thomas Hardy's *A Group of Noble Dames*. The house has magnificent carved-oak panelling, ornate ceilings, grand fireplaces and stone stairs. There is also an impressive collection of art and furniture. The house can be visited at certain times (check the website as these vary) and the gatehouse is available for letting through the Landmark Trust.

3 POUNDBURY

Poundbury is the well-known western extension of Dorchester, constructed on Duchy of Cornwall land as an initiative of King Charles III when he was Prince of Wales. The development was designed in accordance with the prince's town-planning theories, outlined in his 1989 book, *A Vision of Britain*. Building began in 1993 and is due to be completed in around 2025, the target being a total of 2,500 dwellings and a population of about 6,000.

Unsurprisingly, given its high profile, Poundbury has attracted its fair share of critics. However, the theories behind it seem sound. Aiming to create an integrated community of shops, businesses and housing, it comprises many thoughtfully designed buildings. Many of the buildings have handsome Georgian features, but there are also quaint cottages and Victorian-style brick buildings. Thankfully absent are the boxy concrete buildings and shiny glass boxes that dominate so many towns. The streets are planned with people rather than cars in mind, with narrow roads and wide pavements. There is plenty of green space, trees and wonderful parks. In fact, Poundbury has one of the best playgrounds in Dorset, in The Great Field, which also has plenty of open space, exercise equipment and a café. The playground was opened by Prince Charles himself in 2022.

The most alluring parts of Poundbury are the oldest ones, at the Dorchester end. The more time passes the more it settles into the landscape and the more attractive it becomes. People joke about the prescriptive rules residents have to follow, like not being allowed to change the colour of their house without permission, hang washing in public or park a motorhome outside their home, but they do help to keep the town looking lovely.

There are plenty of independent shops in Poundbury, like eco-friendly gift shop, byFoke (Regent House, Crown Sq, DT1 3DY ✆ 01305 602869 ⊘ byfoke.com), founded by husband and wife, Dan and Casey. Every product is selected with sustainability and ethics in mind; most come from small, independent makers. Dan and Casey will happily gift wrap for you. It's a wonderful shopping experience that is, unfortunately, very rare. They also run workshops where you can learn a skill, like making essential-oil candles.

Just to the north of the development lies a much older Poundbury: **Poundbury Hillfort**, a middle Bronze Age enclosure dating from around 1500BC. As well as the relatively simple ramparts of the roughly rectangular fort, the channel of the Roman aqueduct that supplied water to Durnovaria is clearly visible as a terrace in the hillside. The aqueduct cut across the northern and eastern sides of the hillfort's outer defences. On the northern side of the fort, the ramparts slope steeply down to the River Frome and there are good views of Dorchester and the surrounding countryside. It may be much smaller than Maiden Castle, but it is relatively easy to access.

🍴 FOOD & DRINK

A **farmers' market** is held in Queen Mother's Square on the first Saturday morning of each month. Nearby is a village shop.

Café Octagon 4 Pummery Sq, DT1 3GW ✆ 01305 266111. In a handsome octagonal building, owners Mark and Lisa Lovell serve feel-good food like homemade cottage pies and curries.

Fables and Food 7 Dinham Walk, DT1 3WU ✆ 01305 562320. Run by South African couple Natasha and Francel Du Preez-Strauss, this café offers a menu with a South African twist. The lamb bowl is a speciality – barbecue-style lamb served on flatbread. It is in a great location overlooking the fountain and has plenty of free parking.

House of Dorchester 10 Victor Jackson Av, DT1 3GY ✆ 01305 264257. Once you have found this little secret, you will want to keep coming back. This chocolate maker has a seconds shop just near the green. Behind the blue door lies a small room crammed with not-quite-perfect chocolates; whether they be misshapen or close to their best-before date, they still taste delicious and cost far less than usual.

Olives Et Al @ The Potting Shed 81 Poundbury Farm Way, DT1 3RT ✆ 01305 216788 ✆ olivesetal.co.uk. Deli and licensed café run by Dorset company Olives Et Al. Has a great range of local produce and freshly made lunches.

Pavillion in the Park St John's Way DT1 2FG ✆ 01305 259142. Casual, dog-friendly café within The Great Park. Offers breakfast, light lunches and cakes.

4 MAIDEN CASTLE

Free to access, this magnificent earthen fortification around two miles southwest of Dorchester is the largest Iron Age hillfort in Britain. The terraced ramparts, which rise to almost 90ft, enclose an area the size of 50 football pitches. Although it is best known as an Iron Age settlement, the hilltop was first inhabited much earlier, some 6,000 years ago, in the Neolithic period.

Maiden Castle was a bustling settlement populated by the Durotriges tribe. In AD43, the Romans, led by Vespasian, attacked and the Durotriges, armed with only slings and stones, were massacred. A war cemetery excavated near the east gate revealed 34 defenders buried there.

The Romans built a temple on the hilltop, the foundations of which are still visible in the northeast sector. However, they had no real use for an oversized hillfort, so they abandoned the site and established Durnovaria, now Dorchester.

It is a short walk from the car park at the base of the fort to the hilltop. Dorchester and the busy roads around it are clearly visible but are far enough away not to detract too much from the atmosphere of the place. It is only by walking around the site that you can appreciate the scale and complexity of the ramparts and the area they protected. It is easy to imagine how petrified the Durotriges must have been as they saw the advancing Roman armies, and how formidable those ramparts must have looked to the opposition.

Some of the finds from excavation of the site are in the Dorset County Museum (page 129).

5 THE SOUTH WINTERBORNES

The area has two clusters of villages with the 'winterborne' (or winterbourne) prefix to their name, indicating that they lie on a stream that flows only in winter. The South Winterbornes are those west of Dorchester and the North Winterbornes are those near Blandford.

The winterbourne near Dorchester rises above Winterbourne Abbas and joins the River Frome at West Stafford, passing through Winterbourne Steepleton, Winterborne St Martin, Winterborne Monkton and Winterborne Came. The spelling of 'Winterborne' has never been consistent, but traditionally Winterbourne Abbas and Winterbourne Steepleton retain the 'u'.

Attractive **Winterbourne Abbas** is rather spoilt by the A35 running through it. Just west of the village a small Bronze Age stone circle on the edge of a beech wood is known as **Nine Stones**. The canopies of the beech trees cast dappled light over the stones but their proximity to the busy road is unfortunate.

Winterbourne Steepleton has stone or stone and flint cottages with thatched roofs, mostly dating from the 17th and 18th centuries. The delightful little St Michael and All Angels Church is Saxon and Norman; a rare Saxon sculpture of a flying angel hangs on the north wall of the chancel.

Winterborne St Martin, also known as **Martinstown**, is an adorable village, with the stream running down the main street alongside the houses, which are reached by small footbridges over the water. The village still has a post office, pub and a village shop. Eweleaze Dairy (DT2 9JN) has a milk vending machine on the outskirts of the village, where ice cream and local produce are also available.

The **church of St Martin**, which dates from the 12th century, has a square Purbeck marble font dating from around 1125. Nearby the stream crosses under the road, just in front of the Brewers Arms, which was built as a private girls' school in 1848. If you follow the path upstream past the pub you will see the stone **sheep-washing pool**, which was used to wash the sheep before sale, as a higher price could be obtained for clean fleeces. It may look simple but must have been effective as it was in use as recently as the 1960s. Today, the stream outside the pub is the venue for the village's annual yellow-plastic **duck race**, held in May.

From the village it is an easy walk to **Maiden Castle**. The round distance is 3½ miles, although this can be extended by walking around the ramparts of the hillfort. As you walk, look out for the many prehistoric mounds known as tumuli or barrows (set up as tombs and landmarks in the Bronze Age) around the Winterbornes and particularly concentrated around Winterborne St Martin.

¶¶ FOOD & DRINK

Brewers Arms DT2 9LB 🖉 01305 889361. A traditional, dog-friendly pub in the village centre. If you stop at the pub be sure to head up the lane along the stream for a look at the sheep-washing pool (see above).

6 HIGHER BOCKHAMPTON, STINSFORD & SURROUNDS

The hamlets of Higher Bockhampton and Stinsford just east of Dorchester are best known for their links to Thomas Hardy, who was born in a small, highly picturesque cottage in Higher Bockhampton (page 140). He was christened in the **church of St Michael** in Stinsford and attended services there as a child.

Although he was famously agnostic, Hardy loved this peaceful little church and it is easy to see why. The building is largely 13th century, with a 14th-century tower. Above the church door is a relief of St Michael installed in 2011 by local stone mason, Rebecca Freiesleben. It replaced the Saxon version, which is now in the south aisle of the church.

Hardy's family had a long association with the church. Hardy's grandfather, father and uncle all belonged to the parish's string choir, which played from the gallery. Thomas is said to have played the violin

1 Maiden Castle. 2 The medieval and Elizabethan manor of Wolfeton House. 3 Stinsford church is Thomas Hardy's final resting place. 4 Hardy's Cottage in Higher Bockhampton. ▶

with them on occasion. A tablet within the church commemorates the family's participation. Hardy remembered Stinsford and the band with great affection, naming the village 'Mellstock' in *Under the Greenwood Tree*.

Hardy is commemorated in a beautiful stained-glass window of 1930 in the south aisle; it is based on his favourite Old Testament reading, Elijah and the Still, Small Voice (1 Kings 19). Many members of Hardy's family, including his parents, sister, his first wife, Emma, and second wife, Florence, are buried in the churchyard. The Hardy family graves are on the left as you enter from the car park. Hardy's heart is buried alongside Emma but his ashes are in Poet's Corner within Westminster Abbey. Just along from the Hardy graves is the grave of Cecil Day Lewis (1904–72), Poet Laureate and detective novelist.

Hardy's Cottage

Higher Bockhampton DT2 8QJ ✐ 01305 262366; National Trust

It is fortunate that Thomas Hardy was born in a picture-perfect thatched cob cottage with a flower-filled garden, for this must be one of the most photographed addresses in Dorset. The cottage, now held by the National Trust, is nestled at the base of Thorncombe Wood, a five- to ten-minute walk from the car park. You need to buy a timed ticket at the visitor centre before walking to the cottage. The most direct route is along a fairly level but rough track, or there is a pretty, slightly longer and steeper path through the woods.

The cottage was built by his great-grandfather and was Hardy's home, on and off, from his birth in 1840 until he married Emma Gifford in 1874. It gives you an appreciation for how quiet, secluded and reflective Hardy's young life must have been. You have the chance to wander the tiny rooms, negotiate the perilously steep staircase and see where he wrote *Under the Greenwood Tree* and *Far from the Madding Crowd*. The cottage has changed little since he lived here and described it in his earliest-surviving poem, 'Domicilium':

Red roses, lilacs, variegated box
Are there in plenty, and such hardy flowers
As flourish best untrained. Adjoining these
Are herbs and esculents; and farther still
A field; then cottages with trees, and last
The distant hills and sky.

Behind, the scene is wilder. Heath and furze
Are everything that seems to grow and thrive
Upon the uneven ground. A stunted thorn
Stands here and there, indeed; and from a pit
An oak uprises, springing from a seed
Dropped by some bird a hundred years ago.

Kingston Maurward Animal Park & Gardens

DT2 8PY ✆ 01305 215003 ⚲ kmc.ac.uk; free admission

Kingston Maurward House lies between Stinsford and Lower
Bockhampton. It was built in 1720 in the classic Palladian style for
George Pitt, cousin of William Pitt the Elder, who became prime minister
in 1766. During World War II it was occupied by American servicemen
and the estate used as a fuel depot for the D-Day landings. Today,
Kingston Maurward is a well-regarded agricultural college. The gardens
are open to the public and showcase a number of different horticultural
styles, including Arts and Crafts. Although the house is not open to the
public, it is visible from the gardens, elegant but overwhelmingly grey
and rather austere. The animal park is well laid out with a host of pet and
farm animals to delight visiting children. There are indoor and outdoor
play areas and a café.

🍴 FOOD & DRINK

Yalbury Cottage Lower Bockhampton DT2 8PZ ✆ 01305 262382 ⚲ yalburycottage.com. A
highly regarded restaurant with rooms. Owner/chef Jamie Jones uses the excellent produce
available locally to create incredible French-inspired dishes. Jamie has worked in top hotels
around the world, and it shows. His wife, Ariane, takes care of front of house. Dinner is
utterly memorable, starting with pre-dinner drinks in the sitting room. Choose from two or
three courses, with options from the sea, garden and fields. Reservation recommended.

7 MILL HOUSE CIDER MUSEUM & A DORSET COLLECTION OF CLOCKS

33 Moreton Rd, Owermoigne DT2 8HZ ✆ 01305 852220 ⚲ millhousecider.com ⊙ 10.00–
16.00 Tue–Sat & public holidays

This museum north of the A352 features antique cider-making
equipment. In October you can see apples being transformed into cider
using 19th-century machinery. You can even bring your own apples
and have them made into apple juice or cider. Some villages pool their
apples and take them to the museum by the trailer load to produce a

communal supply. Also on site are a shop selling West Country produce and a garden nursery specialising in seed potatoes.

Adjacent, a clock museum houses a collection that includes over 30 grandfather clocks. Beautifully displayed, they will delight anyone with even a passing interest in timepieces.

NORTH FROM DORCHESTER TOWARDS THE BLACKMORE VALE

The A352 runs north from Dorchester to Sherborne and North Dorset. Between Dorchester and Minterne Magna the road runs parallel to the River Cerne through the Cerne Valley. It is along this road that you will see one of Dorset's most distinctive sights, the **Cerne Abbas Giant**.

8 GODMANSTONE

Five miles north of Dorchester, the small village of Godmanstone lies along the River Cerne.

In the centre of the village is a diminutive, single-storey, thatched, mud and flint building dating from 1420 – the Smith's Arms. With a bar measuring just 15ft by 11ft 9in, it once held the title of smallest pub in England.

Tradition has it that King Charles II stopped at a blacksmith's forge in Godmanstone and requested a glass of porter. The blacksmith responded, 'I cannot oblige you Sire, as I have no licence.' The king reportedly granted one on the spot and the Smith's Arms came into being.

In 1982 the licensee of The Nutshell at Bury St Edmunds challenged the Smith's Arms's claim to be England's smallest pub. The rival landlords decided to settle the matter with a football match, which The Nutshell won. The Nutshell has subsequently lost the title to even tinier competitors.

Nearby, a footpath across the River Cerne behind the former mill takes you up on to the hillside for impressive views across the valley. On the other side of the road from the pub a lane leads to a charming, little 11th-century church.

¶¶ FOOD & DRINK

Feed the Soul Green Valley Farm, Longmeadow, DT2 7AE ✆ 01300 342164. Not really what you expect to find on a Dorset farm – this is a vegan café and shop, where the focus is on raw and vegan foods, and superfoods. Speciality coffee is roasted in house, and you will find kefir, kimchi and other healthy fare here. The farm also offers glamping accommodation on site in yurts and bell tents.

9 CERNE ABBAS & ITS GIANT

Travellers along the A352 are treated to a very unusual sight – the 180ft-tall chalk carving of a naked man known as the **Cerne Abbas Giant**. He is also known as 'The Rude Man', for reasons (actually one very obvious reason) that become apparent when you look at him from the roadside viewpoint. I strongly suspect that the postcards of the Rude Man in his birthday suit are the county's best-sellers.

The giant is a Scheduled Ancient Monument that has been in the care of the National Trust since 1920. His age and meaning have long been debated with theories about his identity ranging from ancient fertility

A walk around the giant

OS Explorer map 117; start: Abbey St, Cerne Abbas SY665014; 2½ miles; medium (one steep hill).

The best views of the giant are from the viewpoint on the A352. The giant is fenced off but this walk takes you around him.

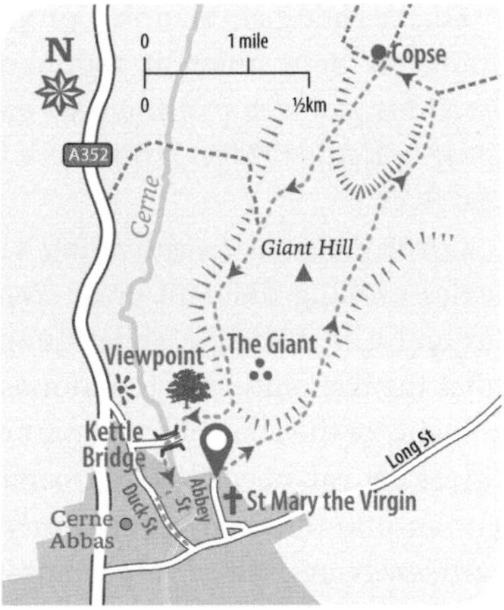

The walk starts at the burial ground at the end of Abbey Street, where a gate in the wall leads into fields. Once through the gate, turn right and head around the base of the woodland, then left up the hill. The climb provides glorious views of the Cerne Valley, where buzzards are frequently seen making good use of the thermals. At the top of the hill cross the field towards the copse, then back to the bottom left corner of the same field. Follow the path downhill and left along the hillside, and you will soon be walking under the giant's feet. Drop down into some woodland and follow the signs for Kettle Bridge, an adorable stone and flint bridge across the River Cerne. Cross the bridge and it is a pleasant, short walk along the river back to the village.

symbol to Oliver Cromwell. One story maintains that the figure was carved around the body of a rampaging giant after he was slain by local people, like a sort of early crime-scene cadaver outline, I suppose! However, recent investigations have brought us closer to the truth than ever. Sediment analysis conducted in 2019 led archaeologists to conclude the giant was probably constructed in the late Saxon period, between AD700 and 1100. This was a surprise to many as most theories had him pegged as either prehistoric or post-medieval. In early 2024, research from the University of Oxford led experts to assess that he was probably carved as an image of Hercules to mark a muster station for West Saxon armies at a time when the area was under attack from the Vikings.

"The rude giant standing proudly in his birthday suit has been many things to many different people over the centuries."

Cerne Abbas being on a main route and with a fresh water source, it was the perfect place to assemble the troops. Apparently, Hercules was well known in 9th-century Britain and had quite the following, so he was the ideal choice to mark the spot and inspire the Saxon armies. In the 11th century, the monks of the village's benedictine abbey re-branded the giant as a depiction of their patron saint, Eadwold (see opposite).

So, the rude giant standing proudly in his birthday suit has been many things to many different people over the centuries. To appreciate him in all his glory, stop at the new parking area on the edge of the village, close to Kettle Bridge. From there it is a lovely walk into the village along the river.

Cerne Abbas is a captivating village with a mixture of architectural styles evoking different eras, from medieval to Georgian. It grew up around a Benedictine abbey founded in AD987 but largely destroyed after the Dissolution of the Monasteries in the 16th century. What little remains of the abbey is now part of a private house at the top of Abbey Street but can be visited for a small fee: the **Abbot's Porch**, built as the entrance to the abbey in the early 1500s, and the **abbey guesthouse**, a rare surviving example of a monastic guesthouse. As you walk up Abbey Street towards the abbey ruins, you will pass a charming duck pond and just beyond it a gate leads into a **burial ground** believed to date from the time of the abbey. Among the gravestones is the medieval **Preaching Cross**, a stone shaft set into a squat hexagonal base, which travelling priests would have used to give communion to local residents.

If you follow the wall on your right as you go into the burial ground you will come to **St Augustine's Well**. Also known as the Silver Well, this is another of the few relics remaining from the days of the abbey. A canopy of trees casts dappled light over the water, which is always cool, and there is a stone bench on which to pause. There is a sense of history as well as beauty here. According to legend, **St Augustine of Canterbury** (died AD604) visited Dorset and met some shepherds in the then uninhabited Cerne Valley. He asked if they would prefer beer or water to quench their thirst. When they replied 'water', the saint struck the ground with his staff and the spring started to flow. Some cynical folk have suggested that the Benedictine monks of Cerne Abbey fabricated the story to attract pilgrims. Regardless, it really does feel like a special place and is a perfect spot for quiet reflection.

Also on Abbey Street, the **church of St Mary the Virgin** was built by the abbey and dates from the 15th century, although the chancel is earlier, being circa 1300, and there were various additions in the 17th

ST EADWOLD – THE HERMIT SAINT

The latest theory about the Cerne Abbas Giant is that he is of Saxon origin but was reinvented by the monks of Cerne's Benedictine abbey as their patron saint, Eadwold. But who was St Eadwold?

He is said to have been born a prince in around AD835, the brother of Saint Edmund, King of East Anglia, who became a martyr after Viking invaders tied him to a tree and peppered him with arrows. Eadwold left his homeland, possibly to get away from the Vikings, and lived as a hermit on the hills around Cerne Abbas. He is said to have lived off bread and water, healed people and performed miracles.

One of his miracles is particularly relevant to the giant. On a hill in the Cerne Abbas area, Eadwold is said to have planted his pilgrim's staff in the ground, at which point the dead wood returned to life, sprouting branches and becoming a living tree. Eadwold then saw a silver fountain where God commanded him to spend the rest of his days in worship. The miracle could have been designed to reinforce the monks' claim that the chalk giant represents Eadwold. The giant's club could have been interpreted as Eadwold's staff blossoming into a tree, and the nearby well fits neatly with the story too.

After his death in AD900, Eadwold was buried in his hermit's cell; his remains were moved to Cerne Abbey in the early 11th century. This association with Eadwold is credited with boosting the monastery's finances immensely, making it the third richest in England. Eadwold was clearly a hugely important figure in medieval Dorset.

and 18th centuries. Opposite the church is a row of wonderfully wonky wooden houses dating from around 1500, known as the **Pitchmarket** because the farmers would pitch their corn sacks here on market days for buyers to inspect.

Heading back towards the A352, along the road known as The Folly, it is worth taking a detour to walk along the footpath marked Barton Farm Meadows, because from the path you get a reasonable view of the **Tithe Barn**. This magnificent barn dates from the 14th century and was probably much longer than the building you see today. It is now a private house and not open to the public.

¶¶ FOOD & DRINK

New Inn 14 Long St, DT2 7JF ⌀ 01300 341274 ⌔ thenewinncerneabbas.co.uk. The restaurant within this 16th-century coaching inn is full of beams and character, and specialises in local fish and game prepared to a high standard. Easily the most upmarket option in town.
Royal Oak 23 Long St, DT2 7JG ⌀ 01300 341797. This ivy-covered freehouse dates from 1540 and serves traditional pub food. It is reportedly haunted by several ghosts.

10 MINTERNE MAGNA

As you travel north from Cerne Abbas towards Sherborne on the A352, you pass through the pretty village of Minterne Magna. The church here, **St Andrew's**, is based on an original Saxon church now incorporated into the chancel. The nave and chancel were built in the early 15th century, while the north chapel was added between 1610 and 1620. Next door to the church is the entrance to **Minterne Gardens** (DT2 7AU ⌀ 01300 341370⌔ minterne.co.uk ⌚ Feb–Nov 10.00–18.00 daily).

Visitors can walk around the impressive garden of this beautiful private home belonging to the Digby family. You will need to leave your car in the car park opposite St Andrew's Church and walk across the road to enter the grounds, which were landscaped in the 18th century in the manner of Capability Brown. The owner at that time, Robert Digby, reportedly used to visit the family home at Sherborne Castle whenever Brown was working there and pick his brain for ideas. Keen gardeners will enjoy walking the mile of paths, which wind through the garden and criss-cross the stream. Himalayan rhododendrons and azaleas

◀ **1** The Cerne Abbas Giant. **2** Buildings on Abbey Street, Cerne Abbas.
3 Minterne Gardens. **4** St Augustine's Well at Cerne Abbas. **5** Cerne Abbas's Tithe Barn.

THE ART OF THATCHING

With Edward Taylor, Master Thatcher

☏ 01297 489528, 07966 209561 ⌂ thatching.biz

A thatched cottage with a rose wandering around the door is one of the quintessential images of English rural living, and with chocolate-box cottages around every Dorset corner thatch is very much part of the landscape and culture.

Dorset master thatcher, Edward Taylor, AKA 'Spike', started his career with a seven-year apprenticeship. Spike explained the craft takes this long to learn because numerous styles, techniques and materials are used and they vary from county to county. Spike works mainly with combed wheat reed and water reed.

Thatching has its own language of ancient terms – thatching wheat is cut with a reaper/binder and the sheaves (bundles) are 'stooked' up in the fields. Eight sheaves make a stook, 16 make a stock. The sheaves are left in the stook for two weeks to dry, then put into the rick before going on the threshing machine or reed comber. Here, the short straws, leaf and flag are combed out and the grain and chaff removed. The long stems are kept perfectly straight. Finally, the straw is trussed up and bundled, ready to use.

Laying thatch is tough physical work. The primary tool is a legget, used to coerce the material into position, a process known as 'dressing'. A 'spar', a branch of split hazel wood tapered to a point at each end and twisted into a V shape, is used to staple the thatch into place. Each course overlaps the one below, providing a continuous depth of straw over the roof. The ridge is where the thatcher can leave his mark; Spike favours the traditional pointed end.

While we all love the look of a thatched roof, people are divided as to whether they would want to live under one. Beauty doesn't come cheap: the roof needs to be re-thatched about every 25 years and the ridge needs to be replaced around every ten years. Depending on the roof and the materials used, re-thatching can cost around £25,000; on top of that there is usually an insurance premium because of a perceived fire risk.

Thankfully, the undeniable charm of a thatched roof means that they will remain part of the rural landscape, just as they have since the Bronze Age.

feature heavily in the design, so it is particularly colourful from March to June. In April and May, bluebells and wild garlic add soft colour and a woodland perfume.

The garden's appeal is greatly enhanced by its location, in a wide valley where sheep graze happily below a band of woodland. Unfortunately, it's not suitable for wheelchairs. The tea terrace serves light lunches, cakes and cream teas.

THE PIDDLE VALLEY & BERE REGIS

The River Piddle (also known far less amusingly as the River Trent) rises near the church in the village of Alton Pancras and flows towards Wareham, entering the sea at Poole Harbour along with the River Frome. The name Piddle is thought to derive from the Saxon, meaning clear water. Many of the villages it passes through are named after the river, creating some of the best village names in existence: Puddletown, Tolpuddle, Piddlehinton, Piddletrenthide, Affpuddle, Briantspuddle and Turnerspuddle. All but two of those names now contain 'puddle' rather than 'piddle'. A popular story tells that the villages were renamed prior to a visit by Queen Victoria to avoid offending her sensibilities, but there is no firm evidence of this. A more prosaic theory is that the names were altered in response to a request from the post office.

11 PIDDLETRENTHIDE & PIDDLEHINTON

Piddletrenthide and its neighbour Piddlehinton are largely made up of stone and flint-banded cottages. Stretched along the river valley and the B3143, **Piddletrenthide** gets its name from the fact that it is on the River Piddle and was assessed for 30 hides in the Domesday Book. A hide was a unit used to measure land value in order to calculate tax, and was originally the amount of land that could be ploughed in a year using one plough and an eight-ox team. The area thus varied with soil quality and a 'hide' could range from 60 to 180 acres. Piddletrenthide has a good village shop and a fine **church** with a splendid tower dated 1487.

The name of the river was a marketing gem waiting to be exploited. In 2002, a micro-brewery was set up in Piddlehinton, the **Piddle Brewery** (⊘ piddlebrewery.co.uk). You will see their beers in pubs and shops throughout the county.

¶¶ FOOD & DRINK

The Blue Vinny Puddletown DT2 8TE ⊘ 01305 848228 ⊘ thebluevinny.co.uk. The clean, fresh interior bodes well and the food doesn't disappoint. Locally sourced ingredients are given a Mediterranean twist. The kitchen takes pride in the way the food is presented, so it looks expensive but is in fact reasonably priced. Reservation recommended.

Puddletown Blueberries Puddletown DT2 8QL ⊘ 07568 099065 ⊘ puddletownblueberries.com. Pick-your-own blueberries available from mid-July until late September.

The Thimble Inn 14 High St, Piddlehinton DT2 7TD ✆ 01300 348270. Word has got out that the food here is excellent, which means it gets pretty busy. It is a proper, thatched country pub with friendly service and a pleasant beer garden with a stream running through it.

12 ATHELHAMPTON HOUSE & GARDENS

Athelhampton DT2 7LG ✆ 01305 848363 🖥 athelhampton.com

Thomas Hardy was a frequent visitor to this beautiful manor house dating from the 15th century, and he referred to it in his writings as 'Athelhall'. The house has been much extended since Tudor times and some of the oldest parts are open to the public, as are the stunning gardens.

A carved stone monkey wearing a chain sits above the front door, and he makes appearances throughout the house, including in its stained-glass windows. He is also said to make ghostly appearances. The story goes that he lived as a pet in the hall in the 15th century but was accidentally imprisoned in a secret passage, starved to death and has haunted the house ever since.

The oak-panelled Great Hall was built in 1485. Hidden in the panels next to the large fireplace is a Tudor doggy door. After the household

THE TOLPUDDLE MARTYRS

In the 1830s life was tough for farm labourers in Dorset. Increased mechanisation of farming in the early part of the 19th century meant landowners became less dependent on labourers and lowered the average agricultural wage. Labourers in Dorset had traditionally been poorly paid in comparison with their counterparts in the rest of England and eventually wages in the county fell to just seven shillings a week. It became impossible for a labourer to support his family.

In 1833, a group of farm labourers from Tolpuddle made representation to their local landowners and employers for an increase in wages. This request was met by a decree that wages would be reduced to six shillings a week.

Under the leadership of George Loveless (a Methodist lay preacher), some of the aggrieved labourers organised themselves into a 'Friendly Society of Agricultural Labourers', effectively an early trade union. The group would meet either under what has now become known as the 'Martyrs Tree' on the village green or in the cottage of group member John Standfield.

Local landowners, led by James Frampton of Moreton House, were determined to quash any uprising, particularly given what had happened to their French counterparts during the French Revolution.

On a cold February morning in 1834, police arrested six members of the group: George Loveless and his brother James, Thomas had finished eating, the dogs would be let in from the wine cellar to clean up the leftovers in the dining hall.

Visitors can wander the 12 acres of Grade I-listed gardens surrounding the house. Largely laid down in the late 19th century, they feature perfect topiary pyramids and colourful herbaceous borders. Highlights include a photogenic 15th-century dovecote and a 19th-century toll house.

In 2019, economist Giles Keating bought Athelhampton and he has been on a mission to make the estate carbon neutral. He has installed a huge solar-panel array, Tesla batteries and ground- and air-source heat pumps. The project required innovative technologies and a sensitive approach to minimise any negative impact on the historic building. You can learn more about the project by taking an Athelampton Zero Tour (book via the website).

⁞⁞ FOOD & DRINK

The Coach House Restaurant Athelhampton House, DT2 7LG ✆ 01305 848363. You don't need to pay the entry fee for the house to eat at the restaurant here, which is in a converted thatched stable block. The menu offers plenty of choice; the food is freshly made and

Standfield and his son John, James Hammett and James Brine. These men were tried at Dorchester Assizes, and found guilty of unlawful assembly and administering an illegal oath. Forming a union had been made legal in 1824, but they had made the mistake of swearing an oath that meant that they could be tried under the Mutiny Act of 1797. Sentencing them to transportation to Australia for a period of seven years, the judge noted he wanted to make an example of them. At the trial, George Loveless reportedly said: 'If we have violated any law, it was not intentionally. We have injured no person or property. We were uniting to preserve ourselves, our wives and our children from utter degradation and starvation.'

The public outcry at the martyrs' harsh treatment, driven by a fledging trade-union movement, was so great that it led to pardons being granted for the labourers in March 1836. Despite this, it was a further three years before the martyrs were brought back to Dorset. During their absence, their families were sustained by the trade-union movement.

The martyrs returned first to Essex, where land had been set aside for them, but several later migrated to London in Ontario, Canada. The only martyr to remain in Tolpuddle was James Hammett, who returned to England a year later than the others and worked as a builder. He died in Tolpuddle in 1891 and is buried in the churchyard.

uses locally sourced ingredients. In the winter, a Sunday carvery roast lunch is available in Athelampton's Long Hall Dining Room. Booking essential.

13 TOLPUDDLE

The small village of Tolpuddle has secured its place in history thanks to the actions of six farm labourers in 1834, now known as the Tolpuddle Martyrs (page 150). The labourers spoke up about their intolerable poverty and took an oath of mutual support, essentially forming an early trade union. This did not go down at all well with the local landowners: the farm labourers were charged with swearing an illegal oath and were transported to Australia. Public outcry eventually led to their pardon and they returned to England.

The village has become a place of pilgrimage for its links to the trade-union movement. The Trades Union Congress (TUC) holds an annual festival here on the third Sunday in July. The festival, which attracts as many as 10,000 people, culminates in a procession through the village by representatives of various trade unions, accompanied by marching bands. There is live music and speeches by prominent socialists.

On the west side of the village are six memorial cottages built by the TUC in 1934 to commemorate the 100th anniversary of the martyrs' transportation and to provide accommodation for retired agricultural trade unionists. In the centre of these is the small **Tolpuddle Martyrs Museum** (DT2 7EH ✆ 01305 848237 ⌂ tolpuddlemartyrs.org.uk ⊙ Apr–Oct Tue–Sun & bank holidays; Nov–Mar Thu–Sun; free admission), devoted to the martyrs and the history of the trade-union movement. This interesting and well laid-out little museum evolved from a library intended for residents of the cottages but that soon became a depository for artefacts, documents and memorabilia relating to the martyrs.

Tolpuddle has a pleasing blend of brick and cob cottages, many of them thatched. Some newer houses have been added, but thankfully in a similar architectural style, and the whole village seems well looked after. At the centre of the village is a small green, on which stands one of the most famous trees in England. This is the tree under which the martyrs used to meet but it seems it was there long before the martyrs came along – the National Trust has dated the tree as having started its life in the

1 Athelhampton House. 2 The ceiling of St John the Baptist Church, Bere Regis. 3 The River Bere at Shitterton. ▶

ALEXANDRA RICHARDS

IAN WOOLCOCK/S

1680s. Next to it is a thatched shelter dedicated to the martyrs, erected as part of the 100th anniversary celebrations in 1934. A new sycamore was planted in 1984 to replace the old one when the time comes.

St John's Church is a striking stone and flint building. Although the original church dates from the 12th century it has been altered and restored over the years, most significantly in 1855. In the graveyard is the grave of the only one of the Tolpuddle Martyrs who returned to live in the village, James Hammett, who died in 1891.

¶¶ FOOD & DRINK

The Martyrs Inn DT2 7ES ☏ 01305 602115. Serves traditional pub food made with ingredients from local suppliers.

14 BERE REGIS

Bere Regis is one of those sprawling villages that used to have a main road running through it, but has now been bypassed, leaving it feeling a little lost. Much of Bere Regis was destroyed in a series of fires, the worst of which occurred in 1788, and as a result it is largely a mixture of 18th-century and more modern buildings. The one exception is the marvellous **church of St John the Baptist**, which dates from 1050.

"The nave has a magnificent 15th-century carved oak ceiling with figures of the Apostles looking down from above. "

The uninspiring approach to the church from the Turbeville Road car park (BH20 7HA) takes you through an estate of modern houses and does not do the church justice, but do persevere. The church bell ringers were in full swing when I visited on a sunny evening in May. A 16th-century tower in flint and stone sets an impressive note, and inside it is even better. Look up as you enter the church and you will see two large iron hooks above the door, an early fire-fighting tool. They date from around 1600 and were placed there for the men of the village to use to pull thatch from the roofs of buildings ahead of an advancing fire. The nave has a magnificent 15th-century carved oak ceiling with figures of the Apostles looking down from above. Much of the wood is painted and gilded: coin-operated lights highlight the ceiling to bring out its colours and detail. The central bosses depict Cardinal Morton, his shield of arms, a Tudor rose and a golden cord, symbolising the marriage he arranged between Henry VII and Elizabeth of York in 1486, so ending the Wars of the Roses.

A small amount of the 1050 church survives at the northeast end of the nave. Just inside the door at the edge of the nave are 12th-century capitals with some curious carvings: the head of a monkey, a king and two people apparently with toothache.

There is a slab in the floor over the entrance to the Turberville vault, which reads '1710 Door of the sepulchre of the ancient family of the Turbervilles'. The manor house at Bere Regis was the home of the Turberville family from the 13th century to the 18th century, when that branch of the family became extinct. It was the fall of the powerful Turbervilles that inspired Thomas Hardy's *Tess of the d'Urbervilles* and Bere Regis featured in the novel as 'Kingsbere'.

In the churchyard, some of the older graves of interest are marked with numbers and boards clarifying their worn lettering. Particularly moving, and apt for the Bere Regis/Shitterton area, is the grave marked number five. According to the inscription on the small headstone Thomas Fry was 'killed by the over-thro of a dung cart June ye 12th 1722 in ye 11th year of his age'.

In 2013, former Queen guitarist, Dr Brian May, CBE, bought 160 acres of farmland just south of Bere Regis and began transforming it into a woodland haven for wildlife, through his Save Me Trust (⌂ savemetrust.org). Over 100,000 trees have been planted, including oak, beech, chestnut and alder. Known as May's Wood, the area is now popular with local walkers.

ᵀ¶ FOOD & DRINK

Royal Oak West St, BH20 7HQ ✆ 01929 472710. A 16th-century coaching inn serving unpretentious pub classics in the pleasant bar area, beer garden or courtyard.

15 SHITTERTON

You won't be surprised to hear that the hamlet of Shitterton, which adjoins Bere Regis, is best known for its name, which appeals greatly to those with a fondness for lavatory humour and ranks at number nine in *Rude Britain: The 100 Rudest Place Names in Britain*. While some prudish folk leave out the 'h', many of the residents are proud to tell you precisely where they live and even emphasise the 'sh'. In a broad Dorset accent, the name has even more of a ring to it.

The heavy stone slab that announces the village's name has a story behind it. Due to frequent theft of Shitterton's previous signs by souvenir hunters, the council gave up replacing it. In July 2010, after nearly three years without a sign, residents, led by chair of the parish council, Ian Ventham, banded together to purchase a slab of Purbeck stone and have it engraved. Of some 50 Shitterton households, well over half contributed and the local council chipped in too. It would take a highly committed souvenir hunter to make off with the 1½-ton stone slab, which now announces, rather grandly, the hamlet's name. In 2012, to commemorate the diamond jubilee of Queen Elizabeth II, Ian arranged for similar stones to be carved and placed at the three entrances to Bere Regis, also funded by local donations.

"A pretty stream runs through Shitterton, although it loses some of its charm when you learn the origin of the hamlet's name."

Shitterton is far more comely than its name may indicate. It was protected by the Bere River from the fires that destroyed Bere Regis, so still retains some older, mostly thatched buildings. A pretty stream runs through Shitterton, although it loses some of its charm when you learn the origin of the hamlet's name, which apparently means stream used as a midden, in other words a dung heap.

THE FROME VALLEY

16 MORETON

This tiny and incredibly pretty village on the River Frome is part of a large estate, owned for centuries by the Frampton family of Moreton House.

The village is firmly on the Lawrence of Arabia trail, for it was in **St Nicholas's Church** that Lawrence's funeral took place on the afternoon of 21 May 1935. It was well attended, including by Sir Winston Churchill, Robert Graves and Siegfried Sassoon. Following his exploits in Arabia, Lawrence had moved to nearby Cloud's Hill (page 160), renting (and later buying) the cottage from his cousins, the Framptons.

Lawrence is buried in the cemetery to the south of the village, next to the Moreton Walled Garden (see opposite). The cemetery's entrance is hard to miss, although it looks more like the Greek-inspired entrance to a public swimming pool thanks to the unusual sky-blue and white porch with white columns on each corner. The porch used to stand about 100yds further north, as the entrance to the Moreton House kitchen gardens. Built into its walls are two tablets that were once at the base of the obelisk on nearby Fir Hill, built in 1784 in memory of James Frampton from the big house, which you may glimpse from the road between Moreton and Wool.

Lawrence's grave is at the far end of the cemetery, on the right. The unpretentious headstone is in the shape of an open book. It records Lawrence's real name, although he had changed his name by deed poll to T E Shaw in 1923 to escape his celebrity status (page 160). The headstone makes no mention of his time in Arabia.

Regardless of its connections to Lawrence of Arabia, St Nicholas's Church is fascinating. The original church was demolished in 1776 and replaced by a Georgian, Gothic building, thanks to the Frampton family.

The church's best-known feature is its unusual engraved windows by Laurence Whistler. The windows were installed in 1955 and 1974–84. A German bomb destroyed the original stained-glass windows on 8 October 1940, along with the north wall of the church. The theme of the replacement windows is light: one depicts candles, another lightning, one the sun, and the effect of the clear glass is striking. You are so accustomed to not being able to see the view from a church, yet this one allows you to enjoy the sky and trees outside and allows light to flood in.

Nearby, there is a ford and a bridge cross the River Frome, which is wide and shallow here. In the summer months locals come here to cool off in the water.

The Walled Garden (DT2 8RG ✆ 01929 462243 ♂ walledgardenmoreton.co.uk ◷ 09.00–17.00 daily) is a very pleasant way to finish off a visit to Moreton. There are five acres of gardens to explore, plants for sale and a café (page 159). A play area and a selection of animals (including pygmy goats, chickens, guinea pigs and rabbits) keep children entertained.

"You are so accustomed to not being able to see the view from a church, yet this one allows you to enjoy the sky and trees outside."

The countryside south of Moreton is remarkably wild and unspoilt; the lanes are lined with ferns, water meadows, heathland and woodland. Much of this internationally important landscape lies within the nature reserves of Tadnoll and Winfrith heaths, which are managed by Dorset Wildlife Trust. In late summer, the heath wears its characteristic purple. The reserves are home to interesting wildlife, including silver-studded blue butterflies,

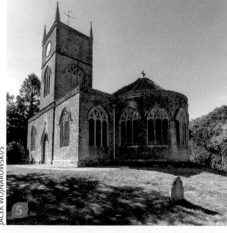

the Dartford warbler and the nightjar, which can be heard making their almost mechanical 'churring' sound after dark.

¶¶ FOOD & DRINK

Dovecote Café The Walled Garden, DT2 8RG ✐ 01929 462243 ⊘ walledgardenmorton. co.uk. This café enjoys a lovely setting in the walled garden next to the stream (but you don't have to visit the garden to go to the café). On offer are homemade meals and cakes, and the Sunday roasts served during winter are popular with locals.

17 SCULPTURE BY THE LAKES

Pallington Lakes DT2 8QU ✐ 07720 637808 ⊘ sculpturebythelakes.co.uk
🕓 10.00–17.00 Tue–Sat.

Peace, beauty and inspiration are the key offerings here, and we all need more of those things. Over 130 contemporary sculptures are displayed with nature as their backdrop, and the path through the sculpture park winds around a series of lakes and along the River Frome, with plenty of places for quiet contemplation or a picnic.

The park was created by Simon and Monique Gudgeon, reflecting their respective passions. Simon is a sculptor who is fascinated by the natural world and Monique is a keen gardener. When they bought the 26-acre site it was a commercial fishery; since then, the Gudgeons have planted over 5,000 trees, shrubs and herbaceous perennials to not only create a landscape to complement the sculptures but to increase biodiversity and provide a habitat for wildlife. Many of the sculptures are by Simon but other artists feature too.

There is a fee to wander around the sculpture park, but entry to the Makers' Yard is free. Within the Makers' Yard are The Gallery with its art exhibitions; The Store, selling creations by over 80 artists and makers from Dorset and beyond; The Pantry selling artisan food and drink; and The Kitchen, a café that features ingredients from the site's impressive kitchen garden.

There is wheelchair access to the sculpture park and Makers' Yard. Children under 14 are not allowed because of the deep water. It's best to buy your ticket in advance.

◄ **1** Sculpture by the Lakes. **2** The village of Moreton. **3** Horseriding across the ford at Moreton. **4** Clouds Hill at Bovington is where T E Lawrence lived between 1923 and 1935. **5** St Nicholas's Church in Moreton. **6** Exhibits at Bovington Tank Museum.

18 CLOUDS HILL

Bovington, near Wareham BH20 7NQ ✆ 01929 405616 ⏱ Mar–Oct Wed, Thu, Sat & Sun; National Trust

This tiny, unassuming former forester's cottage is where T E Lawrence (Lawrence of Arabia; see below) lived between 1923 and 1935 as T E Shaw.

Lawrence first rented the cottage in 1923 while stationed at Bovington Camp with the Tank Corps, and bought it in 1925 from his cousins, the Framptons, the landlords of the Moreton Estate. It was here that Lawrence completed *Seven Pillars of Wisdom* and *The Mint*.

The interior has been recreated to appear as it was when Lawrence lived there. The house is deliberately spartan – Lawrence wrote: 'Nothing in Clouds Hill is to be a care upon the world. While I have it there shall be nothing exquisite or unique in it. Nothing to anchor me.'

The cottage served as Lawrence's retreat, where he read, wrote and listened to music, so it is fitting that his collection of music and books remains. An exhibition provides further insight into Lawrence's extraordinary life.

In 1935, Lawrence left the RAF and retired to Clouds Hill. A few months later, at the age of 46, he was involved in a fatal accident on his Brough Superior motorcycle close to the house.

LAWRENCE OF ARABIA

Thomas Edward Lawrence, also known as Lawrence of Arabia, was born in Wales on 16 August 1888. From the age of eight he lived in Oxford, where he later read modern history at Jesus College.

In 1911, Lawrence worked as an archaeologist in Syria, where he gained knowledge of the Arab culture and language. He made several further trips to the Middle East until the outbreak of World War I.

In 1914, he joined the British Army and was posted to Military Intelligence in Cairo. In June 1916, he was sent to investigate the Arab revolt in the Hejaz, where he formed a bond with the local Arab leader, Amir Feisal. Feisal's troops were committed but ill-disciplined and Lawrence planned to harness their passion by focusing on guerrilla tactics to disrupt the Turkish Army's activities. He led Bedouin tribesmen in guerrilla raids against the Turkish Army, which eventually contributed to British and Arab forces taking Damascus. Lawrence lived the life of a Bedouin, eating what they ate, wearing Arab dress and riding a camel, which earned him an almost mythical status among the Arabs who fought with him.

He returned to Britain in 1918 as Colonel Lawrence and lobbied unsuccessfully for Arab independence. Lawrence attempted to escape from the public eye by changing

19 BOVINGTON TANK MUSEUM

Bovington BH20 6JG ✐ 01929 462359 ✑ tankmuseum.org ◷ 10.00–17.00 daily

The tank museum adjoins Bovington Camp, home of the British Army's Armour Centre. It tells the story of the tank from its invention in 1915 to the present day. The first thing to strike you about this museum is its size – it is vast. Allow at least three hours to get around.

The collection of tanks is one of the biggest and most varied in the world. It was Rudyard Kipling who pressed for the creation of a museum after a visit to Bovington in 1923, when it held a small selection of tanks that had survived World War I. The museum was opened to the public in 1947.

Almost 300 vehicles from 26 countries are on display, each with a story to tell. They include 'Little Willie', the first tracked vehicle, developed in 1915 by the Landships Committee, which had been established by First Lord of the Admiralty, Winston Churchill, to tackle the problems of trench warfare.

The World War I trench experience is particularly moving, taking you from the recruiting office to the front line in the boots of a young soldier. The Battlegroup Afghanistan exhibition shines a light on the work of the Royal Armoured Corps in that area.

his identity and in 1922 enlisted in the RAF as Aircraftman Ross. His alias was soon discovered and he was forced out of the RAF. In 1923, as T E Shaw, he joined the Tank Corps and was stationed at Bovington Camp. He didn't much care for army life and purchased nearby Clouds Hill as a retreat. In 1925, Lawrence rejoined the RAF, and after a spell in Karachi, was posted to Plymouth, where he lobbied successfully for faster rescue boats. He spent the rest of his career developing and testing high-speed rescue boats, which formed the basis of the air-sea rescue service.

Lawrence retired to Clouds Hill in 1935, where, only a few months later, he was involved in a serious collision on his Brough Superior motorcycle. He died six days later in the military hospital at Bovington Camp. Lawrence's mother arranged for his body to be buried at Moreton Church, in the family plot belonging to his cousins, the Framptons of Moreton House.

You can walk the seven mile 'Lawrence of Arabia Trail' tracing his life in the area. It starts at the Bovington Tank Museum and takes in Clouds Hill and Moreton. A leaflet on the trail is available online (✑ visit-dorset.com). If you want to know more but don't fancy the walk, Wareham Town Museum (page 265) has a display devoted to Lawrence.

During the school summer holidays (Mon–Thu) live tank displays take place on the Kuwait Arena and are a big hit with children. It can get very busy at these times. In June, the museum hosts TANKFEST with three days of armoured-vehicle action in the arena.

If you don't have time to explore the tank museum, there is a viewing area on the road between Cloud's Hill (page 160) and the museum where you can watch tanks from Bovington Camp in training. The tank-crossing signs lining the roads around here are a novelty but necessary as you'd be hard-pressed to drive around Bovington and not encounter armoured vehicles.

20 MONKEY WORLD – APE RESCUE CENTRE

Near Wool BH20 6HH ℰ 01929 462537 ℰ monkeyworld.org

In a 65-acre park between Bere Regis and Wool live some unlikely Dorset residents: over 250 rescued and endangered apes and monkeys call Monkey World home. As well as making a perfect day out for children and adults, this is first and foremost a rescue centre and every one of the animals at Monkey World is there because it needs to be. The centre has over 50 chimpanzees living in four social groups, plus orangutans, woolly monkeys, squirrel monkeys, capuchins and more.

New Yorker Jim Cronin started the rescue centre in 1987, on the site of a derelict pig farm. There was a good degree of scepticism in the local community and beyond, but Jim had a vision and the energy to bring it to life. He met his wife Alison when she visited in 1992. She had a background in biological anthropology and animal behaviour, and had been working on the rescue of bears. Jim and Alison married in 1996 and, together with Jim's right-hand man, Jeremy Keeling, continued to rescue primates. Their work and the centre drew international acclaim and touched a wide audience through the television programmes *Monkey Business* and *Monkey Life*. Sadly, Jim died suddenly of cancer in 2007 at the age of 55, a year after he and Alison were awarded the MBE for services to animal welfare. Alison, Jeremy and their team continue the centre's valuable work and the realisation of Jim's vision.

"This programme has broken the cycle of abandonment, and orangutan graduates are now having their own young."

Monkey World was one of the world's first primate rescue centres. Initially its mission was to provide homes for chimpanzees rescued from a miserable life as props for beach photographers in Spain. By necessity, that mission expanded to rescuing primates from circuses, laboratories and the entertainment industry worldwide. Monkey World now works to assist governments around the world to stop the smuggling and mistreatment of primates. The centre also runs important captive-breeding programmes for endangered species, including slow loris and woolly monkeys. It is also home to Europe's official orangutan crèche, where youngsters who have been abandoned or orphaned in zoos or wildlife parks can grow up with their own kind. This programme has broken the cycle of abandonment, and orangutan graduates are now having their own young and successfully rearing the infants themselves.

In January 2008, Monkey World completed the largest primate rescue in history, when 88 capuchin monkeys were rescued from a medical research laboratory in Santiago, Chile. They had been living in solitary confinement in small cages, some for as long as 20 years.

Like the capuchins, many of the rescued primates who arrive at Monkey World have been kept in unnatural conditions, neglected or suffered cruel treatment. They arrive in poor condition, with physical and psychological problems. As you wander around Monkey World, it is a joy to see the rehabilitated animals living in large enclosures with plenty of stimulation and good company. Watching the antics of Monkey World's primates is bound to bring a smile to any visitor's face. The keepers are a devoted bunch, and hold regular, informative talks. Pre-recorded talks are available via QR codes around the park, and are a great accessibility tool, with subtitles for hearing-impaired visitors. Guided tours are available by appointment, or visitors can follow the self-guided tour on their own smartphone. You can even get married here! Monkey World does not receive government funding: it depends on donations and funds raised by opening the rescue centre to the public. By visiting you are helping to support the valuable work conducted here. If you are as moved by the centre's animals as I was, you may wish to consider primate adoption. In exchange for a small fee, you can 'adopt' a particular primate. Monkey World will send you a photograph of your chosen primate, an adoption certificate, three editions of the centre's newsletter and you will receive free entry for a year. Adoption also makes a great gift. Further details are available on Monkey World's website.

BULBARROW HILL, MILTON ABBAS & SURROUNDS

At 902ft, **Bulbarrow Hill** is the third-highest point in Dorset and affords far-reaching views over the Blackmore Vale and towards Somerset. It can be reached on foot from the much-photographed village of **Milton Abbas**, passing Milton Abbey School en route.

21 BULBARROW HILL & WOOLLAND HILL

At any time of year the views from Bulbarrow and Woolland Hill are breathtaking. Up here you can see five counties, namely Dorset, Somerset, Wiltshire, Hampshire and Devon. Bulbarrow is the third-highest point in Dorset and has spectacular views all around: the Blackmore Vale to the north and east and the Dorset Gap (page 165) to the southeast, recognisable as a V-shaped break in a chalk ridge. In summer the patchwork fields of the Blackmore Vale are every shade of green and yellow, while in winter the bare trees stand like skeletons silhouetted against a frosty backdrop. These are views that have been delighting visitors for hundreds of years, at least. Renowned Dorset historian, Reverend John Hutchins, described the view from Bulbarrow as 'surpassing imagination'. In his *Highways and Byways in Dorset*, Sir Frederick Treves (1853–1923) poetically portrayed it as a waving valley of green fields stretching for miles, 'with trees in lines, in knolls, in avenues, in dots; a red roof, the glitter of a trout stream, the trail of a white road, and at the end blue-grey hills so far away that they seem to be made of sea mist'.

Ever popular with paragliders and model-aircraft enthusiasts, **Bulbarrow Hill** has on its promontory Rawlsbury Camp, a five-acre Iron Age hillfort with discernible traces of its twin embankments. The hill was a site for one of the Armada beacons in 1588. Today, at the highest point of the camp is a rustic cross. Also on Bulbarrow are two tall masts that served as radio location posts during World War II. Today they are used by the emergency services.

The road runs straight across the top of Bulbarrow, so if you are short of time you can park quite close to Rawlsbury Camp and walk out towards the cross to admire the earthworks and the views.

Nearby **Woolland Hill** is one of the largest remaining fragments of chalk heath in Dorset at over ten acres. This rare habitat enables acid-loving plants, such as heather, to grow in an alkaline area. Profuse bird and butterfly life includes stonechats and meadow brown butterflies. The small village of Woolland sits at the base of the hill. Sculptor Elisabeth Frink lived here in the 1970s. Her life, art and links to Dorset are celebrated at the Dorset County Museum (page 129).

Close to Bulbarrow Hill is the less well-known Ibberton Hill. It also has excellent walks, far-reaching views and chalk grassland supporting plenty of wildlife. The pretty village of Ibberton sits at its base.

¶¶ FOOD & DRINK

The Ibberton Ibberton DT11 0EN ✐ 01258 817956 ⟋ theibberton.com. A cosy country pub offering traditional pub food and friendly service. With superlative walking all around, the pub makes a great spot for a post-walk lunch. Check the website for opening times as they are limited.

22 THE DORSET GAP, ANSTY & AROUND

Visible from miles around, the Dorset Gap is instantly recognisable as a dip in the chalk ridge known as the Dorset Downs. Being the only low point for miles around, it has always been the easiest and most logical place to cross the ridge. As a result, five ancient routes (now bridleways) converge here. The routes were part of an ancient network that was in frequent use from the Middle Ages (or even earlier) until the 19th century, when other forms of transport became available. For centuries travellers passed through here on foot, pack animals carried goods between settlements,

"Some of the paths around the Dorset Gap have been so eroded by feet and hooves that they have become sunken paths."

and livestock was moved along the routes. Some of the paths around the Dorset Gap have been so eroded by feet and hooves that they have become sunken paths, sheltered between steep sides dotted with ferns and trees laden with moss and lichen.

The Dorset Gap is only accessible on foot or horseback and has probably changed very little since it was a busy crossroads. Standing at the junction of the bridleways, where you cannot see or hear a road, takes us back to an ancient, less complicated era. It has plenty of natural beauty, of course, but it is the history of the place that gives it a really magical quality. You can't help but wonder about the people who passed through this crossroads before you – what were they doing, where were they going and what was their life like at the time? It is such a special place that at the junction of the bridleways there is a visitors' book stowed in a plastic container. People have been recording their passage through here in the books since 1972.

You can reach the gap by walking a 6.2-mile circular route from Lower Ansty through the Bingham's Melcombe estate. It is a beautiful estate, once the country seat of the Earls of Lucan, the most famous of whom was the seventh earl (AKA Lord Lucan) who vanished in 1974 shortly after the family nanny was murdered. This route is described in detail in various places online, including on ⊘ visit-dorset.com. If you wish to shorten the route, you can park at Lower Ansty and walk westwards to the Dorset Gap via Melcombe Park Farm, returning the same way. With both routes starting and ending in Lower Ansty, lunch at the Fox Inn (see below) is a lovely way to finish the walk.

¶¶ FOOD & DRINK

Brewery Farm Shop Ansty DT2 7PN ⊘ 01258 268320 ⊘ breweryfarmdorset.com. The farm's name is derived from the time when the Hall & Woodhouse Brewery was in the village, before moving to Blandford. The farm shop, directly opposite the Fox Inn, is well stocked. There's also luxury wooden self-catering lodges and a campsite.

Fox Inn Ansty DT2 7PN ⊘ 01258 880328 ⊘ foxinnansty.co.uk. A popular, child- and dog-friendly pub. Offers traditional dishes with a creative twist. Also open for breakfast but you need to book ahead. A great starting point for some fabulous walks, including the Dorset Gap (page 165).

23 MILTON ABBAS & MILTON ABBEY
🏠 The Bide

Milton Abbas is typically described with a combination of overused phrases, including 'chocolate-box' and 'picture-postcard'. With its two neat rows of pleasingly uniform white cob thatched cottages on either side of a wide road, it is hard to imagine a village more deserving of those descriptions. It did not evolve but was deliberately planned in the 18th century as an estate village for the nearby Abbey House. The cottages were designed to house two families each and there was a good deal of overcrowding and poverty. Most of them have since been converted to

1 A walk on Bulbarrow Hill provides far-reaching views. 2 The interior of Milton Abbey church. 3 Milton Abbas. ▶

ALEXANDRA RICHARDS

ALEXANDRA RICHARDS

ALEXANDRA RICHARDS

single dwellings. Some house names point to the identity of their original inhabitants: baker, blacksmith and brewer. On the main street there is also a pub, almshouses, a post office and a church. The almshouses, dated 1674, were moved from the original estate village of Middleton.

The Benedictine **Abbey** at Milton Abbas, which grew up around Milton Abbey Church (see opposite), was once one of the richest in the West Country, with estates of over 14,000 acres. King Athelstan, grandson of Alfred the Great, had the original church built in AD933. In AD964, King Edgar founded a Benedictine monastery here with monks from Glastonbury Abbey. The abbey thrived and expanded for six centuries until it was closed during the dissolution of the monasteries in 1539. The abbey and estate were sold in 1540 to Sir John Tregonwell, a lawyer who had helped to arrange Henry VIII's divorce from Catherine of Aragon.

In 1752, the Tregonwell family sold the estate to Joseph Damer (Lord Milton and later Earl of Dorchester). Damer demolished many of the monastic buildings and built a grand Gothic mansion, **Abbey House**, adjacent to the abbey church.

Damer drafted in famed landscape designer Capability Brown to design gardens worthy of his new home. Damer and Brown felt that the town of Middleton was spoiling the view from the big house, so Damer set about demolishing it in order to replace it with an ornamental lake. The only obstacle was what to do with the townspeople, but Damer found a straightforward solution. He commissioned the building of one of the first model villages in order to house the displaced Middletonians. After all, they would still be needed to run the house and the estate. Capability Brown assisted with the design of the new village and Milton Abbas was built in 1780, just one mile from the original town of Middleton. When the last residents of Middleton refused to leave the town, Damer opened the sluice gates of the new dam and flooded the area. Unfortunately for Damer, one of those residents was a lawyer, who sued and won.

"Some house names point to the identity of their original inhabitants: baker, blacksmith and brewer."

Abbey House is now part of **Milton Abbey School**, one of Dorset's many fine private schools. It is easy to see why Damer thought it the perfect spot for a house, nestled in a natural amphitheatre of wooded hills. The lawns in front of the house make an idyllic spot for playing cricket, which is precisely what you will see the schoolboys doing on a summer's day.

Every two years (in odd-numbered years) the villagers hold a **fair** with an 18th-century flavour to celebrate the rebuilding of the village. The main street is closed to traffic, and residents and stallholders dress in 18th-century costume. The day includes traditional music and dancing, local craft stalls and a farmers' market (⌾ miltonabbasstreetfair.co.uk).

Milton Abbey Church

Milton Abbey Church lies within the grounds of Milton Abbey school, but you can take the estate road in to see the church. Additionally, a public footpath leads to the church – from the bottom of Milton Abbas, walk down to the junction, turn right and the signposted path soon goes off on the left, next to Lake Lodge. It's a lovely walk following the outline of the large lake that lies where Middleton once was. When you arrive at the doorway of the church, the building seems far larger than you might

"It is spacious and light floods in through the tall stained-glass windows, making it feel like a miniature cathedral."

expect. It stands in isolation, commanding a view of the valley, and is built of attractive golden stone. It is said that King Athelstan chose this place for the original church because while camping on a hill overlooking this area he had a vision that he would defeat the Danes, and it came true. In gratitude, he founded the church. The Chapel of St Catherine (page 170) is said to sit on the spot where the king had his vision. In 1309, the abbey church was destroyed by fire following a lightning strike, and the current building was begun, although never finished.

To give it its full and rather convoluted title, the Abbey Church of St Mary, St Sampson and St Branwalader is now the chapel of Milton Abbas School but public services are held a few times a year. It comprises a chancel, tower and transepts; the nave was never built and the chapels have been demolished. As it stands today it is large but were it complete it would be enormous. What remains dates largely from the 14th and 15th centuries; the original buildings were destroyed by fire in 1309 after lightning struck the spire.

The interior is breathtaking. It is spacious and light floods in through the tall stained-glass windows, making it feel like a miniature cathedral. The stonework is incredible, especially the intricate 15th-century reredos.

Joseph Damer (page 168) married Caroline Sackville, daughter of the First Duke of Dorset. After her death in 1775 the Italian sculptor, Carlini, was commissioned to make a monument to her. In the north transept of the abbey, the stunning white marble carving depicts Caroline Damer lying on a sofa with her grieving husband beside her, mourning her loss.

A story that is often repeated in connection with the Abbey Church is that of John Tregonwell, son of the owner of the house, who in 1588 and aged five is reputed to have fallen 60ft from the top of the church tower. As was customary at the time, he was wearing several petticoats, which acted as a parachute and he landed on the ground unharmed. He went on to become the High Sheriff of Dorset. Whatever the accuracy of the story, it does conjure up an intriguing image.

The **chapel of St Catherine** stands on a hill within woodland, overlooking the Abbey Church. It is believed to have been built on the spot where King Athelstan had his vision about defeating the Danes. It was once reached by a set of grass steps leading from the garden of the house but the steps are no longer used. The chapel was part of King Athelstan's original construction, although what remains today dates largely from the 12th century and later restoration work. The easiest way to reach it is to park near Steepleton Bill Farm Shop (see below) and walk the 400yds from there.

 ## SPECIAL STAYS

The Bide Milton Meadow, Milton Rd, DT11 0DP ✆ 07905 181385 ⏚ thebide.com.
A contemporary metal and glass box may not sound like a Slow special stay, but this box is nestled in stunning, unspoilt countryside and is a fine example of eco-friendly, sustainable construction. On a working farm, tucked next to woodland, a beautiful 45-minute walk across fields leads to Milton Abbas. Architect Scott and furniture buyer Caroline built The Bide by hand during lockdown using sustainable materials, such as sheep's-wool insulation. It's aimed at couples but can accommodate a cot. There's a deck, wood-fired hot tub and firepit, and a projector screen for rainy-day entertainment. An organic super-king mattress ensures a good night's sleep.

 ## FOOD & DRINK

Steepleton Bill Farm Shop and Café DT11 0AT ✆ 07891 079615. Steve Gould is truly dedicated to this farm shop in the woodland above Milton Abbey School. He sells local groceries and grows much of the fruit and veg himself. He has also spent years developing what he considers to be the perfect pig by crossing different breeds; the pork and marmalade

THE DORSET RED POST

On the A31, between Bere Regis and Wimborne Minster, at Winterborne Zelston, is a distinctive, bright red signpost. It is one of three in Dorset painted that colour, the others being near Evershot and Sherborne.

Although the purpose of these signs is not conclusively known, this sign is believed to have been erected for the benefit of illiterate guards escorting prisoners as they were marched from Dorchester Gaol to Portsmouth for transportation to Australia.

It marked the turning to the substantial barn at Botany Bay Farm, where they would spend the night secured. The barn burnt down in the 1930s and only the base of the walls remains.

sausages are one of his bestsellers. The rows of sweets and crisps might look out of place, but they keep the Milton Abbey School pupils supplied with tuck. The café part is in a rustic outdoor setting among the trees, and in winter Sunday roasts are served in a teepee. There are lots of lovely walks from here.

The View Coffee Shop Milton Abbas Sports Club, Hoggens Down DT11 0BB ✐ 07774 533883. In 2023 a shower block on the edge of the village's sports pitches was converted into a casual coffee shop. Its covered outdoor area has far-reaching views and it's a popular stopping-off point for local dog walkers.

24 THE NORTH WINTERBORNES

Referred to as the North Winterbornes to differentiate them from those southeast of Dorchester, these villages sit at the base of a valley just south of the Blackmore Vale. As their names indicate, they lie near a stream that only runs in winter: Winterborne Houghton, Winterborne Stickland, Winterborne Clenston, Winterborne Whitechurch, Winterborne Kingston, Winterborne Tomson (also known as Anderson) and Winterborne Zelston. The River Winterborne joins the River Stour near Sturminster Marshall to continue its journey to the sea at Christchurch.

The villages are rewarding to potter around, with a mixture of thatched cottages and more modern houses. The busy A354 passes through Winterborne Whitechurch and it's larger than its relatives; the others are relatively unblemished.

Just south of Winterborne Clenston, surrounded by fields, is an adorable church with a dainty spire. Its location seems incongruous, as if it has been accidentally dropped there on its way to the village. It makes this unspoilt valley all the more beautiful, especially in the evenings when the setting sun highlights the stone building against its green backdrop. The church of St Nicholas was built in 1840 of banded flint and Portland stone. Its beauty hasn't gone unnoticed because it was used as the location for the final wedding scene in the 1996 adaptation of Jane Austen's *Emma*.

Winterborne Tomson has a strangely shaped (Norman apsidal) church, St Andrew's (DT11 9HA), which looks rather like an upturned boat. The small weatherboard belfry, resembling a dovecote, dates largely from the 12th century but has undergone various renovations along the way. The church is now in the care of the Churches Conservation Trust and is usually open to visit. Inside you will find total simplicity: whitewashed walls and 18th-century oak pews, screen and pulpit, installed by Archbishop of Canterbury, William Wake, who had grown up in the village of Shapwick. The church was saved from dereliction in the 1920s when it was carefully restored: prior to that it was being used as an outbuilding by the neighbouring farm.

⁉ FOOD & DRINK

East Farm Shop and Tea Rooms Winterborne Whitechurch DT11 9AW ✆ 07966 158831. A small shop on a working farm, selling produce from the farm and surrounding area, including beer from the Cerne Abbas Brewery. It also has a tea room serving homemade cakes.

10% OFF! FOR ONLINE BOOKINGS

Visit Monkey World
Where families Matter!

See over 260 rescued apes and monkeys, including four groups of chimpanzees, and Europe's official orang-utan crèche. **Visit the park to support the rescue work and have a great day out!**

Book Here

MONKEY WORLD
APE RESCUE CENTRE

Monkey World - Ape Rescue Centre
Longthorns, Wareham, Dorset BH20 6HH
01929 462537   www.monkeyworld.org

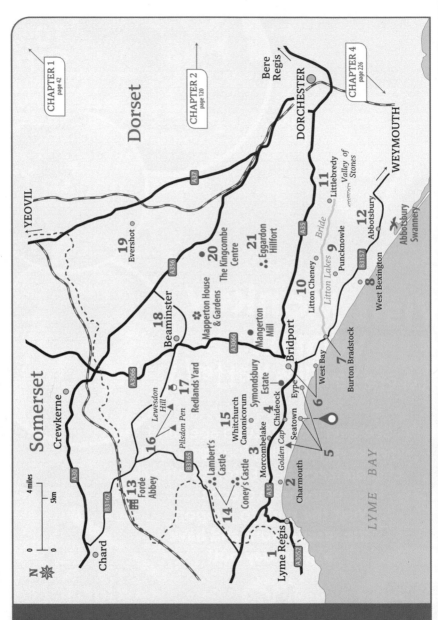

THE MARSHWOOD VALE & WEST DORSET

3

THE MARSHWOOD VALE
& WEST DORSET

West Dorset is endowed with one of the most enticing sections of the
Jurassic Coast World Heritage Site. The Jurassic Coast stretches 95
miles from east Devon along the Dorset coastline to Old Harry Rocks
in the Isle of Purbeck and records 190 million years of the earth's
history. At its heart, just inside the Dorset border, lies the supremely
characterful resort of **Lyme Regis**. Lyme is a popular holiday destination
for its quaint buildings, sheltered beach and fossil hunting. From here
you'll find a choice of excellent walks, notably a particularly beautiful
stretch of the South West Coast Path that
incorporates Golden Cap, the highest point
on the south coast.

The market town of **Bridport** has a
rich food culture and its myriad food and
drink producers are showcased each June
during the annual Bridport Food Festival.

*"As you travel inland
between Lyme Regis and
Bridport the roads turn
quickly to narrow lanes
winding through farmland."*

Bridport's harbour, **West Bay**, marks the start of **Chesil Beach**, a
shingle bank that stretches 18 miles east to Portland and protects a
natural lagoon known as **The Fleet**. The coastline between West
Bexington and Abbotsbury has a rugged, untouched appeal. A journey
inland through the beguiling **Bride Valley** is equally rewarding.

As you travel inland between Lyme Regis and Bridport the roads
turn quickly to narrow lanes winding through farmland – this is the
picturesque **Marshwood Vale**. For exhilarating views over the vale and
towards the coast, you can't beat a walk up **Pilsdon Pen** or **Lewesdon
Hill**, the two highest points in Dorset.

The Dorset Wildlife Trust's **Kingcombe Centre** has the best-preserved
lowland meadow in southern England. The centre offers courses,
such as beekeeping and foraging, or you can simply enjoy seeing the
countryside as it would have looked years ago.

GETTING THERE & AROUND

West Dorset is easily reached from the A35, which links up with the A303.

PUBLIC TRANSPORT

London Waterloo to Exeter services (South Western Trains) call at Axminster in Devon, from where you can catch a bus to Lyme Regis. Alternatively, you can get a **train** from London to Dorchester or Weymouth then hop on a bus.

The **Jurassic Coaster** provides regular bus services (⊘ firstbus.co.uk) along the coastline between Axminster and Poole (X53 Axminster–Weymouth, X54 Weymouth–Poole). The X53 stops at the key places, including Lyme Regis, Bridport, West Bay, Burton Bradstock and Abbotsbury. The X51 links Dorchester to West Dorset, including Bridport and Lyme Regis. The X52 open-top bus travels from Bridport to Monkey World via West Bay, Abbotsbury, Weymouth and Lulworth Cove.

Inland services are limited, although there are regular buses between Bridport and Beaminster.

BY BOAT

Travelling by boat along the Jurassic Coast gives you a real appreciation of the area's geology and its multi-layered cliffs. West Dorset's two harbours, Lyme Regis and West Bay, both have a slipway for public use; visiting craft are welcome but there is a long waiting list for the moorings let on an annual basis. Lyme Regis Sailing Club (⊘ lymeregissailingclub. com) offers temporary membership for visitors. Further information about using the harbours is available at ⊘ visit-dorset.com, while general information about exploring the Jurassic Coast by boat is available at ⊘ jurassiccoast.org.

You can take **fishing, sightseeing and diving trips** from both Lyme Regis and West Bay. Between Easter and October, Lyme Bay RIB charter (⊘ 07971 258515 ⊘ lymebayribcharter.co.uk) operates a **water taxi** between Lyme Regis and West Bay, and cruises from Lyme Regis. Lyme Rib Rides (The Cobb, Lyme Regis DT7 3JJ ⊘ 07790 400300 ⊘ lymeribrides.com) provides similar services. For a bit of variation you can take the Coastline X53 bus from Lyme Regis to West Bay, then the water taxi on your return trip.

CYCLING

West Dorset offers memorable cycling, if you don't mind a few hills. The roads along the coast are crowded in summer but at least there are no big towns or cities to negotiate.

National Cycle Network (NCN) **Route 2** covers 30 miles between Lyme Regis and Dorchester, taking you through the Marshwood Vale, around Bridport and across the Bride Valley, then close to the Hardy Monument and Maiden Castle.

The **West Dorset Pedal** is a series of five cycle routes uncovering West Dorset's finest food and arts. Available from ⏣ dorsetcouncil.gov.uk is a leaflet detailing the routes and describing eateries, farm shops and art galleries found along the way.

The Symondsbury Estate (page 199) near Bridport has a five-mile bike trail, and a cycling shop.

CYCLE HIRE

Bridport Cycles Manor Yard, Symondsbury DT6 6HG ✆ 01308 808595
⏣ symondsburyestate.co.uk. In Symondsbury village, close to the estate's bike trail.

WALKING

Several long-distance trails pass through West Dorset, including the South West Coast Path and the Wessex Ridgeway. Lesser known is the **Dorset Jubilee Trail**, which runs 90 miles from Forde Abbey on the Somerset border across Dorset to Bokerley Dyke on the Hampshire border. The route incorporates the Iron Age hillfort of **Pilsdon Pen** in the Marshwood Vale, and the Dorset Wildlife Trust's reserve at the **Kingcombe Centre** (page 223). The walk was created in 1995 by the Dorset Area Ramblers' Association (⏣ dorset-ramblers.org.uk) to celebrate its 60th anniversary. Details are available on the website.

A walk to the top of **Golden Cap** (page 193) near Seatown will take you to the highest point on England's south coast for breathtaking views, which on a clear day can even include Dartmoor; immediately inland it's interestingly hilly enough for some hugely satisfying round walks linking up with Golden Cap.

One of the most rewarding areas for walking is around **Abbotsbury**, where within a few miles you can walk up on to the hillsides immediately north of the village for glorious views, wander atop ancient Abbotsbury hillfort (page 209), explore the swannery and head out to Chesil Beach.

TOURIST INFORMATION

General information ⟋ visit-dorset.com
Guide to events in Lyme Regis ⟋ whatsoninlyme.co.uk
Bridport Town Hall, South St, DT6 3LF ⟋ 01308 424901 ⟋ bridportandwestbay.co.uk
Lyme Regis Church St, DT7 3BS ⟋ 01297 442138

From the centre of Abbotsbury it's an easy walk up to the hugely atmospheric St Catherine's Chapel (page 212), overlooking the coast.

HORSERIDING

The back of a horse is the ideal vantage point from which to appreciate the fabulous West Dorset scenery, it also allows someone else's legs to do the hard work up the hills. The Wessex Ridgeway is open to horseriders and there are memorable sections around Beaminster and the Marshwood Vale. You can download a trail guide from ⟋ dorsetcouncil.gov.uk.

RIDING STABLES

Bidlake Riding Stables Broadoak DT6 5PY ⟋ 07796 517888 ⟋ bidlakestables.co.uk. Lessons and hacking near Bridport.
Sandford Stables Hawkchurch, Axminster, Devon EX13 5UF ⟋ 01297 639202 ⟋ sandfordstables.co.uk. Family-run stables around three miles from Lyme Regis, offering lessons and hacking.

LYME REGIS TO BRIDPORT & WEST BAY

1 LYME REGIS & SURROUNDS

🏠 **Alexandra Hotel, River Cottage**

Somehow Lyme Regis doesn't look real: with its rows of houses of every shape and size huddled together along the seafront beneath open fields and woodland, it looks more like a painting in a children's book, or perhaps a model town. You might half expect to see an oversized adult bending down peering through the windows of the cottages.

Lyme Regis snuggles up against the Dorset/Devon border, on the River Lim. The Jurassic blue-grey cliffs on either side of the town are filled with layers of fossils, making the beaches of Lyme Regis excellent for fossil hunting. The narrow, twisting (and in parts steep) streets lead down through the town to the attractive seafront and the manmade harbour protected by the ancient breakwater known as the **Cobb**.

There's always plenty going on in Lyme, even outside the summer season. People flock here on New Year's Day for an annual fancy-dress swim in the sea, known as the Lyme Lunge. It is preceded by a rubber-duck race on the River Lim. Lyme likes its rubber ducks – a duck race also features in the annual regatta and carnival, which takes place in August.

The town centre

The town is best explored on foot as the centre is compact, packed with small shops, eateries and art galleries, and there is little room for cars on its narrow roads. At the northern end of the seafront you will find the **tourist-information centre**, which, as well as the usual brochures on accommodation, places to eat and activities can provide tide times – essential if you plan to go fossil hunting. Nearby is the **Marine Theatre** (Church St,

"You might half expect to see an oversized adult bending down peering through the windows of the cottages."

DT7 3QA ✆ 01297 442138 🖳 marinetheatre.com), an active, traditional seaside theatre with regular performances and events.

A little further up the hill is **St Michael's Church**, a charming building with two Norman pillars in the entrance. Inside the church, on the left, is a stained-glass window commemorating fossil hunter **Mary Anning** (page 186). Mary and her brother Joseph are buried in the churchyard almost opposite the window. Their grave is a site of pilgrimage for palaeontologists and geologists, and you will frequently see small fossils found on the beach left on the grave as a tribute.

As you head back down the hill towards the seafront, the eccentric tower of the **guildhall** almost encroaches on to the narrow road; tucked away behind it is the **Lyme Regis Museum** (Bridge St, DT7 3QA ✆ 01297 443370 🖳 lymeregismuseum.co.uk ⊘ closed Mon except during Dorset school holidays). The museum is within a quirky turreted brick building built in 1901 and, like the town, is a warren full of hidden corners to be explored. As you would expect, it has good exhibits on local geology and fossils, and Lyme's literary connections. The museum runs a regular programme of activities, such as guided walks, rock pooling and fossil hunting, which can be booked in advance. Down the hill from the museum the road crosses the river; the bridge is largely medieval underneath but you will need to be looking back from the seafront to see evidence of its age.

The eastern end of the seafront

A promenade leads northeastwards along the seafront from the town centre, past the Marine Theatre in the direction of Charmouth. The cliffs here have long been particularly unstable and in 2014 a sea defence wall was built along this stretch as part of a broader project to stabilise the coastline, prevent erosion and save the houses in the East Cliff area from being washed into the sea. The sea wall provides a wide, elevated and flat platform along which to walk and enjoy the views around the bay to Charmouth and beyond. A large ammonite found during the construction by local consultant geologist Paddy Howe is set into the end of the wall. The structure should also prevent the reoccurrence of an earlier problem: skeletons poking out of the cliff from the graveyard at St Michael's Church. The walk along the wall leads to Back Beach, known for its rock pooling and fossil hunting. On the way you'll pass a statue of pioneering palaeontologist Mary Anning (page 186).

Around the Cobb

Lyme Regis is perhaps at its most enchanting viewed from the **Cobb** at sunset, when the sun illuminates the hills above the harbour and you can see the geological layers within the cliffs, stacked like a deck of cards. Sheltering behind the breakwater is a colourful array of fishing and pleasure boats. The Cobb has been protecting the harbour and the town from erosion since the 13th century. It was originally made from huge boulders inside oak walls and detached from the land at high tide. It was joined to the land in 1756 and rebuilt in Portland stone in the 1820s, as the gently tilting serpentine wall that you see today.

"It was originally made from huge boulders inside oak walls and detached from the land at high tide."

It may look like a tiddler of a harbour but in its heyday Lyme Regis was a major port – the second largest in Dorset in the 14th century. Ships from Lyme Regis traded all over the world until the 20th century. Attached to the front of the Cobb's buildings, near the aquarium (see opposite), is a venerable toll board dated 1879 and entitled 'Rates of

Merchandise'. It lists the amount of tax levied on imports and exports to and from the harbour with incredible detail, such as 'for every barrel of salted beef, cod, herring ... 4d', 'for each horse, mule, cow or ox ... 6d'.

The Cobb has seen its fair share of drama, real and fictional. It was at the Cobb that James Scott, Duke of Monmouth, landed with his followers in 1685, intent on taking the throne from his uncle, James II. Monmouth, the son of King Charles II, chose Lyme Regis because the West Country was strongly Protestant. A month after they landed, Monmouth and his followers were defeated at the Battle of Sedgemoor in Somerset. Following the trial known as the 'Bloody Assizes', which was presided over by the notorious Judge Jeffreys (page 126), 292 Monmouth supporters were executed. A dozen of them were hanged, drawn and quartered on the spot where they had disembarked in Lyme Regis.

You won't be in Lyme Regis for long before finding mention of its connection with John Fowles's *The French Lieutenant's Woman*, the story of a romance between Sarah Woodruff and Charles Smithson, a fossil hunter. Fowles was living in a farmhouse in Lyme Regis when he wrote the book. The Cobb is the setting of the dramatic opening scene of the film, when Sarah, played by Meryl Streep, is standing alone looking out to sea. Lyme Regis's other literary claim to fame involves Jane Austen, who stayed in the town in 1803–04. The Cobb features in her novel *Persuasion*, which describes Louisa Musgrove falling from the steps.

On the Cobb, within a building dating from 1723, is the small, unpretentious **Lyme Regis Aquarium** (✆ 01297 444230 🖥 lymeregismarineaquarium.co.uk ☺ Feb–Nov 10.00–16.30 daily), run by the Gallop family since 1958. It contains a modest collection of species found in the local waters and children will enjoy

"The sand is barely visible beneath the sun-worshippers, the restaurants are buzzing and the shops are crowded with souvenir hunters."

helping to hand feed the mullet or hold a starfish. Alongside the sea creatures is a display of photographs showing films being shot in Lyme Regis, including *The French Lieutenant's Woman* and *Persuasion*. The aquarium was used as a make-up room during the filming of the latter.

Along the seafront (Marine Parade) is a string of pastel-coloured wooden **beach huts**, well equipped and well used. The slightest bit of sun has holidaymakers throwing open their doors. Like magicians pulling

rabbits from hats, they reach into their hut and produce with a flourish a never-ending supply of deckchairs, beach games, umbrellas and, of course, the all-important tea-making paraphernalia. If this prospect tempts you, beach huts are available for daily, weekly or seasonal hire from the council (𝒫 01297 445175 𝒹 lymeregistowncouncil.gov.uk).

As well as the pebble beach, there is a manmade sandy one, complete with sand imported from Normandy, known as **Front Beach**. Lyme Regis is busy in summer and the area around Front Beach is where it shows. The sand is barely visible beneath the sun-worshippers, the restaurants are buzzing and the shops are crowded with souvenir hunters.

The **Langmoor and Lister Gardens** provide a chance to step back from the crowds and admire the views of the Cobb and the coastline.

The Town Mill Complex

Mill Ln, DT7 3PU 𝒫 01297 444042 𝒹 townmill.org.uk ☉ mill tours: Easter–Oct 11.00–16.00 Tue–Sun; Nov–Easter 11.00–16.00 Sat & Sun, plus weekdays during school holidays

Around a cobbled courtyard at the Town Mill Complex, restored mill buildings house shops showcasing local art, crafts and produce, including the popular Lyme Regis Brewery. The self-guided tour of the working watermill (in exchange for a donation) is worthwhile, with its volunteer millers overflowing with knowledge about its history dating back to the 11th century. Powered by the River Lim, the mill continues to produce a small amount of stoneground flour, which is available in the mill shop. It also generates electricity, which powers the site.

Dinosaurland Fossil Museum

Coombe St, DT7 3PY 𝒫 01297 443541 𝒹 dinosaurland.co.uk ☉ variable, check website

This incredible little museum shows what's possible when someone is truly passionate about what they do. It houses the private collection of palaeontologist Steve Davies, who has travelled all over the world collecting fossils and is incredibly knowledgeable. He is usually found behind the reception desk and is very happy to chat about his collection.

◀ **1** Photogenic beach huts, Lyme Regis. **2** The Cobb, Lyme Regis. **3** Take a boat trip from Lyme Regis for a different perspective on the coastline. **4** The pretty harbour in Lyme Regis. **5** Charmouth's beach. **6** Attractive cottages are a key feature of Chideock. **7** Fossil exhibit at the Dinosaurland Fossil Museum.

The building is special in its own right. It's a Grade I-listed former 18th-century Congregational Church, where Mary Anning was baptised and worshipped for most of her life.

There are impressive displays of fossils from the local area, as well as from all around the world. A galleried area houses a collection of dinosaur models that children love. There is also an extensive natural-history section with skeletons (including an impressive and sizeable leatherback turtle), and some taxidermy of British animals.

If you choose to search for fossils without doing a fossil-hunting tour, a visit to the museum will help you understand their formation.

Fossil hunting around Lyme Regis

Made from soft clay layered with a few hard bands of limestone that formed on the bottom of the sea during the early Jurassic period, some 190 million years ago, the grey cliffs of the Lyme Regis area regularly offer up some valuable clues about life on earth in geological ages past. The Jurassic fossils within the cliffs are derived from sea creatures that lived when dinosaurs roamed the land. Landslides and waves cause fossils to fall from the cliffs onto the beaches below, making them prime fossil-hunting territory.

"The grey cliffs of the Lyme Regis area regularly offer up some valuable clues about life on earth in geological ages past."

Heading out with an expert (see opposite) will help you to get the most from your fossil-hunting expedition and give you a greater understanding of how they are formed.

I was lucky enough to go fossil hunting with enthusiastic expert Brandon Lennon. As the son of international geologist, Ian, who also lives locally and fossil hunts, Brandon has a fine fossil-hunting pedigree. He has a small fossil shop at 7 Drakes Way, DT7 3QP.

Brandon started by explaining the origins and significance of the Jurassic Coast; a large map erected by the local council on the seafront provided a handy prop and showed the relative ages of the coastline, with Lyme Regis and Charmouth being the oldest parts of the Dorset section at around 190 million years. As you head eastwards the cliffs are younger, and are a mere 65 million years old at Old Harry Rocks, the most easterly point of the Jurassic Coast.

Brandon led us along Monmouth Beach, west of the Cobb, where we clambered across rocks and trudged through seaweed, keeping an

TIPS FOR FOSSIL HUNTING

Brandon Lennon and the Lyme Regis Tourist Information Centre gave me the following tips for a productive, safe fossil-hunting trip.

- Fossil hunting is usually most productive after stormy weather or rough seas, as cliff falls are frequent and the shingle is rapidly turned over, exposing new fossils.
- Landslides are common, so stay away from the cliffs.
- Sturdy footwear is essential.
- Keep an eye on tide times – you don't want to get stranded. The best time to collect is 1½ hours either side of low tide.
- Only search the loose beach material; never dig into the cliffs.
- Some fossil hunters use hammers. If you hammer at a rock, wear eye protection and gloves, and watch out for flying splinters.
- If you find something of possible scientific interest (a local expert can tell you), you must register it with the Charmouth Heritage Coast Centre (page 190). While it will remain yours, scientists can ask to study it during the six months after registration.

Guided fossil tours are available from Lyme Regis Museum (01297 443370 lymeregismuseum.co.uk; your fossil-walk ticket gives you free entry to the museum), Brandon Lennon (07854 377519 lymeregisfossilsforsale.co.uk) and Charmouth Heritage Coast Centre (01297 560772 charmouth.org/chcc).

eye out for spiral-shaped ammonites and other fossilised creatures. We were heading towards one of the area's best-known fossilised phenomena, the **ammonite graveyard**. About halfway to the headland there was no mistaking that we had found what we were looking for: a ledge of limestone packed with the internal moulds of football-sized ammonites. Brandon explained that a catastrophic event or chemical reaction must have occurred to kill all these creatures at the same time. There were so many, and they were so clearly defined and uniform, that it looked as if an overly enthusiastic wallpaper designer had got carried away with an ammonite-shaped ink stamp. The ammonites of the graveyard are intriguing to admire but you should not attempt to extract them; to do so would be dangerous and would damage this amazing site.

Brandon then handed each of us a sieve and we began sieving sand in rockpools to search for tiny fossils. We hit the jackpot with several

MARY ANNING –
GROUNDBREAKING FOSSIL HUNTER

A female palaeontologist fossil hunter and dealer and palaeontologist who unearthed some of the most significant geological finds ever made, Mary Anning (1799–1847) was ahead of her time. Her discoveries were key to a fundamental shift in scientific thinking about the history of the earth, and challenged religious views.

Mary was born into a humble family of religious dissenters in Lyme Regis. She and her brother, Joseph, were the only survivors of ten children born to Richard Anning, a carpenter and cabinetmaker, and his wife Mary. At the age of 15 months, Mary survived a lightning strike, which killed three others; local legend had it the lightning turned her into a bright and observant child. Mary attended a Congregationalist Sunday School (now Dinosaurland Fossil Museum) where she learnt to read and write. Congregationalist doctrine emphasised the importance of education for the poor, unlike the Church of England at the time. However, the family's position as dissenters against the Church of England caused them further discrimination than poverty alone did.

Richard taught his children how to look for and clean fossils that had been hidden within the cliffs at Lyme Regis. They sold the 'curiosities' they collected to the wealthy tourists who flocked to the town in the summer.

Richard died in 1810, when Mary was 11 years old, and she supplemented the family's meagre income by continuing the fossil trade. It was a dangerous living – landslides, treacherous tides and ferocious seas. In 1833, Mary narrowly avoided being killed by a landslide that buried her constant companion, a terrier named Tray. It has been suggested that Mary was the inspiration for the well-known tongue-twister 'she sells seashells on the seashore', written by Terry Sullivan in 1908.

Mary taught herself geology and anatomy and she, and her family, made some important discoveries. In 1811, Joseph found a skull protruding from a cliff. Over a period of months Mary painstakingly uncovered an almost complete 17ft long skeleton of a 'crocodile'. The specimen was bought by the local lord of the manor, who sold it to William Bullock for his Museum of Natural Curiosities in London. The find brought Mary to the attention of scientific

dainty, little ammonites. Our next find was less appealing – an ancient, fossilised gastropod. It was just as well that we had an expert with us because to the untrained eye it certainly didn't look like anything special, just a rather old and solid snail, and I would have discarded it if it hadn't been for Brandon's enthusiastic reaction.

Brandon skilfully tapped a rock with a hammer to reveal an ammonite and suggested we take it home as a reminder of our day, which we did.

circles. The specimen was later named *Ichthyosaurus*, the 'fish-lizard'.

In 1828, Mary made another important discovery – the first complete skeleton of a flying reptile recorded in England. It was named *Dimorphodon* after its two kinds of teeth and appears to have been a fish eater.

The Anning family had established themselves as fossil hunters but remained very poor. In 1820 one of their patrons, Lieutenant-Colonel Thomas James Birch, organised an auction of specimens he had purchased from them. The sale raised £400, which he donated to the Annings, and the publicity cemented Mary's fame.

Mary's gender and social class meant she could not fully participate in the scientific community of the day. As a woman, she was not eligible to join the Geological Society of London and rarely received due credit for her work. However, she was visited by, and corresponded with, eminent scientists of the time and her opinions were valued. In 1838, Mary was given an annuity raised by members of the British Association for the Advancement of Science and the Geological Society of London.

From humble beginnings she had gained the respect of the scientific community and captured the imagination of the public. Mary may not have been eligible to join during her lifetime but her death was recorded by the Geological Society. In 2010, the Royal Society included Anning in a list of the ten British women who have most influenced the history of science.

Mary died from breast cancer aged 47 and is buried in the churchyard of St Michael's in Lyme Regis, with her brother. A stained-glass window within the church, commissioned by the Geological Society of London and installed in 1850, commemorates her incredible life. On the wall of the Lyme Regis Museum is a blue plaque dedicated to her. The museum is believed to be on the site of Anning's home and her first fossil shop. In 2022, a bronze statue of Anning and her dog was installed not far from the Marine Theatre, at the junction of Long Entry and Gun Cliff Walk, overlooking the beach where she hunted for fossils.

Anning's life inspired the 2020 film *Ammonite*, which was shot in and around Lyme Regis.

He explained to me there is no reason why people should not take small fossils home from the beach. In fact, by taking them home we are saving them from being washed out to sea. The large ones, however, should be left where they are.

Since our outing with Brandon, we and our young dinosaur-loving son, Archie, have enjoyed plenty of fossil-hunting walks along the Jurassic Coast, and we now have quite a collection of tiny treasures.

Cruises, fishing trips & sailing lessons

At the shore end of the Cobb you can arrange fishing trips, Jurassic Coast cruises or a water taxi to West Bay (page 201). Lyme Bay Boat Trips (✆ 01297 642044 ⌂ lymebayboattrips.com) and Jurassic Boat Trips (✆ 01297 642643 ⌂ jurassicboattrips.com ✉ info@jurassicboattrips. com) both offer sightseeing cruises and fishing trips.

Harry May's (✆ 07974 753287 ⌂ mackerelfishinglymeregis.com) mackerel-fishing and deep-sea fishing trips come highly recommended by locals. If you fancy getting in some sea time, a mackerel-fishing

RIVER COTTAGE & HUGH FEARNLEY-WHITTINGSTALL

For details of the busy schedule of events, see ⌂ rivercottage.net

In 1998, TV chef Hugh Fearnley-Whittingstall moved from London to the original River Cottage between Beaminster and Bridport to grow and rear his own food. The TV series following his life on his smallholding was a huge hit worldwide. In 2006, River Cottage moved to Park Farm, just a smidgeon over the border in neighbouring Devon, but I believe Dorset still has a fair claim to Hugh. To this day, the River Cottage principles remain unchanged and are even more relevant than they were when it all started: less dependence on the outside world, food integrity, sustainability, caring for the land, animal welfare, and the consumption of local, seasonal produce.

Park Farm is the venue for events and courses inspired by the philosophy of River Cottage, including foraging, curing, gardening, bread-making and butchery. You can also enjoy an entertaining dinner at Park Farm, where you get to mingle with fellow guests over canapés, then potter around and draw inspiration from the flourishing fruit and vegetable garden and elaborate chicken enclosure, before sitting down to eat. Dinner is at two long tables and each course is accompanied by a talk from the chef, who explains the detail behind the dish. When I went I was struck by the convivial and collegiate atmosphere, although a little intimidated by the serious foodies who took notes throughout the evening. I began to worry that there was going to be an exam at the end of the meal – thankfully not.

Courses and special events need to be booked in advance but you can drop into **The Kitchen and Store at Park Farm** (Park Farm, Trinity Hill Rd, Axminster, Devon EX13 8TB ✆ 01297 630313 ⌂ rivercottage. net ◷ 09.00–17.00 daily, closed Tue & Wed in winter) for delicious food with a view over the glorious countryside. You can also stock up on River Cottage ciders, beers and kombucha here. Accommodation is available at Park Farm on a bed and breakfast basis (see opposite).

trip is a pleasant way to spend an hour pottering around the bay. On a deep-sea fishing trip your catch is likely to be cod, conger and skate.

Sailing lessons are available from Lyme Regis Sea School (lrss.org. uk), and the Lyme Regis Sailing Club (lymeregissailingclub.co.uk) offers temporary membership for visitors.

SPECIAL STAYS

Alexandra Hotel Pound St, DT7 3HZ ℘ 01297 442010 hotelalexandra.co.uk. At the top of Lyme's main street on a clifftop overlooking the bay, this family-run hotel is a fantastic base from which to explore. The 23 rooms are decorated in similar style but vary in size. Opt for one with a sea view if you can – around half the rooms have one. The pick of the rooms is the Countess Room which is spacious and has bay windows with sea views. The self-catering apartments are on the road and have no views, but they're economical for groups. When Lyme is busy it's a joy to be able to retreat to the hotel's garden for a sundowner with views along the coast. There's a good restaurant specialising in locally sourced produce, and the service is professional and friendly.

River Cottage Park Farm, Trinity Hill Rd, Musbury, Axminster EX13 8TB ℘ 01297 630300 rivercottage.net. The white 17th-century farmhouse made famous by the River Cottage TV series now offers homely bed and breakfast accommodation. There is an elegant en-suite master bedroom, plus a twin and a double with a shared bathroom. The inglenook fireplace will be familiar to many as the place where Hugh cooked up many a tempting dish on the TV series, and the sitting room has views over the impressive walled garden, replete with fruit and veg. Adjoining the farmhouse is the two-bedroom Gardener's Cottage. There is also a rustic off-grid cabin for couples. An organic breakfast is served in the Kitchen and Store at the top of the driveway. The location is peaceful with beautiful countryside views, and it's a joy to stay somewhere where sustainability is such an important part of what they do.

FOOD & DRINK

Lyme Regis is packed with cafés and restaurants to suit all budgets and tastes. They are concentrated along the main street and the seafront. Just outside the town is the excellent **Kitchen and Store** at River Cottage headquarters (see opposite).

Amid Giants and Idols 59 Silver St, DT7 3HR ℘ 01297 443791. Towards the top of town. Serves speciality coffee, fine teas, fresh-fruit smoothies, light meals and homemade cakes.
Bell Cliff 6 Broad St, DT7 3QD ℘ 01297 442459. Centrally located restaurant that has stood the test of time. Serves unfussy meals and a good cream tea.

Good Food Store 21 Broad St, DT7 3QE ✆ 01297 442076. A deli, bakery and organic-produce shop, which also has a café. Wholesome, local food and plenty of gluten-free options.

Hix Oyster & Fish House Cobb Rd, DT7 3JP ✆ 01297 446910 ⟨⟩ hixoysterandfishhouse. co.uk. Lyme's best-known and most exclusive restaurant, owned by celebrity chef Mark Hix. Great if you want to treat yourself or someone else, especially if you enjoy fish. At the end of the gardens above the seafront, it has sweeping views over the bay and the service is excellent. There's no parking but you can drop people off and park nearby. Reservation recommended.

Millside Restaurant 1 Mill Ln, DT7 3PU ✆ 01297 445999. In a peaceful location near the old mill, serving a creative menu, prepared to a consistently high standard.

Strawberry Tree Mill Ln, DT7 3PU ✆ 01297 445757. Something a bit different. Giselle Benrimoj and Ed Pemberton created this cosy but smart tapas bar, which is especially popular on a Friday evening.

Swim Marine Pde, DT7 3JH ✆ 01297 442668. Opposite the main beach and with cracking views towards the Cobb, this is a trendy option with a menu boasting plenty of smashed avocado, brioche and sourdough.

Town Mill Bakery 2 Riverside Studios, Coombe St, DT7 3PY ✆ 01297 444754. Bread, pastries, muesli and more, all made on site. Long, wooden tables reminiscent of school mealtimes and the open bakery provide a casual atmosphere. The adjoining deli sells local produce.

2 CHARMOUTH

Smaller than Lyme Regis, Charmouth is billed as the quieter of the two, although the beach can feel pretty crowded in the summer. The bulk of Charmouth is about half a mile back from the sea, spread along either side of the main street, which runs between the coast and the A35. You can drive down to the seafront, where there is ample paid parking close to the beach.

The seafront is decidedly low-key – there is no fancy esplanade lined with shops and hotels; instead there is a pebble beach, fossil-rich cliffs, a fossil shop, a café and the **Charmouth Heritage Coast Centre** (Lower Sea Lane, DT6 6LL ✆ 01297 560772 ⟨⟩ charmouth.org/chcc; free admission). If you plan on collecting fossils or simply want to know more about the Jurassic Coast, the centre is worth a visit. There is a video microscope for you to examine your fossil finds. Displays on the coastal wildlife of the area add another dimension. The centre hosts events, including fossil hunting, ammonite-slice polishing and rock pooling.

At the western end of the village is a turning marked Stonebarrow Lane, which leads to **Stonebarrow Hill** (DT6 6RA). This National Trust land along the coast is a relatively uncrowded and peaceful vantage point from which to take in the sea views, including Golden Cap. Bridleways and the South West Coast Path pass through here and the small National Trust shop does a good trade selling teas, coffees and ice creams to walkers.

¶| FOOD & DRINK

Options are limited at the beach but there are a couple of casual kiosks. A picnic is a good option, or nearby Lyme Regis is crammed with places to eat.

Bank House Café DT6 6PU ℘ 01297 561600. Informal family-run café on the main street, known for its Sunday roasts.
Fernhill Hotel DT6 6BX ℘ 01297 560492 ⊘ fernhill-hotel.co.uk. A smart restaurant, good service and tasty locally sourced food combine to make a meal here a very pleasant experience. The hotel operates a zero-waste kitchen, which means you need to book in advance. The menu is emailed to you on the day and you need to order by 16.00. Owner Jo tells me this system has almost eliminated the hotel's food waste.
Royal Oak The Street DT6 6PE ℘ 01297 560277. A Palmers Brewery pub, offering seaside pub classics like scampi and chips and Palmers beer-battered fish and chips, plus a dedicated gluten-free menu.

3 MORCOMBELAKE

The A35 coastal road passes through the hamlet of Morcombelake; in fact it dominates it. People tend to pass through rather than stop in Morcombelake, but the excellent Felicity's Farm Shop (see below) is worth pulling into. Morcombelake has long been associated with a Dorset icon, for it was here that **Moores Biscuits** (⊘ moores-biscuits. co.uk) opened its bakery in 1880. The company is still going but the Morcombelake bakery closed in 2020 and all manufacturing is now done in their Bridport factory (page 196).

¶| FOOD & DRINK

Felicity's Farm Shop Morcombelake DT6 6DJ ℘ 01297 480930 ⊘ felicitysfarmshop.co.uk. This large, family-run farm shop is conveniently located on the A35 and has plenty of parking (which is important around here). The shop is well stocked with local produce, deli items and gifts. Felicity's son, Tom, raises pigs nearby and his pork, bacon and sausages are deservedly popular. Portland crab is often for sale, and there are tempting locally smoked meats and fish. Stock up here for a picnic or self-catering stay, and if you can't wait to try the food there's a café on site with outdoor picnic tables.

4 CHIDEOCK

As you head eastwards from Morcombelake, the A35 passes through Chideock, a village of attractive golden stone and whitewashed cottages, many of them thatched, and with a couple of decent pubs.

In the centre of the village is the stocky **St Giles Church**. The oldest parts of the church date from the 13th century but what you see today is largely unchanged since the restoration of 1884–85. Its most intriguing feature is not usually visible but it makes an amusing anecdote: the belfry contains a peal of six bells, the oldest of which was cast in 1603 and is inscribed with the unfortunate spelling error 'Love dog'. It's a fine and worthy notion but not what they were going for, which was, of course, 'Love God'.

Behind St Giles Church is a Roman Catholic **memorial chapel**, built in 1852 by Charles Weld of Chideock Manor in memory of his parents. The walls and ceilings are beautifully painted; when it is open (times vary) it is worth a peek inside, or you can make an appointment (⬙ chideockmartyrschurch.org.uk).

"A village of attractive golden stone and whitewashed cottages, many of them thatched, and with a couple of decent pubs."

Catholicism has a strong history in the village, which is displayed in the **museum** (◷ 10.00–16.00 daily; free admission) attached to the **church of Our Lady Queen of Martyrs and St Ignatius** (North Rd, DT6 6LF ⬙ chideockmartyrschurch. org.uk). When Catholicism was banned in England, local Catholics worshipped in secret in a barn that stood on the site of the present-day church. Seven Chideock men were put to death for their faith between 1587 and 1642; the church is a memorial to them and others who shared their fate.

The church is next to Chideock Manor and was designed in Italian Romanesque style by Charles Weld in 1872, who was living in the manor house at the time. He painted much of the decoration himself. Nearby Ruins Lane leads to the site of Chideock Castle, which was destroyed in 1645 and where a cross now stands dedicated to the Chideock Martyrs.

You can visit the gardens of **Chideock Manor** (DT6 6LF ✆ 07885 551795 ⌂ chideockmanorgarden.co.uk ⊙ by appointment only). The gardens are largely formal with parkland, a lake and lovely views.

5 SEATOWN, EYPE & GOLDEN CAP

🏠 **Anchor Inn**

A turning in the centre of Chideock takes you to **Seatown**, a modest seaside hamlet nestled between two of the highest cliffs on the Dorset coast, Golden Cap and Thorncombe Beacon. Seatown consists of a few houses, a pub and a sizeable campsite, all huddled close to a golden shingle beach. It's delightfully unspoilt, with excellent walks along undeveloped coastline in both directions.

The land along the coast around Seatown is owned by the National Trust. The hillside to the east of Seatown is steep and usually dotted with cows of assorted colours and sizes, who casually swagger to the cliff edge and gaze out to sea. From Seatown you can walk eastwards along a rugged, hilly stretch of the South West Coast Path to Eype Mouth, where the small River Eype reaches the sea. It is an up-and-down roller coaster of two miles, which includes Thorncombe Beacon, one of the highest points on the Dorset coast at 515ft. In 1588, a chain of beacons was lit along the south coast to warn of the approaching Spanish Armada, which had been sighted off Plymouth, and Thorncombe was one of these. A short detour inland between Thorncombe Beacon and Eype will take you to Downhouse Farm Garden Café, an excellent stop for refreshments (page 195).

You can also reach **Eype** beach from the village, which is divided into Upper and Lower Eype. A narrow lane leads through the village to a small clifftop car park, from where a steep path takes you down to the shingle beach. The beach is flanked by tall, fossil-rich cliffs topped with farmland and a sizeable campsite. It is a relatively rugged and undeveloped area and tricky to reach by car (plus once you get there the car park is pretty tiny), so it tends to be quieter than other beaches in the area. From Eype it is a glorious walk eastwards along the clifftops to West Bay (page 201).

On the west side of Seatown is **Golden Cap**, which lives up to its name: the top of the cliff has a warm golden glow, which can be seen for miles around, and at 626ft it is the highest point on the south coast of Britain. It can be reached on foot from Seatown (page 194) or from Langdon Hill Wood.

A walk to Golden Cap

✳ OS Explorer map 116 or Landranger 193; start: Seatown ♀ SY420917; 4 miles; difficult (steep climb along the cliff top). Refreshment at the Anchor Inn in Seatown (see below). For an easier walk, avoiding the steep climb, start the walk at Langdon Hill car park ♀ SY412930.

This walk takes you to the highest point on England's south coast and entails an appropriately steep section and far-reaching views. From the car park near the Anchor Inn in Seatown, walk up the hill into the village, climb the stile on the left and join the footpath, signed 'Coast Path Diversion'. Walk across the field, over a stile and through a small woodland. Cross another stile and bear right up the hill, signposted 'Golden Cap'.

Where the track forks, keep left. You will walk through open fields with Golden Cap directly ahead of you. It gets pretty steep in parts but the views give a great excuse for a pause. At the summit you will see a stone memorial to the Earl of Antrim KBE, chair of the National Trust 1966–77. The views of the coastline are spectacular, towards Lyme Regis in the west and West Bay in the east. Once you have had your fill of the view, follow the path down the steep hill to a gate and bear right over the fields towards the ruins of the 13th-century St Gabriel's Chapel. Keeping the chapel on your right, you will pass through two gates. Continue in the direction of Morcombelake. You will pass through Filcombe Farm and around the base of Langdon Hill Wood, which in spring is awash with bluebells and wild garlic. Head down the hill back to Seatown, where the Anchor Inn awaits.

To reach the National Trust car park at Langdon Hill, and the alternative starting point, drive westwards through Chideock on the A35 and turn left at the top of the hill half a mile past the village centre, just before the dual carriageway ends. The turning you are looking for is a tiny, unmarked lane (known as Langdon Lane) just after the turning signposted 'Seatown'. A mostly level walk takes you around Langdon Hill Wood.

 SPECIAL STAYS

Anchor Inn Seatown DT6 6JU ✆ 01297 489215 ⊘ theanchorinnseatown.co.uk. Two hundred years ago, this was a favourite haunt of local smugglers and ruffians, but today it's all far more civilised at this excellent gastropub with three luxurious sea-view rooms. The pub couldn't be closer to the beach and to superb walks along the South West Coast Path. The location is really special, especially when you get up early to enjoy the beach at its most peaceful. The rooms are spacious with roll-top baths and large, comfy beds. Pastel hues and nautical paraphernalia create a relaxed vibe. The highlight of any stay here is waking up to the sound of the sea and stunning views along the coast. The beer garden right above the beach is the perfect spot to enjoy the good-quality traditional pub food, and the menu features plenty of dishes showcasing the area's wonderful local fish. The outdoor tables have uninterrupted views of the sea, so it almost feels wrong to order anything other than fish and chips!

¶¶ FOOD & DRINK

Garden Café Downhouse Farm, Downhouse Lane, Higher Eype DT6 6AH ✐ 01308 421232 ⟡ downhousefarm.org. This outdoor café at the farm serves delicious homemade food. Dishes are prepared using the farm's own organic meats, vegetables and herbs, and there are plenty of vegetarian options. The bubble and squeak is delicious. It's down a very narrow lane if you are driving there, but is easily reached on foot from the South West Coast Path. Dog friendly. It is a magical spot and accommodation is available in a shepherd's hut or cabin.

6 BRIDPORT & WEST BAY
Bridport

Bridport is vibrant, quirky and full of personality. The locals are rightly proud of Bridport's rope-making history, its market, its food culture and its arts scene. Yet Bridport and the surrounding area have to work hard to compete with the likes of Lulworth Cove, Lyme Regis and the coastal towns over the border in Devon. To do that Bridport has had to be a little creative, which is probably one reason why it has a staggering number of events for such a small town. There is the food festival in June, the hat festival in September and the literary festival in November, to name but a few.

The **Bridport Food Festival** (⟡ bridportfoodfestival.co.uk), launched in 2004 by celebrity chef and local food advocate Hugh Fearnley-Whittingstall (page 188), is a fitting way to celebrate the area's local produce. The farms of the fertile Marshwood Vale and the seas off West Bay do their part to contribute, offering up plenty of delicious and natural food.

Bridport is still very much a market town, with street markets held on Wednesdays and Saturdays. The **Saturday market** is crammed with bric-a-brac stalls and attracts bargain hunters from miles around.

Equally popular is the **farmers' market**, held on the second Saturday of each month on Barrack Street.

Perhaps because it is surrounded by inspiring land and seascapes, Bridport has developed a flourishing artistic and literary community. There is a healthy population of art galleries where you can pick up a souvenir of your visit. The **Bridport Arts Centre** (✆ 01308 424204 ⏸ bridport-arts.com) runs free exhibitions and is the home of the literary festival and the coveted Bridport Prize International Creative Writing Competition (⏸ bridportprize.org.uk). The Art Deco **Electric Palace** (✆ 01308 428354 ⏸ electricpalace.org.uk) is one of the best entertainment venues in the region, playing host to theatre, live music, cinema and art exhibitions.

Bridport has had a **rope-making industry** since the 13th century. The town used to produce hangman's ropes, hence the mildly euphemistic saying 'to be stabbed with a Bridport dagger', meaning to be hanged. The long gardens around Bridport were once walks used for making lengths of rope. A **net-making industry** survives in the town, with fishing and sporting nets being made, including the nets for the Wimbledon Tennis Championships. Information about the rope- and net-making industries, and other local history, is on display at **Bridport Museum** (The Coach House, 25 South St, DT6 3NR ✆ 01308 458703 ⏸ bridportmuseum.co.uk ⏲ Apr–Oct 10.00–17.00 Tue–Fri, 10.00–16.00 Sat).

> "Perhaps because it is surrounded by inspiring land and seascapes, Bridport has developed a flourishing artistic and literary community."

Beer has been produced continuously since 1794 at **Palmers Brewery** (West Bay Rd, DT6 4JA ✆ 01308 427500 ⏸ palmersbrewery.com), which claims to be the only thatched brewery in the UK. **Brewery tours** can be booked on the website.

Moores Bakery (202 St Andrews Rd, DT6 3BW ✆ 01308 428526 ⏸ moores-biscuits.co.uk ⏲ Mon-Fri 09.00-15.00) makes its famous biscuits in Bridport and there is a small shop at the bakery where you can buy them. The business began in Morcombelake back in the 1880s and the company is still owned and run by the family. The most

1 The iconic cliffs of West Bay. 2 Alexandra's son Archie walking the atmospheric sunken lanes of the Symondsbury Estate. 3 Taking in the views from Golden Cap. ▶

famous of the biscuit selection is the Dorset Knob, a savoury biscuit baked three times. Originally, they were made from leftover bread dough with added butter and sugar, hand-rolled and left to dry in the dying heat of the oven, which produced a rusk-like biscuit. It even has its own festival, centred around a Dorset Knob-throwing competition (⌀ dorsetknobthrowing.co.uk).

If you are driving in the vicinity of Bridport, keep an eye out for **Colmer's Hill**, a remarkable cone-shaped hill topped with a few windswept pines. It has been used for many years as a local landmark, including by smugglers when they were taking their contraband inland from the shore. You can walk to the top of the hill from the village of **Symondsbury** (opposite).

¶¶ FOOD & DRINK

Bull Hotel 34 East St, DT6 3LF ✆ 01308 422878 ⌀ thebullhotel.co.uk. Centrally located Fuller's Brewery pub. Serves traditional pub dishes with a creative twist and contemporary cuisine.
Dorshi 6 Chancery Ln, DT6 3PX ✆ 01308 423221. This modern east Asian restaurant wouldn't look out of place in London. Specialises in sushi made with local and foraged ingredients.
Green Yard Café 4–6 Barrack St, DT6 3LY ✆ 01308 459466. Casual café with a quiet courtyard area. Simple food prepared with care. Plenty of vegetarian and gluten-free options.
Olive Tree 59 East St, DT6 3LB ✆ 01308 422882 ⌀ olivetreerestaurant.net. Mediterranean-inspired restaurant specialising in seafood. Also cookery courses. Reservations recommended.
Soulshine 76 South St, DT6 3NN ✆ 01308 422821 ⌀ wearesoulshine.co.uk. An unassuming, rustic atmosphere belies the sophisticated dishes that the kitchen turns out. Owners Joel and Andy used to work at River Cottage together and their experience there has served them well. Just like River Cottage, they use local, seasonal ingredients and support artisan producers. The dishes are beautifully presented and exciting, often pairing flavours you wouldn't imagine combining, and the small plates menu means you can try a variety. They also roast their own coffee, which now has quite a following. Check their website for details of supper clubs and events.
Symondsbury Kitchen See opposite.
Washingpool Farm Shop Dottery Rd, North Allington DT6 5HP ✆ 01308 459549 ⌀ washingpool.co.uk. A well-stocked farm shop and licensed restaurant on a working farm. As well as vegetables and meat from the farm, the shop stocks goodies from within a 50-mile radius. A tranquil spot for lunch close to town. There's a farm trail and a children's play area.

Symondsbury Estate

🏠 **Symondsbury Estate**

Bridport DT6 6HG   🖉 01308 424116   ⌀ symondsburyestate.co.uk

The Colfox family has lived in Symondsbury for generations and we can all be grateful that the current custodians of the estate, Sir Philip and Lady Julia Colfox, have chosen to share their beautiful corner of England with the rest of us. In recent years they have opened a superb visitor centre (☺ 10.00-16.00 daily) with information on the estate, walking- and cycling-trail maps, a shop selling books and gifts, and staff on hand to answer questions about the area. There is also a clothing boutique, home and garden shop, and plants for sale.

A deli sells local produce, including the estate's own chutneys, jams and apple juice, which is excellent.

The on-site café showcases produce from the estate's vegetable garden as well as other local, seasonal ingredients, and the sheltered

"The sunken lanes are bewitching, with the high sandstone walls and overhanging trees creating a microclimate."

terrace is perfect on a sunny day. It serves breakfast, brunch, lunch and afternoon tea, and the traditional Sunday lunch is deservedly popular.

Regular workshops are held here, such as willow-weaving and foraging (see website). The Colfox family promotes regenerative farming practices and guided farm tours are available if you'd like to learn more.

There are excellent walks around the estate, which take in the extraordinary holloways (sunken lanes) and Colmer's Hill. The sunken lanes are bewitching, with the high sandstone walls and overhanging trees creating a microclimate and a unique ecosystem. Rare ferns, mosses, insects and fungi flourish in the shade and humidity, and symbols and graffiti are etched into the walls. Some, like the ornate Celtic roses, add to the magical atmosphere, others, like Homer Simpson, do not. It is believed the holloways may have been created when stone from a quarry on a nearby hill was dragged down to the village. They were then used by drovers and locals travelling between Symondsbury and North Chideock. The passage of thousands of feet and hooves, combined with rainwater flowing down the path, wore away the soft sandstone creating deep tunnels.

It is worth walking up to Colmer's Hill for the spectacular views, and simply to satisfy your curiosity about what this strange little hill looks like up close. Caledonian Pines were planted on the hill during World

War I and Monterey Pines were planted in 2006, creating the distinctive outline we see today.

Parking at the estate's visitor centre is free and the friendly farm animals are a bonus. As well as great walks, there is a purpose-built six-mile bike track and bike hire is available in the village (page 177). Symondsbury Estate is a very special place and if you want to extend your stay it offers some charming self-catering properties.

🧳 SPECIAL STAYS

Symondsbury Estate Bridport DT6 6HG ✐ 01308 424116 ⊘ symondsburyestate.co.uk. The Symondsbury Estate lets out houses of varying sizes on the estate, in the village and in Bridport. They range from cute thatched, two-bedroom cottages to Crepe Farmhouse, an impressive Georgian house with eight bedrooms, five bathrooms, cinema room, indoor pool, hot tub and sauna. Lady Colfox told me she personally ensures all the accommodation on the estate is furnished as you would want your home to be. She has selected beautiful furniture, cosy throws and cushions, and makes sure there is more than enough cutlery and crockery for guests to be able to host visitors for meals.

West Bay

A mile from Bridport is **West Bay**, Bridport's harbour, where the River Brit, a tidal river, flows into the sea through the sluice gates and harbour basin. A harbour was first recorded at West Bay in the 13th century and was known as Bridport Harbour until 1884. It was a centre of the boat-building industry until the late 19th century and many ships were built here during the Napoleonic Wars (1799–1815). Although it's popular with visitors and some trendy eateries have popped up in recent years, West Bay has not been primped and preened into a glamorous, tourist honeypot; instead, it continues as a working fishing harbour with a 'what you see is what you get' attitude and where unpretentious fish and chip kiosks are still the lunch venue of choice.

Within a former Methodist church on the beach is the **West Bay Discovery Centre** (The Chapel on the Beach, DT6 4EN ✐ 01308 427488 ⊘ westbaydiscoverycentre.org.uk ☉ 10.00-16.00 Tue–Sun, weekends only in winter; free admission). It is small but a great starting point for a visit to West Bay. There are displays on the geology and history of the

◀ **1** Cone-shaped Colmer's Hill. **2** Exhibits at the West Bay Discovery Centre. **3** Bellows at Mangerton Mill. **4** Canoeing at West Bay.

town, from the formation of the cliffs millions of years ago to the town's starring role in the hugely popular BBC series *Broadchurch,* which first aired in 2013. The crime drama's creator, Chris Chibnall, is from the area and said the series was 'written as a love letter to the scenery of the Jurassic Coast'.

Above the pebbly East Beach tower golden sandstone cliffs, which glow warmly in the setting sun. There are frequent cliff falls here so it's wise not to get too close when on the beach. Walking to the end of the Jurassic Pier provides views along the coastline from the Isle of Portland to Brixham in Devon.

"The waters must be teeming with crabs because it usually only takes a few minutes to get a net full."

A few happy hours can be spent fishing for crabs around the harbour and in summer you'll see many families doing just that. The waters must be teeming with crabs because it usually only takes a few minutes to get a net full. Crabbing nets and bait (squid is a good option) are available at several shops in town, including the Angling Centre (10a West Bay, DT6 4EL).

On the other side of the harbour from East Beach is West Beach. The more protected of the two, it is safer for swimming and tends to be quieter as it's a little further from the centre. From West Beach it's a short but breathtaking walk along the top of the cliffs to Eype (page 193).

At **West Bay River Boat Hire** (⌀ 07875 643700 ⌀ westbayriverboats. info ☉ May–Sep) you can hire a rowing boat to explore the River Brit. The charming wooden boats take up to two adults and two children, and you can even take the dog. They also offer guided canoe tours of the river (⌀ westbaycanoes.co.uk).

⅋ FOOD & DRINK

West Bay is the sort of place where you feel like you really should eat take-away fish and chips on the beach or the pier, and there are plenty of kiosks offering that around the harbour.

Cherries 1 Pier Tce, DT6 4ER ⌀ 01308 301207. It's easy to miss this café on the working harbour, which means it is often less busy than others. The interior is splashed with bright colours and picture windows give views of the boat traffic. Food is homemade and tasty.
Rise West Bay DT6 4EZ ⌀ 01308 422011. Trendy option right on the river with rustic décor, a log fire in winter and water views. It's popular for breakfast, lunch and dinner so it's wise

to book ahead. The menu is casual – think burgers, curries and sandwiches. It also has a bakery/convenience store on the way into West Bay at 16–18 East Road.

Watch House Café West Bay DT6 4EN ✆ 01308 459330 ♺ watchhousecafe.co.uk. In an unrivalled location on East Beach is this sister to the well-known Hive Beach Café at Burton Bradstock (page 204). It has a casual atmosphere and specialises in seafood and wood-fired pizza.

Mangerton Mill

Mangerton DT6 3SG ✆ 01308 485224 ⊙ Easter–Oct; Wed–Sun & Bank Holiday Mon

Tucked away down tiny lanes north of Bridport, this three-storey watermill on the River Manger dates from the 17th century, and has been the home of the Harris family for several generations. Last worked commercially in 1966, the family has restored it and it is now a workable grist mill. It is in a very peaceful location and even the rhythmic churning of the mill wheel is soothing. Visitors are free to explore at their own pace and wonder at the inner workings of the mill, which are surrounded by a collection of household

"It is in a very peaceful location and even the rhythmic churning of the mill wheel is soothing."

and agricultural artefacts arranged in suitably higgledy-piggledy granddad's-shed fashion. There is a tea room and converted outbuildings house artist studios and gift shops.

Trout fishing is available in the lake and there is a quiet, riverside camping area. It is worth walking along the wooded edge of the River Manger to the sluice gates, from where water tumbles into a magical-looking pool shrouded by moss-gilded trees and ferns. It is the sort of scene meditation tracks invite you to imagine.

EAST OF BRIDPORT VIA THE BRIDE VALLEY TO ABBOTSBURY

As you travel east from Bridport you are heading towards some utterly captivating scenery – the Bride Valley, the start of **Chesil Beach** and the village of **Abbotsbury**. The River Bride, which in parts is more a stream than a river, rises in Littlebredy and runs along a 6½-mile course to the sea at **Burton Bradstock**. The surrounding valley is a bucolic blend of rolling hills, woodland and small stone and thatched villages that remain genuine Dorset, and not Dorset dressed up for the tourist trade, with scarcely a trinket shop in sight. Even the wildlife feels unthreatened – walking around the villages of the Bride Valley I saw a stoat, a fox and numerous rabbits all happily going about their business. If you are looking for a quieter base within easy reach of the coast the Bride Valley is a good option.

The **Bride Valley** area provides some good walking country, some of which incorporates Neolithic sites such as the **Kingston Russell Stone Circle** and its neighbour, the long barrow known as the **Grey Mare and her Colts**.

Abbotsbury does get busy during summer but it is a delightful village, best known for its swannery.

7 BURTON BRADSTOCK

The village nestles at the base of the Bride Valley, at the point where the River Bride flows into the sea. Although there has been some modern development on the outskirts, photogenic thatched 17th- and 18th-century cottages remain around the church of St Mary the Virgin.

A shingle **beach** (Hive Beach) lies on the edge of the village, shielded by golden cliffs that regularly yield their fossils. Apart from a National Trust car park and the popular Hive Beach Café (see below), there are no other facilities of note at the beach and it tends to be quieter than the likes of Lulworth Cove or Lyme Regis. The South West Coast Path leads from the beach up onto cliffs and towards West Bay, or eastwards towards West Bexington.

Just outside Burton Bradstock on the Bridport road is the **Bridport and West Dorset Golf Club** (Burton Rd, DT6 4PS ✆ 01308 421095 ⬦ bridportgolfclub.org.uk). Founded in 1891, it's the oldest club in Dorset. If you play here and find you are off your game, you can always use the excuse that you were distracted by the spectacular views across Lyme Bay. Visitor tee times can be booked online.

ⵌ FOOD & DRINK

Anchor Inn High St, DT6 4QF ✆ 01308 897228. Behind the typical pub exterior hides a clean, comfortable restaurant divided into several small rooms, which creates an intimate atmosphere. The menu is creative, with a focus on seafood. Reservation recommended.
Hive Beach Café Beach Rd, DT6 4RF ✆ 01308 897070 ⬦ hivebeachcafe.co.uk. The name is misleading, for this is not your average beachside café. Trendy, well known and with a reputation for superb seafood, it draws quite a crowd. It has its own range of beer, cider and

wine. The café is committed to sustainable fishing and prioritises locally sourced ingredients. No reservations.

Modbury Farm Shop Modbury Farm, Bredy Rd, DT6 4NE ✆ 07514 614231 ⌂ modburyfarmshop.co.uk. This well-stocked shop on a working farm is found two miles from Burton Bradstock on the Litton Cheney road. As well as West Country produce there are plenty of gluten-free items.

The Parlour Restaurant Bredy Farm, Bredy Ln, DT6 4ND ✆ 01308 897899 ⌂ theparlour-bredyfarm.com. The unusual approach through the farmyard lets you know this is a special place. Owner and chef Simon Payne has impressive credentials and a wealth of experience. He works his magic on top-notch local ingredients, including fish that's as fresh as it gets. He caters to a range of tastes and budgets, from pizzas cooked on the wood-fired oven to sophisticated Italian-inspired fish and game dishes. Simon opened the restaurant on the farm of his old school friend, Charlie, who runs the on-site cider-making business and adults-only camp site. They've gained a strong and loyal following with their Friday music nights and summer music festivals proving popular. If you're staying in the area it is worth setting aside an evening to eat here, but book ahead as it is deservedly popular.

The Seaside Boarding House Cliff Rd, Burton Bradstock DT6 4RB ✆ 01308 897205. The restaurant and bar of this smart hotel provide an upmarket dining option overlooking the sea. Unfussy food is prepared to a high standard. It does a super afternoon tea (bookings required).

CHILLIES FROM DORSET

Sea Spring Farm, West Bexington DT2 9DD ✆ 01308 897898 ⌂ seaspringseeds.co.uk

Dorset is well known for its cream teas, its cheese and its apple cake. It is less well known for its chillies, yet one of the hottest chillies in the world, the **Dorset Naga**, was first grown in a polytunnel in a nursery behind a bungalow in West Bexington.

The Dorset Naga is the creation of Joy and Michael Michaud. The couple, who both have doctorates in agronomy, began growing chillies at West Bexington in the early 1990s and are widely acknowledged as the first commercial chilli-growers in the UK. Although the Dorset Naga is frequently referred to as the hottest chilli in the world, it is a title Joy shies away from, as there are a few other 'superhot' chillies and, depending on growing conditions, one could be hotter than the next in any given season. One thing is for certain, annual tests since 2005 have consistently shown that the Dorset Naga is exceptionally fierce

Joy and Michael have helped to put Dorset on the chilli-growing map. The **Great Dorset Chilli Festival** (⌂ greatdorsetchillifestival. co.uk) is held annually in August.

8 WEST BEXINGTON

West Bexington is a small settlement tucked away off the B3157 between Burton Bradstock and Abbotsbury. A lane leads down to a car park that extends over the pebble beach, making it one of the most accessible beaches for those with limited mobility.

West Bexington is popular with beach fishermen, who can be seen casting their lines into the sea whatever the weather.

On the B3157, in the area known as Swyre, is **Vurlands Animal Farm** (DT2 9DB ✆ 01308 897160 ⌂ vurlandsanimalfarm.co.uk ◷ 10.00–17.00 daily). Visitors can wander between the paddocks and meet the farm animals, and there are good views of the Bride Valley. There is an indoor soft-play area, pedal carts and the Eggcup Tearooms (see below).

¶¶ FOOD & DRINK

Chesil Beach Manor House Hotel Beach Rd, DT2 9DF ✆ 01308 897660. Within a 16th-century building five-minutes' walk from the beach, this hotel has a pleasant restaurant with a flagstone floor, plus an outdoor eating area. The menu is simple pub fare cooked to a high standard.

The Club House Beach Rd, DT2 9DG ✆ 01308 898302 ⌂ theclubhousewestbexington. co.uk. Another venture by the owners of Hive Beach Café (page 204) and Watch House Café (page 203). What was a humble café in a bungalow opposite the beach has been transformed into a restaurant with a retro feel. The atmosphere is casual and the menu is, unsurprisingly given the location, fish-centric. Gets very busy at times. Reservation recommended.

Eggcup Tearooms Coast Rd, Swyre DT2 9DA ✆ 01308 897160. Tea room at Vurlands Animal Farm (see above), serving homemade lunches, cakes and roasts on Sunday in winter. The outdoor area has views of the Bride Valley.

Tamarisk Farm Shop Beach Rd, DT2 9DF ✆ 01308 897781 ⌂ tamariskfarm.co.uk. If you are lucky enough to be passing when the farm shop is open it is worth popping in. This family farm is in a spectacular seaside location overlooking Chesil Beach and was one of the country's first certified organic farms. They breed sheep and handsome Red Devon cattle, and grow organic cereals and vegetables. In the quirky shop behind the blue door you'll find their meat, stoneground flour, sheepskins and wool.

9 PUNCKNOWLE

Despite its spelling, Puncknowle is pronounced 'Punnel'. There is no agreed explanation for the 'Punck' part of the name but the second part is believed to refer to the knoll to the south of the village. On top of the knoll is a small, mysterious **stone house**. No-one is certain of its origins but its positioning high above the coast means it has long been used as a land- and sea-mark. In 1794 the knoll was the site of a signal station, one of a chain along the coast, and it has been suggested the house may have been associated with it. The house is built on a Bronze Age barrow and a cremation urn, now in the County Museum in Dorchester (page 129), was found under its foundations.

The **village** has a simple charm – narrow roads lined with thatched, stone cottages and farm buildings. Behind the high walls in the centre is the manor house, and next to it the church. Their positioning side by side is a reminder of how dominant the church and the big house were in England's rural villages.

> *"No-one is certain of its origins but its positioning high above the coast means it has long been used as a land- and sea-mark."*

⑂ FOOD & DRINK

Crown Inn Church St, DT2 9BN ✆ 01308 897711. A thatched 16th-century inn run by Palmers Brewery. It serves tasty, traditional pub food and has a community shop selling local produce and household essentials.

10 LITTON CHENEY

The road from Puncknowle to Litton Cheney takes the most extraordinary route right through the centre of the farmyard of Looke Farm. Around the village several pretty stone bridges span the River Bride. Litton Cheney is another picturesque Bride Valley village with 17th- and 18th-century cottages reached by crossing the flagstones that lie over the stream running in front of them.

South of the village is **Litton Lakes** (DT2 9DH ✆ 07983 450401 ⌂ littonlakes.co.uk), a campsite that is open to visitors, who can buy a pass to enjoy the 1½-acre lake. It is a good spot to swim and a local company hires out stand-up paddleboards. There is also a café overlooking the lake.

⑂ FOOD & DRINK

Ford Farm Cheese Ford Farm, Ashley Chase Estate, DT2 9AZ ✆ 01308 482580 ⌂ fordfarm. com ⏰ 09.00–16.30 Mon–Fri. Just outside the village, this large cheese-making operation has a tiny on-site shop where you can pick up some of their delicious cheeses at great prices.

Head up the steps to reception and they'll point you in the right direction. The cheddar and the goat's cheese aged in Wookey Hole Caves are my favourites.

White Horse Inn DT2 9AT ✆ 01308 482539. An old-school country pub through and through, from the décor to the menu. Pub classics have been adapted so there are gluten-free and vegan options. The beer garden lies next to the village stream and is fun for children and dogs. Live music every Sunday in summer.

11 LITTLEBREDY

At the head of the Bride Valley, Littlebredy is an idyllic hamlet in a magical setting. As I approached the village on my last visit the unmistakable Englishness of the scene struck me – the green rolling countryside, the neat hedgerows and the buzzards shrieking above.

Only cars belonging to Littlebredy's 85 residents are allowed into the community, so you will need to park and walk, but on foot is the best way to appreciate this special place. The road above the church is a good place to leave the car. With its dainty spire, the **church of St Michael and All Angels** stands out against the deep green of the hill behind, making it look superimposed on the scene. The church was largely rebuilt in 1850 and the spire was added to the 14th-century tower.

There is a very pleasant circular walk from here, into the grounds of Bridehead House then along the River Bride and back up the hill to the church. Bridehead House was the manor house at the centre of the estate; it stands behind the village cricket ground and can be glimpsed from the road. Incidentally, the cricket ground has to be one of the most picturesque in England.

"As I approached the village on my last visit the unmistakable Englishness of the scene struck me."

The lake in the grounds was formed by damming the springs that are the start of the River Bride. Water tumbles from the lake down a waterfall and into the river, which passes in front of Littlebredy's cottages. From the waterfall a footbridge takes you across the river, which is small at this stage, and on to a path that runs beside the water. You will pass thatched, stone cottages built in the 19th century but in the medieval style – essentially this is an early Victorian model village. Even the village hall (once a school), which is near the church, looks like a cottage. You come to a **Victorian walled garden** (✆ 01305 898055 ☉ Easter–Sep, 14.00–17.00 Wed, Sun & bank holidays), which belonged to the local estate. The gardens and walls have been restored to their former glory by a not-for-profit community interest venture. You can visit for a small fee and tea, coffee and cake are available. It's a beautiful garden in a stunning setting, and enthusiastic volunteers are on hand to tell you about its history.

The **Valley of Stones National Nature Reserve** lies on the southeastern edge of Littlebredy and its 24 acres are pleasant for walking and horseriding. It is named for the sarsen stones that have tumbled down the valley. The stones were formed at the end of the last ice age as the tightly cemented sandstone that capped the chalk hilltops gradually fragmented under freeze/thaw conditions. The chalk grassland is home to wildflowers and butterflies, and scarce lichens and mosses grow on the sarsens. In 2023, a rare discovery was made here: a 'polissoir' or polishing stone, believed to have been used 5,000 years ago by Neolithic people to sharpen stone tools. It is only the second polishing stone found earthfast (stuck in the earth in its original position) in England. It may look like just a boulder among many others but the smooth, shiny dip in the top of it gives away its former use. It was found by chance when volunteers were clearing vegetation from the sarsens. It is incredible to think of the role this stone performed for early communities.

12 ABBOTSBURY

Approaching Abbotsbury by road from the west is an absolute delight, as you gaze down towards Chesil Beach, which is watched over by St Catherine's Chapel. There are a few lay-bys where you can pull over and admire the view but it can all get a bit frantic if there are streams of traffic in both directions. A more relaxing option is to head up to **Abbotsbury hillfort** to take in the views at your leisure. Before you begin the descent to Abbotsbury, take the small turning on your left. It is worth the short detour to the top of the hill, where you can park and walk along Abbotsbury hillfort for practically aerial views of **Chesil Beach** and the lagoon it shields, known as **The Fleet**. The hill forms the western end of the ridgeway, which protects Abbotsbury from the worst of the weather and gives it its own microclimate. The fort would have been of great strategic importance to the Iron Age population as news of any seaward invasion could be passed to the region's other hillforts, including Maiden Castle (page 136).

As the name indicates, Abbotsbury was the site of an abbey, built in 1044 around the church of St Peter and populated with Benedictine monks from Cerne Abbas. It was destroyed in 1539, during the Dissolution, and some of the stone was used to build the village you see today. Near the church and Abbey House you will see other scattered ruins of the abbey, but the most obvious reminder of the monastic days is the **Tithe Barn**, which now lies at the heart of the **Abbey Farm** complex ($\mathcal{O}$ abbeyfarmabbotsbury.co.uk). The barn was built in the 14th century to store the tithe payments (a tenth of the harvest) paid by local farmers to the abbot and at 272ft is the longest tithe barn in England. Its thatched roof covers only half the building but even that takes around three years and 11,000 bundles of reeds to re-thatch. Reed is still cut at Abbotsbury and used to thatch the Ilchester Estate buildings, including the barn. It is fascinating to think that the building must have been re-thatched by many hands over the centuries, yet always with reeds from the same stretch of land.

"It is fascinating to think that the building must have been re-thatched by many hands over the centuries."

Today the Tithe Barn is an atmospheric venue for events. The buildings around it have been converted into small, independent shops and a café. It is an idyllic setting, nestled next to the village pond.

On the other side of the pond is **Abbey Farm Flowers** ($\mathcal{O}$ abbeyfarmflowers.co.uk), the clever and colourful creation of Amy Ralph. It's a pick-your-own flower garden where visitors can choose and cut their own bunch of flowers.

One of the best views of the Tithe Barn is from Abbey House, where you can have lunch or afternoon tea in the garden (page 214). In the corner of the garden is the Old Mill House, believed to be the only surviving Benedictine watermill in England. The **church of St Nicholas**, parts of which were built around the same time as the Tithe Barn, features some bullet holes in the pulpit. These are not the result of a violent reaction to a particularly dreary sermon, but rather they were caused when the Parliamentarians expelled a Royalist garrison from the church during the Civil War.

While Abbotsbury can get very busy during the day in summer, the crowds are largely made up of day trippers who perform a mass exodus

1 Abbotsbury Subtropical Gardens. **2** The curious stone building atop the knoll at Puncknowle. **3** Nesting swans at Abbotsbury Swannery. **4** St Catherine's Chapel awards visitors with outstanding coastal views. ▶

shortly after 17.00, making it a more pleasant place to stay than you might expect. The village has model looks; it is crammed with golden stone cottages, many topped with thatched roofs and decorated with window boxes full of colourful flowers. Most of Abbotsbury is owned by Ilchester Estates (page 222) and only around 15 houses are freehold. Residents credit Ilchester Estates with keeping Abbotsbury beautiful because any repairs and alterations are completed in harmony with the village.

St Catherine's Chapel

This lonely building dominates the village from its position high on a hill and beckons you to walk up to it for stunning views of the coastline. From Market Street in the centre of the village, take Chapel Lane and follow the path up the hill, passing pretty stone walls and looking back for views over the village. From this angle it is easy to appreciate the vast size of the Tithe Barn.

The chapel was built in the 14th century and may have been used as a chantry by the monks. When they built St Catherine's Chapel they certainly meant it to last – it is constructed entirely of stone, including the roof, with walls 4ft thick. It survived the Dissolution, probably because of its importance as a seamark for shipping.

St Catherine is the patron saint of spinsters and for centuries unmarried women have climbed up to the chapel to pray for a husband:

A husband, St Catherine; a handsome one, St Catherine; a rich one, St Catherine; a nice one, St Catherine; and soon, St Catherine!

When I last visited, there were several handwritten prayers in the wall of the building asking for husband-hunting help, and the resident white doves seemed to be a good omen. Non-denominational services are held monthly in summer and, should your prayers to St Catherine bear fruit, it is good to know that you can get married here.

From the chapel there are far-reaching views of Chesil Beach and The Fleet, and you can walk half a mile down the hill to the swannery and the beach from here.

Abbotsbury Swannery

New Barn Rd, DT3 4JG ✆ 01305 871858 ✍ abbotsbury-tourism.co.uk ⊙ mid-Mar–Oct 10.00–17.00 daily

By far Abbotsbury's best-known attraction is the swannery on The Fleet lagoon, which is home to around 600 swans (and various other canny birds who have taken up residence and exploit the very pleasant living conditions). It was established by Benedictine monks during the 1040s, when they farmed the swans for food. Sir Giles Strangways bought the swannery from Henry VIII in 1543 and it is still owned by his descendants, Ilchester Estates (page 222), making these the only swans in England not owned by the monarch.

Clearly the swans you see here today won't end up on anyone's plate – this is a sanctuary – and you won't usually see swans in pens, they are free to roam. The visit begins with a film and an exhibition about swans and the swannery. You can then wander along the paths among the nesting mute swans, and hides allow you to watch them and other waterfowl out on the lagoon. On display over the waterways are some rather dastardly looking old-fashioned duck traps.

"You can then wander along the paths among the nesting mute swans, and hides allow you to watch them on the lagoon."

Children can help with feeding at noon and 16.00, and mid-May to late June is a particularly exciting time to visit as this is when the cygnets hatch. Also on site are a well-stocked gift shop, a café and go-karts.

Abbotsbury Subtropical Gardens

Bullers Way, DT3 4LA ✆ 01305 871387 ⌖ abbotsbury-tourism.co.uk ⊘ 10.00–17.00 daily

This is far from a traditional English garden. In fact, it feels like you've entered another world. With hills to the north sheltering the site, and moist sea air, tropical plants thrive here. It was originally established in 1765 by the first Countess of Ilchester as a kitchen garden, then developed over time into a colourful 30-acre garden of rare and exotic plants from all over the world. Many of the plants were first introductions to Britain, discovered by the descendants of the countess. Paths wind their way through lush, tall trees, palms and notable rhododendron, camellia and hydrangea collections. It is divided into geographical zones but feels very natural and organic. A fallen oak bearing the dates 1828–2010 has been carved with an impressive series of countryside scenes, featuring an otter, fish, duck, owl and hound pursuing a fox. The rope bridge across the pond is a fun addition. The plant centre sells some of the plants on show in the garden, and there's a restaurant.

¶ FOOD & DRINK

Abbey House Church St, DT3 4JJ ☎ 01305 871330. Teas and lunches around the fireplace or on the lawn, with views of the millpond and Tithe Barn.

Cherries Abbey Farm, Church St, DT3 4JJ ☎ 01305 873925. At the heart of the Abbey Farm complex, this licensed café serves a creative menu and excellent cakes.

Old Schoolhouse Tearooms 1 Back St, DT3 4JP ☎ 01305 871808. This quintessential tea room is in a suitably quaint building in the village centre, with additional seating in the garden. Good homemade light lunches, cream teas and cakes, plus a range of preserves on sale.

FROM THE SOMERSET BORDER TO THE MARSHWOOD VALE

Once part of a wealthy monastic estate with Forde Abbey at its heart, the area between the Somerset border and the A35 coastal road remains remarkably unspoilt. The accurately named **Marshwood Vale** is marshy and wooded, which has protected it from the development of large settlements; instead the bowl-shaped valley has just a few scattered farms and hamlets. It is encircled by hills, including Dorset's two highest points: **Pilsdon Pen** and **Lewesdon Hill**, which make for superb walking country.

13 FORDE ABBEY

Forde Abbey, near Chard TA20 4LU ☎ 01460 221290 ⏁ fordeabbey.co.uk ☉ gardens, tea room & shop: Mar–Oct 10.30–17.00 daily; house: Apr–Oct noon–16.30 daily

Founded by Cistercian monks 900 years ago, Forde Abbey became one of the richest monasteries in the country. It was transformed into a private house in 1649 and lies at the heart of a family-run estate. The house is surrounded by 30 acres of beautiful gardens. If it inspires you to start your own garden makeover, there is a small garden nursery on site. Central to the garden are its lakes. Several times a day, the centenary fountain is turned on in the Mermaid Pond in front of the house and throws water 160ft into the air for 15 minutes, creating a good photo opportunity. It is the highest powered fountain in England.

You enter the house via the Great Hall, one of the remaining monastic rooms. Upstairs is the Saloon with its wall-hanging Mortlake Tapestries depicting scenes from St John's Gospel. The tapestries were made in London around 1620 as copies of those woven in Brussels a hundred years earlier for the Sistine Chapel at the instigation of Pope Julius II; elsewhere are family heirlooms and some evocative 18th-century bedrooms. Aside from the Great Hall, other remnants of the house's monastic days remain: the chapel, the monks' dormitory, the cloisters and the undercroft, which now houses a tea room.

14 CONEY'S CASTLE & LAMBERT'S CASTLE

🏠 **Mallinson's Woodland Retreat**

Those Iron Age folk certainly kept themselves busy, for not far from Pilsdon Pen and Lewesdon Hill are two further Iron Age hillforts. Tucked away down narrow lanes near the village of Fishpond Bottom, they are preserved by the National Trust. They lie about a mile apart and are linked by a road and a footpath. As well as fine walking spots, they are ideal for a picnic overlooking the Marshwood Vale.

Both Coney's and Lambert's castles may have been built as border posts between the neighbouring tribes, the Durotriges (eastwards) and the Dumnonii (southwest), or as status symbols for local chiefs. More recently (from 1709 to 1947), Lambert's Castle was used as the venue for a fair, with the hilltop serving as a racecourse.

These hillforts are at their best when wearing their spring finery in the form of a layer of bluebells, particularly Coney's Castle with its magical woodland enveloping the ramparts. Lambert's is larger and less wooded than Coney's Castle and as a result the views of the surrounding countryside are clearer.

🧳 SPECIAL STAYS

Mallinson's Woodland Retreat Yonder Hill, Holditch TA20 4NL ✆ 01460 221102 ⏚ mallinson.co.uk. Woodworker Guy Mallinson has created three luxurious treehouses with all sorts of extras like roll-top baths, hot tubs, wood-fired pizza ovens and coffee machines. They are designed for couples and are romantic and private. They are architecturally fascinating and have won awards for their cutting-edge design. Cars are parked a five-minute walk from the treehouses, so it feels like you are immersed in nature. Children and dogs are not allowed.

15 WHITCHURCH CANONICORUM

A village of farms and cottages tucked back from the coast at the southern edge of the Marshwood Vale, Whitchurch Canonicorum has a **church** with an unusual dedication – to St Candida, also known as

St Wite. Within the church is the 13th-century shrine containing St Wite's remains. The three oval openings were originally designed for the sick to insert their ailing limbs into, or if they couldn't make it to the church a handkerchief was inserted and taken to them. Today the openings are used for depositing prayers handwritten on small cards, and there were plenty of them when I was last there. The shrine is a rare survival as most were destroyed during the Reformation and this is the only church in England, other than Westminster Abbey, that still contains the original medieval shrine and relics of the saint to whom it was dedicated. St Wite has not conclusively been identified: one theory is that she was a Saxon woman killed by the Danes in one of their raids on Charmouth.

"The three oval openings were originally designed for the sick to insert their ailing limbs into."

Near the altar is a rather splendid shrine to 'S John Ieffrey of Catherstone, Knight', who died in 1611. The recumbent stone figure dressed in a knight's armour is in excellent condition.

Buried in the churchyard (not far from the entrance) is **Georgi Ivanov Markov**, the Bulgarian dissident writer who died in London in 1978 after being stabbed with an umbrella that was used to insert a ricin pellet into his calf. His assassination was allegedly organised by the Bulgarian Secret Police, possibly with the help of the Soviet KGB. It was their third attempt to dispose of him, and several prominent KGB defectors, including Oleg Gordievskiy, have asserted that the KGB assisted with the killing. The inscription on Markov's gravestone states that he died 'in the cause of freedom'. He was buried here at the request of his English wife, whose family is from the area.

16 PILSDON PEN & LEWESDON HILL

Pilsdon Pen and Lewesdon Hill are the two highest points in Dorset. No-one ever seems quite sure which of the two is actually the higher, although I am reliably informed Lewesdon narrowly takes the title at 915ft. These neighbouring hills have a lot in common: both were once Iron Age hillforts, both were once used as beacon sites to warn

---

1 View west from Eggardon Hillfort. **2** St Wite's tomb, Whitchurch Canonicorum. **3** Forde Abbey. **4** Mapperton House & Gardens. ▶

of impending invasion and both provide magnificent views of the Marshwood Vale. A round walk from Broadwindsor, incorporating both Pilsdon Pen and Lewesdon Hill, takes about four hours.

Pilsdon Pen is particularly easy to access and makes a brief but satisfying walk on its own. There is a car park opposite the start of the walk, on the B3164. From there it is a short, steep climb up the hillside until you reach the flat top where the Iron Age settlement stood.

¶¶ FOOD & DRINK

Shave Cross Inn Shave Cross DT6 6HW ☎ 01308 868358 🖫 shavecrossinn.co.uk. A characterful 14th-century thatched inn with a lovely beer garden. The menu isn't huge but the portions are generous. Reservations recommended.

17 REDLANDS YARD

Broadwindsor DT8 3PX ☎ 01308 285001 🖫 redlandsyard.co.uk

Former farm buildings house a series of small independent shops and a restaurant in the village of Broadwindsor, east of Beaminster. At the heart of the centre is Foxy Cottage, a large gift shop selling country-style gifts, homewares, clothing and food; in the lead-up to Christmas there is a huge and colourful range of Christmas decorations. In the surrounding buildings, formerly pig pens, are individual shops, many of which have a homemade crafts and gifts focus.

The restaurant serves homemade light lunches and cakes, and is a popular pit stop for walkers tackling Pilsdon Pen and Lewesdon Hill. There is plenty of free parking and the centre is wheelchair accessible. It has been part of the local farming community since 1986 and owner Sarah Williams comes from a local farming family. The centre's farming links contribute to its charm.

EASTWARDS FROM BEAMINSTER

18 BEAMINSTER & SURROUNDS

Beaminster, a market town since 1284, positively glows on a sunny day thanks to the golden hamstone from which much of the town is built. If you look closely you may see ammonites and other fossils in the walls of the buildings, as stone from nearby Horn Park Quarry, from which much of the town is constructed, is rich in them. Narrow lanes of terraced cottages converge in the market square.

At the centre of **The Square** is a covered market cross known as the Julia Memorial. This was erected in 1906 by Vincent Robinson of Parnham House, which lies south of the town, as a memorial to his sister, Julia.

St Mary's Church faces a row of pretty terraced cottages of assorted shapes, sizes and colours. The community has come up with an ingenious solution to the problem of getting an ageing population into church. A small stone building at the end of the churchyard contains a lift allowing those with limited mobility or in wheelchairs to avoid the steps. Volunteers are usually on hand to guide visitors and the community has done an admirable job conserving and restoring the church and deservedly won an award for their efforts. The volunteer who showed me around told me proudly that they had installed underfloor heating,

"If you look closely you may see ammonites and other fossils in the walls of the buildings."

when each of the original flagstones was painstakingly lifted and replaced. Sadly, the pews had to be removed due to wood rot, and have been replaced with chairs. The tower, which dates from the 1500s, is one of the most elaborate in the West Country: every three hours the church clock plays the hymn tune known as 'Hanover'. Within the church are large memorials to the Strobe family who once lived in Parnham House, while the embroidery screen near the organ, which depicts nearby scenes, was made by local ladies as part of their millennium celebrations.

Beaminster has a small, local **museum** (Whitcombe Rd, DT8 3NB *𝒹* 01308 863623 *𝒸* beaminstermuseum.co.uk ☉ Easter–Oct 10.30–16.00 Tue, Thu, Sat & bank holidays, 14.00–16.30 Sun) telling the history of the town and surrounding villages. There are some fascinating Stone Age, Bronze Age, Iron Age and Roman artefacts that have been found locally. Fossils found at nearby **Horn Park Quarry** are on display. The quarry lies between Beaminster and Broadwindsor on the B3163 and is the country's smallest national nature reserve. It contains fossils dating back 170 million years, including what geologists have described as the most significant examples of ammonites in Britain. To arrange a visit you need to contact the Jurassic Coast Trust (*𝒸* jurassiccoast.org), or the museum can assist. You can see the fossils in situ and chat with experts, but fossil-collecting is not allowed.

Mapperton House and Gardens

DT8 3NR ✆ 01308 862645 ⌖ mapperton.com ◷ garden: Apr–Sep 10.00–17.00 Sun–Thu; house: Apr–Sep noon–16.00 Sun–Thu, guided tours only, 11.00, noon, 13.00 & 14.00

The Mapperton Estate, home of the Earl and Countess of Sandwich, lies in a gloriously bucolic landscape two miles east of Beaminster. The first Earl of Sandwich is, of course, famously credited with the inspired idea of putting a slice of roast beef between two pieces of bread.

The estate's garden, hidden in a narrow, steep-sided valley below the house, is fascinating for its amalgamation of three styles at the hands of three different owners. The banks, terraces and long, rectangular fish ponds date from the Elizabethan period but in the 1920s a wealthy widow, Ethel Labouchère, created an Arts and Crafts garden in the Italianate style on the highest of the terraces, into the banks of which she built little rooms, complete with fireplaces for taking afternoon tea. It's possible she was influenced, or helped, by Harold Peto, creator of the (Arts and Crafts Italianate) garden at Iford in Wiltshire. The present custodians and residents of the main house are Viscount and Viscountess Hinchingbrooke. The viscount's grandfather (Victor Montagu, the tenth Earl of Sandwich) bought the property in the 1950s and made several important additions to the garden, including a classical-style orangery, overlooking Mrs Labouchère's fountains and topiary, and a pergola. He also converted one of the Elizabethan fish ponds into a swimming pool of near-Olympic proportions. It is still used for swimming, mostly by Viscountess Hinchingbrooke and the family's turtle, Splurtle. In the wild, stream-fed valley below the pool the tenth earl planted an arboretum with some notable specimen trees, which are now a good size. Over the past few decades the planting on all three levels has been much enhanced under the expert guidance of the Countess of Sandwich. Head gardener, Susie, told me the garden is special because it still feels very much like the garden of a family home, and because of how incredibly peaceful it is. Susie loves to see people relaxing in the garden, sitting on the lawn in the sun, reading a book.

"It is still used for swimming, mostly by Viscountess Hinchingbrooke and the family's turtle, Splurtle."

The manor house dates from the 1540s with various more recent additions. It can only be visited by guided tour, and it is advisable to book ahead. The family moved here with an impressive collection of art and the pictures on display include works by Lely, Reynolds and Hogarth. You can also visit All Saints' Church, which stands beside the manor house and is of medieval origin.

The Mapperton Estate extends to some 2,000 acres. In recent years, hundreds of acres have been set aside for a vast rewilding project. You can book a guided tour of the Mapperton Wildlands (⌀ mappertonwildlands.com) or take a self-guided walk. The project includes the use of conservation grazing by heritage breeds and has seen the introduction of White Park cattle, Exmoor ponies and Tamworth pigs. In 2022, they introduced two beavers, appropriately named Woody and Twiggy. Beavers are native to the UK but were hunted to extinction in the 1600s.

There are two well-designed children's play areas, one near the café for younger children and one in the woods. You can visit the café and one of the play areas without buying entry to the house and gardens if you don't have time for an extended visit. The website has details of ticketed events at the house, such as Shakespeare in the gardens, plant fairs and the Christmas market.

There are two beautiful self-catering cottages, and you can even rent the main house; see website for details.

⑪ FOOD & DRINK

The small, independent shop seems to have survived better in Beaminster than elsewhere. Around The Square are several selling locally grown food, such as **Nick Tett Family Butchers** and **Fruit n' Two Veg**. Just around the corner, on Hogshill Street, is the **Village Bakery** – irrepressibly quaint and old-world.

Brassica 4 The Square, DT8 3AS ⌀ 01308 538100 ⌀ brassicarestaurant.co.uk. Upmarket restaurant in the market square, created by chef Cass Titcombe who co-founded Canteen Restaurant in London. The menu has a Mediterranean flavour but dishes are prepared using Dorset produce wherever possible. Elevenses are served 11.00–noon and the fixed price lunch menu is good value. It also has a homewares shop across the road.

Café @ Cilla and Camilla 22 The Square, DT8 3AU ⌀ 01308 863477. A casual café at the back of a shop and in a pleasant courtyard behind it. Much of the food is sourced from suppliers within the town.

Coach House Café Mapperton House and Gardens, Mapperton DT8 3NR ⌀ 01308 862645 ⌀ mapperton.com. The coach house and stable block at Mapperton (page 220) have been carefully converted into a café and events space. The café serves light lunches, sandwiches (of course!), coffee and cake, and endeavours to source its food locally. There is a play area inspired by Mapperton's beavers, where children can play with water and build dams, and the home of the estate's resident tortoise is close to the cafe. You can visit the café and play area without paying the admission fee for the house. It is a beautiful, historic and peaceful setting.

The Ollerod 3 Prout Bridge, DT8 3AY ✐ 01308 862200. A smart restaurant within the hotel in the centre of town. Specialises in local, seasonal produce, including veg from its own garden.

19 EVERSHOT

♠ Summer Lodge Country House Hotel, Restaurant & Spa

Evershot is the second-highest village in Dorset, after Ashmore, although unlike Ashmore it doesn't feel particularly high. It is also where the River Frome rises, just behind St Osmund's Church in Back Lane.

Much of the village's charm derives from its mixture of architectural styles, from tiny 17th-century cottages to large Georgian houses. Although the main street is largely residential, Evershot has managed to keep its village shop, and the excellent bakery is thriving. The pavement is raised on one side of the village street; this protected pedestrians and residents of the more upmarket side of the street from the muck that collected in the road, presumably mostly donated by the local bovine population. The houses on the raised pavement side were therefore considered more desirable and expensive.

On the edge of Evershot is the heart of the vastly wealthy Ilchester Estates, which owns 15,000 acres of West Dorset, including Abbotsbury and Chesil Beach, and 40 acres of central London, including Holland Park. The estate is currently owned by Charlotte Townshend and, as the owner of the Abbotsbury Swannery (page 212), she is the only person in the country, other than the monarch, who is allowed to own swans.

SPECIAL STAYS

Summer Lodge Country House Hotel, Restaurant & Spa 9 Fore St, DT2 0JR ✐ 01935 482000 ⊘ summerlodgehotel.co.uk. A pleasingly old-school, luxury hotel surrounded by stunning countryside. Once home to the Earls of Ilchester, Summer Lodge retains the feel of a fine country home thanks to its lofty ceilings, polished antiques, and artwork featuring handsome horses and gun dogs. As well as elegant rooms in the main house, there are upmarket self-contained cottages in the village. The four-acre gardens are just as impressive as many you might pay to visit. There are surprisingly few spa hotels in Dorset, so the spa and indoor pool are a big draw.

The fine-dining restaurant offers slick service and an award-winning wine selection. Meals are taken in the conservatory, restaurant or cosy bar, and afternoon tea is served daily in the drawing room. The Acorn Inn in the village has the same owners and also offers very comfortable accommodation.

⫴ FOOD & DRINK

Acorn Inn 28 Fore St, DT2 0JW ✆ 01935 83228 ⬧ acorn-inn.co.uk. A 16th-century coaching inn with excellent food and service. The restaurant is elegant without being pretentious, and prides itself on using the freshest local ingredients. The bars offer a huge range of drinks, including Dorset ales and gins.

Evershot Village Bakery 18 Fore St, DT2 0JW ✆ 01935 83379. A tiny bakery that does big things. Spelt and sourdough breads sell briskly, alongside a range of pizzas and sweet treats.

Summer Lodge Country House Hotel, Restaurant and Spa See opposite.

20 THE KINGCOMBE CENTRE

Lower Kingcombe DT2 0EQ ✆ 01300 320684 ⬧ dorsetwildlifetrust.org.uk/Kingcombe
⊙ visitor centre: Feb–Dec 10.00–16.30 daily; nature reserve: year-round daily

The Dorset Wildlife Trust manages almost 1,000 acres of meadows and nature reserve at Kingcombe and Powerstock. The Kingcombe site was formerly a well-managed organic farm, owned by the Wallbridge family, and is now rich in wildflowers, butterflies and birdlife. Grazing is an important element of the conservation of this land, so you can expect to see livestock as well as wildlife. You can simply wander and experience the English

"Grazing is an important element of the conservation of this land, so you can expect to see livestock as well as wildlife."

countryside as it used to be, have lunch in the café or take part in one of the many activities or courses on offer, such as beekeeping, hedge laying and wildlife tracking.

I spent a wonderful and informative day on a **foraging course** with John Wright (page 27), known for his appearances on television's *River Cottage*. By the end of a day, I was surprised I had survived my childhood. As an only child and a tomboy, I spent many hours building camps in the countryside surrounding our house, collecting all manner of leaves and berries for my 'tea parties'. By sheer fluke it seems, I managed to steer clear of the various toxic plants that John took care to point out on his course. As he said, 'it is just as important, if not more so, to know the plants you can't eat as it is to know the plants you can'.

John describes himself as one of those lucky people who has turned a hobby into a job. I had assumed he must have had some sort of botany studies background but he was actually a cabinetmaker, whose passion for mushrooms led him to become a self-taught forager. John runs fascinating foraging courses, covering hedgerow, seashore, fungi and more. He maintains an interesting and helpful website (⌂ ediblebush. com) and has written many books.

21 EGGARDON HILLFORT

This impressive Iron Age hillfort, four miles east of Bridport, has superb panoramic views and is one of the most accessible hillforts in Dorset. On a clear day you can see across Lyme Bay to south Devon, and across the Marshwood Vale to Pilsdon Pen.

The fort covers 20 acres of the hilltop. Its impressive ditches and banks seem to ripple as shadows cast by the clouds drift across them. The interior contains a large octagonal earthwork, thought to be the result of tree planting by a smuggler who owned the land and used the formation as a seamark for his ships.

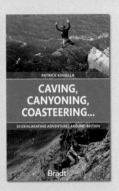

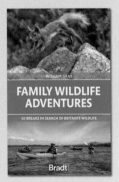

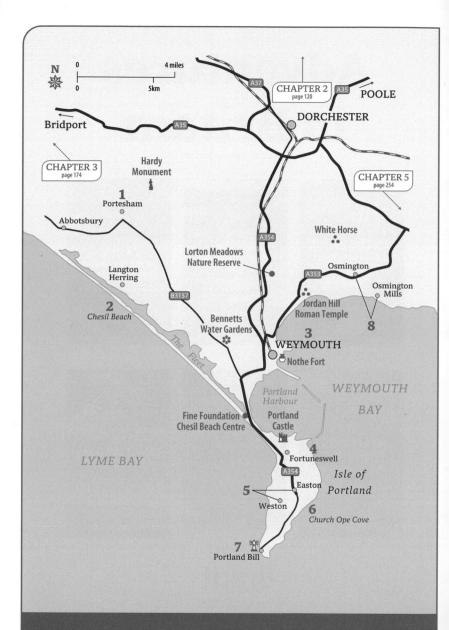

WEYMOUTH & THE SOUTHERN COAST

4
WEYMOUTH &
THE SOUTHERN COAST

Along this portion of the Dorset coast the huge shingle bank of **Chesil Beach** stands separated from the mainland by a lagoon, The Fleet, creating a strange, but entirely natural, visual phenomenon. At the beach's southeastern end are the town of Weymouth and the peninsula known as the Isle of Portland. Depending on how you look at it, **Weymouth** is either confused about what it wants to be or multi-talented, having to juggle being a working town, a port and a seaside resort. In 2012 it added yet another achievement to its CV – Olympic venue. It was quite a coup for Weymouth, and for Dorset, when the Weymouth and Portland National Sailing Academy (WPNSA) was chosen to host the sailing events for the London 2012 Olympic and Paralympic Games. Thanks to the WPNSA, the area now has world-class facilities to complement its superb sailing waters.

> *"Depending on how you look at it, Weymouth is either confused about what it wants to be or multi-talented."*

Linked to Weymouth by a causeway is the **Isle of Portland**, famed for its stone quarries and its lighthouse at Portland Bill, which warns shipping to steer clear of Dorset's southernmost point. A highlight is Portland Castle, an extraordinarily well-preserved fort built by Henry VIII in the 1540s.

Smuggling became rife along the south coast after an act was passed in 1751 that dramatically increased the tax levied on spirits. Weymouth and the surrounding area was a smuggling hotspot, with a notorious gang operating around **Osmington Mills**. The quiet waters of **The Fleet** behind Chesil Beach were ideal for stowing contraband for collection at a more convenient time.

The **South Dorset Ridgeway** is a ridge of chalky downland running parallel to the coast from **Abbotsbury** to Osmington. It's extraordinarily rich in prehistoric sites and offers exceptional walks.

GETTING THERE & AROUND

Reaching Weymouth and Portland by road can be irksome, as the main route from Dorchester gets very congested in summer. There is a park and ride at Mount Pleasant, off the A354.

PUBLIC TRANSPORT

Weymouth is three hours from London Waterloo by **train** (South Western Railway) and is connected by train to Dorchester, Wareham, Poole and Bournemouth.

The **Jurassic Coaster** (⊘ firstbus.co.uk) bus services link Weymouth to the main stops along the coast. The X53 travels westward to Abbotsbury, West Bay, Bridport, Chideock, Charmouth, Lyme Regis and Axminster. The X54 links Weymouth to Poole via Osmington, Durdle Door, Lulworth Cove, Wool and Wareham.

First Buses are useful for getting around Weymouth and Portland. From Easter to September open-top buses (501 AKA Portland Coaster) run from Weymouth Esplanade to Portland Bill.

Information about local bus services and how to link up with the South Dorset Ridgeway is available at ⊘ travelinesw.com.

BY BOAT

A summer **ferry** (⊘ coastlinecruises.com) operates from Weymouth (Brewers Quay) to Portland Castle, taking around 40 minutes.

Also during summer, local boatmen operate **rowing-boat ferries** across the harbour from near the ferry terminal. This is a novel way of getting from the town to Nothe Fort and saves you the walk up to the Town Bridge. The service has been operating for over 60 years and the traditional clinker-built wooden boats have a nostalgic quality. Numerous **cruises** along the Jurassic Coast also depart from Weymouth.

⚓ **CRUISE OPERATORS**

Coastline Cruises Brewery Quay, DT4 8TJ ⊘ 01305 785000 ⊘ coastlinecruises.com. Cruises along the coast from Weymouth Bay. Also a Portland ferry service and private charter.
MV Freedom 11 Redcliff View, DT4 8RW ⊘ 07974 266867 ⊘ mvfreedom.co.uk. Trips along the Jurassic Coast or around Portland Harbour in a boat specifically equipped for the disabled.

TOURIST INFORMATION

Weymouth has a tourist-information centre (98 St Mary St, DT4 8NY ✆ 07886 086812 ⌕ love-weymouth.co.uk). There is also a small visitor-information centre at the Heights Hotel in Portland (page 244), where you can pick up brochures and maps. For general information, see ⌕ weareweymouth.co.uk and ⌕ portlandtourism.co.uk.

Weymouth Bay Rib Charters ✆ 07983 022227 ⌕ weymouthbayribcharters.co.uk. High-speed rigid inflatable boat rides around the bay.

Weymouth Portland Boat Trips Weymouth Harbour, DT4 8ED ✆ 07899 725107 ⌕ weymouthportlandboattrips.co.uk. Offers one-hour boat trips from just near Weymouth Pavillion. They depart every 30 minutes from 10.00 and you don't need to book in advance.

CYCLING

Just as driving around Weymouth can be problematic due to traffic, so can cycling. Cycle-friendly routes are outlined in **brochures** available from tourist-information centres and ⌕ visit-dorset.com. The **Jurassic Cycle Trails** (⌕ love-weymouth.co.uk) are three easy routes around Weymouth, Portland and Lodmoor. The **Rodwell Trail** (⌕ sandsfootcastle.org.uk) follows the track of the old Weymouth and Portland railway, and is open to cyclists and walkers.

The **South Dorset Ridgeway** (⌕ dorset-nl.org.uk) has good off-roading with fantastic views and a chance to stop off at the numerous prehistoric sites.

 CYCLE HIRE

Ebike Café Custom House Quay, DT4 8BG ✆ 01305 786839 ⌕ ebikecafe.co.uk. Café offering e-bike hire.

Weymouth Bike Hire 23 Melcombe Av, DT4 7TH ✆ 07548 254634 ⌕ weymouthbikehire.co.uk. A wide range of bikes, including child trailers and tandems.

Weymouth E-bike Hire 40a St Thomas St, DT4 8EH ✆ 01305 564563 ⌕ weymouthebikehire.co.uk. Electric bike hire.

WALKING

The South West Coast Path runs along this stretch, diverting inland around Weymouth and passing above the **White Horse** near Osmington. A four-mile circuit from Osmington works well through fields to Sutton

Poyntz, then up on to White Horse Hill for the high-level section on the coast path before dropping down into Osmington.

The **South Dorset Ridgeway** is part of the South West Coast Path and runs from West Bexington to Osmington Mills. Glorious views of the Jurassic Coast, chalk downland and river valleys are not its only draw as this is an area packed with archaeological delights, reminders that the land has been inhabited for over 6,000 years. You can download information, maps and suggested walking routes from the Dorset National Landscape website (♂ dorset-nl.org.uk).

The We Are Weymouth website (♂ weareweymouth.co.uk) suggests various themed trails. The **Rodwell Trail** (♂ rodwelltrail.org.uk) follows the track of the old Weymouth and Portland railway and links to the South West Coast Path.

Portland is easy to explore on foot and a nine-mile path runs around the peninsula. The southern tip around Portland Bill makes a perfect three-mile circuit past the three lighthouses. Southwell is a useful starting point, giving the pleasure of arriving at the Bill on foot, and taking in decayed quarries with rusting cranes and derricks, and a huge blowhole on the east coast.

HORSERIDING

Weymouth Beach is popular with local horse riders. Note that you cannot ride on the beach between 1 April and 30 September between 09.00 and 19.00. For further information visit ♂ weymouthtowncouncil.gov.uk.

🜹 RIDING STABLES

Chesil Equestrian Sweet Hill Farm, Portland DT5 2DS ♪ 01305 823719 ♂ chesilequestrian.co.uk. Hacking on the Isle of Portland with impressive sea views.
Rosewall Equestrian Osmington Mills DT3 6HA ♪ 01305 833578 ♂ weymouthcamping. com. BHS-approved riding school offering hacking for most abilities.

WESTWARDS FROM WEYMOUTH, INCLUDING CHESIL BEACH

1 PORTESHAM & SURROUNDS

The village of Portesham snuggles up against the base of the chalk hills of the South Dorset Ridgeway. **St Peter's Church**, which is largely 12th and 13th century, is reached over a flagstone across the flower-topped stream that flows gently alongside the main street. The handsome 18th-century **Portesham House** is where Vice Admiral Sir Thomas Masterman Hardy once lived.

Standing high above Portesham on Black Down Hill is the **Hardy Monument** (National Trust). It is not, as you may at first assume, a monument to the novelist Thomas Hardy but to the vice admiral who served aboard Nelson's HMS *Victory* during the Battle of Trafalgar in 1805. During the battle the French and Spanish fleets were defeated but Nelson was fatally wounded. It was to Hardy that Nelson reputedly uttered his famous last words, 'Kiss me, Hardy'. Hardy spent his childhood in Portesham until joining the navy as a 13-year -old captain's servant. The monument is a 72ft Portland stone tower built in 1844. It certainly isn't a thing of beauty, looking rather like a factory chimney protruding from the hilltop: its shape was intended to represent a telescope of the type Hardy may have used at sea. Once you know that, it doesn't seem so out of place. It is well worth climbing the 120 steps to the top of the monument for spectacular views. That said, the views from the base are splendid, without the climb, so visitors with limited mobility can still appreciate a visit here. The heathy surroundings make great strolling terrain, with the South Dorset Ridgeway passing the monument. Free parking is available at the visitor area, which also has picnic areas.

"The heathy surroundings make great strolling terrain, with the South Dorset Ridgeway passing the monument."

From the Hardy Monument, you have several options for **walking**: one of the most pleasing (around seven miles) is to start from Portesham and walk up, then carry on eastwards on the well-marked track along the ridge of Bronkham Hill with its spectacularly profuse series of prehistoric tumuli, and down to Corton Farm, then back to Portesham by lanes and footpaths.

FOOD & DRINK

Duck's Farm Shop Bramdon Ln, DT3 4HG ✎ 01305 534111. A farm shop selling local produce and essential supplies for self-catering, plus a surprisingly large amount of West Country alcohol. It also has a café.

Kings Arms 2 Front St, DT3 4ET ✎ 01305 871342. Freshly cooked pub food. The large beer garden with wood-fired pizza oven is popular in the warmer months.

2 CHESIL BEACH

Stand on Portland Heights or outside St Catherine's Chapel high above Abbotsbury and look out to sea and you will be treated to the most extraordinary sight – a wide, golden, shingle bank rising out of the water and running along the coastline, with a lagoon sheltering sheepishly behind it. If you saw such a thing in Dubai you might assume it was the zany creation of a capricious sheikh, but this is Dorset and Chesil Beach is all natural.

Stretching for 18 miles between West Bay and Portland, Chesil Beach is the largest of three major shingle structures in Britain. The shingle bank reaches around 40ft at its highest point, around the height of three double decker buses. It was formed by rising seas at the end of the last Ice Age. Its approximately 180 billion rounded pebbles have been graded in size by strong tidal currents; they are as small as peas at the western end and the size of oranges at the Portland end. For centuries the size of the pebbles has been helping locals, mostly smugglers and fishermen, pinpoint where they are landing on the beach. It isn't until you get up close to Chesil Beach that you can truly appreciate how large it is and, in some parts, how steeply it rises from the water. It is very impressive to look at but tricky to walk on as the pebbles shift endlessly beneath your feet. Wherever you are on Chesil Beach you can hear the sound of shifting pebbles as the waves roll up and back across the stone.

The lagoon, known as **The Fleet**, extends from Abbotsbury to Portland and contains a mixture of salt- and freshwater. It is the largest tidal lagoon in the UK. Home to an abundance of birdlife, wading birds can be seen all year, while brent geese from Siberia and red-breasted merganser (fish-eating duck) visit in winter. The birds' ancestors must have had quite a shock back in 1942–43, when Barnes Wallis's famous bouncing bomb was tested on The Fleet in preparation for the Dambusters raids.

At the southern end of The Fleet, just before you head over the causeway from Weymouth to Portland, is the **Fine Foundation Wild Chesil Centre** (Portland Beach Rd, DT4 9XE ✆ 01305 206191 🖥 dorsetwildlifetrust.org.uk/wildchesilcentre) and a pay-and-display car park with direct access to Chesil Beach. The centre is run by Dorset Wildlife Trust and provides information on Chesil Beach, the Fleet and Portland. Binoculars allow you to watch seabirds feeding on the sand flats and there is live video from cameras on the bed of the lagoon.

There are educational displays for children and a small shop. It is worth checking whether any sections of the beach are closed, as during nesting season (usually April to August) parts are off-limits to avoid disturbing the birds. The centre also runs a programme of events (see website for details), and there is a café with views of the lagoon and beach. From the centre is a boardwalk leading to Chesil Beach.

Since Chesil Beach is almost physically impossible to walk along, the South West Coast Path follows the inland side of The Fleet, midway along which **Langton Herring** makes a handy access point for the water's edge.

Glass-bottom boat trips run by DWT provide the opportunity to explore The Fleet and get a closer look at its bird- and sealife (The Fleet Explorer, Ferryman's Way, Wyke Regis, Weymouth DT4 9YU ✆ 01305 206191 ✍ dorsetwildlifetrust.org.uk ☉ Easter–Oct daily). The trips last one hour and can be booked at the Fine Foundation Wild Chesil Centre.

¶¶ FOOD & DRINK

Cafe at the Wild Chesil Centre Portland Beach Rd, DT4 9XE ✆ 01305 206196. The café at the visitor centre uses as much locally sourced food as possible. You can watch the birdlife on The Fleet as you eat.

3 WEYMOUTH

A busy seaside town of around 55,000 people, Weymouth attracts thousands of holiday-makers in summer, earning it the rather dubious nickname of 'England's Bay of Naples', or more recently 'Weybiza'. It has an active harbour, constantly criss-crossed by fishing vessels and pleasure craft, and a large, sandy beach.

Plague port & royal resort

Weymouth began as two medieval ports on either side of the mouth of the River Wey. The two towns, Weymouth and Melcombe Regis, were joined in 1571 by royal charter and a bridge was later built across the harbour between them. The portion now referred to as the town centre, which lies north of the River Wey, was actually Melcombe Regis, which has a grim claim to fame, for it was here that the bubonic plague, or Black Death, entered England in 1348.

During the 18th century Weymouth, like many coastal towns, was touted as a health retreat. King George III came to Weymouth in 1789 to try out one of the first bathing machines, a hut on wheels drawn into the water by horses where one could bathe supervised by an attendant. It is said that while he bathed 'God save the King' was dutifully sung from another hut. A replica of the bathing contraption is now displayed on the seafront, alongside a **statue of George III** erected in 1809 to mark the 50th anniversary of his succession. The king visited regularly until 1810, a fact which is commemorated by a chalk carving on a hillside at Osmington depicting the monarch on horseback (page 250). The promise of healing properties and royal patronage made Weymouth highly fashionable and rows of smart houses sprung up along the esplanade to cater for well-to-do visitors. Those wonderful, characteristically Georgian houses still define the seafront today, although their elegance is somewhat undermined by the abundant amusement arcades, bars and bucket-and-spade shops.

At the end of King Street, is the colourful **Jubilee Clock**, which was built in 1887 to commemorate 50 years of the reign of Queen Victoria. A bronze **statue of Queen Victoria** sits in front of **St John's Church**, a fine Portland stone building completed in 1854. During World War II, Weymouth featured prominently in the D-Day landings in Normandy as a departure point for many British and American soldiers. A **memorial** on the esplanade, opposite the Royal Hotel, records that 517,816 troops and 144,093 vehicles embarked at Weymouth between 6 June 1944 and 7 May 1945. The hotel itself was requisitioned for use as the local headquarters of the United States military. Weymouth's military importance made it a target for German bombing, and over 500 bombs were dropped on the town. Over a thousand homes were lost and the High Street was so badly damaged that much of it had to be demolished after the war.

The seafront

Today, handsome Georgian terraced houses and some sizeable hotels line Weymouth's seafront. The earlier terraces have iron balconies, while the later ones (1820s) have bay windows. In summer the long sandy beach is given over to the usual seaside entertainment, including a

1 Look for red-breasted merganser at The Fleet, Chesil Beach. 2 The Hardy Monument crowns Black Down Hill. 3 Chesil Beach. 4 Bearded tits are frequently seen at Radipole Lake. 5 Weymouth harbour. ▶

funfair, traditional Punch and Judy show and the ever-popular donkey rides. A **land train** (⊘ weymouthlandtrain.com) operates between Easter and the end of October from the seafront across the Town Bridge to Hope Square on the other side of the harbour. **Hope Square** is a busy part of town packed with restaurants.

For over a hundred years, visitors to Weymouth have been treated to amazingly intricate sand sculptures on the beach. Today these are primarily the work of Mark Anderson. It's incredible what he can create with just sand and water. On one of my visits in 2023, I was wowed by his intricate sculpture of King Charles III in his coronation regalia. Mark learnt from his grandfather, Fred Darrington, who began creating sand sculptures here in the 1920s. Mark's sand sculptures can also be seen at **Sandworld** (Lodmoor Country Park, DT4 7SX ✆ 07411 387529 ⊘ sandworld.co.uk ⊙ Easter–Oct 10.30–15.30 daily), which he co-founded in 2011.

"The sound of the wind rustling through the reeds is absorbing and it's easy to forget you're just on the edge of town."

Lodmoor Country Park is a 350-acre park to the north of the town centre. It is set up for picnics and barbecues, and contains numerous attractions, such as minigolf, a miniature railway (⊙ Easter-Oct), playgrounds, Weymouth Sea Life Centre and Sandworld. Adjacent to Lodmoor is a Royal Society for the Protection of Birds (RSPB) nature reserve with observation hides and boards detailing the various species that can be seen.

Although relatively small, **Weymouth Sea Life Centre** (Lodmoor Country Park, DT4 7SX ✆ 01305 671070 ⊘ visitsealife.com ⊙ 10.00–17.00 daily) is one of the town's best-known attractions. As well as the displays of colourful fish you may expect, there are seals, sharks, otters, rays, fairy penguins and rescued green sea turtles. Many of the creatures were rescued and cannot be released, or were bred at the park as part of its conservation work. You might like to plan your visit around particular feeding times or keeper talks (details on the website), and to take along swimwear and towels for the water rides. Admission is costly but various vouchers (available in local tourism magazines) offer reduced rates and booking ahead online is cheaper.

Continuing north along the seafront you come to **Bowleaze Cove**. The beach here tends to be slightly quieter than the beach in the centre of town, although in summer there is a funfair and across the road is a very large caravan park. Heading eastwards from Bowleaze Cove there is wonderful walking along an unspoilt stretch of the South West Coast Path. A very pleasant but hilly walk takes you through Osmington Mills and past Durdle Door to Lulworth Cove.

Radipole Lake

Returning towards the town centre and heading away from the esplanade along King Street you will come to the Swannery car park, where an open-air **market** is held on Thursdays between Easter and autumn. This is also where you will find the visitor centre for the **Radipole Lake RSPB Reserve** (℘ 01305 778313 ◈ rspb.org.uk), a peaceful pocket of nature in the middle of town. The lake – which flows into Weymouth Harbour – and the surrounding wetland with its dense reed beds are home to an impressive line-up of bird species, including rare bitterns, Cetti's warblers, bearded tits and marsh harriers. You don't need to be a knowledgeable ornithologist to enjoy the reserve – the visitor centre (◷ 09.30–17.00 daily, till 16.00 in winter) and handy display boards make it accessible to everyone. The sound of the wind rustling through the reeds is absorbing and it's easy to forget you're just on the edge of town. Children can be entertained with specially created trails, bird events, and during the summer, family activities such as pond dipping and bug hunts, while paths make the reserve accessible to wheelchairs and pushchairs.

Around Weymouth Harbour

More low-key than the seafront, **Weymouth Harbour** is a pleasant place to wander, divided into two distinct halves by the River Wey, as it was when it was two communities prior to 1571. On the old Melcombe Regis (north) side is **Custom House Quay**, where the buildings that were once at Weymouth's commercial shipping heart now stand at the centre of an area dominated by restaurants and shops. Being an old mariners' haunt, there is no shortage of historic pubs along this stretch. From here you can watch the fishing and pleasure boats on the harbour and explore the narrow streets that lead back into the town centre. Many of the buildings lining the water are painted in cheerful colours, making this one of the most photogenic parts of town. **Custom House** is a fine brick building, as is the George Inn, which towers over its neighbours. The **Royal Dorset Yacht Club** (11 Custom House Quay, DT4 8BG ℘ 01305

786258 ☞ royal-dorset.com) occupies a chapel-like building, which was once an institute for seamen, known as the Sailor's Bethel.

The squat stone building at the end of Maiden Street is the original **Fish Market**, built in 1855, and appropriately still sells fish. It is worth taking a short walk along Maiden Street for a closer look at the stone building on the corner of St Edmund Street. I wouldn't ordinarily suggest people take a closer look at a **public convenience**; however this one has a cannonball lodged in the wall above the first-floor window, believed to have been fired during the Civil War.

In summer, you can cross to Nothe Gardens on the other side of the harbour using a rowing-boat ferry from the ferry terminal. Alternatively, you can take the **Town Bridge**, a bridge that lifts every two hours during the day to allow tall ships to pass through. The bridge is reputed to be in the same place as the wooden one constructed in 1597 after Melcombe Regis and Weymouth were united.

Holy Trinity Church, erected in the 1830s, is one of the first buildings you are likely to see if you come across the bridge and it gives its name to Trinity Road, which runs alongside the harbour. This side of the harbour has more residential buildings than the other, giving it a homely, village-like feel. Set back from the harbour is **Tudor House** (3 Trinity St, DT4 8TW ☎ 01305 779711 ☞ weymouthcivicsociety. org ☉ May–Oct 10.30–16.00), one of Weymouth's few remaining Tudor buildings. It is decorated and furnished in the style of a 17th-century middle-class home and guided tours provide an insight into domestic life at that time.

"In summer, you can cross to Nothe Gardens on the other side of the harbour using a rowing-boat ferry from the ferry terminal."

Nearby Hope Square is dominated by **Brewers Quay**, the converted buildings of the Devenish Brewery. At the time of writing Brewers Quay was being redeveloped and is set to provide residential properties, as well as a new site for the Weymouth Museum. Continuing along the peninsula, Nothe Gardens offer a peaceful retreat from the town, plenty of parking and views of the harbour. It is here that you will find **Nothe Fort**, part of Weymouth's 19th-century defences, now a museum (see opposite).

Continuing towards Portland, **Sandsfoot Castle** (☞ sandsfootcastle. org.uk; free admission) sits across Portland Harbour from Portland Castle (page 244). The two were built by Henry VIII to protect against

French and Spanish invasion after his divorce from Catherine of Aragon and his break with the Catholic Church. Unlike Portland Castle, Sandsfoot is a ruin, largely because the cliff on which it sits has been progressively eroded by the sea, although the construction of the Portland Breakwater in 1849 helped to slow the erosion. The ruin sits precariously on a clifftop and in recent years stabilisation work has been carried out and attractive gardens laid down on the approach to it. It is fenced off because it is unstable. The castle and gardens are peaceful with views of the harbour, and the small café makes a good pit stop on the Rodwell Trail (page 230).

Nothe Fort

Barrack Rd, DT4 8UF ✐ 01305 766626 ⊘ nothefort.org.uk ⊙ Mar–Oct daily, & at specified times during the rest of the year – see website

At the end of a promontory on the south side of the entrance to Weymouth Harbour, Nothe Fort was built between 1860 and 1872 by the Royal Engineers with the help of inmates from Portland Prison. It was part of England's coastal defences and remained in active service until 1956. It is one of the best-preserved forts of its kind.

Today, it is an absorbing museum, displayed over three levels, charting its own history and Weymouth's, with particularly detailed information on the town's role in World War II. The Fort Artillery in their splendid Victorian artillery uniforms put on displays of musketry and cannon firing on alternate Sundays throughout the year and during special events.

The fort is still worth visiting on a rainy day as much of it is under cover. In better weather, however, you can take in the views of the harbour from the picnic areas on the ramparts. The fort is wheelchair accessible and has a good café.

Lorton Meadows Nature Reserve

Lorton Ln, Upwey DT3 5QH ✐ 01305 816546 ⊘ dorsetwildlifetrust.org.uk

On the northern edge of Weymouth, this is a Dorset Wildlife Trust reserve of 462 acres of unimproved grassland, woodland and wetland with views over Portland and Weymouth Harbour. Don't be put off by the uninspiring approach – it is quite different when you arrive. The grassland attracts a variety of bird and butterfly species, including marbled white, common and holly blues, and small and large skipper. A series of marked trails take you around the reserve, and there is a pleasant picnic area. The DWT website also has suggested walking routes. Events are held in the conservation centre at the site – see website for details.

Bennetts Water Gardens

Putton Ln, Chickerell DT3 4AF ✆ 01305 785150 ⬦ bennettswatergardens.com ☺ Apr–Sep 10.00–16.00 Sun–Thu

A series of ponds in gardens of eight acres holds over 140 cultivars of water lilies. The centrepiece is a Monet-style bridge above a pond of yellow and pink water lilies. The garden was created in 1957 from a former clay pit by the Bennett family, who still run it today. It is tranquil and beautiful, with impressive mature trees providing the backdrop to the lilies. There is a good café overlooking the ponds. Dogs are not allowed.

Boating, fishing & diving around Weymouth

For information on sailing, watersports and angling, see ⬦ weareweymouth.co.uk

From Weymouth you can take boat trips of varying durations, including along the Jurassic Coast.

With superb sailing waters, and having hosted the 2012 Olympic sailing, it is unsurprising that there are numerous sailing schools in the area. If you want to try your hand at **performance yachting**,

"It is tranquil and beautiful, with impressive mature trees providing the backdrop to the lilies."

Weymouth Sailing (✆ 07970 122718 ⬦ weymouthsailing.co.uk) offers groups of up to eight people the opportunity to have a go on a state-of-the-art yacht. Sailing is either around Weymouth and Portland or along the Jurassic Coast to Swanage. The Andrew Simpson Sailing Centre (WPNSA, Osprey Quay, Portland DT5 1SA ✆ 01305 457400 ⬦ aswc.co.uk), a not-for-profit that encourages young people to sail, offers **sailing and powerboat courses**, as well as kayaking, windsurfing and stand-up paddle boarding. Details of charter boats can be found at ⬦ deepsea.co.uk. Sirius Charters (✆ 07767 305073 ⬦ siriuscharters.co.uk) offers day charters of a motor boat for up to five passengers.

Weymouth and Portland are also popular for other **watersports**, including windsurfing, canoeing and diving. A permit is required for waterskiing in specially designated areas of Weymouth Harbour, available from the Harbour Master's Office (13 Customs House Quay, DT4 8BG ✆ 01305 838423). Underwater Explorers (Unit 1, Maritime Business Centre, Portland DT5 1FD ✆ 01305 824555 🖮 underwaterexplorers.co.uk) is one of Dorset's largest dive schools. C-Waves Diving (✆ 07973 209034 🖮 c-wavesdiving.com) also offers diving around Weymouth and Portland.

The best source of information on **fishing** is Weymouth Angling Centre (✆ 01305 777771 🖮 weymouthangling.com). Weymouth has one of the largest charter angling fleets in Britain, with turbot, brill, bass, plaice, pollack, cod and ray fishing available. The following offer deep-sea fishing charters:

Amarisa Weymouth Cosens Quay Car Park, DT4 8AQ ✆ 07976 520607 🖮 amarisaweymouth.co.uk.
Atlanta 59 Abbotsbury Rd, DT4 0AQ ✆ 01305 839899 🖮 atlantafishing.co.uk.

🍴 FOOD & DRINK

Weymouth Harbour and the seafront are overflowing with eateries. Cheap and cheerful cafés and fish and chip shops dominate but there is the odd upmarket restaurant too.

Blagdon Fruit Farm Coldharbour, Chickerell DT3 4BG ✆ 07557 337679. Pick-your-own farm growing lots of fruit and vegetables, as well as a lovely tea room serving excellent cream teas.
Crab House Café Ferry Man's Way, Portland Rd, Wyke Regis DT4 9YU ✆ 01305 788867. Located at the Weymouth end of Ferry Bridge (to Portland), this unassuming little shack has earned an enormous reputation for excellent seafood. It is run by father and son team, Nigel and Charlie Bloxham. They own oyster beds just in front of the café, so the oysters are as fresh as they get. The views of The Fleet and Chesil Beach are the perfect accompaniment to the seafood dishes. Reservation recommended.
Les Enfants Terribles 19 Custom House Quay, DT4 8BG ✆ 01305 772270. Across the road from the harbour, this upmarket restaurant is run by French chef Eric Tavernier, who specialises in seafood dishes with a French influence.
Lookout Café Bowleaze Cove DT3 6PL ✆ 01305 833459. Casual café with lots of outdoor seating on a hill overlooking Weymouth Bay. Popular with dog walkers. The bubble and squeak with poached egg makes a great brunch.
Oliveto Pier Bandstand, DT4 7RN ✆ 01305 839888. An upmarket Italian in the enviable location of the Weymouth Pier Bandstand. Sea views and beautifully presented food make meals here memorable.

Upwey Wishing Well 161 Church St, DT3 5QE ✆ 01305 814470 ⬦ upweywishingwell. co.uk. A café set in pretty subtropical water gardens. The 'well' is actually a natural spring, the source of the River Wey. It has been attracting visitors since the 18th century; local legend holds that the water has healing properties, particularly for eye problems. George III apparently enjoyed visiting and the stone seat next to the water is said to have been installed for him. He drank the waters from a special gold cup, which became the original prize for the Ascot Gold Cup horse race. The menu is varied and they do an excellent afternoon tea.

THE ISLE OF PORTLAND

Despite its name, the Isle of Portland is a peninsula connected to the mainland by Chesil Beach and the A354, which runs along it. A place of maritime history and quarrying, Portland is a term familiar to many, either via the BBC's shipping forecast or linked to its most famous product, Portland stone.

As a Royal Manor, Portland has its own court leet and crown court. A popular car sticker has been seen around this part of Dorset, proclaiming 'Keep Portland Weird'. Evidently it has been that way for some time, which is perhaps why it feels like you are entering another country when you arrive here. Reverend John Hutchins (1698–1773), the Dorset historian, wrote:

> **The people are a stout, hardy, industrious race and in general better informed than most labouring people; very healthy, but not long-lived, for, though at 60 many of the men appear strong and robust, they soon drop off and there are no instances of longevity, which may be accounted for from too great a use of spirits.**

By all accounts they were not a friendly bunch: Portlanders used to throw stones at outsiders, whom they called 'kimberlins', to keep them from setting foot on their island. Hutchins commented:

> **The natives are jealous of strangers coming to settle in the Island and... in consequence they marry and intermarry so much among themselves that most of the Islanders are related.**

They reportedly followed a bizarre marriage custom, whereby women did not marry until pregnant, at which point:

> **She tells her mother, the mother tells her father; her father tells his father and he tells his son that it is then the proper time to be married.**

STONE ISLAND

The Isle of Portland has been quarried since the 17th century. In his 1793 paper on Dorset, written for the Board of Agriculture and Internal Improvement, John Claridge wrote:

> As to quarries, the whole island of Portland seems to be one mass of the most beautiful stone, chiefly used in the metropolis and elsewhere for the most superb buildings, and universally admired for its close texture and durability, surpassing any other. The raising of it, is a laborious business, sometimes employing upwards of a hundred men, to break down a large jam of it, afterwards it is divided into blocks and then conveyed in cars by horses to the shore.

Indeed there is plenty of Portland stone to be admired in the 'metropolis' today, including St Paul's Cathedral, the Bank of England and the British Museum. The island still has working quarries; those which are disused have been colonised by plants and wildlife creating mini nature reserves.

The system, perhaps predictably, broke down when 'kimberlins' got the local Portland ladies pregnant and then reneged on the deal to marry them.

Thankfully Portland has come a long way since Hutchins's days, the locals no longer throw stones at outsiders and its rugged curiosity value (rather than beauty) makes it worth a visit. Portland should perhaps be more attractive than it is – after all it is surrounded by the sea, overlooks Chesil Beach and there is no shortage of beautiful stone with which to build. While there are some attractive buildings of Portland stone, the island also has many rows of boxy-looking houses and most of the villages turn their back on the sea.

The whole of Portland is a solid block of limestone, windswept and industrial in feel, owing to its many quarries, extant and defunct. Its long and fascinating history is neatly summarised in the island's museum (page 249); finds from the Culverwell Mesolithic site indicate that it is the oldest known settlement in Britain. The peninsula is easily explored on foot, along the nine-mile coast path. Several of its disused quarries, including Broadcroft, Kingbarrow and Tout (page 245), are now nature reserves, colonised by plants and wildlife.

> *"The whole of Portland is a solid block of limestone, windswept and industrial in feel."*

4 FORTUNESWELL & SURROUNDS

The drive across the causeway, shielded on one side by the vast Chesil Beach, makes a memorably strange approach to Portland. Chesil Beach is so high at this point that it resembles an enormous desert dune and you might half expect to see a camel lolloping over the hill.

The modern complex on your left as you arrive on the Isle of Portland is **Osprey Quay**, home to the **Weymouth and Portland National Sailing Academy** (Osprey Quay, DT5 1SA ✐ 01305 866000 𝄢 wpnsa.org.uk). It occupies the site of the former Royal Navy air station, and breathed new life into the area when it was founded in 1999 as a not-for-profit company to promote sailing at all levels and make the sport more accessible to a wider group of people. The academy has superb facilities and direct access to Weymouth Bay and Portland Harbour, reputed to be some of the best sailing waters in the world.

The road climbs to the top of a hill through Portland's largest residential settlement, known as Fortuneswell. From just in front of the Heights Hotel there are expansive views over Chesil Beach and Portland Harbour. It isn't exactly a beautiful view – the dense mass of housing and modern harbour buildings see to that – but it gives you your bearings. At one end of the Heights Hotel is a **visitor information centre**, where you can pick up brochures and maps. On Tuesdays in summer you may encounter the Portland **market** (🕑 09.00–16.00), in the New Ground Car Park behind the hotel. Also nearby, on the island's highest point, **Verne Citadel** was built between 1848 and 1869 as a fort and became a prison in 1949. In 2014 it was turned into an immigration removal centre, but reverted again to a prison in 2018.

Portland Castle

Liberty Rd, Castletown DT5 1AZ ✐ 01305 820539 🕑 daily most of the year, weekends only in winter, parts are closed at times for private events; English Heritage

It may not be huge but Portland Castle is one of English Heritage's best-preserved Tudor monuments, and is absolutely worth a visit. It overlooks the harbour, just beyond the National Sailing Academy and is juxtaposed with a series of ultra-modern buildings. It was built in the 1540s by Henry VIII to protect against French and Spanish invasion after his break from the Catholic Church.

A short, squat building, designed to make it less of a target, it has a rounded wall facing the sea to deflect incoming artillery. If you walk through the hole in the wall from the car park you will come to the water and can appreciate the building's robust exterior. Its surroundings are unexceptional – the modern buildings tower over it – but once you are inside the castle walls it is a different story. The castle is, of course, built of Portland stone, which seems to be tough stuff as it remains in superb shape. I doubt the modern buildings around it will fare as well over the next 550 years.

The other reason Portland Castle is well preserved is that it saw less battle action than Henry VIII had perhaps anticipated. During the Civil War the Parliamentarians and Royalists alternately occupied the castle, and in the 19th century it became a private house. During World War I it was a sea-plane station, and during World War II it was used as a base in preparation for the D-Day landings.

You are free to wander through the castle at your own pace (the audioguides help to bring it to life) and browse a series of exhibits on its history. The rooms overflow with atmosphere, especially the Great Hall, and the enormous fireplaces the size of a modern apartment's kitchen transport you back to the time of Henry VIII. This is a great castle for firing up the imagination of children, who will enjoy the arrow slits, cannons and life-sized model of Henry Tudor. There are also plenty of activities for children, including dressing up in costume and playing Tudor board games. The gardens make a pleasant and peaceful place to sit, and there is a café on site.

5 EASTON, WESTON & SURROUNDS

The unimaginatively named villages of Easton and Weston lie on the plateau in the centre of the island. They are not particularly appealing in their own right but there are a couple of interesting places to visit.

As you travel southwards along Wide Street from Fortuneswell, towards Weston, you will see on your right the turning to **Tout Quarry**

DON'T MENTION THE 'R' WORD!

Whatever you do while on Portland, don't mention the 'R' word. The use of the word is taboo because rabbits have long been associated with bad luck, and instead locals refer to them as 'underground mutton', 'long-eared furry things' or 'bunnies'. The superstition is thought to derive from quarry workers, who would see rabbits rising from their burrows immediately before a rockfall and blamed them for increasing the likelihood of landslides.

(Tradecroft Industrial Estate, DT5 2LN ✆ 01305 826736 ⌂ learningstone. org; free admission). The road takes you into an industrial estate and an abandoned stone quarry that has been turned into a nature reserve and a sculpture park with a difference. You can wander through it on foot and look at the sculptures carved into the rock, and you may see local stonemasons at work. There are spectacular views along the coast from the cliffs at the back of the quarry. Stone-carving courses are available; details are on the website.

A little further south, off Weston Road, is the sizeable and commanding **St George's Church**, which appears almost as if it has been superimposed against the backdrop of a quarry and residential streets. It was consecrated in 1766 and replaced the church of St Andrew above Church Ope Cove, although St George's is now itself redundant. It is under the care of the Churches Conservation Trust and helpful volunteers are on hand to show you

"There are spectacular views along the coast from the cliffs at the back of the quarry."

around. Built from Portland stone, the nave exudes residential rather than ecclesiastical style, but the belfry and steeple are more intricate and are reminiscent of St Paul's Cathedral. The interior is unusual, with the box pews arranged so everyone faces the twin pulpits in the centre of the chancel. The graveyard is packed tightly with over 2,000 sturdy headstones in assorted shapes, with many of the deaths related to seafaring or quarrying. Only one headstone is not made from Portland stone: the black granite headstone marks the grave of William Pearce who was killed by lightning in 1858 on Portland Beach. Some locals theorise that the dark-coloured stone was chosen to symbolise the fact that the lightning turned him black. A leaflet in the church provides details of some of the more interesting graves, including those of the victims of the **Easton Massacre**. When a press gang came to Portland in 1803 to take men to join the military, the locals resisted, believing that they were exempt because they had paid 'quit rent' as a substitute for military service, as was the right of people living in a Royal Manor. In the ensuing struggle with the press gang just near the church, three Portland men and one woman were shot and killed.

◀ **1** Portland Bill Lighthouse. **2** Tout Quarry nature reserve and sculpture park. **3** Church Ope Cove.

South of Easton are two Grade II-listed windmills, which date from at least 1608, although their exact date of construction is unknown. They were used to mill flour until the late 1890s. Today they appear as cylinders, are rather overgrown, and sadly they are frequently vandalised.

6 CHURCH OPE COVE & SURROUNDS

Church Ope Cove is a small pebbly bay on the east side of the island, which can only be reached on foot. Haphazardly dotted around the bay are a mismatched selection of wooden beach huts. You can park opposite Pennsylvania Castle (a large private house) and follow the path down the steep hill, through the ruins of the medieval **church of St Andrew**. Dating from the 12th century, it was abandoned in 1756 and is Portland's earliest surviving building. The path takes you through woodland, then rather eerily through the middle of the plant-covered ruins and between the gravestones. There is an easier path just near the Portland Museum, along Church Ope Road.

That easier path takes you past the remains of Rufus Castle, also known as Bow and Arrow Castle, which sits on top of the cliff above Church Ope Cove. What little there is of the structure is largely shrouded in vegetation. An arched stone bridge spanning Church Ope Road remains and hints at the building's former glory. The castle is believed to have been built by Richard, Duke of York between 1432 and 1460 as a coastal defence against the French during the final stages of the Hundred Years War. It is thought it replaced an earlier castle dating back to the 11th century.

"The path takes you through woodland, then rather eerily through the middle of the plant-covered ruins and between the gravestones."

Not far from Church Ope Cove on the way to Portland Bill is a viewpoint at **Cheyne Weares** with views as far as St Aldhelm's Head near Swanage, and a different perspective on the ruins of Rufus Castle.

HM Portland Prison in the village of The Grove was established in 1848 to provide labour to quarry the island's stone. Artefacts and photographs from the prison's early days make an interesting display at the Portland Museum and at the **Grove Prison Museum** (104 Grove Rd, DT5 1DL ✆ 01305 715726 ⊙ 10.00–14.00 Thu–Sun; free admission). The museum, which is in the former deputy governor's house, is small but crammed with information. It is run by former prison officers who have plenty of interesting insights.

Portland Museum

217 Wakeham, DT5 1HS ✐ 01305 821804 ✍ portlandmuseum.co.uk ☉ Easter–Oct 10.30–16.00 daily

The museum is built around two tiny 17th-century cottages and a small garden above Church Ope Cove. For a little island, Portland has a big history and this museum covers it from Jurassic fossils, through prehistoric inhabitants, to the more recent maritime links, prison and Portland stone. The displays on finds from archaeological digs on the island are fascinating and include information on the important Mesolithic site at Culverwell. There are also some interesting items from the days when the Romans inhabited the island, including a beautiful duck brooch inlaid with blue and cream enamel, and the sarcophagi in the garden of the museum. Other highlights include rare Iron Age ingots, which date from around 500BC, paraphernalia from the island's prison, and a fossilised freshwater turtle unearthed in 2010.

7 PORTLAND BILL & SURROUNDS

Portland Bill is a narrow promontory that forms the most southerly part of the Isle of Portland. Before you reach Portland Bill's lighthouses, you will pass the **Culverwell Mesolithic site**, which provides evidence that Portland has been inhabited for between 8,000 and 8,300 years, making it the oldest known site of permanent residence in Britain. The site was discovered in 1967 and excavated over the course of 30 years. One of the most exciting discoveries was a stone floor from the period, which represents the earliest known use of Portland stone for building purposes. It used to be possible to visit Culverwell but in 2021 the decision was made to close it and backfill the site in order to preserve it. You can learn more about the site and see some of the items uncovered here at the Portland Museum (see above).

"It guides vessels bound for Portland and Weymouth through the strong currents and acts as a marker for ships navigating the English Channel."

Of the three lighthouses on the promontory, one is still operational. The red-and-white striped **Portland Bill Lighthouse** (DT5 2JT ✐ 01305 821050 ✍ trinityhouse.co.uk ☉ varied, check website) was built in 1906 and is 115ft high. It guides vessels bound for Portland and Weymouth through the strong currents and acts as a marker for ships navigating the English Channel. A visitor centre inside the former lighthouse keepers' cottages has information on the lighthouse, its keepers and the Isle of Portland. Tours are informative and you can walk the 153 steps up to the light itself (provided you are at least 3.6ft tall), which gives spectacular views of the Jurassic Coast. Behind the lighthouse is the much photographed and climbed Pulpit Rock, a manmade stack of rock left in the 1870s after a natural arch was cut away by quarrymen. The slab leaning against the main stack is said to represent an open bible.

One of the disused lighthouses, built in 1788, has been transformed into the **Portland Bird Observatory and Field Centre** (The Old Lower Lighthouse, DT5 2JT ✐ 01305 820553 ✆ portlandbirdobs.com), with basic hostel-style accommodation. The other, **Old Higher Lighthouse**, is a private residence but offers guest accommodation in two cottages.

¶¶ FOOD & DRINK

The Heights DT5 2EN ✐ 01305 821361. It doesn't look like much from the outside, and the bistro has a bit of a chain-restaurant feel, but it does have expansive views over Chesil Beach and Weymouth Bay.

Lobster Pot Restaurant Portland Bill DT5 2JT ✐ 01305 820242. The location is the big selling point here – right next to Portland Bill Lighthouse with amazing sea views. Good, simple fare, including lovely cream teas.

EAST OF WEYMOUTH

Leaving Weymouth and heading east you are welcomed back into wild, untouched Dorset landscapes. Inland lies gentle chalk downland, river valleys, farms and scattered villages, while the coast here features austere cliff faces.

8 OSMINGTON & AROUND

Although just four miles from Weymouth, Osmington seems a world away from the bustling town. Its narrow street is lined with thatched cottages and the backdrop of verdant hills leaves you in no doubt that you have re-entered rural Dorset. To the north of the village of Osmington is the **White Horse**, a depiction of George III on horseback, carved into the chalk hillside. It was created in 1808 in honour of the

---

1 Kayaking at Ringstead Bay. **2** Osmington's White Horse. **3** The SWCP dips down to The Smugglers Inn. **4** Jordan Hill Roman Temple. ▶

king, to commemorate the summers he had spent in the Weymouth area. Sadly, due to ill health, the king never returned to see it completed. At 279ft long and 327ft high, the carving is clearly visible from the A353 to the east of Weymouth. A walk from Osmington or the nearby village of Sutton Poyntz allows a closer view.

On the coast is **Osmington Mills**, which has a rugged coastline and spectacular views towards Portland. The South West Coast Path runs along the top of the cliffs here, dipping down to the **Smugglers Inn**, a very popular pub with an inviting garden. It is easy to see why this building, parts of which date from the 13th century, has a long association with smugglers as its location is perfect for bringing contraband ashore – right on the coast at the bottom of a gulley. In the 18th and 19th centuries it was home to one of the area's most notorious smugglers, Emmanuel Charles; a file on the inn's history available at the bar makes interesting reading.

East of Osmington Mills is **Ringstead Bay**. The beach here is popular with local families as a far quieter alternative to Weymouth. There are just a few houses and farms behind the beach, and the cliffs of White Nothe at the eastern end. It is predominantly shingle with some patches of sand and some rock pools at low tide. The water is generally pretty calm, so it is popular with swimmers, including the hardy cold-water lovers who come here in winter to enjoy the serenity. There is a car park close to the beach but it's expensive unless you plan to spend the whole day; the alternative is to park at the top of the hill in the National Trust car park and walk down the steep path to the beach, enjoying the views of the bay on the way.

JURASSIC SAFARIS – 4X4 TOURS

07872 471973 ⊘ jurassicsafari.co.uk

Husband and wife team Gary and Carol Fry offer 4x4 tours of the Bride Valley, exploring beautiful villages and seeking out spectacular views. Both from farming families, Gary and Carol have lived in Dorset all their lives and have devised routes that take you off the beaten track, along country lanes and ancient byways. Gary provides an enthusiastic commentary, using his local knowledge to full effect.

They also offer tours of th eir 52-acre family farm, looking for wildlife and discussing life on a working farm. In 2024 they introduced a vintage tractor-driving experience.

Jordan Hill Roman Temple

DT3 6PL; free admission; English Heritage

On a hill at the back of a residential area between Weymouth and Osmington, off the A353, are the foundations of a 4th-century Romano-Celtic temple. All that remains of the building are the stone foundations in the form of a square. Built during the Roman occupation of the area, the temple would have served the local farming and fishing communities, and would have been visible from the sea.

Excavations of the site located a large cemetery to the north of the temple, where more than 80 skeletons were found, some originally in wooden coffins, others in stone cists. Various personal objects were buried with them, including pots, combs, jewellery, arrowheads and an iron sword; some are now on display in the County Museum in Dorchester (page 129).

¶¶ FOOD & DRINK

Craig's Farm Dairy East Farm, Osmington DT3 6EX ✆ 01305 834591 ⬧ craigsfarmdairy. co.uk. Tea rooms and farm shop on a working dairy farm, where the dairy's own ice cream is sold.

The Smugglers Inn Osmington Mills DT3 6HF ✆ 01305 833125. A perfect stop-off for walkers on the South West Coast Path, this large pub has lots of separate eating areas and a huge beer garden on either side of the stream, and its menu offers plenty of variety. There is a fee for the car park but you can redeem it at the bar for orders over £15. Dogs are welcome. Gets very busy in summer.

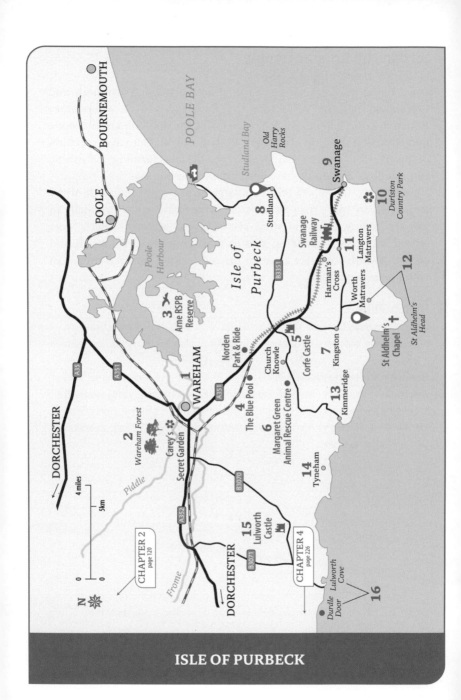

ISLE OF PURBECK

5

ISLE OF PURBECK

One glance at the map tells you that the Isle of Purbeck is not actually an island, but a peninsula of some 60 square miles bordered to the south and east by the English Channel and to the north by Poole Harbour and the River Frome. Nevertheless, I wouldn't be surprised to wake up one morning to the news that residents of the Isle of Purbeck are lobbying for independence from the rest of Britain. And I for one wouldn't blame them. The people who live here will proudly tell you how lucky they are to dwell in this enchanting corner of England. When extolling the virtues of the peninsula, locals may tell you that it inspired some of Enid Blyton's stories and that it has its own microclimate. Both claims are evidently true: Blyton was a regular visitor to the area from 1931 and the Isle of Purbeck does indeed have one of the highest sunshine records in England.

The peninsula is dissected by the **Purbeck Hills**, a chalk ridge that runs westward from the sea near Old Harry Rocks across the Isle of Purbeck to Lulworth Cove, and whose shape hints at the origin of the name 'Purbeck' – supposedly from the Saxon 'pur', meaning bittern or snipe, and beck meaning 'beak'. **Purbeck marble** has been quarried from the Isle of Purbeck's coastal plateau, especially the area between Swanage and **St Aldhelm's Head**, since Roman times and can be seen in many of England's grandest buildings.

In 2020, the Purbeck Heaths National Nature Reserve was established. It brings together land owned by seven different organisations, including the National Trust, RSPB, Dorset Wildlife Trust and Forestry England. In total it covers over 8,000 acres and is the UK's first 'super' reserve. It is primarily lowland wet and dry heath, but also covers areas of grassland, woodland, coastal salt marsh and mudflats. The area includes RSPB Arne, which is a delight to visit.

Wareham, a pleasing ancient market town within Saxon earthen defences, marks the obvious gateway to the Isle of Purbeck and Poole Harbour. In the centre of the peninsula the towering ruins of **Corfe Castle** constitute one of Dorset's most-visited landmarks. **Studland Nature Reserve** provides beautiful sandy, unspoilt beaches and heathland. Nearby **Swanage** is a busy seaside resort with all the associated entertainment. On the town's outskirts is **Durlston Country Park**, which offers unmissable coastal walks.

Off the coast from Studland the chalk stacks known as **Old Harry Rocks** mark the eastern end of the **Jurassic Coast**. The military training area around East Lulworth encompasses the fascinating deserted village of **Tyneham**, which can be visited when the firing ranges are not in use. Nearby are two of Dorset's most photogenic landmarks, **Lulworth Cove** and **Durdle Door**.

You'll chance across plenty of opportunities here for Slow Travel, including a ride through the peninsula on the **Swanage Railway**, and ideal country for **cycling** and **walking**. The South West Coast Path traces the outline of the peninsula and footpaths and bridleways criss-cross the hills. For me, the highlight has to be **horseriding** along Studland Beach as the sun is setting, illuminating the pale faces of Old Harry Rocks.

GETTING THERE & AROUND

The A351 runs along the spine of the peninsula between Wareham and Swanage and minor roads branch off it. Crowds are drawn to Swanage and Studland in summer and the roads can become congested. Leaving the car at Purbeck Park (formerly Norden) to catch the Swanage Railway heritage service to Swanage is therefore a good option.

Information on travelling sustainably in the Purbeck Heaths is available at ⌀ purbeckheaths.org.uk.

PUBLIC TRANSPORT
Three handy entry points to the Isle of Purbeck – **Wareham**, **Wool** and **Bournemouth** – have mainline **train stations** with connections to London. From Wareham you can access the main attractions by **bus**, including Corfe Castle, Swanage and Lulworth Cove. The Purbeck Breezer (⌀ purbeckbreezer.co.uk) provides several useful bus services. Route 50 links Bournemouth and Sandbanks to Studland and Swanage, crossing from Sandbanks to Studland on the **chain ferry** (see opposite); during spring and summer most buses on this route are open-topped.

Route 40 links the peninsula to Poole via Wareham all year round. In summer, the Jurassic Breezer (route 30/31) travels from Swanage to Weymouth via Corfe Castle, Wareham, Lulworth Cove and Durdle Door.

The **Jurassic Coaster X54 bus** (page 176) stops at Wareham and link buses provide access to Corfe Castle and Swanage.

A memorably vintage way to travel is by the **Swanage Railway** (page 286), a heritage train service between Purbeck Park, Corfe Castle, Harman's Cross, Herston and Swanage. Many families heading to the beach opt to leave their car at Purbeck Park and catch the train to Swanage. Another great use of this train is to walk from Swanage to Corfe Castle along the Purbeck Ridge then catch the steam train back.

BY BOAT

A **chain ferry** (⌗ sandbanksferry.co.uk), which takes cars, buses and foot passengers, connects Studland and Sandbanks and has been operating since 1926. An area highlight in itself, it neatly avoids heavy traffic around Poole and Bournemouth. Crossings are every 20 minutes in the daytime, with the first leaving from the Sandbanks side at 07.00 and the last from the Studland side at 23.10. Cars can spend over an hour queuing to get on to the ferry at busy times but foot and bus passengers and cyclists can usually board straight away. From Sandbanks you can hop on another ferry to Brownsea Island (page 324).

You can hardly miss the crowds of **sailing** enthusiasts who teem in the waters around the Isle of Purbeck. An idyllic way to arrive in the peninsula is to sail from Poole Harbour along the River Frome to Wareham Quay; Wareham has a public slipway and there is right of navigation on both the Frome and Piddle rivers. The Environment Agency controls over a hundred moorings on the River Frome; call to check availability (⌗ 01392 352223).

If you don't have your own boat but want to get out on the river, you can **hire small craft** at Wareham Quay or take a cruise from Wareham or Poole Quay (page 258).

Short cruises operate from Swanage to Brownsea Island and Poole, providing magnificent views of the Jurassic Coast, including Old Harry Rocks. Specific **Jurassic Coast cruises** allow you to spend more time taking in the views of the cliffs and pinnacles, which are particularly impressive from sea level as their true size becomes apparent.

⚓ BOAT HIRE

Poole Boat Hire Cobbs Quay Marina, Poole BH15 4EL ☏ 07866 732537 ⌂ pooleboathire. co.uk. Self-drive boat hire from Poole, which gives the opportunity to take a boat up the River Frome to Wareham Quay, or to Arne.

Wareham Boat Hire Abbots Quay, Wareham BH20 4LW ☏ 01929 550688
⌂ warehamboathire.co.uk ◷ Mar–Sep, daily; Oct–Feb, by appointment. Hire canoes, kayaks, stand-up paddle boards, rowing boats and self-drive motorboats, as well as a wheelchair-friendly self-drive motorboat. Also offers kayak and canoe tours on the River Frome, and canoeing lessons.

⚓ CRUISE OPERATORS

City Cruises Swanage Pier, BH19 2AW ☏ 02077 400400 ⌂ citycruises.com. Sightseeing cruises from March to October between Poole Quay and Swanage Pier. The Sea Train Adventure Cruise from Poole to Swanage links up with the Swanage Railway. There is also an evening cruise from Poole Quay to Wareham. The birdwatching cruise, which if you are lucky includes seeing puffins (page 292) close to Swanage, departs from Poole and stops at Swanage Pier before continuing on. Passengers can embark at either place.

Dorset Cruises Parkstone Bay Marina, Turks Ln, Poole BH14 8EW ☏ 01202 844199
⌂ dorsetcruises.co.uk. Cruises and charters on a vintage motor yacht, *Dorset Queen*, originally built in 1938. Destinations include Wareham. Also offers themed trips showcasing local produce.

Greenslade Pleasure Boats Poole Quay, BH15 1HJ ☏ 01202 669955
⌂ greensladepleasureboats.co.uk. Offers cruises of Poole Harbour and from Poole Quay along the River Frome to Wareham.

Marsh's Boats The Stone Quay, Swanage BH19 2LN ☏ 01929 427309 ⌂ marshsboats. co.uk. Cruises along the Jurassic Coast from Swanage, including birdwatching cruises.

CYCLING

The Isle of Purbeck's roads get busy in summer but there are some good off-road options, such as the **Sika Trail** (7 miles) at Wareham Forest (page 267) and the **Rempstone Ride** (12 miles) between Purbeck Park and Studland or Shell Bay.

Bikes can be taken on the chain ferry between Studland and Sandbanks for a small fee, and on the Swanage Railway.

Beryl Bikes (from the nationwide bike-sharing scheme) are available to hire at Studland and on the other side of the chain ferry in the Bournemouth/Poole area. Exact locations are available at ⌂ beryl.cc/ where-you-can-hire. Beryl bays are available in the four National Trust car parks around Studland (Shell Bay, Knoll Beach, Middle Beach and South Beach).

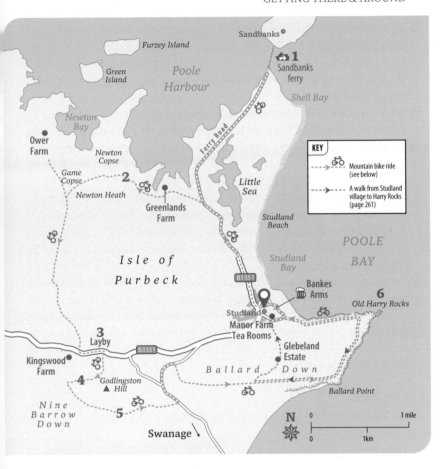

A mountain-bike ride on the Isle of Purbeck

Paul Connor

❋ OS Explorer map OL15; about 15 miles; start: Sandbanks Ferry Terminal; ♀ SZ 0372 8707; moderate

1 Jump the traffic queue at Sandbanks by taking your bike on the chain ferry (⌖ sandbanksferry. co.uk) to the Isle of Purbeck. Breathe in the sea air and the views during the quick crossing before hopping on your bike along a straight stretch of road for two miles. Half a mile after the road curves to the left take a sharp right turn. Don't go through the gate but take the gravel track towards Greenlands Farm. Turn left as you approach the farm (which is to your right) and the track soon bends to the right and fords a stream.

2 Stay on the bridleway through Newton Heath and Newton Copse, towards Game Copse, and you will see views of Newton Bay. After Game Copse the track gradually curves to the left, joining another track (leading away from Ower Farm) before meeting a crossroads. Turn left and follow this track south for one mile then take a short dogleg turn to continue southeast towards Kingswood Farm.

3 Turn left onto the B3351 for a few hundred yards of tarmac riding. Pause at the lay-by on your left for great views across the harbour before turning sharp right up the bridleway. (If you wish to cut the ride short and avoid the steepest hills continue along the B3351 from here to Studland.)

4 The bridleway goes through a gate and up through woodland thick with the smell of wild garlic in spring. The track steepens before emerging on the ridgeway.

5 Turn left, heading east along the top of Nine Barrow Down and soak up the amazing views – small wonder this was chosen as a burial site in Neolithic times. The bridleway soon heads down Godlingston Hill. Be sure your brakes are in good order for this fast and at times bumpy descent. Turn left when you reach the road and after 500yds on the tarmac turn right for the last steep climb, up a bridleway.

6 The ride from Ballard Down to Old Harry Rocks is a joy – a gentle sweeping ride downhill with panoramic views all around and The Needles just off the Isle of Wight in the distance. Pause a while at Old Harry Rocks before following the track to Studland. Where the track joins a lane, turn right. You pass the Bankes Arms, a tempting spot for a break, before turning left onto Rectory Lane, left onto Beach Road and then right (signposted Poole, Bournemouth) to join the road back to the ferry.

CYCLE HIRE

The Bike Shop Swanage 5 Queens Rd, Swanage BH19 2EQ ✆ 01929 423215
⌂ thebikeshopswanage.com.

Cyclexperience Purbeck Park, Corfe Castle BH20 5DW ✆ 01929 481606 ⌂ cyclex.co.uk.
Bikes can be hired from Purbeck Park. If booked in advance, delivery may be possible.

WALKING

The Isle of Purbeck offers the nearest really challenging coastal walking to London; a microcosm with extraordinary variety in a small area – within miles you can be walking through remote-feeling heathland around Agglestone Rock, past prehistoric burial mounds on Nine Barrows Down and up on to Ballard Down for views of Old Harry Rocks and Swanage.

Studland is the starting point of the **South West Coast Path**, which traces the outline of the peninsula and runs all the way to Minehead in Somerset (a total of 630 miles). The **Purbeck Ridge**, which forms the spine of the peninsula, provides far-reaching views of the surrounding countryside and the coastline. **Swanage to Corfe Castle** along the Purbeck Ridge is a classic walk, and if you run out of steam you can switch to another form of steam and catch the Swanage Railway heritage train on the way back. Even a short walk, such as the one to **Old Harry Rocks**, will reward you with an exhilarating panorama of Studland Bay, Poole Harbour and the Jurassic Coast towards Swanage (see below). The walk from Worth Matravers to the clifftop **St Aldhelm's Chapel** has a stunning coastline as well as an air of mystery (page 296). For a short coastal walk you can't beat the stretch between **Lulworth Cove** and **Durdle Door** (page 302). The **Range Walks** through the military firing ranges around Lulworth and **Tyneham** offer some very well-preserved countryside. They are open when the ranges are not in use, which is most weekends of the year; opening times are available at ✂ gov.uk/ government/publications/lulworth-access-times and are signed at the entrance.

A walk from Studland village to Old Harry Rocks

❀ OS Explorer map OL15; start: Bankes Arms ♀ SZ 038824; 3 miles; easy.

Although the beaches at Studland provide a view of Old Harry Rocks, the chalk stacks are much more impressive up close. This can either be done by boat from the sea or by walking out along the chalk ridge towards the cliffs along a section of the South West Coast Path. There is a National Trust car park next to the Bankes Arms, where you can leave your car.

Early morning, in time to see the first rays of sunshine hitting the cliff faces, is a beautiful time of day for this walk. The waters are at their calmest then and the views towards the Isle of Wight at their clearest. After a short descent and climb at the start, it is a mostly level walk along the chalk ridge. There are opportunities for bird- and butterfly- watching on the way, as well as views of Studland Bay and Poole.

You can return the same way or extend the walk by heading up the hill, following the coastline to the summit of Ballard Down. As you approach Ballard Point, the South West Coast Path continues on towards Swanage. To walk back to Studland you need to head through the gate on the right. After the descent past the Glebeland Estate, you arrive at the edge of Studland. **Manor Farm Tea Rooms** (page 281) is a good spot to reward yourself with a cream tea. There are many other longer variants, such as walking through Studland Heath, past the prominent Agglestone Rock, then on a path southwest over the heath before climbing up onto the western end of Ballard Down and following the ridge to the clifftop, for a grand coast-path finale past Old Harry Rocks and back to Studland.

TOURIST INFORMATION

General information 🖱 visit-dorset.com, virtual-swanage.co.uk, visitpurbeckdorset.co.uk
Swanage White House, Shore Rd, BH19 1LB 📞 01929 766018

HORSERIDING

The Isle of Purbeck is blessed with a network of outstanding **bridleways**. Trails through **Wareham Forest** allow horse and rider to explore the heathland and mingle with wildlife (page 267). **Studland Beach and Nature Reserve** are criss-crossed with bridleways and provide a rare opportunity to ride along a sandy beach. A permit from the National Trust is required to ride your own horse on the beach, or you can head out on a ride with Studland Trekking Centre (page 280).

For **hacking** in the Lulworth area, try Lulworth Equestrian Centre (Kennel Farm, Coombe Keynes BH20 5QR 📞 01929 400396 🖱 lulworthequestriancentre.co.uk).

WAREHAM TO SWANAGE & NORTH OF THE A351

The A351 cuts through the centre of the Purbeck peninsula, linking Wareham to **Swanage** and passing through **Corfe Castle** en route. The area north of the A351 is unspoilt, much of it being heathland, and is bordered to the north by the sheltered waters of Poole Harbour. It is here that you will find Arne RSPB Reserve, a wildlife-rich pocket of heathland and old oak woodland (page 268). The Purbeck Ridge stretches to the sea at Handfast Point, near Studland, where the chalk stacks known as **Old Harry Rocks** stand proudly in the water.

An alternative to arriving on the peninsula via the A351 is the **chain ferry** from Sandbanks to Studland (page 257). As you cross from the glamorous, built-up side of the harbour, it is as if you are venturing to another country as the wild heathland and Purbeck Ridge rise up before you.

1 WAREHAM

Although north of the River Frome and so not strictly in the Isle of Purbeck, Wareham is considered the gateway to the area. It is an ancient market town on the watershed of the Frome and Piddle rivers, surrounded on three sides by Saxon earthen defences; its fourth side is protected by the River Frome. Known as the **Town Walls**, these were a Saxon solution to the problem of Viking raids and were likely built in the 9th century as part of Alfred the Great's series of 'burh' (fortified) towns across Wessex. It seems Alfred was on to something, as the walls have lasted extraordinarily well, despite being tinkered with over the years. They were variously beefed up by the Normans, halved in size by Cromwell's troops during the Civil War and heightened on the west side during World War II to protect against tank attacks.

The Town Walls aside, Wareham may not strike you as particularly ancient. That is because much of the town centre was rebuilt in the Georgian style following a ferocious fire in 1762. However, the strict grid pattern of the streets following the points of the compass was laid out in Roman times, and some notable early buildings have survived, including medieval almshouses and one of Dorset's finest Saxon churches.

St Martin's on the Walls

☺ if closed, you can borrow the key during shop hours from A F Joy Outfitters at 35 North St

As you enter Wareham by road from the north, you cross the River Piddle then pass through a gap in the Town Walls and it is at this point that the history of the place resonates. Up on the walls to the left is the church of St Martin's on the Walls. If the church is open, there will be a steward on hand to guide you around. Most visitors to the church come to see the life-sized effigy of Lawrence of Arabia, but the church is enchanting in its own right.

"It seems Alfred was on to something, as the walls have lasted extraordinarily well, despite being tinkered with over the years."

Dating from 1030 and the best-preserved Saxon church in Dorset, it contains fragments of **murals** of various ages. Painted above the chancel is the coat of arms of Queen Anne and the Ten Commandments, dated 1713.

To the left of the altar a remarkable 12th-century mural depicts the **story of St Martin**, who was born to pagan parents in AD316 and joined the Roman army at around 15 years of age. He is shown giving half of his cloak to a naked beggar; as the story goes, he later saw Christ wearing the cloak in a vision and converted to Christianity. One of the reasons for its survival is that the mural was made by fixing crushed stone into plaster, rather than painted. The Portland Stone **effigy of**

Lawrence of Arabia is the work of Eric Kennington and was installed in 1939. The effigy was homeless for some time after its completion. Kennington had designed it as a national memorial for Westminster Abbey but as there was already a Kennington bust of Lawrence in St Paul's crypt it was not accepted. Lawrence's brother bought the effigy, which eventually ended up at St Martin's, an appropriate choice because Lawrence, who lived locally at Clouds Hill (page 160), had contributed to the church's restoration. He had reportedly wanted to be buried here but is instead buried at nearby Moreton (page 156).

Around the Walls & quay

St Martin's Church is a logical point to begin the **Walls Walk**. This well-signed 1½-mile walk leads you around the town atop the grassy Saxon defences. Highlights include passing along Wareham Quay and the views of the River Piddle, the water meadows and, in the distance, Wareham Forest. The walk also takes you through some rather unexciting modern housing estates, providing a rather disappointing backdrop to the romantic Saxon walls. Nowadays, one imagines the only Scandinavian invaders here are of the flat-packed furniture variety.

As you walk around the town, don't get too excited about the signs to Wareham Castle in the southwest quarter of the town. All that remains of the Norman castle is a mound, on which stands a Victorian house.

Wareham was an important port until the 14th century, when Poole, with its much larger harbour, replaced Wareham in that role. The **quay** remains a focal point of the town but it is understated and has in no way suffered from overdevelopment. Here you can **hire a boat** to potter along the River Frome (page 258), either heading inland, where it is quiet and wildlife sightings are likely, or towards Poole Harbour, where you can admire the yachts moored along the river.

If you don't fancy taking to the water, there is a footpath along the riverside.

Wareham Town Museum

East St, in the Town Hall building ✆ 01929 553448 ⌂ greenacre.info/wtm ☺ Apr–Oct 10.00–16.00 Mon–Sat; admission by donation

◀ **1** The Quay at Wareham. **2** Wareham Forest. **3** Carey's Secret Garden. **4** Look for Dartford warblers at RSPB Arne.

This small museum tells the story of the local area and its inhabitants through the ages. It has archaeology, geology and local history but the most detailed exhibit is that on Lawrence of Arabia. The **almshouses** opposite the museum date from 1741.

The venerable Rex

Rex Cinema 14 West St, BH20 4JX ✆ 01929 552778 ⌂ therex.co.uk

Wareham's cinema is something of an institution. It began life in 1889 as the Oddfellows Hall, providing a venue for travelling theatre shows, concerts and banquets, and has operated as a cinema since 1920. In 2009, following a period of uncertainty about its future, the Rex was bought by the Purbeck Film Charitable Trust.

Full of character, the Rex still has its original gas lights and although they are no longer used, as you walk up the stairs you can see the black marks where they used to burn.

Carey's Secret Garden

⌂ careyssecretgarden.co.uk ⊙ 10.00–16.00 Wed–Sat

Close to Wareham, in a secret location, this garden was hidden from the world for decades until just a few years ago. When the current owners, the Constantine family, took possession of the estate in 2019 they had no idea that a wonderful walled garden was hiding in woodland under around 40 years' worth of brambles and ivy. They were exploring their new home when they came across a padlocked gate in a brick wall virtually hidden by vegetation. They began uncovering and restoring the garden, which is surrounded by a tall 150-year-old brick wall on three sides.

"This garden was hidden from the world for decades until just a few years ago."

As you walk from the car park along the gravel track to the garden, you walk through forest which, surprisingly, contains heavily graffitied remnants of the Berlin Wall, bought from a salvage yard. The wooded location seems unusually remote for a walled garden and at 3½ acres it's large. The open side of the garden faces water meadows, allowing cold air to flow out.

At the centre of the garden is a copper sculpture by local artist Ted Edley. From there a formal garden radiates out with rosebeds featuring prominently. Beyond the formal area lie a vegetable garden, permaculture areas, a small orchard and a wildflower garden. A stumpery of old tree stumps and willow arches creates a natural play area. A former potato store has been turned into a small shop/café, where tasty treats from the excellent Salt Pig (see below) in Wareham are served.

In 2022 a pair of ospreys raised two chicks close to the garden, becoming the first breeding ospreys in southern England for over 200 years. Osprey tours are now available and led by a guide from Birds of Poole Harbour ($\mathcal{O}$ birdsofpooleharbour.co.uk).

Visits must be booked in advance, at which point you will be sent directions. Between April and September, the head gardeners provide free guided tours on a Friday at 11.00. There are regular workshops and events – see website.

¶¶ FOOD & DRINK

There is a small farmers' market at the Town Hall on the second and fourth Thursday of the month from 09.00 to 13.00, and a small weekly produce market at the United Reform Church on Church Street on Thursdays. A larger, general market operates on Saturdays at the quay from 08.00, with plenty of food stalls.

Old Granary The Quay, BH20 4LP $\mathcal{O}$ 01929 552010. A Hall & Woodhouse pub-restaurant within an attractive former granary overlooking the River Frome. The deck is a great spot to sit and watch the river traffic.

Orchard Café West Holme Farm, BH20 6AQ $\mathcal{O}$ 01929 554716 $\mathcal{O}$ holmeforgardens.co.uk. On the B3070 Lulworth road is this garden centre with a farm shop and café run by the team from Salt Pig (see below). Local produce features in both the shop and the café.

The Priory Church Green, BH20 4ND $\mathcal{O}$ 01929 551666. Fine-dining restaurant overlooking the beautiful hotel gardens, which run down to the River Frome. The French chef takes his inspiration from French and international cuisine.

Salt Pig 6 North St, BH20 4AF $\mathcal{O}$ 01929 550673 $\mathcal{O}$ thesaltpig.co.uk. An urban farm shop selling a tempting selection of Dorset produce, including fresh local fish. The popular café serves good, simple food, such as pies and quiches. Owner, James Warren, previously worked as a shepherd and has a passion for local produce. He accurately describes the food as 'not frilly, not chefy'. It gets busy at lunchtimes, so a good option is to get a take-away and eat it at the quay.

2 WAREHAM FOREST

A large heathy, pinewood expanse north of Wareham, Wareham Forest is dominated by commercial forestry but is varied enough for some pleasant walks and bike rides. Horseriders need a permit from Forestry

England (⟨⊘⟩ forestryengland.uk). The **Sika Trail** runs for seven miles (mostly level) around the forest, and takes its name from the sika deer, which you may well spot along the way. Roe deer are also present, as are Dartford warblers, nightjars and all six native species of reptile (adders, grass snakes, smooth snakes, slow worms, common lizards and sand lizards). You can camp within the forest (⟨⊘⟩ warehamforest.co.uk).

3 ARNE RSPB RESERVE

RSPB Arne, Wareham BH20 5BJ ⟨⊘⟩ 01929 553360 ⟨⊘⟩ rspb.org.uk/arne

Strikingly remote and peaceful, despite its proximity to Poole, Arne is a peninsula jutting out into Poole Harbour east of Wareham. The RSPB reserve, comprising heathland, wetland, mudflats and old oak woodland, provides a habitat for wildlife, including sika deer, all six of the UK's reptile species, and rare birds, such as the Dartford warbler and nightjar.

A very pleasant few hours can be spent wildlife spotting along the trails (guided or unguided) and then relaxing on Shipstal Beach, which is usually delightfully uncrowded.

The visitor centre shows footage from cameras in the nesting boxes around the reserve. There are educational activities and trails for children. Dogs are allowed but must be kept on a lead.

Arne is part of the UK's first 'super' reserve. Created in 2020, the Purbeck Heaths National Nature Reserve (⟨⊘⟩ purbeckheaths.org.uk) links Arne with neighbouring reserves (page 255) creating one vast protected area of over 8,000 acres.

4 THE BLUE POOL NATURE RESERVE & TEAROOMS

BH20 5AR ⟨⊘⟩ 01929 558150 ⟨⊘⟩ bluepooltearooms.co.uk

First opened as a tourist attraction in the 1930s, the pool is a former clay pit on the privately owned Furzebrook Estate between Wareham and Corfe Castle. The fine clay particles in suspension in the water give it its characteristic turquoise-blue colour. Walking through the 30 acres of heath and woodland that surround it, it is hard to imagine this was once an industrial site, as the plants have done such a good job of colonising the area. In recent years a lot has been done to enhance the biodiversity here, including the introduction of wild ponies, mangalica pigs and bees.

ARNE'S GLORIES

Paul Morton, Warden, Arne RSPB Reserve

Come to Arne at any time of the year, and you will be treated to some real wildlife spectacles. In spring all six native British reptiles can be seen emerging from their winter lairs, while our iconic Dartford warblers will be singing their scratchy song from the top of a gorse bush. When summer arrives the reserve explodes with life as hundreds of dragonflies emerge from our heathland ponds, many of them World War II bomb craters. Rare silver-studded blue butterflies carpet the illuminated purple bell heather, hobby can be seen dashing about in their aerial display and magical sunsets are elevated by the sound of churring nightjars.

Autumn is my favourite time because it hosts the osprey. Poole Harbour is a magnet for these majestic 'fish eagles', which can be seen carrying large mullet to favourite eating posts. Migration is also in full swing and birds you wouldn't normally see, such as redstarts, pied flycatchers and wrynecks, can be found. Autumn is also when all manner of fungi appear across the reserve. If you think winter is quiet, then think again. Poole Harbour and Arne host some of the largest winter wader flocks in the UK. We're lucky enough to have the UK's largest winter avocet flock, thousands of brent geese and a multitude of wildfowl.

The original 1935 tea room remains and the fun, art-deco interior is a nod to its heritage. It has been joined by a gift shop.

Dogs are welcome but the water is not safe for swimming, for dogs or for humans.

5 CORFE CASTLE

The hilltop ruins of Corfe Castle are magnificent from every angle (page 271) and for most people are a must-see on a visit to Dorset. Nestled at their base is the village of the same name, built in the local grey limestone, some of which was salvaged from the ruins of the castle. The village thrived between the 12th and 14th centuries thanks to the Purbeck marble quarries. Stone was brought to the village to be worked and they made good use of it – many of the stone houses also have stone roofs.

Aside from the road running through it, the village has a tremendous sense of history commensurate with its position at the foot of the castle. Some curious traditions survive here. On Shrove Tuesday the **annual meeting of the Ancient Order of the Purbeck Marblers and Stonecutters** is held at Corfe Town Hall. Following the meeting, members kick a football three miles from the Town Hall to Ower Quay on Poole Harbour to preserve the right of way along which the quarried stone was transported. The tradition dates from 1695, when the company agreed to pay landowner John Collins a pound of pepper and a football in exchange for the right of way. Today the football is kicked into the sea and has pepper tipped over it, symbolising the peppercorn rent.

Small shops and pubs huddle around the village square, with the castle looming above. At the centre of the square stands the medieval cross and pump. For centuries the square would have come alive for the weekly market, crammed with livestock, fish, fruit and vegetables; families chattering; and the smell of cooking in the air. The **model village** (page 273) gives an idea of what the village would have looked like prior to the Civil War. The **Town Hall** on West Street is reputed to be the smallest in England. It houses a tiny, one-room, walk-through **museum** (admission by donation) in what was once a gaol. The exhibits include a stained-glass window panel from Corfe Castle showing the royal coat of arms and dating from the 1500s. One of the strangest objects on display is the Poole punt and wildfowling gun, a contraption that allowed the hunter to lie flat on a narrow boat fitted with an enormous gun capable of killing 20 to 30 ducks with one shot.

At the base of the castle lies Boar Mill, which operated until 1914 but is now a private home. The building you see today dates from the 18th

THE PURBECK FILM FESTIVAL

Julie Sharman, Administrator, Purbeck Film Festival

🖑 purbeckfilm.com

The Purbeck Film Festival is the largest rural film festival in the UK.

In October each year the festival puts on around a hundred performances at venues throughout Purbeck and at the Lighthouse in Poole. The main cinema is the historic Rex in Wareham (page 266) but films are also shown at local village halls and more unusual venues, such as Bovington Tank Museum. Wherever we can find a 13-amp plug and an enthusiastic local organiser, we can show a film.

The festival was set up to increase tourism outside the main season and to celebrate a hundred years of cinema. The first event was so successful that it continued and a Lottery grant gave the stability that was needed. The Purbeck Film Festival serves an important purpose – bringing the community together and taking film to rural venues.

century but records indicate there has been a mill on this site since at least 1510.

Also in the centre of the village is the **church of St Edward the Martyr**, dedicated to a Saxon king who is said to have been murdered at Corfe Castle in AD978 (page 272). On the east gable of the church is a statue of the martyr. During the Civil War, Cromwell's men occupied, vandalised and stabled their horses in the church. They used the 14th-century Purbeck marble font with its carved octagonal bowl and stem as a horse trough. Thankfully it has now reverted to its original purpose.

There is little room for parking in the village. There is a National Trust visitor centre and car park opposite the castle on the way into the village. From there it is about a ten-minute walk to the village centre and castle. The other option is the Purbeck Park park and ride. It is here that you will find the volunteer-run Purbeck Mineral and Mining Museum (BH20 5DW ✆ 01929 481461 ◈ purbeckminingmuseum. org ◷ see website; admission by donation), which allows visitors to explore part of the old Norden clay works, including a reconstructed narrow-gauge railway.

"Small shops and pubs huddle around the village square, with the castle looming above."

Just south of the village is Corfe Common, Dorset's largest common and a Site of Special Scientific Interest for its wildflowers and insects. There are several Bronze Age round barrows here (burial mounds), which date back around 3,000–4,000 years. It is crisscrossed by holloways, sunken paths created by centuries of use.

Corfe Castle: the castle itself
✆ 01929 481294 ◷ daily; National Trust

Corfe Castle is everything you want a ruined castle to be: built of moody grey stone, towering high on a conical mound and reached across a stone bridge. So it is unsurprising that its image adorns countless calendars, postcards and book covers. It was also reputed to be the inspiration for Kirrin Castle, which featured in Enid Blyton's *The Famous Five* series of children's books. Blyton did spend a lot of time in Purbeck and is known to have visited Corfe Castle for the first time in 1931. Her description of Kirrin Castle in *Five on a Treasure Island* certainly could apply to Corfe as you see it today: 'Broken archways, tumbledown towers, ruined walls – that was all that was left of a once beautiful castle, proud and strong.'

THE MURDER OF EDWARD THE MARTYR

Saxon King Edward, great-grandson of Alfred the Great, was murdered at Corfe Castle in AD978 and the prime suspect was his stepmother. Edward's father, King Edgar, died suddenly in AD975 leaving two sons, Edward by his first marriage and Ethelred by his third. England's ruling nobles chose 13-year-old Edward as king, much to the disgruntlement of Ethelred's mother. She formed an alliance with anti-monastic noblemen who opposed Edward's close relationship with the Church. Since Ethelred was too young to replace Edward as ruler, she would rule as regent until he was ready to take over, so she devised a plan to get Edward out of the way.

Edward, who was hunting in the area, accepted an invitation from his stepmother to visit her at Corfe Castle, unaware of her plans for his demise. According to the 12th-century chronicler, William of Malmesbury, he was still on horseback when she:

> allured him to her with female blandishment and made him lean
> forward, and after saluting him, while he was eagerly drinking from
> the cup which had been presented, the dagger of an attendant pierced
> him through.

Edward fled on his horse but fell. His foot caught in the stirrup and he was dragged through the woods until he died.

He was initially buried at Wareham Priory but following a series of miracles and a growing number of pilgrims his body was moved to Shaftesbury Abbey. The first miracle is said to have occurred the night Edward died, when the blind woman in whose house the body was laid regained her sight. Edward was canonised circa 1008 and became St Edward the Martyr.

The building oozes history and drama and a wander around the ruins cannot help but stimulate the imagination. Just thinking of the characters who have lived and died here, and the momentous events that have taken place here, can induce the odd shiver.

The castle's location is no accident – it guards the only break in the Purbeck Ridge. The Domesday Book records a castle at this site and attributes its construction to William the Conqueror. It was one of the first castles to be built of stone, rather than timber. Later kings, including Henry I, John and Henry III, put their own stamp on the place, modifying and fortifying as they went.

By the 13th century, the castle was being used as a treasure storehouse and prison. High-ranking, wealthy prisoners were held in the keep (the highest tower of the current ruin), but the less privileged died a slow and miserable death in the dungeon under the Butavant Tower. In 1635, ownership of the castle passed to the Bankes family – Sir John Bankes was Charles I's Attorney General.

During the Civil War the castle was courageously held for the king by Lady Mary Bankes, who became known as 'Brave Dame Mary'. She, along with her daughters, servants and a garrison of five men, successfully defended it for three years. Corfe Castle eventually fell victim to betrayal in 1646 when one of her ladyship's own men smuggled in Parliamentarian troops. Later that year the castle was blown up by order of the House of Commons so that it could never again stand as a Royalist stronghold. A combination of undermining and explosives left the previously impregnable fortress in the ruined state in which it remains today. It is astounding that the gatehouse and outer towers have not tumbled down the hills during the intervening years, as their remains seem to be leaning out at impossible angles over the mound's steep slopes.

The views from the castle are magnificent – the higgledy-piggledy village beneath it, the neat fields around it and the pretty village of Kingston (page 274) in the distance.

While it may have been reduced to a skeletal impression of its former self, the castle, clinging tenaciously to the hilltop, maintains an air of majesty and enduring strength.

The Model Village

The Square, BH20 5EZ ⌁ 01929 481234 ⌂ corfecastlemodelvillage.co.uk ⏳ Feb–Oct daily

If you find it hard to imagine what Corfe Castle would have looked like before Cromwell's troops got their hands on it, then you may like to head to the Model Village. It recreates the castle and the village as they would have been before the events of 1646.

Being in the shadow of the real castle, it allows for an intriguing visual comparison of the two. The 1:20 scale model was begun in 1966 and took two years to complete. The detail is extraordinary: the roofs, like those *"The detail is extraordinary: the roofs, like those in the real village, are made of Purbeck stone tiles."* in the real village, are made of Purbeck stone tiles, there is livestock in the fields, a stream running through the village and people sitting in their gardens. There is a wedding taking place at the church and music plays from the church as you walk by.

The model sits in an acre of garden with the Corfe River running along its edge. Benches beside the river invite you to sit and watch the local wildlife. There is plenty to interest children, including giant outdoor games and a fairy garden. There's a café on site where you can enjoy a cup of tea with views of the castle ruins.

¶¶ FOOD & DRINK

Corfe Castle Tearooms The Square, BH20 5EZ ☎ 01929 481294. National Trust tea rooms in an 18th-century building. You can take your tea in the garden, right at the base of the castle.
Greyhound The Square, BH20 5EZ ☎ 01929 480205. This pub sits beneath the castle, and its garden looks up to the ruins. Local produce is used and there are good vegetarian and gluten-free options.
Lentenbury Farm Soldiers Rd, Norden BH20 5DU ⬈ purbeckfood.co.uk. Pick-your-own berries, vegetables and sunflowers during the summer.
Mortons Manor Hotel 45 East St, BH20 5EE ☎ 01929 480988. Fine-dining, 2-AA rosette restaurant within a handsome Elizabethan manor house.

6 MARGARET GREEN ANIMAL RESCUE CENTRE

Church Knowle BH20 5NQ ☎ 01929 480474 ⬈ margaretgreenanimalrescue.org.uk
🕑 11.00–16.00 Thu–Tue; admission by donation

Margaret Green Animal Rescue is a charity with three sanctuaries in Devon and Dorset. They do exemplary work caring for domestic and farm animals in need – cats, rabbits, goats, chickens and ponies among them – finding new homes for them where possible. The sanctuary at Church Knowle is open to the public and visitors have the satisfaction of knowing their donation goes to a very worthy cause.

¶¶ FOOD & DRINK

New Inn Church Knowle BH20 5NQ ☎ 01929 480357. The Estop family has run the New Inn since 1984. Licensee records for the pub date back to 1881 and, amazingly, Estop is only the fourth name on the licence in over 160 years. The team prides itself on serving reasonably priced traditional pub food and seafood. Their Blue Vinny (Dorset blue cheese) soup is legendary.

7 KINGSTON

Two miles south of Corfe Castle lies a less well-known but similarly pretty village built of Purbeck Stone, Kingston. One of the main reasons to come here is to enjoy the beer garden at the Scotts Arms (see opposite), which has superb views of Corfe Castle and allows you to fully appreciate its position plugging a gap in the Purbeck Ridge.

The church of St James was built in 1880 and is surprisingly large and elaborate for the size of the village. It is built from local Purbeck stone; the pink colouring is caused by algae. The church is the starting point for The Commoners Ways walk – a 5½-mile circular walk that takes you via Corfe Common and Corfe Castle. You can download a leaflet on the walk from ∂ dorsetcouncil.gov.uk.

¶¶ FOOD & DRINK

The Scotts Arms West St, BH20 5LH ∂ 01929 480270. The beer garden at this pub must have one of the finest views of any in the country: over unspoilt countryside towards Corfe Castle and the Purbeck Hills. Landlady Nicki is originally from Jamaica, and on weekends in summer Kingston, Dorset takes on the flavours of Kingston, Jamaica when the Jerkshak in the garden serves spicy Caribbean food.

8 STUDLAND
♠ Pig on the Beach

My Australian friends are always teasing me that British beaches are ugly, covered in lumpy pebbles and devoid of sand. Studland is one beach to prove them wrong. A four-mile, sheltered stretch of sand with views of Old Harry Rocks and the Isle of Wight, Studland Beach really is beautiful. The water here is shallow a long way out, so is ideal for families, and there are plenty of watersports available. A large area of protected heathland, woodland and sand dunes behind the beach adds greatly to its appeal and provides for walking, cycling and horseriding.

Although Studland attracts large numbers of visitors each year, it is largely undeveloped because the area is owned and protected by the National Trust. In 1981, landowner Ralph Bankes died and bequeathed his 16,000-acre estate, which included Kingston Lacy, Corfe Castle and

"The water here is shallow a long way out, so is ideal for families, and there are plenty of watersports available."

Studland, to the National Trust. It was one of the largest gifts the trust has ever received. For many years prior to that, the Bankes came down from Kingston Lacy to spend their summers at Studland, based at their impressive beach house, which is now the Pig on the Beach Hotel.

The beach is divided into four areas: South Beach, Middle Beach, Knoll Beach and Shell Bay. South Beach is the smallest and most rugged, and tends to be the quietest. It is reached down a gravel path along a stream and has no facilities aside from Joe's Café (page 281). Next to it is Middle Beach, which has watersports and the Sandy Salt Pig café (page 281). Knoll Beach is the biggest and the most accessible from its large car park. It has a National Trust shop and watersports. At Shell Bay a chain ferry covers the short distance to Sandbanks (page 257). There are wooden beach huts spread along the beaches. Beach-hut hire can be arranged through the National Trust office (✆ 01929 450500).

The beaches at Studland have been popular with **naturists** since the 1920s. Those pioneering naturists were taking a risk greater than just sand in places where sand shouldn't be because in those days exposure was illegal. Naturists can now relax on the right side of the law in a designated zone on **Knoll Beach**. Signs clearly mark the naturist area, including the instruction 'naturists please dress before passing this point'. I've always found this request strangely immaterial because it is not as if there is a giant curtain across the beach shielding the naturists from the view of the 'textiles' (the term naturists use to refer to the clothed masses).

"Behind Knoll Beach is Little Sea Lagoon, which was closed to the sea by the dunes around 1880 and now contains fresh water."

Behind Knoll Beach is **Little Sea Lagoon**, which was closed to the sea by the dunes around 1880 and now contains fresh water, being stream fed. Over 3,000 waterfowl spend the winter in this 79-acre body of water, including tufted ducks, pintails and pochards. Little egrets and teal are present all year round, and bird hides are strategically positioned around the lagoon. It is hard to believe that just a short distance away is Wytch Farm, western Europe's largest onshore oilfield; thankfully, the refinery is well hidden in a pine forest on Wytch Heath.

In 2019, Studland Bay was designated a Marine Conservation Zone. The Seahorse Trust (⌖ theseahorsetrust.org) and its partners are working to restore and protect the bay's seagrass meadows and improve the habitat for species that live here, including spiny seahorses. To minimise the damage from the increasing boat traffic, The Seahorse Trust has installed eco-moorings. These permanent moorings mean that the seagrass is not damaged by the dropping of anchors.

1 Corfe Castle. **2** The village of Corfe. **3** Agglestone Rock stands proud on the heathland at Studland. **4** Knoll Beach, Studland. ▶

RICHARD MURGATROYD

PATRYK KOSMIDER/S

PHILIP HECTOR/S

VISIT DORSET

In summer, when the heather is flowering, **Godlingston Heath** is glorious. The mass of yellow gorse flowers in spring is equally spectacular.

From a mound in the midst of the heathland, **Agglestone Rock** proudly surveys its surroundings. Also known as 'Devil's Nightcap', this 400-ton sandstone rock gets geologists excited. Local legend has it that the devil was sitting on The Needles off the coast of the Isle of Wight and, in a characteristically demonic temper tantrum, threw his cap at the mainland. Its intended target was Corfe Castle but it fell short and landed in its current position. The geologists' explanation for its presence is less colourful – it is a natural rock outcrop made of Agglestone grit, which was left behind when softer layers of rock around it eroded. The reserve around it is a haven for rare wildlife, including Dartford warblers, nightjars and all six British reptile species (adders, grass snakes, smooth snakes, slow worms, common lizards and sand lizards).

Most people bypass Studland village in favour of the beach. The houses are spread over a wide area, although the centre of the village is tiny and consists mostly of Edwardian buildings. Studland village was apparently the inspiration for Toy Town in Enid Blyton's Noddy books. The **church of St Nicholas** dates from the 11th century; it blends Saxon and Norman architecture and is featured in Simon Jenkins's excellent book *England's Thousand Best Churches*. The original building was almost entirely destroyed by the Vikings but was later rebuilt by the Normans. The short, squat tower is the most striking architectural feature; it is thought the foundations could not support a full-sized one. Between Middle Beach and The Pig on the Beach Hotel is the adorable, thatched Groom's Cottage, which houses a second-hand bookshop. The cottage was used by the Bankes's family's groom when the family came down to their summer residence. Within the cottage are information boards explaining its history.

"The reserve around it is a haven for rare wildlife, including Dartford warblers, nightjars and all six British reptile species."

During World War II Studland was used as a training ground for the D-Day landings. A relic from this time is **Fort Henry**, a concrete bunker on top of Redend Point, on the edge of the bay beneath the Pig on the Beach Hotel. It was from here in April 1944 that King George VI, Winston Churchill, General Montgomery and General Eisenhower watched troops training for the landings in an exercise known as

Operation Smash. Sadly, during the exercise the sea became rough and six tanks sank, killing six crew members. You can simply wander in and stand where those leaders stood in 1944 to look out through the slit across the bay. Studland was also identified as a possible site for a German invasion, so concrete defences known as Dragon's Teeth were installed and remain between Middle Beach and Fort Henry. There are also some defensive pillboxes dotted around, including on South Beach.

To the west of Studland is the **Isle of Purbeck Golf Club** (BH19 3AB ℘ 01929 450361 ⌀ purbeckgolf.co.uk), which was once owned by Enid Blyton and her husband. There is a nine-hole course for golfers of all abilities and an 18-hole course for more accomplished players. The courses wind through the heathland and have expansive views over both the nature reserve and the sea.

Old Harry Rocks

Studland, just near South Beach, is the starting point for walks to **Old Harry Rocks**, the stark white chalk stacks that stand in the water just off the cliffs at Handfast Point. Carved by millions of years of erosion by the sea, Old Harry Rocks mark the most easterly point of the Jurassic Coast, which is also the youngest. They are said to take their name from a 15th-century pirate, Harry Paye (page 316), who regularly attacked ships leaving Poole Harbour. Standing at Handfast Point on a clear day you can see a similar chalk formation off the coast of the Isle of Wight, called **The Needles**. They serve as a physical reminder that the Isle of Wight was once joined to the mainland at

"Carved by millions of years of erosion by the sea, Old Harry Rocks mark the most easterly point of the Jurassic Coast, which is also the youngest."

this point by a chalk seam, of which both Old Harry Rocks and The Needles were part. A further reminder is visible at **Redend Point**, at the northern end of Studland's South Beach. This small headland of brown, reddish and yellow sandstone bears a striking resemblance to the multicoloured sand cliffs at Alum Bay on the Isle of Wight.

Horseriding at Studland

A National Trust permit is required to ride your own horse on the beach at Studland and the relevant forms can be downloaded from the National Trust website (⌀ nationaltrust.org.uk). It is advisable to contact the National Trust's local office ($\mathcal{J}$ 01929 450500) to discuss availability before applying. A limited number of daily and annual permits are issued per year and you will need to allow a few days for processing.

If you don't have access to your own horse, never fear because **Studland Trekking Centre** (see below) has a yard full of horses and ponies to suit all abilities. If you have always dreamt of riding on the beach, this is a great opportunity to do so.

RIDING STABLES

Studland Trekking Centre Ferry Rd, BH19 3AQ $\mathcal{J}$ 01929 450273 $\mathcal{O}$ studlandstables.com. For riders of all abilities. Clifftop rides with superb views, heathland rides, forest rides, beach rides (Oct–Jun) and rides through the dunes of Knoll Beach (Oct–Jun). If you prefer to bring your own horse, the centre can provide DIY livery. There is no accommodation for owners on site but you can stay nearby.

Watersports around Studland

The waters off Studland offer some great opportunities for the watersports enthusiast, from boat cruises along the coast to windsurfing and waterskiing.

WATERSPORTS & ACTIVITIES PROVIDERS

Fore Adventure Middle Beach, BH19 3AP $\mathcal{J}$ 01929 761515 $\mathcal{O}$ foreadventure.co.uk. Activities include kayaking, snorkelling, coasteering, foraging, rock climbing and bushcraft.
Shell Bay Sailing Ferry Rd, BH19 3BA $\mathcal{J}$ 01258 880512, 07853 986345 $\mathcal{O}$ shellbaysailing. co.uk $\odot$ Apr–Sep daily. A small sailing school with dinghy hire and courses for adults and children. Sailing is in the south of the harbour, between Brownsea Island and the Studland peninsula.
Studland Watersports Knoll Beach, Ferry Rd, BH19 3AQ $\mathcal{J}$ 07980 559143 $\mathcal{O}$ studlandwatersports.co.uk. Offers waterskiing, sailing, windsurfing, paddleboarding and kayaking.

SPECIAL STAYS

Pig on the Beach Manor Rd, BH19 3AU $\mathcal{J}$ 0845 0779494 $\mathcal{O}$ thepighotel.com. This characterful, higgledy-piggledy manor house was once the summer residence of the Bankes family. Today it is one of the Pig group of hotels and offers 28 luxurious guest rooms full of thoughtful touches. Key to the Pig philosophy are sustainability, the relationship between the hotel garden and the kitchen, and the use of local produce. It is worth popping into the carefully tended walled garden – the produce grown here is the star of the excellent restaurant. The large lawn in front of the hotel has views of the sea and Old Harry Rocks, and shepherds' huts in the grounds are used for spa treatments. Antique and upcycled furniture complement the building and creates a homely feel, and there are several snug areas and a cosy bar to retreat to. The rooms have everything you would expect from an upmarket hotel. Room 16 is particularly spacious and has a large bathroom with a clawfoot bath with a view of Old Harry Rocks – the extra space means it's the best option for families. For couples, Room 14 is a romantic option with expansive sea views. The closest rooms to the sea are the shepherds' huts – each room consists of two huts, one with the bedroom and bathroom and the other with a cosy snug and terrace.

The hotel restaurant is in an orangerie and the shabby-chic tables with mismatched chairs have lovely views over the gardens to Studland Bay. Uncomplicated seasonal dishes are prepared using ingredients from the kitchen garden, or from within a 25-mile radius. An extensive wine menu means you can find just the right pairing for your food. Any meal here feels like a special occasion and that is partly due to the excellent service. There is a wood-fired pizza oven in the garden for more casual dining, and a cosy bar.

🍴 FOOD & DRINK

Bankes Arms Manor Rd, BH19 3AU ✆ 01929 450225. Traditional pub atmosphere and food in a 16th-century local-stone building a short walk from South Beach. Across the road is a large beer garden with water views. This is also the home of the Isle of Purbeck Brewery. Perfectly placed for the start or finish of a walk out to Old Harry Rocks.

Joe's Café South Beach, BH19 3AU ✆ 07931 325243. A modest café in a priceless location on South Beach. Serves the usual beach-kiosk fare, like sandwiches, burgers and ice cream, but endeavours to provide as much fresh, homemade and local food as possible. Packaging is recyclable. It has a selection of buckets and spades available to borrow if yours has been forgotten.

Manor Farm Tea Rooms Church Rd, BH19 3AT ✆ 07947 554955. Delightful tea rooms in converted farm buildings. Light lunches, cakes and cream teas at reasonable prices.

Pig on the Beach See opposite.

The Sandy Salt Pig Middle Beach Car Park, BH19 3AP. Part of the local Salt Pig brand founded by former shepherd, James Warren. Offers top-quality, simple food (like pies, sausage rolls and cakes) made from local ingredients and eaten on outdoor tables overlooking Middle Beach.

Shell Bay Seafood Restaurant Ferry Rd, BH19 3BA ✆ 01929 450363 ⌂ shellbay.net. This restaurant is in a fantastic location, right on the water overlooking Brownsea Island and Poole Harbour, 250yds from the Sandbanks ferry. The menu features some creative seafood dishes and a few options for non-seafood eaters. The restaurant sometimes has to close in bad weather and gets very busy in good weather, so it's worth booking ahead.

9 SWANAGE

If you have spent some time enjoying the slow pace of rural Dorset you may need to be prepared for a change of gear because Swanage's atmosphere of seaside-holiday jollity can come as a bit of a shock. Swanage is a typical British seaside town, complete with amusement arcades and beach crowds. Take some time to get to know Swanage, however, and the deeper aspects of its personality emerge.

With this in mind, I took time to wander the town's out-of-the-way places, as well as the seafront, and found that there is much to like about Swanage. For a start, there is a lovely sandy **beach**, which is where the British seaside town bit comes in. It has everything you would expect – deckchairs, beach huts, a Punch and Judy show and tacky souvenir shops. It is a wide sweeping bay, with chalk cliffs at the northern end leading out to Old Harry Rocks, and on a clear day you can see the Isle of Wight from the beach.

In summer it gets very busy on the beach in the main part of town, but there are usually spare patches of sand at the northern end.

At the southern end of the beach is the typically ornate **Victorian pier**, which was constructed in 1896 for shipping stone from local quarries. Horses were used to pull carts of stone along the narrow-gauge tramway which ran along the seafront and on to the pier. In 1994, the Swanage Pier Trust took control of the structure, which was by then in a sorry state, organised extensive repairs and has since managed to keep it open. Today, you can walk out along the pier for a small charge, which goes towards its upkeep.

Above the pier, **Prince Albert Gardens**, a hillside park, makes a very pleasant spot for a picnic overlooking the bay. Within the gardens is the Swanage Ampitheatre, where open-air performances are held with the bay providing a splendid backdrop. Immediately behind the gardens are the Swanage Downs, which offer clifftop walks and a break from the

SWANAGE CARNIVAL & REGATTA

Swanage comes into its own at the end of July/early August each year, when it holds the annual Swanage Carnival and Regatta (⊘ swanagecarnival.com). The week's events include various sporting competitions (including a half marathon, swimming and sailing), a carnival procession, sand-sculpture competition and spectacular fireworks on the main beach. Swanage is even busier than usual during carnival week, so be prepared.

crowds on the seafront. Walking across the downs takes you to the most southerly point of Swanage Bay, Peveril Point, from where you can walk along the South West Coast Path to Durlston Country Park (page 287).

Peveril Point is the location of the **Swanage Lifeboat Station** (𝒮 01929 423237 𝒶 rnli.org), opened in 1875 at the request of local residents. Consisting of a boathouse and slipway, it is open to visitors from April to October (see website for timings, usually noon–16.00 daily). As you head northwards along the seafront from the pier, you pass the **Mowlem Theatre** (𝒮 01929 422239 𝒶 themowlem.com), a venue for theatre and film since 1967. It is by no means a handsome building but has become one of the town's landmarks, and the upstairs bar has views of the bay.

"Take some time to get to know Swanage, however, and the deeper aspects of its personality emerge."

Before it was a seaside resort, Swanage was a quarrying and fishing town. Stone and building contractor John Mowlem (1788–1868) and his nephew George Burt (1816–94) were highly influential in the town's development – so much so that George Burt is referred to as 'the king of Swanage', a nickname supposedly bestowed by Thomas Hardy.

The town owes its most interesting architectural features to Mowlem and Burt, who scavenged them from London when they delivered their stone there. The elaborate façade of **Swanage Town Hall** once adorned the Mercers' Hall in London and looks rather out of place in Swanage High Street. It dates from 1670 and was brought to Swanage in 1883. The **Wellington Clock Tower** at **Peveril Point** came from the old London Bridge. The clock tower was erected at one end of London Bridge in 1854, but apparently caused traffic chaos so was removed and brought to Swanage in 1863. **Purbeck House** (now a hotel) in the High Street, which has obvious castle aspirations, was the house George Burt built for himself using marble chippings from the Albert Memorial. The house also includes a bollard from Millbank Prison, an archway from Hyde Park Corner and floor tiles from the Palace of Westminster.

Behind Swanage Town Hall is a small stone **lock-up** inscribed 'Erected for the Prevention of Vice and Immorality by Friends of Religion and Good Order – 1803'. It used to stand in the St Mary's churchyard and was considered a necessary measure for dealing with the town's rowdy

revellers. It looks to me as if it would have served as an extremely powerful deterrent. **St Mary's Church** is near to the pretty, spring-fed millpond. Apart from the 14th-century tower, the church is largely 19th and 20th century.

The High Street is lined with tempting shops and places to eat, such as the **Mulberry Tree Gallery** (57 High St), selling local and locally themed art and ceramics. The **Tilly Mead** area on Commercial Road is a complex of small, independent shops, including local handmade chocolate company **Chococo**. It is a pleasant area to wander and, if you need to buy a gift for the cat-sitter, dog-sitter or house-sitter, you are likely to find one here.

Swanage Museum and Heritage Centre (The Square, BH19 2LJ ✐ 01929 421427 ☉ Easter–Oct daily; free admission) is housed in the old market building on the seafront. It shows an informative film on the Isle of Purbeck and displays depict the local shops as they may have looked in the early 1900s.

Water-based activities around Swanage

For those who tire of lying on the beach and wandering the shops, there are plenty of water-based activities. If you fancy fishing, the **Swanage Angling Centre** (✐ 01929 424989) at the pier end of the High Street can arrange bait, tackle and a skipper. You can fish from the pier but you will need to pay the fee for accessing the pier and a small additional rod fee. Durlston Bay and Durlston Head are also popular fishing spots for bass, mullet, wrasse and conger eels.

If you bring your own boat to Swanage you can launch it from the slipway next to the lifeboat station. The waters around Swanage, in particular beneath the pier and the local shipwrecks, are popular with divers.

BOAT TRIPS, WATERSPORTS & FISHING

City Cruises Poole Quay BH15 1BQ ✐ 0207 7400400 ⥀ cityexperiences.com. Many options, including a cruise from Swanage to Poole and back. The birdwatching cruises depart from

---

◄ **1** Old Harry Rocks viewed looking towards Poole. **2** Exploring Studland on horseback.
3 Kayaking allows you to get up close to Harry Rocks. **4** The Swanage Steam Railway.
5 The world's last sea-going paddle steamer sometimes calls at Swanage Pier. **6** The annual carnival in Swanage is a riot of colour.

Poole and Swanage, and offer the chance to see the large guillemot colony at Durlston Country Park (see opposite) and puffins (page 292).

Ocean Bay Waterports North Beach, Ulwell Rd, BH19 1LH ℘ 07721 938949. Offers jet-ski, pedalo and kayak hire, as well as deckchair and beach-hut hire.

Paddle Steamer Waverley ⌁ waverleyexcursions.co.uk. Waverley, the world's last seagoing paddle steamer, departs from various ports around the UK. In previous years its itinerary has included departures from Swanage Pier. Check the website for timetables.

Swanage Sea Fishing Pier Approach, BH19 2AP ℘ 07939 649007 ⌁ swanageseafishing. co.uk. Fishing trips in fully equipped boats catering for all levels of experience. Also offers sightseeing and wildlife cruises.

DIVE OPERATORS

Divers Down The Pier, BH19 2AR ℘ 01929 423565 (Apr–Oct) ⌁ diversdownswanage. co.uk. Established in 1958, this is reputed to be the oldest dive school in England.

Swanage Boat Charters Larks Rise, 279b High St, BH19 2NH ℘ 01929 427064 ⌁ kyarra. com. Caters for novice to experienced divers, visiting wrecks, reef, scenic and drift-dive sites.

The Swanage Railway

Station House, BH19 1HB ℘ 01929 425800 ⌁ swanagerailway.co.uk

You don't need to be a train buff to be charmed by the lovingly restored steam and diesel trains of the Swanage Railway. The railway operates over almost six miles between Swanage and Norden, which is just northwest of Corfe Castle and four miles from Wareham. Trains first ran to Swanage in 1885 and continued until 1972, when the line closed. The painstaking restoration, reopening and maintenance of the railway is the work of the Swanage Railway Trust.

"You don't need to be a train buff to be charmed by the lovingly restored steam and diesel trains of the Swanage Railway."

Every summer thousands of families use the railway to travel to and from the beach, parking at Purbeck Park (Norden) and taking the train to Swanage via Corfe Castle, Harman's Cross and Herston. The train travels at no more than 25mph and provides views of Corfe Castle and the surrounding countryside. The railway stations and staff uniforms are those of a bygone age

Around 450 volunteers keep the railway functioning, and they do a fantastic job. The railway holds special events throughout the year (see website). One favourite is the Christmas special, when families clamber aboard and eagerly await Father Christmas.

¶¶ FOOD & DRINK

Swanage has a good selection of places to eat, and plenty of casual fish bars. A market is held every Friday in the main beach car park on Victoria Avenue (BH19 1AN). The Isle of Purbeck produces some wonderful food, such as Robert Field honey and the ubiquitous Purbeck Ice Cream. These and other local delicacies are available from the **Purbeck Deli** (26 Institute Rd, BH19 1BX ✐ 01929 422344) from where you can pick up a selection and head to Prince Albert Gardens or Durlston Country Park for a picnic.

The Cabin The Beach, BH19 1LW ✐ 07342 322162. Café right on the beach under The Grand Hotel. It may not look like much but it does simple, fresh food very well, including famously good crab sandwiches.

Chococo Central Commercial Rd, BH19 1DF ✐ 01929 408288 ⊘ chococo.co.uk. Chococo makes delicious handmade chocolates from quality ingredients. The business started here in 2002; production has moved to a bigger unit elsewhere and this is now a small chocolate shop and café. Also on offer are excellent homemade cakes, sandwiches and, of course, superb hot chocolate. It is worth the short walk from the beach just to sample one of their hot chocolates.

Gee Whites 1 High St, BH19 2LN ✐ 01929 425720. Popular open-air fish bar and ice-cream parlour near Swanage pier. The place for lunch on a sunny day.

Java Independent Café Commercial Rd, BH19 1DF ✐ 07464 873427. The fun, quirky décor is the first thing you notice – an eclectic mix of vintage items. Has a reputation for excellent coffee, vegan options and homemade cakes.

Love Cake 42 High St, BH19 2NX ✐ 01929 475664. Not just excellent cake, but light lunches too. Lovely, welcoming atmosphere.

The Salt Pig Too 7A Station Rd, BH19 1AB ✐ 01929 423616. The Swanage outpost of the well-known Salt Pig in Wareham. Takes provenance seriously, only using meat from the Isle of Purbeck and fish from the surrounding waters. Delicious salads and pies.

10 DURLSTON COUNTRY PARK & NATIONAL NATURE RESERVE

Lighthouse Rd, Swanage BH19 2JL ✐ 01929 424443 ⊘ durlston.co.uk; free admission, paid parking

Within a few hundred yards of the hilly, southern fringes of Swanage, Durlston Country Park has 320 acres of countryside with meadows and coastline ideal for walking, wildlife watching and picnics. The logical starting point is the **visitor centre** within Durlston Castle, another of George Burt's legacies and more of a seaside villa than a castle. The centre has displays on the area's natural history; you can watch Durlston's nationally important guillemot colony via a live video feed and listen to sounds from the seabed picked up by an underwater microphone. There is a café with sea views, which is handy for post-walk refreshments. The website provides details of ranger-led guided walks and events run throughout the summer.

Durlston is rare among England's national nature reserves because of the diverse habitats and geology it contains: sea cliffs, coastal limestone downland, haymeadows, hedgerows and woodland. It has been owned by Dorset County Council since the 1970s and at one point narrowly escaped being turned into a housing estate. And thank goodness for that, because it really is a very special place.

The walk along Durlston's cliffs in the direction of Anvil Point is one of my favourite family walks. The path is gravel (and pushchair and wheelchair friendly) most of the way to Anvil Point but then it turns to a rough and steep track to reach the lighthouse. If you want to turn around at that point it is still a satisfying stroll and you can see the lighthouse from a distance. Starting from the visitor centre, the first point of interest on the walk is the **Great Globe**, a handcrafted Portland limestone representation of the world. It is set into an alcove carved in the solid rock and decorated with interesting facts and inspirational quotations. Burt had it created to attract people to the area and at 10ft in diameter it is one of the largest stone spheres in the world. From the globe the gravel path, bordered by a low wall of local stone, hugs the cliff. As you walk, look out to sea for **bottle-nosed dolphins**; Durlston is reputed to be one of the best places in Britain for spotting them. The coastal path passes **Tilly Whim Caves**, former limestone quarries. Originally excavated during the Napoleonic Wars, they were used up until the early 20th century. The extracted stone was winched down the cliffs to barges waiting below, then taken to Swanage.

"It is not far from here that Dorset's resident puffins have made their home on a rock ledge."

Durlston has the second largest **guillemot colony** on the south coast with some 400 individuals. It is not far from here that Dorset's resident **puffins** have made their home on a rock ledge. The best way to view these seabirds and their clifftop homes is on a birdwatching cruise (page 292).

From Durlston it is a six-mile round walk to Dancing Ledge (page 291) along some spectacular, undeveloped coastline.

BEYOND SWANAGE TO LULWORTH COVE

Some of the most exciting **walking** in southern England can be found on this stretch of coast, with its demanding hilly cliff paths and intriguing military ranges inland.

The area between Swanage and St Aldhelm's Head is known for its Purbeck stone quarries and the coast here has an irrepressible bleakness. **Lulworth Cove** and **Durdle Door** are, justifiably, both tourist magnets and very busy in the summer months. Large tranches of the countryside around East Lulworth are within the army ranges, including the fascinating deserted village of **Tyneham**, empty since its compulsory evacuation in 1943. Although the warning signs look forbidding, military occupation has preserved the landscape in time, making for some hugely rewarding walks within the ranges (the Range Walks), obviously only open when the firing ranges are not in use (most weekends and at certain times during school holidays).

11 LANGTON MATRAVERS

The area around Langton Matravers and Worth Matravers has long been the heart of Purbeck's quarrying industry. These two appealing villages are a living illustration of the uses of Purbeck stone, being constructed largely of that material. The fields surrounding them are separated by stone walls.

There are around a dozen different types of Purbeck stone but by far the best known is **Purbeck marble**. Just as the Isle of Purbeck isn't really an island, Purbeck marble isn't really a marble, but a hard limestone made up of river mud and packed with the shells of millions of freshwater snails that lived in the great river that once flowed through the south of the peninsula. It takes its name from the fact that it can be polished. Purbeck marble is usually blue-grey but can have a green or reddish tint. It has been quarried from this area since Roman times, when it was the material of choice for tombstones. Widely used in the Middle Ages, Purbeck marble can still be seen in churches, abbeys and cathedrals throughout England, as fonts, altar

"These two appealing villages are a living illustration of the uses of Purbeck stone, being constructed largely of that material."

tables, flooring and columns. Some of its most notable appearances are in Durham Cathedral, Westminster Abbey, and Salisbury Cathedral.

In a former coach house in Langton Matravers, the tiny **Purbeck Stone Museum** (St George Close, BH19 3HZ ✆ 01929 423168 ✦ langtonia.org ☉ Apr–Sep 10.00–noon & 14.00–16.00 Mon–Sat) tells the story of the local geology, stone and quarries. Following World War II, three local men (Jim Bradford, John Dean and Reg Saville) began separate collections of items relating to the history and geology of the area. Their combined collections now form the bulk of the exhibits in the museum, which also has a reconstruction of a section of an underground quarry. Reg Saville explained to me that the museum was created in response to local demand when, in 1960, the tradition of underground quarry mines (begun in the late 17th century) was stopped by order of the Privy Council for reasons of safety. The local community was eager to ensure that the hardships of the past should not be forgotten.

"The local community was eager to ensure that the hardships of the past should not be forgotten."

If you are inspired to unleash your creativity on a slab of Purbeck stone, **Burngate Stone Carving Centre** (Kingston Rd, Langton Matravers BH19 3BE ✆ 01929 439405 ✦ burngatestonecentre.co.uk) offers stone-carving courses from beginner to advanced. A have-a-go course takes just two hours. Details of the courses are on the website; book in advance.

Also in Langton Matravers is **Salt Pig the Farm (Putlake)** (✆ 01929 422917 ✦ thesaltpig.co.uk). As well as farm animals, there is an indoor play area.

South of Langton Matravers is Spyway (an area owned by the National Trust), which is the the best starting point for walks to see fossilised dinosaur footprints at Keates Quarry and the cliffs of Dancing Ledge. To reach the dinosaur footprints, park at the National Trust car park (BH19 3HG) then follow the gravel path south towards the sea, turning right onto the Priests' Way. This three-mile walking route connecting Swanage, Langton Matravers and Worth Matravers, was once used by medieval priests to travel between their churches. After about three quarters of a mile the dinosaur footprints are signposted on the right, beyond the turning for Acton. You'll pass working quarries on the way. The path is gravel almost the whole way

– only the last bit is across a field – so it is possible to do most of the walk with an off-road pushchair or wheelchair.

The fossilised footprints were discovered by quarrymen in 1997 when the quarry was still being worked. More than a hundred dinosaur tracks dating from 145 million years ago are preserved in a flat layer of rock. It is likely they were left by giant sauropods, such as brachiosaurus; long-necked herbivores that could weigh as much as 50 tonnes. The sheer number of footprints has led experts to conclude there was probably a watering hole here. The footprints they left in the soft mud were covered by layers of rock and preserved. At the time they roamed here Purbeck would have been covered with subtropical forests and swamps. It is mind blowing to be able to walk in the footsteps of these giants and to imagine Purbeck during the Jurassic period. My dinosaur-mad five-year-old thought it was simply amazing.

Walking back to the path from the footprints, you have wonderful views of the fields divided by Purbeck stone walls and the sea beyond. You can walk back the way you came or continue along Priest's Way to Worth Matravers.

DANCING LEDGE

When you walk to the dinosaur footprints, you pass a turning on Priest's Way signed 'Dancing Ledge'. You can walk to Dancing Ledge from Durlston Country Park (page 287), but the easiest route is from Spyway. The route takes you through a rich grassland habitat, where in spring and summer you will be greeted by orchids and butterflies, perhaps including the rare Adonis blue and Lulworth skipper which are known to frequent the area. As you near the cliffs, look out for guillemots, puffins, shags, razorbills and peregrine falcons.

At Dancing Ledge is a former cliff quarry and a natural, flat sea ledge that is very popular with experienced climbers (page 292). Care must be taken here – to reach the sea ledge it is a steep scramble down and back up again, and it is certainly not safe when the sea is rough. On the lowest ledge is a pool, blasted into the rock in the early 20th century at the request of Tom Pellat, the eccentric headmaster of the former Durnford Preparatory School in Langton Matravers (now Langton House). He asked local quarrymen to create the pool so that his schoolboys had somewhere to swim. One of those boys was Ian Fleming, author of the James Bond novels. It is still possible to swim in the pool at low tide.

THE PURBECK PUFFINS

'Puffins? Are you sure? In Dorset?' This is the response I usually get when I tell people my family and I spotted puffins near Swanage. But I can assure you we did, much to our delight.

Puffins are one of the world's favourite birds. Their colourful beaks, comical manner and apparent kindness towards each other combine to make this a bird everyone would like to see at least once in their lifetime. The possibility of spotting puffins was forefront in our minds as my family and I boarded the City Cruises birdwatching boat in Poole one sunny June evening.

We headed out through the second largest natural harbour in the world, gazing at the vast, glass-fronted waterside mansions on one side and, in stark contrast, magical, unspoilt Brownsea Island on the other. We passed through the narrow stretch of water we'd crossed so many times before on the Sandbanks chain ferry and headed out to open water. I was slightly apprehensive as we passed the naturist beach at Studland, but I suspect that by evening they had retreated. Besides, our attention was fixed on Old Harry Rocks, which looked magnificent, glowing in the soft evening light. It seemed so much larger viewed from water level than from the land.

We moored briefly at Swanage Pier to pick up more passengers, including guides from Durlston Country Park, who provided helpful commentary on the birdlife and

Adding to the interest of this place are sea caves (most now sealed off for safety) and ammonites fossilised within the ledge. It is thought the name Dancing Ledge comes from the way the ledge appears to dance when the water washes over it at certain stages of the tide.

The name Spyway harks back to the days of smuggling along the coast here. Once quarrying at Dancing Ledge ceased, the caves around it were perfect for hiding contraband, and the easy landing point made this a natural route for transporting goods from the sea and up over the hill. Smugglers could hide contraband (and themselves) in the network of quarry caves and tunnels.

ADVENTURE SPORTS AT DANCING LEDGE

Dancing Ledge is popular for climbing and coasteering. There are various providers who can organise these activities, including the below.

Cumulus Outdoors Cobbler's Ln, Swanage, BH19 2PX ✆ 01929 422480
🖰 cumulusoutdoors.com
Jurassic Watersports ✆ 01202 985196 🖰 jurassicwatersports.co.uk

geology of the Isle of Purbeck. My nature-loving, dinosaur-mad five-year-old, Archie, peppered our guide with questions, and it was clear he knew his stuff. We spotted a peregrine falcon perched at the top of a cliff. Archie was delighted – as the fastest member of the animal kingdom, it has long been on his list of 'cool' species. The boat paused opposite the Durlston guillemot colony, which, with some 400 individuals is the second largest on the south coast. They were crammed onto ledges at various heights in the cliff, jostling for the most desirable spot in their noisy, high-rise residence. We also spotted kittiwakes, shags and razorbills. But secretly we were holding out for the puffins…We reached the instantly recognisable Dancing Ledge (page 291) and marvelled at the daredevil climbers who were spending their Friday evening dangling from the cliff. Then finally, we glimpsed the puffins. They seemed just as kind and comical in real life, snuggling up gently to their mates on their rocky ledge. The Purbeck puffins come in from the sea to the same spot only for around three months each year and it's a very small colony, making any sighting particularly special. Thankfully, the guides know exactly where to look.

The City Cruises (⌀ cityexperiences.com) birdwatching trip departs every Friday from May to July at 18.00 from Poole Quay and picks up passengers at 19.00 from Swanage Pier. The cruise lasts four hours to/from Poole and two hours to/from Swanage.

Land & Wave Unit 14 Jaden Centre, Victoria Av, Swanage, BH19 1EJ ✎ 01929 423031 ⌀ landandwave.co.uk

12 WORTH MATRAVERS & ST ALDHELM'S HEAD

From Langton Matravers fields lined with grey stone walls lead you to **Worth Matravers**, the last settlement before the coast. The village is more beautiful than Langton Matravers, with stone cottages huddled around a duck pond that was formerly part of Worth Manor Farm. Not far from the duck pond is the well-known and highly idiosyncratic **Square and Compass pub** (page 298). The Newman family has held the licence here since 1907 and current licensee, Charlie Newman III, represents the fourth generation. Charlie is passionate about palaeontology and attached to the pub is a small museum. In 2017, a newly discovered extinct species of rat-like creature was named *Durlstotherim newmani*, in honour of Charlie. Palaeontologists from the University of Plymouth identified the small nocturnal mammal from a handful of fossilised teeth collected from early Cretaceous rock near Swanage. They concluded the creature lived around 145 million years ago, which makes it the earliest

HELEN HOTSON/S

THE ETCHES COLLECTION

ALEXANDRA RICHARDS

ALEXANDRA RICHARDS

COLLINS UNLIMITED/S

mammal in a line that eventually leads to humans. Charlie had helped collect the samples and opened his pub to the team, who in turned named the creature after him.

Behind the pub, Charlie has created 'Woodhenge', a version of Stonehenge created from tree trunks. He built it in 2016 just before the summer solstice. Initially the council asked for it to be dismantled as it contravened planning rules, but support from residents and tourists meant it was granted a reprieve and allowed to stay.

Charlie told me that his mother's family has lived in the village since 1660. Sadly, long-term residents like Charlie's family have become a rare breed in this village, where over 60% of the houses are now holiday homes.

In the graveyard of the **church of St Nicholas** is the tombstone of Benjamin Jesty, who in 1774 became the first person to inoculate against smallpox when he administered a low dose of the milder cowpox to his family. As a farmer, he (like many other country folk) had seen that milkmaids who contracted cowpox through their contact with cattle were protected from smallpox. At the time he was living in Yetminster and he was hounded by his neighbours who thought his inoculation of his family disgusting. They left and moved to Worth Matravers. Jesty did not publicise his work and the credit for developing a smallpox vaccine went to Dr Edward Jenner in 1796, some 20 years later. Jesty's groundbreaking move is yet another in Dorset's long list of bizarre claims to fame.

"The chapel has a mystical quality, perched on the cliff and often shrouded in sea mist."

St Aldhelm's Head & Chapel

Worth Matravers is the starting point for walks to St Aldhelm's Head, for sweeping views of the coast and a visit to the clifftop **St Aldhelm's Chapel**, dedicated to the first bishop of Sherborne, St Aldhelm. The chapel has a mystical quality, perched on the cliff and often shrouded in sea mist. The square, squat shape is very unusual for an ecclesiastical building, which is one of the reasons why many people believe its original purpose was not as a place of worship. As experts point out,

◀ **1** Kimmeridge Bay. **2** St Aldhelm's Chapel. **3** Look for puffins from the water around the Isle of Purbeck. **4** Exhibits at The Etches Collection Museum of Jurassic Marine Life. **5** Walk in the footprints of dinosaurs at Spyway.

A walk to St Aldhelm's Head & Chapel

OS Explorer OL15 or Landranger 195; start: Renscombe Farm SY964774; approximately 3½ miles; difficult (some steep hills).

From the car park at Renscombe Farm, west of Worth Matravers, it is around one mile to St Aldhelm's Head. Next to the map displayed in the car park is a pedestrian gate. Head through the gate and diagonally across the field in the direction of **Chapman's Pool**. When you reach the coast (after about a quarter of a mile) you will be looking down (from around 400ft) over Chapman's Pool, a brilliantly clear bay with a jumble of fishing huts on one side. Low rumblings from the Lulworth army range can often be heard echoing around the hills.

Turn left and head along the **clifftop path**, bordered by a drystone wall. The farmland here runs almost to the edge of the cliffs, and it seems not an inch of land is wasted. You may well encounter some very contented cows along the way, as I did.

You will come to a memorial to members of the Royal Marines killed between 1945 and 1990 that includes stone benches and a table, where you are invited to sit and take in the scene.

The cliffs are steep and dramatic here and care needs to be taken. You will come to a long set of steps that run down and up a deep 'v' between hills. The part heading up the hill is extremely steep and has no handrail – if you don't like heights you probably won't enjoy this section.

there is no tradition of ecclesiastical buildings being square in England and the corners point to the cardinal points of the compass, which is unheard of in a medieval sacred building.

Although little is known about the chapel's origins, it is possible that it was built as a lookout for Corfe Castle. The first known mention of it was during the reign of King Henry III (1216–72), when it was referred to as a chapel served by a chaplain. The mounds around the chapel suggest it is on the site of a pre-Conquest Christian enclosure and that it probably rests on an earlier timber building. The vaulting is 12th century and there are medieval graves outside. By the 17th-century the chapel was falling into disrepair and appears to have gone out of use; however, the initials and dates from that period carved into the stonework indicate that it was still visited. The central column was evidently used as a wishing pillar, mostly by young ladies who would drop a pin into it

At the top of the hill you will see white coastguards' cottages built in 1834 and the tiny St Aldhelm's Chapel.

To head back to the car park without retracing your steps, take the track that runs between the chapel and the line of coastguards' cottages. When the track divides, bear left. You will pass a small working quarry en route to the car park.

You can extend the walk to five miles by carrying on along the coast from the chapel for another mile and then turning inland up **Winspit Bottom**, a steep-sided dry valley with its slopes etched in outstanding medieval terracing known as lynchets. At the road at Worth Matravers, turn left to Renscombe Farm.

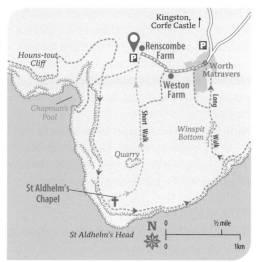

through a hole and typically wish for a suitable husband. The building was restored in the 19th century and church services were held again from 1874. In 2005, a new altar made of stone from St Aldhelm's Quarry was installed. Today services are held on special occasions, and you can get married here.

A local legend has evolved to explain the chapel's presence: when in 1140 a bride and groom were sailing around the headland watched by the bride's father, their boat capsized and they were drowned; the father is said to have built the chapel in their memory.

Near the chapel are a modern coastguard station and a **memorial to the radar research station** at Worth Matravers. The station's work in developing radar between 1940 and 1942 was crucial to turning the tide of World War II and was critical to the development of modern telecommunications.

⊞ FOOD & DRINK

Square and Compass Worth Matravers BH19 3LF ☎ 01929 439229. A delightfully quirky pub run by Charlie, the fourth generation of the Newman family to hold the licence here. Charlie is a keen amateur palaeontologist (page 293) and archaeologist. A small museum within the pub contains fossils found by Charlie and his father. Some of Charlie's archaeological finds are also displayed. The pub is lacking something that would be considered essential in most pubs – a bar – but customers are served through a small hatch in the wall. Food is limited to homemade pasties and pies, which you can wash down with the pub's homemade cider. The pub is popular with walkers and locals and has regular live music.

Worth Matravers Tea & Supper Room Weston Rd, Worth Matravers BH19 3LQ ☎ 01929 439368. It has the feel of a traditional tea room but serves far more than you'd expect, including excellent lunches. Charming atmosphere with vintage crockery and a pretty garden. Reservations recommended for weekend meals.

13 KIMMERIDGE

The small village of Kimmeridge lies about a mile from the bay of the same name and consists of a clutch of stone and thatched cottages in the midst of some fine farmland. The bay is part of a privately owned estate and you pay a toll to drive on the road from the village to the bay, where there is plenty of parking.

Kimmeridge Bay lies within the **Purbeck Marine Wildlife Reserve**, one of the first underwater reserves in the country. It is wide and sheltered, backed by dark shale cliffs and with calm waters for swimming: the shallow waters mean this is fine rock-pooling country. The **Fine Foundation Wild Seas Centre** (BH20 5PF ☎ 01929 481004 ⊘ dorsetwildlifetrust.org.uk/kimmeridge ☉ Apr–Oct 10.30–17.00 Tue–Sun), run by the Dorset Wildlife Trust, has displays on the local marine life and organises events for children.

Archaeological evidence indicates that Iron Age residents of the area manufactured and exported jewellery, such as rings and bangles, made from Kimmeridge shale on rudimentary lathes.

The oil field at Kimmeridge is part of BP's Wytch Farm operation; its 'nodding donkey' has been pumping continuously since 1961, making it the UK's oldest working oil pump.

On top of the cliff to the east of Kimmeridge is **Clavell Tower**, its soft pink-and-cream colouring and its Tuscan colonnade combining to give it a certain wedding-cake quality. It was built as a folly in

1830–31 by Reverend John Richards, who took the name Clavell when he inherited the Smedmore Estate. The three-storey tower fell into disrepair and due to coastal erosion ended up perilously close to falling into the sea. Between 2006 and 2008 the Landmark Trust dismantled the tower, repositioned it 82ft further back from the cliff and restored it. Since completion it has been available to rent as luxury holiday accommodation.

Seen from the road to the east of the village is **Smedmore House** (BH20 5PG ✆ 01929 480719 ⌂ smedmorehouse.com), an impressive country home constructed of Portland stone and set in the midst of an 18,000-acre estate. It is available for short-term rental and is also used as a wedding venue.

The Etches Collection Museum of Jurassic Marine Life

BH20 5PE ✆ 01929 270000 ⌂ theetchescollection.org ⏱ 10.00–17.00 daily

Local man, Steve Etches, found his first fossil when he was just five years old. That find ignited a lifelong passion. Steve spent years collecting fossils in the Kimmeridge area and in 2016 he opened this museum to display some of his collection.

The museum is modern and at one end of the main gallery is Steve's workshop, where he can often be seen preparing fossils. The focus is marine dinosaurs, and there are some impressive large ichthyosaur and plesiosaur fossils, as well as rare pterosaur (flying reptile) fossils. In 2024 a new star was added to the gallery – the skull of a pliosaur that Steve and his team had painstakingly extracted from a nearby cliff. The skull was high up in the cliff, meaning they had to abseil down to work on it. Their mission to extract the massive predator's skull was the subject of the BBC documentary *Attenborough and the Giant Sea Monster*. The team spent ten months cleaning and preparing the fossil for display, and it looks magnificent.

⅋⅋ FOOD & DRINK

Clavell's Restaurant BH20 5PE ✆ 01929 480701. This charming cottage is part of the 2,000 acres farmed by the Hole family. Much of the produce is grown on the farm and the fish is local too. There are options to suit most tastes, including a vegan menu; the ploughman's is tasty, complete with homemade scotch egg. The restaurant welcomes dogs, who even get their own menu. Look out for evening events held here during the summer.

14 TYNEHAM

Ministry of Defence Ranges, East Lulworth BH20 5QF ♿ tynehamvillage.org ☺ Tyneham village & the footpaths through the surrounding firing ranges (the Range Walks) are open to the public on certain weekends, when not being used by the army (check ♿ gov.uk/government/publications/lulworth-access-times); free admission, donation for parking

In November 1943, 106 households in this area, including all the houses in Tyneham, received notice from Winston Churchill's war cabinet that they had one month to leave their homes as the area was to be used as an army-training facility. It was meant to be a temporary arrangement but in 1948 the village was compulsorily purchased by the British Army and the villagers were never to return. Most of its buildings are now ruined, although the schoolhouse and church are preserved as museums showing what life was like in the village prior to the evacuation. The Tyneham Valley has escaped any form of development and is essentially frozen in time. It has become a haven for wildlife living among the ruined buildings.

A visit to Tyneham is a fascinating and moving experience, showing how the villagers lived and how their lives were thrown into disarray by World War II. Each of the ruined dwellings contains a board with a description and photographs of the family who lived there. The **schoolhouse**, built in 1856, is as it would have been when the villagers left, right down to the children's names on the coat hooks. Being such a small community, the school catered for children aged four to 14 in the same classroom: a school photo from 1928 and children's school work bring the history to life.

When the villagers left they pinned a note to the door of the church:

> **Please treat the church and houses with care; we have given up our homes where many of us have lived for generations to help win the war to keep men free. We will return one day and thank you for treating the village kindly.**

The **church** contains the names and photographs of local inhabitants at the time of the evacuation. In the gallery is the restored Bible that was last used in the church and a list of the parishioners. There is also a touching memorial to an Elizabeth Tennant, who died in 1769 and was a servant to the lady of the manor house: 'servant to Mrs Bond of Tyneham in which station she continued 34 years. To the memory of her prudence, honesty and industry this monument is erected'.

The history is what draws people here, but it is a beautiful setting regardless of the history. The village is nestled in a narrow valley between two ridges of the Purbeck Hills, with a pretty stream running through it. In spring the area is carpeted with wild garlic and daffodils.

On the other side of the car park from the main part of the village is an abandoned farm, in which is displayed vintage agricultural machinery and used ordnance. From there it is a ¾-mile walk to the stunning **Worbarrow Bay**. On a sunny day the water here can be so clear and blue, offset against the crisp white of the cliffs, that it could almost be the Mediterranean. As the shingle bay can only be accessed on foot, it tends to be quieter than other beaches in the area. It is a hilly four-mile walk along the coast from the bay to Lulworth Cove.

"The village is nestled in a narrow valley between two ridges of the Purbeck Hills, with a pretty stream running through it."

Both Tyneham and Worbarrow make excellent picnic spots if you come prepared. In summer there is a mobile café at Tyneham, operated by the company behind the Salt Pig in Wareham (page 267).

Above Tyneham, **Whiteways Viewpoint** provides far-reaching views towards Poole and Studland. From here it is a short drive to East Lulworth; the 'tank crossing' signs you pass en route are a reminder of this area's primary use.

15 LULWORTH CASTLE

East Lulworth BH20 5QS ✆ 01929 400352 ⬦ lulworth.com ⊙ Mar–Dec 10.30–17.00 Sun–Thu (check website as it closes for weddings); English Heritage

Square with round towers in each corner, this pleasingly symmetrical building was built in 1608 as a hunting lodge in the form of a stylised castle. The property was bought by Humphrey Weld in 1641 and has remained in the family, at the centre of a 12,000-acre estate, ever since. The castle was gutted by fire in 1929 and lay exposed to the elements for 70 years. What you see today is the result of extensive restoration work completed in 1998. Nevertheless, the castle is really just a shell and the only recognisable rooms inside are a cellar and kitchen.

The burnt-out upper floors have not been replaced, creating a cavernous space inside. Visitors who are happy to brave the steep staircase can climb the **tower** to take in spectacular 360° views of the surrounding countryside from the roof. Within the castle are information boards and displays of memorabilia that give you an idea of what the castle would have been like in its heyday. It certainly played host to its fair share of royalty over the years, including King Charles II who came here in 1665 to escape London during the Great Plague.

It is worth mentioning that you can visit the grounds, woodland, playground and picnic areas without paying the admission for the castle. You just need to pay for parking. We like to finish our visits here with a cup of tea in the gardens, looking back up at the castle. And it is also worth going to the loo just to admire the impressive basement!

"The rest of the church was rebuilt in 1864 in line with plans drawn up by Thomas Hardy when he was a young architect."

The **chapel of St Mary** (1786) in the grounds was the first free-standing Roman Catholic church built in England after the Reformation. George III approved the building on condition that it did not look like a chapel. He is reputed to have said, 'build a mausoleum and you may furnish it inside as you wish'. It looks more like a Georgian house than a chapel from the outside but the inside is more ecclesiastical, with a large, painted dome.

Also in the grounds is the charming St Andrew's Church, whose 15th-century tower predates the castle. The rest of the church was rebuilt in 1864 in line with plans drawn up by Thomas Hardy when he was a young architect.

The Weld family built themselves a new house in 1977, Lulworth Castle House, which adjoins the grounds of the original castle.

16 LULWORTH COVE & DURDLE DOOR

The Lulworth Estate covers some 20 square miles and includes Lulworth Cove and Durdle Door, two of the most spectacular and best-known features of the Jurassic Coast World Heritage Site. Lulworth Cove is scallop-shell shape (almost a full circle) sculpted by the sea, which broke through a fault in the limestone beds at the mouth of the cove and ate away at the soft clay inland. Durdle Door, an impressive limestone arch eroded by waves, lies a mile to the west.

The hilly coastline and looping bays backed by pale-coloured cliffs are topped with grassland and colourful flowers. Spring is the perfect

1 Durdle Door. 2 Ruined buildings in the abandoned village of Tyneham. 3 Lulworth Castle. 4 Lulworth Cove. ▶

time to walk this section of the South West Coast Path, before the summer crowds arrive. The stretch west from Lulworth Cove over Hambury Tout to **Man o' War Bay** and Durdle Door is only 1¼ miles. It is steep in parts but at the top of those climbs you are rewarded with almost aerial views of the coastline. You can park either in the car park above Durdle Door or at Lulworth Cove but bear in mind that the refreshments are at the Lulworth Cove end. Another popular walk from Lulworth Cove is the one eastwards to the **Fossil Forest**, which can be done only when the Lulworth Range Walks are open (page 261). The 'forest' is a ledge in the Purbeck limestone cliff made up of doughnut-shaped layers of mud and algae, in the centre of which trees once grew.

The approach to West Lulworth and Lulworth Cove is via a narrow lane; there is a car park at Lulworth Cove but like all car parks on the estate it is expensive. The **Lulworth Heritage Centre** (BH20 5RH ✆ 01929 400587) near the car park makes a handy starting point. The free exhibition contains information on the geology, geography and social history of the area, including its long farming tradition. You won't be surprised to learn, given the shape of the cove, that it was a popular haunt for smugglers, who exploited its seclusion. The heritage centre stocks local maps, walking guides and wildlife-identification guides, which can come in handy when exploring the area.

From there it is a short stroll to **Lulworth Cove** along a narrow street lined with the usual trappings of a seaside touristy spot – guesthouses, tea rooms and shops selling brightly coloured buckets, spades and rock-pooling nets. Thankfully, however, it lacks that slick, smarmy, touristy feel and instead retains the scruffy charm of a fishing village enhanced by the presence of rickety rowing boats lying at odd angles beside the street. Running down one side of the street is a stone wall and on the other side a stream, one of the many springs that feed the cove and make its waters some of the coldest in Dorset. The water pools in a pond part way down the hill.

"You won't be surprised to learn, given the shape of the cove, that it was a popular haunt for smugglers, who exploited its seclusion."

As you walk down the hill you will see a mint-coloured cottage, the **Dolls House** (✆ 01929 400587), which is said to have been brought from Canada and rebuilt here in 1860. Within is a delightfully old-fashioned fudge shop. In the 1920s and 1930s, the cottage was reportedly home to one Jimmy Carter, not the former US president but a fisherman renowned for smearing his boat with dripping to keep tourists from sitting on it. Tourists are given a much warmer welcome today and can take tea in the courtyard here.

At the cove, boats lie scattered around the slipway and moored in the calm water, reinforcing that fishing-village feel. The cove is ringed by a well-sheltered shingle beach and the waters are popular with swimmers and snorkellers.

Walk up the grassy hill towards the sea and look back down over the cove to fully appreciate its scallop shape. This is also where you will find Stair Hole, a geologist's dream with its arches, caves, a blowhole and the adorably named Lulworth Crumple. The crumple consists of alternating bands of limestone and shale – the layers resemble a cross-section of a collapsed cake.

The bulk of the village of **West Lulworth** lies a mile back from the sea and contains a mixture of architectural styles, including thatched cottages and grand Victorian stone villas.

The car park above **Durdle Door** is reached by driving through the large Durdle Door Holiday Park. On a clear day the views from here along the coast stretch as far as Portland. It is a steep walk down (and back up!) to Durdle Door, where there is a pebbly beach. The sea washes back and forth through the arch, making a washboard of the rocks below. Adventurous visitors can be seen swimming or kayaking through the arch, but it is a risky pastime. On the way down to the beach is a lookout point with views of Durdle Door in one direction and **Man o' War Bay** in the other. The beach at Man o' War Bay is accessible only at low tide.

Before you head to Lulworth Cove and Durdle Door it is useful to be aware that when the army ranges are in use, firing may be heard.

OUTDOOR ACTIVITIES & WATERSPORTS

The area around Lulworth offers excellent mountain biking, walking and watersports. Due to restricted access you need prior permission to launch a boat in Lulworth Cove, but moorings are available (⊘ lulworth.com).

Lulworth Outdoors West Lulworth, BH20 5RQ ✆ 01929 400155 ⊘ lulworthoutdoors. com. Offers guided hikes, mountain biking, coasteering, archery, orienteering and bushcraft.

¶¶ FOOD & DRINK

Many of the shops in this area sell **Purbeck Ice Cream** (⊘ purbeckicecream.co.uk). Like many dairy farmers, Peter and Hazel were driven to diversify when milk quotas were introduced; Purbeck Ice Cream was the result. It is made at Kingston, near Corfe Castle.

Boat Shed Café Main Rd, West Lulworth BH20 5RQ ⊘ 01929 400810. The location is hard to beat – right on the bay with al fresco dining. Simple, light lunches and homemade cakes.
Castle Inn Main Rd, West Lulworth BH20 5RN ⊘ 01929 400311. A traditional thatched pub near Lulworth Castle, dating back to 1660. Known for its food and variety of local beers and ciders. Extremely dog-friendly – there are even dog treats at the bar.
Limestone Hotel Restaurant Main Rd, West Lulworth BH20 5RI ⊘ 01929 400252. Set on a hill at the entrance to the village, with views of West Lulworth and surrounding countryside. Carefully created modern dishes featuring local produce.
Lulworth Cove Inn Main Rd, West Lulworth BH20 5RQ ⊘ 01929 400333. A popular Hall & Woodhouse pub in a prime location, just a few hundred yards from Lulworth Cove. Thoughtfully decorated and has a large beer garden.
Lulworth Lodge Bistro 38 Main Rd, West Lulworth BH20 5RQ ⊘ 01929 400252. Fresh modern décor and a varied menu with standard fare like fish and chips, plus more creative dishes. There is no parking so you will need to park in the main Lulworth Cove car park.

The award-winning Slow Travel series from Bradt Guides

**Over 20 regional guides across Britain.
See the full list at bradtguides.com/slowtravel.**

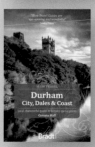

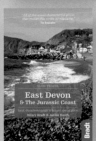

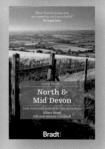

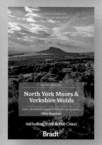

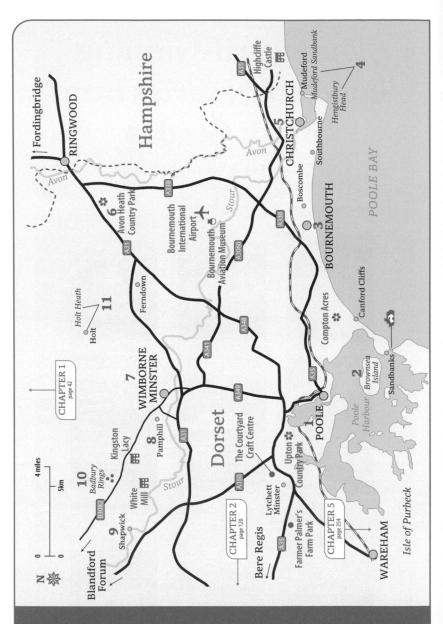

N

Fordingbridge

RINGWOOD

Hampshire

Avon

Highcliffe Castle

Mudeford Sandbank

Mudeford

CHRISTCHURCH

Hengistbury Head

4

A35

5

Southbourne

Avon

Boscombe

POOLE BAY

A338

Avon Heath Country Park

6

A31

A338

Bournemouth International Airport

Bournemouth Aviation Museum

A3060

BOURNEMOUTH

3

Stour

Canford Cliffs

A348

Compton Acres

Holt Heath

11

Holt

Ferndown

A341

WIMBORNE MINSTER

7

A349

POOLE

A35

Brownsea Island

Sandbanks

Poole Harbour

2

CHAPTER 1
page 42

4 miles

5km

0

0

Kingston Lacy

10

Badbury Rings

8

Pamphill

Dorset

The Courtyard Craft Centre

A31

Upton Country Park

1

White Mill

A350

Stour

Lytchett Minster

Blandford Forum

9

Shapwick

CHAPTER 2
page 120

Bere Regis

Farmer Palmer's Farm Park

CHAPTER 5
page 254

WAREHAM

Isle of Purbeck

B3082

6
POOLE, BOURNEMOUTH & THE EAST

Poole and Bournemouth, Dorset's two largest towns, virtually combine into one large conurbation, with Christchurch as an appendage to make this by far the most densely populated part of Dorset. Although heavily urbanised, it has Slow corners to be discovered and I hope to help you find them.

The historic town of **Poole** sits on the second-largest natural harbour in the world, after Sydney, and its sheltered waters offer ideal conditions for all manner of watersports. Eight islands are dotted around the harbour, most of them privately owned, but the National Trust's **Brownsea Island** is open to the public and provides an unblemished, car-free sanctuary and a vantage point from which to watch the harbour's abundant birdlife. Many visitors, however, are drawn to the island by the possibility of catching a glimpse of the red squirrel as this is one of the few places in Britain where it remains.

Seven miles of sandy beaches stretch around Poole Bay from Sandbanks to Hengistbury Head near Bournemouth. **Sandbanks** is a small spit jutting out across the mouth of Poole Harbour, mirroring Studland on the Isle of Purbeck; a useful chain ferry links the two and replaces a long drive around the harbour. Sandbanks is the pick of the Poole Bay beaches: glamorous and well known for its exclusive real estate.

Bournemouth and Christchurch are relative newcomers to Dorset – until 1974, when the county boundary was moved, they were part of Hampshire. It is said that in Dorset terms it takes around 40 years to be accepted as a local, so they should be feeling just about settled by now. **Bournemouth** was created as recently as the 19th century and quickly developed all the accoutrements of a British seaside town: the pier, beach huts and souvenir shops. **Christchurch** has a very different feel as it dates from Saxon times, lies on the sedate rivers Stour and Avon and has as its focal point the magnificent Priory Church.

Rural East Dorset offers a pleasing mix of open rolling countryside, cherished heathland and forest, while just over the border into Hampshire is the gorgeous New Forest National Park. **Wimborne Minster** is an attractive historic town with a minster church dating from the 8th century. A short distance from Wimborne Minster is the National Trust's **Kingston Lacy Estate** with one of Dorset's most imposing houses at its centre. **Badbury Rings**, an Iron Age hillfort, lies on the estate and offers some pleasant walking.

GETTING THERE & AROUND

Bournemouth International Airport (⌖ bournemouthairport.com) lies north of Christchurch and links Dorset to other UK and European cities; an airport shuttle operates to Bournemouth town centre.

The A35 links Poole, Bournemouth and Christchurch but traffic can be frustratingly heavy, particularly during summer, so you may wish to consider some car-free options.

PUBLIC TRANSPORT

South Western Railway connects London Waterloo to Christchurch, Bournemouth, Poole and Weymouth. If you arrive in Poole by **train**, a **Plus Bus** ticket gives you unlimited bus travel on most local bus services around the urban area of Poole, Bournemouth and Wimborne (⌖ plusbus.info).

Information on buses is available at ⌖ morebus.co.uk. Poole's distinctive sky-blue **town centre bus** (route 1; Mon–Sat) loops around the major attractions. Parking in Sandbanks in summer can be troublesome but there are buses from Bournemouth and Poole. Regular buses link Poole and Bournemouth to Wimborne Minster, and to Swanage on the Isle of Purbeck.

A land train (☉ Apr–Oct daily; Nov–Mar Sat & Sun) runs from Bournemouth Pier to Branksome Chine on the edge of Poole via Durley Chine and Alum Chine, and in the other direction to Boscombe Pier via Toft.

BY BOAT

If you are arriving in your **own boat**, Poole Quay Boat Haven (☏ 01202 649488 ⌖ poolequayboathaven.co.uk) has serviced pontoon berths for visitor use and is within walking distance of the town centre. Permanent berths are also available. The harbour master can answer any queries about navigation and regulations (✆ 01202 440200 ⌗ phc.co.uk). Further east, mooring is available at the Christchurch Sailing Club (✆ 01202 483150 ⌗ christchurchsailingclub.co.uk).

Sailing is part of the area's identity and regattas are held throughout the summer. At the heart of it all are Poole Yacht Club (⌗ pooleyc.co.uk), Parkstone Yacht Club (⌗ parkstoneyachtclub.com), Royal Motor Yacht Club (⌗ rmyc.club) and Christchurch Sailing Club (see above).

Small ferries provide a time-saving and enjoyable way to get around the Poole and Christchurch harbours; bikes and dogs are usually welcome on board. From Sandbanks you can hop on a chain ferry to the quieter side of the harbour, Studland, in the Isle of Purbeck (page 257). Poole Quay is the departure point for ferry cruises around the harbour and along the Jurassic Coast. You can reach Brownsea Island via ferry from Sandbanks or Poole Quay. A short ride from Christchurch Quay or Mudeford Quay to Mudeford Sandbank avoids the drive around the harbour, and from the sandbank you can walk up on to Hengistbury Head.

⚓ BOAT OPERATORS

The following offer ferries to Brownsea Island and/or boat cruises.

Brownsea Island Ferries Poole Quay and Sandbanks ✆ 01929 462383 ⌗ brownseaislandferries.com. Provides ferries half-hourly from Poole Quay and Sandbanks to Brownsea Island, from March to October. Also harbour cruises, Jurassic Coast cruises and trips to Swanage. A Wareham River cruise from Poole Quay takes around 75 minutes. In winter there are RSPB-guided birding trips.

City Cruises Poole Quay BH15 1BQ ✆ 0207 7400400 ⌗ cityexperiences.com. Many options, including Jurassic Coast cruises and Swanage day cruises, with the option of connecting with the Swanage steam train. The pick of the cruises has to be the evening birdwatching cruise, which offers the chance to see the large guillemot colony at Durlston Country Park (page 287) and puffins (page 292).

Dorset Cruises Poole Quay BH15 1HJ ✆ 01202 724910 ⌗ dorsetcruises.co.uk. Private charters of a vintage motor yacht, and a variety of ticketed events.

Greenslade Pleasure Boats Poole Quay BH15 1HJ ✆ 01202 669955 ⌗ greensladepleasureboats.co.uk. Brownsea Island ferries, plus harbour cruises, river cruises to Wareham, coast cruises, Swanage cruises and birdwatching trips. Private hire also available.

Paddle Steamer Waverley ⟨⟩ waverleyexcursions.co.uk. *Waverley*, the world's last seagoing paddle steamer, departs from various ports around the UK. In previous years its itinerary has included departures from Poole Quay. Check the website for timetables.

BOAT HIRE & WATERSPORTS PROVIDERS

Watersports are big business in Poole Harbour and there are plenty of companies offering everything from windsurfing to waterskiing. Hiring a boat or kayak is a relaxing way to explore Poole Harbour and get up close to the birdlife.

Castaway Boat Charters Poole Quay BH15 1HJ ⟨⟩ 07860 793450 ⟨⟩ castawaycharters. co.uk. Full-day, half-day and evening charters exploring the harbour aboard a 45ft cruiser. Also fishing and diving charters.

Poole Boat Hire Cobbs Quay Marina, Poole BH15 4EL ⟨⟩ 07866 732537 ⟨⟩ pooleboathire. co.uk. Powerboat hire for up to six people; no experience necessary.

Poole Harbour Watersports School 284 Sandbanks Rd, Poole BH14 8HU ⟨⟩ 01202 700503 ⟨⟩ pooleharbourwatersportsschool.co.uk. Kayak and stand-up paddle board harbour tours, plus windsurfing and kitesurfing. Hire also available.

Rockley Watersports 13 Parkstone Rd, Poole BH15 2NN ⟨⟩ 01202 677272 ⟨⟩ rockley.org. Sailing, windsurfing, kayaking and powerboating courses.

Superhawk Marine Charters Cobbs Quay Marina, Poole BH15 4EL ⟨⟩ 01202 694427 ⟨⟩ superhawkmarine.com. Sunseeker luxury powerboat charters for up to 12 passengers. Experienced skipper provided.

Watersports Academy 15 Banks Rd, Sandbanks BH13 7PS ⟨⟩ 01202 708283 ⟨⟩ thewatersportsacademy.com. Dinghy lessons and hire, kayak hire, yacht charter, power boating, windsurfing, kitesurfing, wakeboarding, paddle boarding and waterskiing. Also bike hire.

CYCLING

You may think that the built-up area along the coast would be unsuitable for riding but there are off-road cycle routes and cycling does present the opportunity to avoid the traffic. Poole has around 48 miles of cycle network and the town is well equipped with bike stands. A 7½-mile **Heritage Cycle Route**, part of National Cycle Route 25, takes you around places of historical interest in Poole and alongside the harbour to Upton Country Park. The **Castleman Trailway** runs almost 17 miles along the route of the defunct Southampton to Dorchester railway, linking three country parks: Avon Heath, Moors Valley and Upton. It also allows you to ride from Upton Country Park to Wimborne Minster. The trailway is open to walkers and cyclists, and part of it to horseriders too. The **Bourne Valley Greenway** for walkers and cyclists runs 4½ miles from Canford Heath in Poole to Bournemouth seafront, taking you through heathland and past the Alder Hills Nature Reserve.

Bournemouth has a good **promenade** for cycling, although you can't ride on it between 10.00 and 18.00 in July and August due to the high volume of pedestrians. You can cycle from Bournemouth Gardens to Hengistbury Head along the seafront, and extend it by continuing down Harbour Road and through Wick to Tuckton Gardens on the River Stour. Alternatively, you and your bike can catch the **ferry** from Mudeford Sandbank to Christchurch. Hengistbury Head has sealed bike paths that make for easy cycling to Mudeford Sandbank – a popular activity for families.

For a full day out, you can take bikes on the train from Bournemouth to Brockenhurst for riding the hundred miles of cycle paths around the **New Forest National Park**.

CYCLE HIRE

Poole, Bournemouth, Christchurch and Wimborne Minster all have Beryl Bikes available to borrow. For details see ♦ beryl.cc.

Front Bike Hire The seafront, Bournemouth BH2 5AA ♦ 01202 373280 ♦ frontbikehire. co.uk. A few hundred yards from the pier.
Kool Cycle Hire 4c West Cliff Rd, Bournemouth BH2 5EY ♦ 07594 505776 ♦ koolcyclehirebournemouth.co.uk
On yer bike 88–90 Charminster Rd, Bournemouth BH8 8US ♦ 01202 315855 ♦ onyerbike.co.uk
Shore Thing The Hobie Centre, Rockley Park, Poole BH15 4LZ ♦ 01202 671661 ♦ shorething.co.uk. E-bike hire. Pre-booking recommended.
Wheelie Bike Hire 15 Banks Rd, Poole BH13 7PS ♦ 01202 708283 ♦ wheeliebikehire.com.

WALKING

This bit of Dorset is by no means as rich in great walks as the county is further west, with most of the coast built up – but the waterside provides plenty of interest, notably around Poole Harbour, which can be explored by a series of scenic trails (♦ pooleharbourtrails.org.uk). The **Cockle Trail** follows a series of brass plaques around Poole and helps you

TOURIST INFORMATION

Bournemouth Pier Approach, BH2 5AA ⌀ 01202 123800 ⌂ bournemouth.co.uk
Christchurch 51 High St, BH23 1AS ⌀ 01202 499199
Poole The Quay, BH15 1GZ ⌀ 01202 128888 ⌂ pooletourism.com
Wimborne Minster 29 High St, BH21 1HR ⌀ 01202 882533

uncover the town's heritage with points of interest explained. You can download the trail from ⌂ pooletourism.com.

A stroll around **Brownsea Island**, perhaps followed by a picnic, is a memorable way to spend a day and provides the opportunity for wildlife watching and views of Poole Harbour from a different perspective.

The **Stour Valley Way** follows the river for 64 miles from its source in Stourhead to the sea at Christchurch, with some rewarding sections at the Christchurch end of the walk. The path ends at **Hengistbury Head**, which provides pleasant walking and excellent views of Christchurch Harbour and along the Bournemouth coastline. If you park at the base of the head you can walk over the headland to **Mudeford Sandbank** and catch the land train along the harbour on the way back. From Mudeford Sandbank you can catch a ferry either to Christchurch Quay or to Mudeford Quay, where local fishermen sell their daily catch (page 337).

The Stour Valley Way runs through the village of Shapwick, from where a short detour leads to the Iron Age hillfort of **Badbury Rings**; the site is imprinted with history and atmosphere and provides good views of the surrounding countryside. The nearby **Kingston Lacy Estate** is criss-crossed with footpaths and bridleways – ⌂ nationaltrust.org.uk has some suggested walks.

HORSERIDING

Rural East Dorset offers some decent riding, including the opportunity for beach rides; horseriding is allowed on **Highcliffe and Mudeford beaches** but horses are not permitted on the seashore between Easter and October from 10.00 to 21.00. Also suitable for riding is the Castleman Trailway, a 16½-mile route linking Avon Heath Country Park, Moors Valley Country Park and Upton Country Park.

Ringwood, which lies near the Dorset/Hampshire border, is the gateway to the **New Forest**'s superb riding (itself not in Dorset and therefore outside the scope of this book), and there are no restrictions for riding across New Forest District-covered beaches (Barton on Sea, Calshot, Milford on Sea or Hordle Cliffs). Between April and July, New Forest stallions are let out into the forest to breed with the mares and it is best to keep your distance from them. Another thing to be aware of is that the New Forest Hounds drag hunt on Tuesday and Saturday from November until the end of February, so unless you are content to join the chase involuntarily, those days may be best avoided. The Forestry Commission has produced a code of conduct for riding in the forest, available online (thenewforest.co.uk).

The **Kingston Lacy Estate** near Wimborne Minster has 22 miles of wonderful public bridleways with shared access for cyclists.

RIDING STABLES

Arniss Farm Godshill, Fordingbridge SP6 2JX 01425 654114 arnissequestrian.co.uk. Hacking in the New Forest without having to venture on to roads. Runs summer camps for children.

Bagnum Riding Stables Charles Lane, Ringwood BH24 3BZ 01425 476263 bagnumequestrian.co.uk. New Forest rides all levels of experience.

Burley Villa Bashley Common Rd, New Milton BH25 5SH 01425 610278 burleyvilla. co.uk. English and Western riding in the New Forest.

Eastmoors Riding School Ringwood Rd, St Leonards BH24 2SB 07904 902188 eastmoorsridingschool.com. Woodland treks from 30 minutes to four hours.

Fir Tree Farm Equestrian Centre Ogdens, Fordingbridge SP6 2PY 01425 654744 fir-tree-farm.org.uk. Has direct New Forest access; also offers Equine Assisted Learning and reiki for humans and horses.

Honeybrook Riding Stables Wimborne BH21 4JD 01202 028406 honeybrookridingstables.co.uk. Pony experiences for children.

POOLE & SURROUNDS

Poole Quay and **Poole Old Town** offer some good pottering territory – historic buildings, numerous eateries, independent shops and the chance to gaze with envy at the fabulous Sunseeker motorboats under construction there.

Poole Harbour's 110 miles of coastline, shallow waters and eight islands are a haven for wildlife, in particular birds. The best place to appreciate the area's flora and fauna is **Brownsea Island**, where the Dorset Wildlife Trust manages a conservation area with hides overlooking the lagoon. This wonderful, car-free island also offers the chance to see rare red squirrels.

The harbour draws almost as many watersports enthusiasts as it does wildfowl and plays host to a number of sporting events throughout the year, including windsurfing and kitesurfing championships.

The **beaches**, in particular Sandbanks, attract people to the area but if they get too busy there are some waterside parks where you can relax and admire the harbour. The best of these is **Upton Country Park**.

1 POOLE

Although modern development dominates Poole, a historic core remains around the quay and Poole Old Town, testament to the town's long seafaring history. The earliest evidence of that history was discovered in 1964: a 33ft boat hollowed from an oak tree found preserved in mud off Brownsea Island and dated to around 295BC; it is now on display in Poole Museum. While being on the sea has its advantages, it has also meant the town had its fair share of seaborne invasions – both the Romans and the Vikings landed here. The Romans took over an Iron Age settlement at Hamworthy on the western side of the harbour and built a road between it and their settlement at Badbury Rings. In 1015 Canute used Poole Harbour as a convenient base from which to attack Wessex. Poole began to emerge as an important port in the 12th century and, gradually taking over from Wareham, was the biggest port in Dorset by 1433. In the 18th century it was the main British port trading with North America, bringing great wealth to its merchants. It was central to the Newfoundland trade, whereby Poole's

HARRY PAYE

One particularly lively event on Poole's calendar takes place in June when the Harry Paye Charity Fun Day brings assorted crowds of sightseers and 'pirates' to the quay, with various forms of re-enactments and children's entertainment. It gives a nod to local boy Harry Paye, a colourful privateer and pirate who led naval raids along the coasts of France and Spain in the late 14th and early 15th centuries. He caused a fair amount of mayhem, capturing ships, razing cities and holding prisoners to ransom. In 1406 he captured 120 French and Spanish vessels in an expedition, brought them back to Poole and distributed the booty to the residents. It is said the wine from one of the ships kept the people of Poole happy for a whole month.

ships sailed to Newfoundland laden with salt and provisions, collected salted cod caught off Newfoundland and delivered it to the West Indies and southern Europe, then returned with wine, salt and olive oil. More recently, Poole played an important role as one of the principal departure points for the World War II D-Day landings.

Poole suffered some bombing during World War II, and in the 1950s and 1960s over half the buildings dating from before 1850 were demolished. In 1975, a conservation area was established around the southwest end of High Street and across to West Street, in order to preserve the remaining old buildings. Within this zone, known as **Poole Old Town**, some medieval buildings survive but the predominant style is Georgian. Church, Market and Thames streets in particular have some fine Georgian buildings, many of which were houses built in the 18th century to accommodate the town's prosperous middle class, made wealthy by sea trading. **Poole House** in Thames Street has a typically flamboyant façade, while another highly decorative example sporting Baroque decoration is **West End House** in St James Close; built in the early 18th century for Newfoundland merchant, John Slade, in the late 19th-century it was home to the Carter family, founders of Poole Pottery.

At the end of Market Street, the **guildhall** dates from 1761, with twin exterior flights of steps curving up to the first floor, which once housed the courtroom; the ground floor was originally open and occupied by market stalls. Behind the guildhall in 1886, Alderman Horatio Hamilton, once mayor of Poole, was shot repeatedly by John King, a disgruntled harbour pilot following a dispute over a boat; you may be able to spot the bullet holes.

The large **St James's Church** was built in 1820 from Purbeck stone, although there has been a church here since the 13th century. The interior has a nautical feel: its grainy wooden pillars, which arrived on ships from Newfoundland, are reminiscent of the masts of sailing ships, and galleried seating extends all around. The American flag was presented by American naval forces based in Poole during World War II, who used the church.

The quay

A colourful variety of fishing boats are moored in this lively, industrious part of town, and early risers will see the daily catch of crabs and flat fish. Mussels are also regularly farmed and clams are racked within the harbour. Poole still has a thriving fishing industry with a strong fleet of some 80–90 professional fishermen.

The quay is also the departure point for **boat trips** around the harbour, to Brownsea Island and along the coast. A statue of Robert Baden-Powell gazes out from the quay towards Brownsea Island, where he held the first scout camp.

"You pass a series of historic pubs that have served Poole's thirsty seafarers for centuries."

At the western end of the quay is the **Town Bridge**, a lifting bridge built in 1927 and sporting green copper cladding, which gives access to Hamworthy, where Sunseeker builds its luxury powerboats and the ferry port operates services to France and the Channel Islands. **Hamworthy Park** (Lulworth Av, BH15 4DH) is on the waterfront and has views of the harbour, a small sandy beach, tennis courts, playground facilities and a café. It is lesser known than Poole Park (see opposite) and thus tends to be quieter.

On the oldest part of the quay, at the edge of Poole Old Town, stands the Georgian, Grade II-listed **Custom House**, which now houses a restaurant. In front of it is the beam that was once used to weigh goods for customs duty. In 1747, following the seizure of one of their shipments, the notorious Hawkhurst Gang of smugglers raided the Custom House to retrieve their contraband. The shipment from Guernsey contained about 30 hundredweight of tea, 39 casks of brandy and rum, and a bag of coffee; it had been destined to land at Christchurch Bay when it was intercepted off the coast. About 30 members of the gang broke into the Custom House and escaped on horseback with the tea; several of them were later captured and hanged.

Nearby, in one of the 19th-century warehouses that once served the busy port, **Poole Museum** (4 High St, BH15 1BW ✆ 01202 262600 ☉ Mar–Oct 10.00–17.00 daily; free admission) houses exhibits on the area's history and prehistory. At the time of writing it was closed for refurbishment but when it reopens it is likely that Poole's seafaring history will continue to feature prominently. The museum's star attraction has long been the log boat dating from around 295BC that was found off Brownsea Island in 1964 (page 316).

On the quay is Sir Anthony Caro's 35ft tall Sea Music Sculpture, created in 1991. The sculpture is inspired by the waves and sailing boats of the harbour. You can walk up the metal stairs to the platform next to it for views of the harbour.

Heading eastwards along the quay you pass a series of historic pubs that have served Poole's thirsty seafarers for centuries, and the old seaman's mission, which is reputed to be haunted. Witnesses have reported seeing the ghostly apparition of an old man with a long grey beard and cloth cap sitting in a chair. The front of the Poole Arms is covered with tiles made a little further along the quay by the forerunners of the famous Poole Pottery, 'Carter's Industrial Tile Manufactory', who also made many of the tiles used in London underground stations. Until 2017 Poole Pottery had a shop on the site of the original factory on the quay, but sadly it closed after more than 140 years. Production ceased when the company went into administration in 2006 but it was subsequently taken over and the pottery is now produced in Stoke-on-Trent and available to order online (⊘ poolepottery.co.uk).

At the eastern end of the quay, in the boathouse where Poole lifeboat station was based from 1882 to 1974, **is Poole Old Lifeboat Museum** (Fisherman's Dock, BH15 1HU ✆ 01202 666046 ⊘ poole-lifeboats.org. uk ⊙ Apr–Dec 10.30–16.00 Mon–Sat, 13.00–16.00 Sun; free admission). It tells the story of the Royal National Lifeboat Institution (RNLI) and has a shop selling RNLI memorabilia. The centrepiece of the museum is the *Thomas Kirk Wright*, one of the first lifeboats to reach Dunkirk on 30 May 1940. She was one of the flotilla referred to as 'Dunkirk's Little Ships', sent to rescue members of the British Expeditionary Force from the beaches. On her third and final rescue voyage she was hit by German gunfire but managed to limp back to Poole on one engine; she returned to service at Poole until 1962. The RNLI has its headquarters in Poole at West Quay Road (BH15 1HZ) and maintains a library and archive on its work, which you can visit by appointment.

Poole Park, to the east of the town centre, is a green open space that snakes around a large saltwater lake separated from the sea by a thin strip of land where the railway runs. The lake has plenty of wildfowl, including some curious Canada geese, and is popular for watersports. Rockley Watersports (✆ 01202 677272) has a boathouse here offering all manner of water-based activities. For landlubbers there are tennis courts, a cricket pitch and children's play areas.

Poole's beaches

Poole is blessed with some fine, golden-sand beaches. Heading east from the town the first beach you come to, **Shore Road**, lies within the harbour

and has a dedicated launch zone for kitesurfers and windsurfers. The next beach along is Poole's best known, **Sandbanks**, a sandy peninsula stretching across the harbour mouth and connected to Studland on the Purbeck side of the harbour by a chain ferry (page 257). Sandbanks is well known for its luxurious, ultra-modern homes and is reputed to be the most expensive coastal location in the UK. Though it may exude an air of exclusivity, it gets packed in summer. The beach ranks among the finest on the south coast; the water is clean and shallow for around 200yds offshore, making it popular with families.

In July the beach plays host to Sandpolo ($\mathcal{O}$ sandpolo.com), the **British Beach Polo Championships**, which draws top national and international teams, and is coupled with music events in the evening. The polo is played in an arena with an oversized orange ball, designed not to get lost in the sand; spectators are close to the action and get a real appreciation of the speed and skill involved.

The stretch of sand continues from Sandbanks in the direction of Bournemouth and includes the beaches of **Canford Cliffs**, **Branksome Chine** and **Branksome Dene Chine**. Although officially belonging to Poole, the Branksome beaches seem more part of Bournemouth because of their location; the surrounding area is largely residential, with wooded hills running down to the beaches. Beach huts are available for hire at most of the beaches (to book visit $\mathcal{O}$ pooletourism.com). Canford Cliffs has the oldest ones, dating from 1927.

If you are looking for a **dog-friendly beach**, the main beaches are closed to dogs between May and October but you can always take your dog to Rockley Point at Hamworthy, the beach at Hamworthy Park, Branksome Dene Chine or the western end of Sandbanks.

Upton Country Park

BH17 7BJ $\mathcal{O}$ 01202 262753 $\mathcal{O}$ uptoncountrypark.com $\odot$ park: 09.00–dusk daily (free), house: certain Sun, see website

This tranquil space lies just four miles from the town centre. You can walk or cycle through the 160 acres or so of lush gardens, parkland, woodland and coastline, or simply have a picnic. You can download a

---

◀ **1** The stunning gardens of Compton Acres. **2** Poole's Sandbanks beach. **3** Poole Old Town. BROWNSEA ISLAND: Look out for **4** red squirrel, **5** reed bunting, **6** little stint and **7** sika deer among other species.

map of the park from the website, and there's a helpful visitor centre. Throughout the year there are regular family-friendly activities, such as a popular Easter egg hunt.

The park has just over 1½ miles of shoreline and plenty of opportunity for watching birds on the harbour. There is a large bird hide overlooking the salt marsh and intertidal mud flats of Hole Bay Nature Reserve, a 707-acre protected area.

"There is a large bird hide overlooking the salt marsh and intertidal mud flats of Hole Bay Nature Reserve."

In the restored **walled garden** is the tea room and above it an art gallery, **Gallery Upstairs** (⌂ thegalleryupstairs.org.uk).

The park is extremely dog friendly. There are enclosed off-lead areas and a self-service dog wash at the visitor centre.

The Grade II-listed Upton House makes an impressive backdrop for a picnic. It was built in 1816 and is now an events venue; it's usually closed to the public but guided tours are available on certain dates (see website). The house was built for Christopher Spurrier, one of the many Poole merchants made wealthy by the lucrative Newfoundland trade (page 316). He was declared bankrupt in 1830 after trade plummeted and things didn't get better – he reputedly managed to gamble away the family silver by losing a bet on a maggot race.

Compton Acres
164 Canford Cliffs Rd, BH13 7ES ✆ 01202 700778 ⌂ comptonacres.co.uk

Between Poole and Bournemouth and covering ten acres, this garden displays over 3,000 species and is enhanced by views of Poole Harbour, Brownsea Island and the distant Purbeck Hills. A margarine entrepreneur bought the property in 1920 and four years later created a garden to reflect his worldwide travels. It's divided into themed areas, including Italian, Japanese and heather gardens. Plants and gifts are on sale and there is a fully licensed cafe and a bakery.

Farmer Palmer's Farm Park
Wareham Rd, Organford BH16 6EU ✆ 01202 622022 ⌂ farmerpalmers.co.uk
⊙ 09.30–17.00 daily

Off the A35 between Poole and Bere Regis, this farm park evolved from a working farm and is aimed at children under eight. The barn has farm animals, pets and plenty of interactive experiences.

The Courtyard Craft Centre

Huntick Rd, Lytchett Minster BH16 6BA *∂* thecourtyardcraftcentre.co.uk

West of Poole, this complex of converted farm buildings houses a variety of independent shops. Many are craft-related and include a pottery, where you can take classes (*∂* tradpots.com). The restaurant offers hot meals, as well as cream teas. The centre runs classes and events, and is pet-friendly. Many of the units close on Mondays.

¶¶ FOOD & DRINK

Poole market takes place on the High Street on Thursday and Saturday, while a farmers' market is held in Falkland Square (outside the Dolphin Shopping Centre) on Thursday (⊙ 09.00–14.00). Unsurprisingly, Poole does seafood very well; **Frank Greenslades** (16 New Quay Rd, BH15 4AF *∂* 01202 672199) has been selling freshly caught seafood since 1884, including local crab, lobster and scallops. Poole Quay has plenty of casual cafés, pubs and restaurants.

Barn Café Bere Farm, Wareham Rd, Lytchett Matravers BH16 6ER *∂* 01202 900131. Tucked away off the A35 near Lytchett Matravers. A charming café in a courtyard of former farm buildings now housing shops and businesses. Quirky décor and a peaceful patio area. Unpretentious food in generous portions and an extensive gluten-free menu.

Courtyard Tearooms 48a High St, BH15 1BT *∂* 01202 922470. Tea rooms in a 16th-century building in the Old Orchard Plaza. Serves a huge range of teas, homemade cakes and light lunches.

Custom House The Quay, BH15 1HP *∂* 01202 073295. An à la carte restaurant upstairs and a more casual café/bar downstairs. Serves modern English and French cuisine and seafood specialities. Good views of the quay, and the Georgian building has an elegant atmosphere.

Da Vinci's 7 The Quay, BH15 1HJ *∂* 01202 667528. Outdoor tables on the waterside at Poole Quay are the big attraction at this Italian. Enjoy watching the boat traffic, or even do a spot of crab fishing, while you wait for your meal. Serves excellent pizza.

Deli on the Quay D17 Dolphin Quays, The Quay, BH15 1HU *∂* 01202 660022. A smart deli and café overlooking the quay. Wholesome food and a welcoming atmosphere.

Guildhall Tavern 15 Market St, BH15 1NB *∂* 01202 671717. Upmarket seafood restaurant known for its tasty, beautifully presented dishes. Gets busy so it's a good idea to book.

Rick Stein 10–14 Banks Rd, Sandbanks BH13 7QB *∂* 01202 283000. A swish Rick Stein restaurant with views of Poole Harbour and Brownsea Island, across the road from Sandbanks Beach in a row of shops. The ground floor is a casual bar area while upstairs is more formal dining. The menu features plenty of Stein's famous fish dishes. Also does breakfast or just a coffee. Take-away available.

South Deep Café Parkstone Bay Marina, Turks Lane, BH14 8EW ✆ 01202 733155. It's not the easiest to find but once you've discovered it you'll be glad you did. An informal, licensed café at the marina, overlooking the water. Food and service is of a good standard and they serve a tasty fish and chips. There is a limited amount of indoor seating but more outside. Reservation recommended.

2 BROWNSEA ISLAND
⚊ Brownsea Island Campsite
✆ 01202 707744 ⊙ Mar–Oct; landing fee payable on arrival; foot-passenger ferry from either Poole Quay or Sandbanks (page 311); National Trust

A car-free haven for wildlife (including the charming red squirrel), as well as the starting point of the Boy Scout movement, Brownsea is the largest of the islands in Poole Harbour and one of Dorset's treasures. The journey to the island gives the impression that you are travelling to a magical, faraway land; arriving by boat, the first thing you see is the island's few stone houses and the castle, with a backdrop of woodland. The first castle on Brownsea was built in the time of Henry VIII as one of a string of defences; in the 18th century it was rebuilt as a residence. In the late 19th century it burnt down and was again rebuilt; today the John Lewis Partnership rents it as a hotel for its employees and it is not open to the public.

The **visitor centre** is a good starting point and provides information on the island's history, flora and fauna. Exploring the island independently is straightforward and rewarding; you can download a walking trail from the National Trust website. Alternatively, you can take a **guided walk**. Off-road prams and buggies are available, which is really handy as some of the paths are a bit rough.

There really is great pleasure in walking around an island where there are no roads and no traffic, and absorbing sea views. Around the quay and visitor centre are traces of the communities that have lived here, including **St Mary's Church**, built in 1853 by the island's then owner, Colonel Waugh. The church has remained virtually unchanged since its construction and there is no electricity and no water supply, but its services are often well attended. A service is held every Sunday at 15.00 from May to September. The woods around the church are one of the areas where you may well spot red squirrels.

The island was the site of Major-General Robert Baden-Powell's original experimental scout camp in 1907, which gave rise to the international scouting movement. A **memorial** commemorates the first camp and a permanent campsite now exists on the island.

The island has plenty of space for picnics, or there is a National Trust tea room near the ferry. In summer, the **Brownsea Island Theatre Company** (✆ 07845 782924 ⬀ brownsea-theatre.co.uk) puts on open-air productions. You can prolong your stay at Brownsea by renting one of two National Trust cottages or by camping (page 326).

Wildlife on the island

Indications are that the island was inhabited as early as the 5th century BC. Until the 16th century it was mostly heathland but successive owners farmed the island, planted deciduous and coniferous woodlands, reclaimed marshland from the harbour, created meadows and excavated peat bogs to form two large lakes. The National Trust acquired Brownsea Island in 1963, after the last owner, Mrs Bonham-Christie, died in 1961. She had owned the island since 1921 and virtually lived as a recluse; she ordered almost everyone off the island, reducing its population from 70 to six. She let the island run wild, free from farming and forestry, and in part that is what preserved it.

"The journey to the island gives the impression that you are travelling to a magical, faraway land."

The whole island, with its combination of woodland, heathland, wetland, seashore and lagoon, is rich in wildlife. Over a hundred native and introduced species of trees grow on Brownsea, providing a shady canopy for walks. Pheasants roam the woodland, the descendants of those introduced for shooting parties, while the pine forest is the domain of goldcrests, woodpeckers, nuthatches and treecreepers. The open heath supports diverse butterfly species, common lizards and nightjars.

The northern half of the island, including the lagoon, is managed by Dorset Wildlife Trust (DWT) and you can enter this area for a small fee, which goes towards the trust's conservation work. A large part of their work has been the removal of the rhododendrons that have spread invasively throughout the island. This is one of the areas where you are most likely to catch a glimpse of **red squirrels**, a key attraction for many visitors. Food is put out for them at The Villa, which serves as the DWT's visitor centre providing detailed information on the wildlife.

Poole Harbour islands, including Brownsea Island, and the Isle of Wight are the only natural locations in southern Britain where red squirrels live. At the time of writing the population of red squirrels here was around 200. They flourish on the island because the mature pine trees provide an ideal habitat and their competitor, the grey squirrel, has never been introduced here. The squirrels are most active at sunrise and sunset for about three hours, they sleep during the day and shelter when the weather is inclement or very hot. One of the best times of year to see them is autumn, when they spend a good deal of their time on the ground gathering nuts.

You may also see **sika deer** – they were introduced to the island from Japan in 1896 and were one of the first populations in the country. The deer are quite shy so are usually found hiding in dense vegetation.

A series of hides allows you to watch the lagoon's abundant and diverse **bird population**. The lagoon was reclaimed from the harbour in the 1850s to create 70 acres of farmland; from the 1930s it was rarely drained, creating a rich non-tidal wetland. In spring and autumn waders stop off during their migration, including little stint, curlew sandpiper, ringed plover, spotted redshank and ruff. Also in spring, common and sandwich terns return from overwintering off the western coast of Africa and nest on gravel islands in the lagoon. Each pair usually rears two chicks and from May to September you can see them diligently feeding their young. From autumn to early spring large flocks of waders, including avocets and black-tailed godwits, make their home here, as do spoonbills. Colourful shelducks are present all year.

A freshwater marsh is home to an entirely different array of bird species, including water rail, reed bunting and reed warbler, an African migrant that spends the summer here. The marsh also supports many insects, including 24 species of dragonfly.

SPECIAL STAYS

Brownsea Island Campsite BH13 7EE ⬦ nationaltrust.org.uk ☺ Mar–Sep. Camping never used to be allowed on Brownsea, aside from scout camps, but the National Trust recently opened a campsite on the south side of the island. And as campsites go it is pretty incredible – delightfully car-free and with beautiful views over the water towards the Purbeck hills. You can either bring your own tent or book one of the on-site bell or tree tents. There is something magical about being on the island in the quiet of the evening, once the day visitors have left. There are only 40 camping pitches so the island doesn't feel

BIRDS OF POOLE HARBOUR

◈ birdsofpooleharbour.co.uk

Paul Morton

Birds of Poole Harbour is a charity dedicated to boosting the profile of bird observation, conservation and education around Poole Harbour.

The charity has a wide breadth of work consisting of detailed surveying of Poole Harbour's bird populations, setting up visitor access points, habitat restoration, and a busy engagement and education program, including popular birdwatching boat trips.

The charity is best known for the Poole Harbour Osprey Reintroduction Project in partnership with the Roy Dennis Wildlife Foundation. It began in 2017 with the aim of restoring a breeding population of ospreys to the south coast after an absence of 180 years. In 2022, the team saw initial success when a pair of ospreys raised young for the first time, and it is hoped that more pairs will establish and spread across the south coast in the coming years. This is a project that's really captured the public's attention.

We also work closely with The Roy Dennis Wildlife Foundation and Forestry England's sea-eagle team to monitor and track the now-established white-tailed eagles that frequent Poole Harbour, which arrived as a result of a reintroduction that started on the Isle of Wight in 2019.

With its rich and varied mosaic of habitats, Poole Harbour is an incredibly important area for birds from all over Europe and beyond. The landscape plays host to vitally important over-wintering and breeding populations and is therefore afforded multiple protections including the Poole Harbour Special Protection Area, multiple sites of Special Scientific Interest and a RAMSAR designation. With several conservation organisations and forward-thinking landowners driving nature recovery at a landscape scale in Dorset, Birds of Poole Harbour are not alone in protecting this beautiful place for wildlife.

Our website has useful information on birdwatching in the area. You can also view the osprey-nest webcam and book events, including birdwatching trips.

crowded in the evenings, and you can have some memorable wildlife encounters. It is about a 20-minute walk from the ferry to the campsite, so pack lightly. The campsite has toilets, showers, drinking water, cooking facilities and a small shop.

BOURNEMOUTH & CHRISTCHURCH

Colourful, vivacious, even shameless, **Bournemouth** is what you may have come to expect from a British seaside resort; what you may not expect is the high quality of the beaches, which draw crowds of eager sun-worshippers in summer. **Christchurch** is more refined, imprinted with history spanning generations and with the wonderful **Christchurch Priory** at its heart. The River Stour meets the sea here and you can spend a very sedate afternoon pottering along the river in a boat hired from the quay. Small ferries cross the harbour, providing plenty of opportunity for relaxing, car-free travel.

The area is within easy reach of the peaceful and beautiful New Forest National Park, with its excellent walking and horseriding, although as it is in Hampshire I don't discuss it in detail here.

3 BOURNEMOUTH

There is little truly 'Slow' about Bournemouth, a large and relatively new settlement that has exploded around the coastal resort, but I have endeavoured to uncover the elements that give Bournemouth its distinctive character.

Prior to 1810, the area where Bournemouth now stands was little more than rugged heathland leading down to a deserted coastline. Smugglers landed their contraband here and took advantage of the chines (small ravines running down to the sea, carved into the cliffs by streams) to hide their illicit goods. The smuggling activity and threat of invasion by Napoleon's forces prompted the government to authorise the protection of the coast by Dorset Volunteer Rangers. The commander of the local Cranborne troop was Captain Lewis Tregonwell, who is credited with founding Bournemouth. Tregonwell took a liking to the area, built a summer residence here and planted the valleys with pine trees. The Victorians considered the sea air scented with pine to be therapeutic, in particular for those suffering with tuberculosis, and a series of villas sprung up to cater for wealthy, ailing visitors. The villas are still visible at the southern end of Tregonwell Road and Tregonwell's house has been incorporated into the Royal Exeter Hotel.

"The Victorians considered the sea air scented with pine to be therapeutic, in particular for those suffering with tuberculosis."

Hotels specialising in seawater treatments followed, such as the Mont Dore, built in the 1880s and now part of the town hall. One of those who came for rehabilitation was **Robert Louis Stevenson**, who wrote *Kidnapped* while living in Alum Chine Road. As well as creating grand villas, the prosperous Victorians added expansive parks and **gardens**, which, along with the pine trees, are characteristic of Bournemouth. The Lower, Central and Upper gardens break up the urban sprawl and maintain a Victorian feel, while Alum Chine has tropical gardens by the sea.

For many years, Bournemouth was considered a retirement town but the council has taken steps to attract other demographics. The university and a large number of schools teaching English as a foreign language have brought young people but it lacks that seat-of-learning atmosphere, perhaps because the institutions are relatively new and have not yet become an integral part of the town's identity. With students and youngsters comes a lively **nightlife** and in summer stag and hen parties invade the town. It also has a strong **gay** scene, similar to Brighton but on a smaller scale.

Bournemouth is subject to incessant entertainment, with events running throughout the year; one of the best known is **Bournemouth Air Festival** (⊘ bournemouthair.co.uk), held over four days in August when aircraft display teams provide an exciting spectacle, and there is live music, fireworks and outdoor films.

The seafront

Bournemouth's main draw is its sandy **beaches**, with views across the bay towards the Isle of Wight. The beaches referred to as Bournemouth's (as opposed to Poole's) lie at the centre of the seven-mile stretch of sand that runs from Sandbanks to Hengistbury Head. As a general rule, the further you head east (towards Hengistbury Head) from Bournemouth, the quieter the beach. For the full English-seaside experience, you can hire **beach huts** by the day, week or month, or even buy one (⊘ 0845 0550968 ⊘ bcpcouncil.gov.uk). Over 250 beach huts stretch across the seafront from Alum Chine to Southbourne and come equipped with four chairs, a gas ring and curtains. Boscombe Beach has a modern take on the beach hut: beach pods designed by fashion guru Wayne Hemingway, which come complete with kitchenette, French doors and private balcony. Between May and September, **dog-friendly beaches** are at Alum Chine, Middle Chine, Fisherman's Walk and Hengistbury Head.

"Boscombe Beach has a modern take on the beach hut: beach pods designed by fashion guru Wayne Hemingway."

A **land train** (⊘ bournemouth.co.uk ⊙ Easter–Oct daily) runs along the seafront from Bournemouth Pier to Branksome Chine on the edge of Poole, via Durley Chine and Alum Chine, and in the other direction to Boscombe via Toft Zig Zag, the path down to East Cliff Beach.

Bournemouth's **pier** (⊘ thebournemouthpier.com) has a cheap-and-cheerful flavour. The council operates a pier toll from April to October. For a small fee you can buy a ticket for the whole season that allows you to walk to the end of the pier, where entertainment includes a restaurant, a climbing wall and a zipline back to the beach. These can be booked online (⊘ rockreef.co.uk).

The town centre

The busy commercial centre of the town is slightly inland, around **The Square**, where varied architecture adds interest. An attractive Victorian arcade leads through to a pedestrian shopping mall, where you will find the usual high-street shops and the odd stoic independent.

If you enjoy Victorian churches, have a look in **St Stephen's**, north of The Square and widely recognised as Bournemouth's most interesting. It was designed by renowned architect John Loughborough Pearson and built in 1881–98. According to John Betjeman in 1952, 'it was worth travelling 200 miles and being sick in the coach' to view the interior. Light and airy, it features towering columns, dramatic stone vaulting and a decorative wrought-iron screen, which separates the chancel from the main body of the church. The floors of the choir, sanctuary and lady chapel contain around 60 different types of coloured marble. The stained glass is reputed to be the best in Bournemouth; the life and death of St Stephen are depicted in the west window and a rose window in the north transept commemorates the first vicar here.

The Grade II-listed **Lower Gardens**, between The Square and the seafront, maintain a Victorian feel: there's a bandstand where you'll often hear live music, the River Bourne meanders through the gardens, and wide paths and bridges are ideal for promenading. There are refreshment kiosks, an aviary, minigolf, and art exhibitions in summer. The gardens draw a crowd at Christmas when they are transformed with dazzling decorations and an ice rink.

---

1 Aerial view over Hengistbury Head. 2 Lower Gardens, Bournemouth.
3 Bournemouth pier. 4 The main hall in the Russell-Cotes Art Gallery & Museum. ▶

The Bournemouth Natural Science Society and Museum (39 Christchurch Rd, BH1 3NS ✐ 01202 553525 ⬙ bnss.org.uk ◷ 10.00–16.00 most Tue & special events) houses its collections in a handsome Victorian building. Enthusiastic and knowledgeable volunteers are on hand to explain the exhibits.

Boscombe & Southbourne

To the east of Bournemouth, **Boscombe** developed from the middle of the 19th century and has a neat seafront and a wide, sandy beach. The pier is free to stroll along and gives good views along the coast and towards the Isle of Wight. You can fish from the pier although you will need to pick up a permit from the Boscombe Beach Office first (call ✐ 01202 123 800 to arrange payment). To the east of the pier is The Overstrand, a complex of shops, places to eat and a surf school. This is where you'll find the Wayne Hemingway-designed beach pods. You can also hire surfboards, paddleboards and kayaks here. There are some pleasant gardens, including the Italianate Gardens, Boscombe Cliff and Boscombe Chine. The A35, Christchurch Road, is dotted with antique shops.

Boscombe is having to work hard to shake off its long-held reputation as the seedy end of Bournemouth. The seafront is pleasant enough during the day and its lively atmosphere attracts a young, student crowd, but it is not worth going out of your way to visit. Inland Boscombe still has a seedy element, which means it is best avoided at night.

East of Boscombe towards Hengistbury Head is **Southbourne**, where a funicular railway built in 1935, **Fisherman's Walk Cliff Railway**, runs the 128ft between the coastal road and the promenade. Similar railways can be found at West Cliff and East Cliff, and opened in 1908. All three railways operate between April and October, labouring up their respective hills and looking as if they are about to run out of energy before they reach the top. In 2016 the East Cliff railway was closed due to a landslide and has remained closed since.

The Oceanarium

Pier Approach, West Beach BH2 5AA ✐ 01202 311993 ⬙ oceanarium.co.uk
◷ 10.00–17.00 daily

This oceanarium on the seafront displays aquatic creatures from around the world. A walk-through tunnel passes underwater allowing you to see sharks, turtles and other fish. The most endearing residents are the Humbolt penguins. You may wish to time your visit around daily feeding presentations, details of which are on the website.

Russell-Cotes Art Gallery & Museum

East Cliff Promenade, BH1 3AA ✐ 01202 451858 ♂ russellcotes.com ⊙ 10.00–17.00 Tue–Sun & Bank Holiday Mon

Sir Merton Russell-Cotes was a mayor of Bournemouth (1894–95) and a local philanthropist. Built in 1901, this extravagant Victorian house contains artwork and souvenirs collected by the Russell-Cotes family during their worldwide travels in the late Victorian era. The abundance of statues, paintings and gold paint gives an effect somewhere between grand and gaudy. Regular exhibitions provide the opportunity to purchase artwork by local and other artists. On a hillside above the beach, the shaded gardens and views of the coastline are a highlight and there is a good café.

▯▯ FOOD & DRINK

Bournemouth is packed with bars, restaurants and nightclubs, concentrated around the town centre and along the seafront. Boscombe has a fresh food market on Thursday and Saturday (⊙ 09.00–17.00) in the pedestrianised section of the High Street.

All Fired Up 35–37 Bourne Av, BH2 6DT ✐ 01202 558030. Just off The Square, this is a café where you can paint your own ceramics.

Chez Fred 10 Seamoor Rd, Westbourne BH4 9AN ✐ 01202 761023. Serves ethically sourced fish and chips; eat-in or take-away.

Larder House 4 Southbourne Grove, BH6 3QZ ✐ 01202 424687. A wood-fired oven is at the heart of things here, producing artisan breads and pizzas. Sharing plates are popular.

Russell Cotes Café East Cliff Promenade, BH1 3AA ✐ 01202 451858. One of the most picturesque and peaceful coffee spots in town. You don't have to pay admission to the museum to visit the café here. It has a sunny terrace with sea views.

West Beach Pier Approach, BH2 5AA ✐ 01202 587785. A modern, relatively upmarket restaurant and bar with sea views. Fresh, local seafood is the star of the menu.

4 HENGISTBURY HEAD & MUDEFORD SANDBANK

One of the few uninhabited parts of this built-up coastline, the sandstone promontory known as **Hengistbury Head**, a nature reserve, offers a quiet retreat for walking, cycling and wildlife watching. It has hidden depths too – as a place of great archaeological significance.

A sleek, modern **visitor centre** (BH6 4EN ✆ 01202 451618 🖱 visithengistburyhead.co.uk; free admission). provides information on the area's intriguing archaeology and natural history.

Archaeological investigations of the headland have revealed a wealth of activity from at least 10500BC. Its visible lumps and bumps include Bronze Age barrows and Iron Age earthworks dating from its time as a busy cross-Channel trading centre. Italian amphorae, Breton pots and raw purple glass are among the imports that have been unearthed here, some of which are on display in the visitor centre.

Heath, grassland, woodland, reed beds and water meadow are all present on the headland, which supports 500 plant species and over 300 bird species, including Dartford warbler and skylark. In 1989 the endangered natterjack toad was reintroduced to Hengistbury Head, where temporary pools near sand dunes and heathland are ideal for breeding. At dusk you may hear the call of the male natterjack, so loud it can be heard from over a mile away. Human activity in the 19th century left acidic ponds on the head, now a significant element of the nature reserve and home to 16 species of dragonfly.

The headland and the long sand spit trailing from the end of it (Mudeford Sandbank) provide natural protection for Christchurch Harbour. The unspoilt sandbank has a spine of colourful beach huts running along it, reputed to be some of the most expensive in Britain. The beach here is a good vantage point for watching the harbour's birdlife. Facilities are limited but there is a good restaurant, **Beach House** (page 342), with a small shop adjoining it.

The headland and sandbank are easily reached from both the Christchurch and Bournemouth sides. A ferry shuttles visitors the short distance to the sandbank from Mudeford Quay on the northeastern side of Christchurch Harbour (Mudeford Ferry ✆ 07968 334441 🖱 mudefordferry.co.uk ☉ Easter–Oct 10.00–17.00 approx every 15 mins; winter weekends weather permitting; bikes and dogs allowed). Bournemouth Boating Services (✆ 01202 429119 🖱 bournemouthboating.co.uk ☉ Easter–Oct) operates a vintage ferry between Tuckton Tea Gardens, and Mudeford Sandbank, stopping at Wick Ferry and Christchurch Quay.

From the large car park at the base of Hengistbury Head you can walk or catch the land train to **Mudeford Sandbank**. It is a very pleasant walk or bike ride on a sealed track around the harbour. A more strenuous option is to walk up over the headland, where the views of Christchurch, Bournemouth and the Isle of Wight make it worth the climb.

The car park has a café and is the departure point for the **land train** ($\mathcal{O}$ 01202 425517 ☉ summer 10.00–16.00 daily; school summer holidays 10.00–17.00 daily; winter 10.00–15.00 daily, weather & numbers permitting; dogs allowed). Trains depart every 30 minutes and run 1½ miles around the harbour to the sandbank.

5 CHRISTCHURCH & SURROUNDS

Although a close neighbour, the delightful, historic town of Christchurch, on the rivers Stour and Avon, is a world away from the bustle and modernity of Bournemouth. It is worth visiting for its attractive riparian scenery and historic buildings, the most notable of which is its medieval church, Christchurch Priory.

Christchurch Priory (page 339) lies in a park-like area on the River Avon and the town's key historic features are conveniently clustered around it. Christchurch's bowling green must surely have the best outlook of any of its kind, for it stands amid the ruins of **Christchurch Castle**, probably built by the Normans in around 1100 to protect the town's river access. The castle was taken by Cromwell's troops during the Civil War and when hostilities ended Cromwell had it torn down, leaving it in the ruined state in which it remains. Steps lead to the top of the motte on which the castle was built and it is worth the short climb to see the remaining stonework and for the views over the town.

Within the castle precinct beside the river are the roofless remains of **Constable's House**, a 12th-century chamber block with a rare surviving Norman chimney. From here you can walk along the mill stream (Convent Walk) past the priory and onwards to the point where the stream meets the River Stour, near Place Mill. In

"Christchurch's bowling green must surely have the best outlook of any of its kind, for it stands amid the ruins of Christchurch Castle."

the **Priory Gardens** is a handsome mausoleum for a Mrs Perkins, who died in 1783. She reportedly had a horror of being buried alive and so asked that she be laid to rest in the mausoleum at the entrance to the school so she could be heard if she revived. She left instructions that the coffin should not be sealed and she should be able to unlock the door of the mausoleum from the inside. Her wishes were carried out but when her husband died in 1803, her body was removed, the mausoleum sold and re-erected here.

A sculpture by Jonathan Sells in the gardens has a humorous take on the history of the priory; the images include one monk climbing on the shoulders of another to feed birds. It was erected in 1994 to commemorate the priory's 900th anniversary.

Place Mill (BH23 1BY ✆ 01202 487626 ☺ Apr–Oct 11.00–17.30 Tue–Sun & bank holidays) was used to grind corn until 1908 and, although no longer in working order, it has been restored and opens in spring and summer as an art gallery and craft workshop. It is listed in the Domesday Book of 1086 as Prior's Mill. Near Place Mill is the quay, where you can **hire small boats** and potter upstream along the River Stour. I spent a very relaxing

"I spent a very relaxing hour taking a boat up the river, which flows gently at this point, passing carefree swans, ducks and moorhens."

hour taking a boat up the river, which flows gently at this point, passing carefree swans, ducks and moorhens drifting in and out of the reeds and golden water lilies. The river gives you a totally different perspective on the town and you can't help but covet the houses with gardens running down to the water and private moorings. You can also hire a self-drive motor boat or a rowing boat further upstream from **Tuckton Tea Gardens** (✆ 01202 429119 ☺ Feb–Dec), a riverside café. Boat hire is also available at Wick, outside the Captain's Club Hotel. The **Wick Ferry** (✆ 01202 429119 ☺ Easter–Oct 10.00–17.30 daily; Nov–Mar 10.00–16.00 Sat–Mon) runs across the River Stour between Wick Village (on the Hengistbury Head side of the harbour) and Christchurch. Simply beckon to the ferryman and he will gladly pick you up. A **vintage ferry service** (✆ 01202 429119 ⌖ bournemouthboating.co.uk ☺ Easter–Oct 10.00–17.00 daily) operates boats built in 1934–35 between Tuckton Tea Gardens, Wick Ferry, Christchurch Quay and Mudeford Sandbank.

From the quay you can often see ponies or cattle grazing on the meadows almost surrounded by water, creating the illusion of an island inhabited by marooned livestock. Behind the meadows, **Stanpit Marsh Nature Reserve** juts out into the harbour on the northern side, giving the waterway its narrow appearance. A visitor centre fleshes out detail on the resident wildlife of this habitat, made up of salt marsh with creeks and salt pans, reed beds, freshwater marsh, gravel estuarine banks and sandy scrub. Although it is boggy in parts, you can walk through the reserve. In the 18th century Stanpit Marsh was a favourite haunt of smugglers, who landed their contraband at Mudeford Quay and brought it across the harbour and up the narrow channels that cut across the marsh.

Christchurch town centre is a pleasing blend of Georgian and older buildings, such as the delightfully wonky, thatched 13th-century building at 11 Church St. It is distinguishable by its medieval timber frame and thatched roof. On the other side of the road is Ducking Stool Walk, which leads along the river to a replica **ducking stool**, installed in 1986. Records show that the ducking stool was used in Christchurch from at least the mid 14th century. It was a humiliating punishment largely reserved for scolds (women accused of verbal abuse or other anti-social behaviour). The last recorded use of a ducking stool in England is 1809.

It is worth popping into the **Red House Museum and Gardens** (Quay Rd, BH23 1BU ✆ 01202 482860; free admission) for an insight into the archaeology and social history of the area. The building was constructed in 1764 as a workhouse; upstairs is a collection of finds excavated during the building of Bournemouth, while the ground floor has an array of more recent items and changing art and photography exhibitions.

A pleasant coastal walk leads from **Mudeford Quay**, a working quay piled high with lobster pots, to **Highcliffe Beach**. The beach stretches for four miles and is divided into areas known as Avon, Friars Cliff, Steamer Point and Highcliffe Castle. You will pass colourful beach huts and have views across to the Isle of Wight and The Needles; a couple of cafés along the way provide handy stopping-off points. Avon Beach offers excellent windsurfing.

St Catherine's Hill Nature Reserve (BH23 6BQ) lies north of the town and provides commanding views of the town and surrounding area. It has probably served as a lookout point since prehistoric times and there is evidence of Bronze Age and Iron Age settlement here. The heathland and coniferous forest provide a habitat for smooth snakes, sand lizards, Dartford warblers, nightjars and abundant butterflies. You can leave your car in the small car park at the bottom of St Catherine's Hill Lane, or on surrounding residential roads, and walk up from there.

"You will pass colourful beach huts and have views across to the Isle of Wight and The Needles."

STEVE POWELL

DORSET COUNCIL

RED HOUSE MUSEUM AND GARDENS/HCT

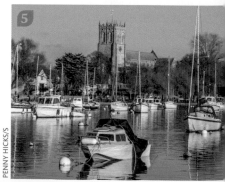

PENNY HICKS/S

Christchurch Priory

christchurchpriory.org ⊙ 10.00–17.00 daily

A characterful cobbled street lined with shops and restaurants leads to the longest parish church in England – it is so long it looks almost as if it has been stretched lengthways. There is so much to see within that it is just as well there are hugely knowledgeable volunteer guides on hand to point you in the right direction. The church has been considerably added to since it was first built in the 11th century and therefore displays a catalogue of architectural styles from Norman to Renaissance. Thankfully, during the Dissolution Henry VIII abandoned his plans to pull down the church in a merciful response to a plea from the townspeople, instead giving permission for it to be used as the parish church.

At the end of the 11th century Ranulf Flambard (later Bishop of Durham) decided to build a church to replace the 7th-century Saxon one that existed on the site of the current priory but he elected to build it on St Catherine's Hill, about two miles away, so that the new Norman church would be visible for miles around.

The townspeople objected – they wanted the church built in the town on the same spot as the Saxon one. Flambard ignored their wishes and in 1094 preparations began to build the church on St Catherine's Hill. After the stones that were laid out on the hill were repeatedly moved overnight to the site of the Saxon church, Flambard conceded to build the church there, citing divine intervention.

"It is said that a mysterious carpenter helped with the building and was never present for meals or to collect wages."

Talk of miraculous happenings continued throughout the construction. It is said that a mysterious carpenter helped with the building and was never present for meals or to collect wages. Then there is the **miraculous beam**, still visible at the rear of the lady chapel – a large beam was cut from the New Forest for the roof but when it was brought to the church it was found to be too short. The workers returned the following morning to find it was the perfect length and already installed in its intended position. The mysterious carpenter was not seen again

◀ **1** The River Avon flows through beautiful Christchurch. **2** Bournemouth Aviation Museum. **3** Pond dipping at Avon Heath Country Park. **4** The Red House Museum, Christchurch. **5** Christchurch Priory is the largest parish church in England.

and was assumed to be Jesus. Until that point the intended name was church of the Holy Trinity but because of the miracles it became known as Christchurch.

The **lady chapel** was completed and vaulted early in the 15th century, and features what is thought to have been the first pendant vault (a decorative pendant hanging from the vaulted ceiling) in England. Above the lady chapel, reached by climbing 75 steps, is St Michael's Loft, originally a school for novice monks and later for local boys; it now contains a **museum** on the history of the priory (☉ May–Oct).

The absorbing **reredos** behind the high altar is essentially Jesus's family tree caricatured – it illustrates the prophecy in the book of Isaiah: 'And there shall come forth a shoot out of the stem of Jesse, and a branch shall grow out of his roots.' It dates from around 1350 and is remarkably well preserved.

The oak **misericords** are mostly from the 1520s, although four date from the early 13th century and are thought to be the oldest in England. Misericords are seats designed to prevent monks falling asleep during services – if they did so, the seats fell forward with a loud crash. Each seat has a carving, either human or animal or a blend of the two. Look out for the depiction of a fox in the pulpit and geese underneath, a cheeky ecclesiastical metaphor.

"Look out for the depiction of a fox in the pulpit and geese underneath, a cheeky ecclesiastical metaphor."

The large **memorial** of 1500 to Margaret, Countess of Salisbury, is ornately carved and exquisite but tells a chilling tale. The countess was punished for the sins of her son; Henry VIII had her beheaded at the age of 74 because her son had published criticisms of the king. Henry VIII refused to allow her to be buried in her chantry in Christchurch and she was interred in the Tower of London's cemetery for traitors.

For a small fee, you can do a private tour which includes climbing the 176 steps to the top of the 15th-century **tower** accompanied by a steward; you are rewarded with memorable views over the town, harbour and surrounding countryside.

Boating around Christchurch

The boating companies at the quay provide boat hire for pottering along the River Stour and some also offer cruises. Most boat-hire companies only operate between Easter and October.

⚓ BOAT HIRE & CRUISES

Bournemouth Boating Services 323 Belle Vue Rd, Bournemouth BH6 3BA ✆ 01202 429119 ⊘ bournemouthboating.co.uk. Operates the Wick Ferry between Wick village and Christchurch. Hires self-drive motorboats for exploring the river from Christchurch Quay, Tuckton Tea Gardens and near the Wick Ferry. Rowing boats are also available for hire at Tuckton Tea Gardens, near the café (⊙ Feb–Dec). In summer it offers hour-long boat cruises followed by a barbecue.

H2O Powerboat Experience Christchurch Quay, Christchurch, BH23 1BY ✆ 07547 188633 ⊘ h2opowerboatexperience.co.uk. Offers blasts in a RIB to the Isle of Wight or Old Harry Rocks.

Mudeford Ferry Mudeford Quay ✆ 07968 334441 ⊘ mudefordferry.co.uk. Offers trips across to Mudeford Sandbank as well as themed cruises.

Quay Leisure Hire Christchurch Quay, BH23 1BY ✆ 07582 969151 ⊘ willowwaymarina. co.uk. Hires out self-drive boats for up to six people to explore the River Stour.

Fishing around Christchurch

Anglers are well catered for, with opportunities for excellent sea, coarse and fly fishing in and around Christchurch. The harbour is good for bass and mullet during spring and summer, while Mudeford and Hengistbury Head yield mackerel, sea bream, wrasse and the occasional cod. Some of the best river fishing in England is available at the acclaimed Royalty Fishery (⊘ swlakestrust.org.uk) on the River Avon and the Throop Fishery on the Stour, where you can expect to hook barbel, chub, roach, carp and pike. Permits are available from Davis Tackle (75 Bargates, BH23 1QE ✆ 01202 485169 ⊘ davistackle.co.uk).

Highcliffe Castle

Rothesay Dr, Highcliffe BH23 4LE ✆ 01202 093377 ⊘ highcliffecastle.co.uk ⊙ house: 10.00–16.00 Sun–Thu; gardens and tea rooms: from 07.00 daily

There can be few stately homes with a better location than Highcliffe, which stands looking out to sea from its clifftop. The house was built in the 1830s by Lord Stuart de Rothesay, an eminent diplomat, using materials salvaged from medieval French buildings, including gargoyles and coloured glass windows. It is this Norman and Renaissance carved stone, along with the castle's Gothic revival features, that makes it appear older than it is. It remained a family home until the 1950s but was severely damaged by fire in the following decade, and only the shell of the building remains. Nevertheless, it is widely recognised as one of the best surviving houses in the Romantic and Picturesque styles of architecture. Highcliffe was bought and renovated by Christchurch Borough Council and now hosts a range of events throughout the year, from concerts to murder-mystery suppers. You can linger in the 14-acre clifftop grounds and walk down the steps to the beach below.

The tea rooms serve Dorset cream teas, cakes and light lunches.

Bournemouth Aviation Museum

Merritown Ln, Hurn BH23 6BA ✐ 01202 473141 ⊘ aviation-museum.co.uk

On the B3073 Bournemouth International Airport perimeter road, this is a hands-on museum, run as a charity and staffed by enthusiastic and knowledgeable volunteers. You are encouraged to climb into aircraft and twiddle the knobs; a flight simulator allows you to play pilot. Expect excited children clambering into the helicopter, fighter planes and double-decker bus and wrestling with the controls. The aircraft are scattered in a field, rather than in a hangar, and the planes taking off and landing at the airport add to the atmosphere.

⅋ FOOD & DRINK

A market is held every Monday (◔ 09.00–16.00) in Saxon Square. An annual food festival in May (⊘ christchurchfoodfest.co.uk) features demonstrations and special offers in the town's eateries.

Beach House Mudeford Sandbank, Hengistbury Head BH6 4EN ✐ 01202 423474. An excellent casual restaurant among the beach huts on Mudeford Sandbank, with views across Christchurch Harbour to the Priory. Specialises in fresh seafood. Adjacent, a small shop sells essentials and take-away food. If you arrive in your own boat, you can moor outside the restaurant. Pet friendly. Gets very busy so booking is recommended. There are late ferries back to Mudeford Quay (◔ 22.00 or 23.00) in summer.

Boat House 9 Quay Rd, BH23 1BU ✐ 01202 480033. In an enviable position on the quay, close to the priory. The menu is creative but unfussy and has something to suit most tastes, from scallops to burgers.

Cat and Fiddle Farm Lyndhurst Rd, Hinton BH23 7DS ✐ 01425 672451. A farm shop, café and pick your own (fruit and vegetables) two miles from Christchurch.

Coast Coffee Co 74 High St, BH23 1BN ✐ 01202 096260. Owner Sally prides herself on her coffee, including exotic single-estate coffees, and her locally sourced light lunches and cakes.

The Jetty 95 Mudeford, BH23 3NT ✐ 01202 400950. Smart but not over-the-top waterfront dining at the Christchurch Harbour Hotel & Spa. Fresh fish is the speciality.

Noisy Lobster Avon Beach BH23 4AN ✆ 01425 272162. In a super location with views of Mudeford Bay and the Isle of Wight. Specialises in locally caught seafood, but there are plenty of non-fishy options.

The Paddle 397 Waterford Rd, Highcliffe BH23 5JN ✆ 01425 275148. A relaxed and popular café, where homemade cakes and wood-fired pizzas take centre stage.

Soho 7 Church St, BH23 1BW ✆ 01202 496140. Close to the priory church, this restaurant has a moody interior and transforms into a popular bar in the evenings. It sits at the base of the castle and at the rear of the restaurant there are views upwards towards the ruins. It serves good pizzas in fancy flavours and other light meals.

Sopley Farm Sopley, Christchurch BH23 7AZ ✆ 01425 672451 ⊘ dantanners.co.uk. A farm shop, bakery and pick your own (berries and vegetables) on the edge of the New Forest.

Tuckton Tea Gardens 323 Belle Vue Rd, Tuckton BH6 3BA ✆ 01202 429119. A riverside café in a peaceful setting, offering minigolf and boat hire. On a sunny day, sit in the gardens and watch the boats go by.

6 AVON HEATH COUNTRY PARK

BH24 2DH ✆ 01425 478082 ⊙ 08.00–dusk daily; visitor centre 11.00–16.00 daily; admission is free but parking is charged

Two miles west of Ringwood off the A31, Avon Heath is an important area of lowland and wet heath, acid grassland and heather. Managed by Dorset County Council in conjunction with the RSPB, the 580 acres are home to rare species, including Dartford warblers, nightjars and woodlarks.

You can walk or cycle along marked trails, and for families there are activity trails and play equipment. A visitor centre provides information on the park and there are live feeds from wildlife cameras, plus a hide for watching the wildlife visiting the feeders. It's dog-friendly, and you can picnic or use the café.

WIMBORNE MINSTER & SURROUNDS

Wimborne Minster is an attractive riverside town with an impressive minster church. Nearby is the National Trust **Kingston Lacy Estate** with its manor house, parkland and **Badbury Rings**, an Iron Age hillfort in an appealing countryside setting. Kingston Lacy has the distinction of being the National Trust's largest lowland property, with a working estate encompassing three villages, a dozen farms, a farm shop and an extensive network of footpaths and bridleways. It is well worth a visit.

7 WIMBORNE MINSTER

If you're arriving from the north, Wimborne Minster, usually shortened to Wimborne, is the last pleasantly sized Dorset town before you hit the heavily populated area around Poole and Bournemouth. Although just five miles north of Poole, it retains a rural flavour and streets full of character. History and tree trails are available from ⊘ wimbornehistorytrail.uk to help you explore.

The town stands on the confluence of the rivers Stour and Allen and dates back to the early 8th century. It became an important market town although trade had slowed by the 18th century when John Hutchins noted in his *History of Dorset*, 'the town of Wimborne is much more remarkable for what it was formerly than for what it is now'.

Whatever the changing fortunes of the town, its principal feature has remained constant through the ages, the **minster of St Cuthburga** (see opposite), the two towers of which dominate the town's skyline.

Narrow streets following medieval lines lead away from the minster to the well-preserved town centre with its abundance of historic buildings. One of them, a townhouse dating from the 16th century, contains the **Museum of East Dorset** (page 347).

The square is a natural focal point and is surrounded by some elegant Georgian buildings. A farmers' market is held here on the third Saturday of the month (⊙ 09.00–13.00).

Leading away from the square is Mill Lane, which takes you to the River Allen. The **Town Mill** at the end of the lane was erected as a corn mill in 1771, but was severely damaged by fire in 1952.

The town is blessed with some good **independent shops**, such as Gullivers Bookshop (47 High St, BH21 1HS ✆ 01202 882667 ⊙ 09.00–17.30 Mon–Sat), which has been selling books on Dorset, as well as maps, jigsaw puzzles and stationery, since 1969. As you wander the town centre, you may hear the bellowing tones of the local **town crier**, Chris Brown, also known as DJ Dapper Dan. He is always happy to stop for a chat and is a great source of knowledge on the area. When not performing his town-crier role, he is a DJ with a special interest in reggae music.

To the northwest of the minster, the **Cornmarket** with its market house of 1738 is the original marketplace. Nearby is **Dreamboats** (Tarrant Close, BH21 1QU ✆ 07761 816796 ⊘ dreamboats.org; ⊙ May & Jun 11.00–17.00 Sat, Sun & public & school holidays; Jul–Aug daily;

Sep Sat & Sun), where you can hire a rowing boat, paddleboard, kayak or canoe and mess about on the River Stour. It is a registered charity staffed by volunteers and was created in 2000 to promote enjoyment of the river, in particular for children.

Wimborne always seems to have plenty going on. The **Tivoli Theatre** (West Borough, BH21 1LT ☎ 01202 885566 🖥 tivoliwimborne.co.uk) is a very active Art Deco cinema and theatre built in 1936 in a Georgian townhouse.

A highlight on the local calendar is the annual **Wimborne Folk Festival** (🖥 wimbornefolk.co.uk) in June, one of the largest folkdancing and music events in the country.

Wimborne has a rather grim skeleton in its closet: it was the birthplace of one of the chief suspects in the Jack the Ripper murders. **Montague John Druitt** was born in Wimborne in 1857 into a medical family – his father William was the town's leading surgeon. They lived at the substantial Westfield House, which has now been converted into flats; he was educated at Winchester College and New College, Oxford and went on to become a schoolmaster and a barrister. Druitt was found drowned in the River Thames on 31 December 1888, believed to have committed suicide; his death coincided with the cessation of the Jack the Ripper murders. Druitt is buried in Wimborne Cemetery, now something of a macabre tourist attraction.

"As you wander the town centre, you may hear the bellowing tones of the local town crier, Chris Brown, also known as DJ Dapper Dan."

The minster

🕑 09.30–17.30 Mon–Sat, 14.30–17.30 Sun; guides available in summer

As you approach the minster church in summer, pink flowering chestnuts provide a decorative surround. Its foundations date back to around AD705, when Cuthburga, sister of Ine, king of the West Saxons, founded a nunnery here. In its heyday it housed around 500 nuns (there was also a monastery) but it was destroyed by the Danes in 1013 and never rebuilt. The Saxons obviously considered the church significant as King Alfred buried his brother Ethelred here in AD871 after he was mortally wounded in a battle near Cranborne.

The largely Norman building dates from around 1120 to 1180, although the transepts are 14th century and the western end is from 1500. On the northern exterior of the west tower a **quarter jack** strikes his bells every quarter of an hour. He was created in 1612 and reportedly began life as a monk but during the Napoleonic Wars was given a makeover to create the appearance of a grenadier. Attached to the quarter jack on the inside of the tower is a colourful **astronomical clock** built in the 14th century by a monk at Glastonbury in Somerset. Its rudimentary depiction of the solar system is rather beautiful and resembles a drawing from a children's storybook in its simplicity, but its operation is remarkably clever. The sun points to the time of day and the gold-and-black sphere represents the moon; both move around the face of the clock. The sphere shows the moon's phases with appropriate portions showing black and gold: when there is a full moon it is completely golden and when there is a new moon it is completely black.

"Its rudimentary depiction of the solar system is rather beautiful and resembles a drawing from a children's storybook."

Opposite the clock is the simple memorial to **Isaac Gulliver**, better known as 'the King of the Smugglers'. In 1782, the government offered a pardon to smugglers who joined the navy, or who could find substitutes to undertake military service on their behalf. For a man of Gulliver's means, buying a substitute was no problem and thus he cleared his name and became a respected member of Wimborne society. It is also said that he uncovered a French plot to kill King George III and this contributed to his receiving a pardon.

The minster contains other fascinating tombs, such as that of **Anthony Ettricke**, known as 'the man in the wall', whose plans to be interred in Wimborne Minster on his death were scuppered when he fell out with church authorities and announced he would not be buried either in the church or outside it. He subsequently relented but to save face was buried in the wall. All in all his demise was rather farcical: he had predicted he would die in 1693 and had that date engraved on his memorial but ended up living until 1703 and so the date had to be altered. In the north chapel is an ornate and colourful monument of 1606 to **Sir Edmund Uvedale**, whose effigy is lying on his side in full armour and appears to have two left feet. While it would nice to think this was a hint that he was an appalling dancer, it is believed to have been the result of a restoration by a sculptor who was having a bad day.

Above the choir vestry and reached via a spiral staircase is the **chained library** (☺ times vary), established in 1686. It is one of just five surviving chained libraries in the world and with over 400 leather-bound books it is the second largest of its kind in England. It was one of England's first public libraries. The books weren't always chained because originally only people who worked in the church could read them. In 1695, a Middle Temple lawyer called Roger Gillingham came up with the idea of attaching each book to a chain so that local shopkeepers or the 'better class of person', could study in the free library and perhaps make a better life for themselves. The library holds some literary treasures, including the Regimen Animarum or Direction of Souls manuscript written in 1343 on vellum (lambskin) with a quill pen and ink made from oak apples. Only two other copies survive and this one is believed to be the finest of the three. Also in the library are the collected works of St Anselm of 1495, some of the earliest printings of the Gospels, Bibles in Hebrew, Greek and Latin, and a book bound for the court of Henry VIII. Another notable item is Walton's Polyglott Bible in no fewer than nine languages.

Museum of East Dorset

23–27 High St, BH21 1HR ✐ 01202 882533 ✐ museumofeastdorset.co.uk ⊙ 10.00–16.00 Mon–Sat

A characterful building dating from the 16th century houses this museum dedicated to local history. A series of galleries shows the area through various eras, including finds from the excavation of a nearby Roman site. The childhood gallery has a colourful array of toys and games, which might hold a few surprises for today's children. The long, narrow garden running down to a stream behind the house has a wealth of traditional, mature fruit trees and colourful flowerbeds – this is also where you will find the tea room.

Wimborne Model Town

16 King St, BH21 1DY ✐ 01202 881924 ✐ wimborne-modeltown.com ⊙ Apr–Oct 10.00–17.00 daily

This intricately detailed 1:10 scale model of Wimborne Minster was begun in the 1940s and finished in 1951. It depicts the town in the 1950s and yet it still bears a striking resemblance to the town today, aside perhaps from the goods on sale in the shops. Seeing what was on offer in a rural town centre in the post-war years will be quite a revelation for many. The model is surrounded by beautiful gardens

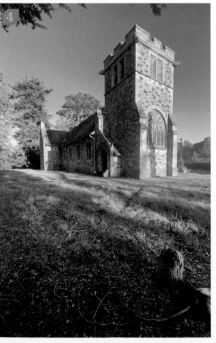

CHRISDORNEY/S

ROGERMECHAN/S

WALFORD MILL CRAFTS

ALEXANDRA RICHARDS

ALEXANDRA RICHARDS

TERRY YARROW/S

and the tea rooms are good value. In the mid-1980s the model town had fallen into disrepair and a group of townsfolk managed to save it from developers; they found a new site for it and it reopened here in 1991.

Deans Court

BH21 1EE ✆ 01202 849314 ⬧ deanscourt.org ☉ guided tours only, selected dates; see website for details

On the outskirts of town, south of the minster, an elegant house lies at the heart of the Deans Court estate, which has been owned by the Hanham family since 1548. The house and grounds can only be visited by guided tour on certain days of the year (see website). The guided tours focus on the family history and some impressive ancestral portraits help to tell the story.

The estate hosts events and courses and some of the outbuildings have been converted to provide a vintage shop and small café (page 350). The rivers Allen and Stour meet at Deans Court, and you can fish for trout here (book via the website).

Walford Mill Craft Centre

Stone Lane, BH21 1NL ✆ 01202 841400 ⬧ walfordmillcrafts.co.uk ☉ 10.00–17.00 Tue–Sat, 11.00–16.00 Sun

Just north of Wimborne on the River Allen, this converted mill provides a peaceful setting for its exhibitions of crafts, plus a craft shop and cafe (page 350). Some of the artisans, including a silk weaver and printmaker, have studios on site and you can see them at work. The centre also runs craft workshops and there are craft markets on the second Saturday of the month.

⑪ FOOD & DRINK

A market is held on Friday at The Allendale Centre on Hanham Road (BH21 1AS).

The Cloisters 40 East St, BH21 1DX ✆ 01202 880593 . A homely café serving tasty food made from scratch with locally sourced ingredients. Takes pride in the quality of its coffee.

◀ 1 Wimborne Minster town centre. 2 Crafting at Walford Mill Craft Centre. 3 The Chained Library in the minster at Wimborne Minster. 4 St Stephen's, Pamphill. 5 Kingston Lacy House & Estate. 6 Visit Abbot Street Copse, Pamphill in May for wonderful bluebell displays.

Deans Court Cafe Deans Court Ln, BH21 1EE ☎ 01202 639249. A 1932 squash court has been reinvented as a homeware shop with a vintage flavour. It's in a quiet spot, with a pleasant courtyard and small café in a converted garage. The café sources food locally, and there are vegan and gluten-free options.

Little Pickle Café Walford Mill Crafts, Stone Ln, BH21 1NL ☎ 07961 347721. In a delightful riverside location at the Walford Mill Craft Centre, you can enjoy local produce and good homemade food in a peaceful setting. Very dog-friendly. It is family run and there is a genuine emphasis on being local and sustainable.

Number 9 on The Green 7 Cook Row, BH21 1LB ☎ 01202 887765. This café is conveniently located in a characterful building opposite the minster and offers tasty breakfasts, light lunches and cream teas.

Riverside Café 10a The Old Mill, Mill Lane, BH21 1LN ☎ 07816 462184. An informal, friendly café on the River Allen, with indoor and outdoor seating. It serves unpretentious, traditional dishes and is a good option for the budget-conscious. The building is reputedly haunted by a 15-year-old girl who worked at the mill and drowned in the mill race while trying to escape the unwanted advances of the miller.

Trehane Nursery Staplehill Rd, Wimborne BH21 7ND ☉ trehaneblueberrypyo.co.uk. Pick-your-own blueberries in July and August. There is a café on site. Cut flowers are also sold in summer.

The Wimborne Pig 26 West Borough, BH21 1NF ☎ 01202 888565. Run by a mother and son team, this is a small restaurant with a big reputation. It showcases local, seasonal produce with flair. Many of the vegetables come from their own allotment and they smoke local meat and fish in their smokehouse.

8 PAMPHILL

Around a rambling green in this delightful village of the Kingston Lacy Estate huddles a group of 17th- and 18th-century cottages, many of them thatched. St Stephen's Church at the northern end of the green was built in 1907 in Arts and Crafts Gothic style as a memorial to Walter Ralph Bankes, who left £5,000 in his will for the purpose of 'building and endowing a church at Kingston Lacy'. The interior is simple with fine carved oak from the Kingston Lacy Estate. In the grounds are mature trees and behind the church is a small woodland, which you can walk through to reach the farm shop (see opposite).

"A bridge leads over the river to Eye Mead, a wetland habitat with abundant birdlife."

The nearby Pamphill First School and Nursery began life as an almshouse and school in 1698, and the 17th-century manor house was built by a steward to the Bankes family. In spring, Pamphill's **Abbott Street Copse** is awash with bluebells, offering up an unmistakably English scene.

It is a short stroll along quiet lanes from the village to the **River Stour** (or you can drive and leave your car in the parking area just off Cowgrove Road), where there is an inviting picnic spot at **Eyebridge**. A bridge leads over the river to Eye Mead, a wetland habitat with abundant birdlife. National Trust signs suggest walks along the river, including towards Cowgrove, another small village on the Kingston Lacy Estate.

¶¶ FOOD & DRINK

Pamphill Dairy Farm Shop and Café Pamphill BH21 4ED ✆ 01202 857131 ⬦ pamphilldairy.co.uk. Close to the church in a converted dairy, this complex comprises a well-stocked farm shop, butcher, café and various independent outlets. Products on sale at the butcher include Red Devon beef produced on the Kingston Lacy estate. The café serves wholesome, farmhouse cooking. There is a vending machine on site selling milk from the local Allen Valley herd, and their delicious ice cream is also on sale.

Vine Inn Pamphill BH21 4EE ✆ 01202 882259. A classic country pub offering local cider, simple food and two tiny, characterful bars.

Kingston Lacy House & Estate

Wimborne Minster BH21 4EA ✆ 01202 883402 ⊙ house: usually 11.00–17.00 daily (top floor closed Nov–Mar); garden: 10.00–18.00 daily; National Trust

One of Dorset's grandest houses, Kingston Lacy was the home of the Bankes family from 1665 until 1981, when Ralph Bankes bequeathed the magnificent 8,500-acre estate to the National Trust. Today it draws a steady flow of visitors for its sumptuous interior, outstanding collections of art and Egyptian artefacts, and serene grounds.

The house was built in 1665 for Sir Ralph Bankes after the family's original home, Corfe Castle, was destroyed by Cromwell's troops during the Civil War. It was significantly altered in 1835 at the behest of William Bankes, who employed the noted architect Sir Charles Barry (whose other projects included work on the Houses of Parliament and Westminster Bridge) to refurbish it in flamboyant Italian Renaissance style. The house's lavish interior is in large part the legacy of William Bankes, who was an avid traveller, collector and Egyptologist and who enjoyed displaying his trinkets at the family home. From 1841 he lived in Italy, where he had fled to avoid prosecution for homosexual acts, but he continued to collect and send back furniture and fittings for the house, and may have made the occasional clandestine visit to his beloved Kingston Lacy.

A grand marble staircase leads from the entrance hall; William Bankes bought it in Italy and it was part of Barry's brief in the refurbishment that he alter the house to accommodate it. Perched in niches in the walls on the first floor loggia are bronze statues of King Charles I, Sir John Bankes and Dame Mary Bankes. Dame Mary is depicted holding the keys to Corfe Castle, which she successfully defended during the Civil War until Cromwell's men gained access via subterfuge and destroyed the building (page 273). The real keys to Corfe

"The house's lavish interior is in large part the legacy of William Bankes, who was an avid traveller, collector and Egyptologist."

Castle hang over the fireplace in the library, which is adorned with family portraits and Guido Reni's ceiling fresco, *The Separation of Night and Day*. Still sporting their 18th-century design are the library and saloon, created when Henry Bankes (William's father) renovated the house in the 1780s. The saloon contains some of the house's exceptional art collection, including paintings by Rubens and Titian. In the dining room, look out for the walnut shutters featuring ornate carvings of food. Designed by William Bankes, the detail is incredible – look carefully and among the fruit you'll even spot a bee. William built the oppressively flamboyant Spanish room to display his Spanish art collection; the room is a monument to opulence, with gilded leather wall hangings and a gilded ceiling taken from a Venetian palace. The Egyptian room contains objects Bankes collected while on expeditions in Egypt and represents the largest private collection of Egyptian artefacts in the UK. The Egyptian theme extends to the grounds of the house, where an obelisk from the 2nd century BC has stood since 1827. Its journey from Egypt to Kingston Lacy reportedly took 20 years and a team of 19 horses was needed to haul it into place.

The house is surrounded by formal gardens and 250 acres of landscaped parkland, grazed by Red Devon cattle. The garden features an Edwardian Japanese area and a Victorian fernery, which contains over 20 varieties of ferns. Paths lead from the formal gardens through

1 The 16th-century stone bridge at White Mill. **2** Badbury Rings. **3** St Bartholomew's Church, Shapwick. ▶

the park and woodland, awash with daffodils and bluebells in spring. Across the lane is the impressive kitchen garden, where there is a playground and mobile café. Hidden within the woodland not far from the house is a larger playground. Multiple longer walks, bridleways and cycleways lead around the estate, and are mapped in a leaflet available at Kingston Lacy. The red-brick stables of 1880 house a café that serves a wealth of local food, including the estate's Red Devon beef. There is no mistaking that this was the stables as the original stable dividers, hay racks and feeders remain. At Christmas the house and grounds are beautifully decorated and visitors come from miles around to soak up the festive atmosphere.

White Mill

Sturminster Marshall BH21 4BX ✆ 01258 858051 ☉ Apr–Oct noon–17.00 Sat, Sun & bank holidays; National Trust

Even if it isn't open, it is worth driving along the narrow road past White Mill and over the charming bridge nearby to enjoy the incredibly picturesque riverside scene they create. Made of red brick, this former corn mill on the River Stour has a doll's-house quality. Just over half a mile west of Pamphill, White Mill was last rebuilt in 1776 and was worked by tenants of the Kingston Lacy Estate until the late 19th century. The National Trust took over the mill when it was given the estate but it was not until the early 1990s that efforts were made to conserve it, using a photograph from 1900 to assist in the accurate restoration of the exterior; even the dovecotes on the wall are copies of those seen in the photograph. Although some restoration work has been done on the interior, the wooden drive gear, which dates from the 1776 rebuilding, is too fragile to work. The wheels are thought to

"Local legend tells that the bells from the ruined church at Knowlton were stolen and dropped into the millpond by the thieves."

be elm, which is resistant to water and to vibration, while the teeth are likely made of apple wood. Apple was traditionally used to make the teeth as it is more fragile than elm and should anything go wrong the teeth would shear off before more substantial parts were damaged. Local legend tells that the bells from the ruined church at Knowlton were stolen and dropped into the millpond by the thieves, and that they can still be heard ringing.

The statuesque eight-arch **stone bridge** near the mill is thought to date from the 16th century, but its predecessor is referenced in documents from 1175 as 'a bridge on the River Stour adjacent to the White Mill'. Carbon dating of the wooden pilings on which it stands indicate they are 12th century, making this the oldest bridge site in Dorset. A plaque warns: 'Any person wilfully damaging any part of this county bridge will be guilty of felony and upon conviction liable to be transported for life by the court'. The bridge is the ideal vantage point for views along the river, which flows freely here and on the mill side divides around an island draped with silvery willows.

9 SHAPWICK

Across the B3082 from Badbury Rings is the turning to the small village of Shapwick, which lies just over a mile down the lane. On the River Stour, it is an ideal spot to stop off during a walk along the **Stour Valley Way**. Opposite the Anchor pub is the village cross, believed to be of Saxon origin. In 1880 it was destroyed in a brawl and in 1920 the remains were converted into a war memorial.

"Little did the unsuspecting occupant know that they were going to receive an impromptu burial at sea."

St Bartholomew's Church was originally built in the 11th and 12th centuries near an old Roman ford, where the Dorchester to Old Sarum road crossed the river. It is remarkably close to the river and has been known to flood, including during a funeral in 1870 when a torrent of water carried the coffin off down the river, never to be seen again. Little did the unsuspecting occupant know that they were going to receive an impromptu burial at sea. The tower, with its heathstone and flint banding, is thought to have been added in the 14th century, when the height of the roof was raised: coffin lids from that period can be seen supporting the north wall of the nave. Much restored in the late 19th century, the church was until the Reformation connected with a priory. Henry VIII expelled the prior and gave the land and houses to 'my belovit cousin Hussey, the little man but a great General'. The Commissioners of Henry VIII left 'ye one silver cuppe'; this is probably the chalice still used in the church today, which dates from 1527, and is one of the finest of its type in England. In the floor of the church, near the altar, is a gravestone bearing the inscription, 'Anne Butler here beneath is laid, a pious prudent modest maid – 1659': an epitaph of which any girl could be proud.

¶¶ FOOD & DRINK

The Anchor at Shapwick West St, DT11 9LB ℘ 01258 857269. A refurbished gastropub with a sophisticated modern British menu. An ideal stop-off for those walking the Stour Valley Way.

10 BADBURY RINGS

The road to Badbury Rings announces that you are in for something special, with the stately avenue of beech trees along the B3082 providing a fitting approach. It stretches for over two miles and is made up of 731 trees planted in 1835. Sadly, the trees are nearing the end of their natural lives and gaps in the avenue are starting to appear.

Badbury Rings is a memorable spot for a stroll, with far-reaching views from the ramparts of the surrounding countryside, and an abundance of wildflowers, including 14 species of orchid. The Iron Age hillfort was built on a site that was occupied much earlier, as evidenced by the four Bronze Age (2200–800BC) round barrows, the most notable of which are the three that lie just to your right as you travel up the track to the car park. The hillfort itself consists of three concentric, circular ditches with high walls that protect a large central area where the settlement would have been. From the bottom of the ditch to the top of the rampart would have reached a height of some 40ft and, even accounting for 2,000 years of erosion, the ditches are still formidable today. Above the rampart a timber palisade would have been constructed to further protect the settlement on top of the hill, now covered by a small wood. The circular depressions visible in the ground, roughly 10ft in diameter, are evidence of the wattle-and-daub roundhouses.

"Point-to-point racing is steeplechasing for amateurs and has its origins in fox hunting."

Badbury Rings is believed to have been one of several settlements in the area belonging to an ancient Dorset tribe known as the Durotriges. It would almost certainly have fallen to the invading Romans, and was probably taken by the Second Legion Augusta, led by Vespasian under Emperor Claudius. Evidence of the important Roman road from Old Sarum to Dorchester can be seen running to the west of the hillfort; the 22-mile portion of the road from Old Sarum to Badbury Rings is known as Ackling Dyke and is visible as an embankment. To the north this crosses a north–south road, which probably ran from Bath to Poole.

The Romans are thought to have built a town just outside the rings, which they called Vindocladia – the place of white walls. It has been suggested that Badbury Rings could be the Mons Badonicus, where King Arthur and his army defeated the invading pagan hordes of the early 5th century, the Jutes, Angles and Saxons. Ravens, which have always been associated with Arthur, bred here until the late 19th century.

Just below the rings is the **point-to-point** racecourse, the scene of much drama and excitement during the season. Point-to-point racing is steeplechasing for amateurs and has its origins in fox hunting. The sport dates back to 1836 when hunting men used to race their horses from church steeple to church steeple — hence the name 'point-to-point'. The link between these two country sports still exists today: all of the horses that race in a point-to-point have to be qualified out hunting and all of the jockeys have to be a member or subscriber of a hunt.

11 HOLT & HOLT HEATH

Holt was originally the centre of the Royal Forest of Wimborne, mentioned in the Domesday Book, and the area is still well wooded. The **church of St James** is unusual for Dorset, being of red brick. It was completely rebuilt in 1836 but records show a church was repaired here in 1493 so that inhabitants would not have to walk to Wimborne Minster for services.

At 1,200 acres, **Holt National Nature Reserve** is one of Dorset's largest areas of lowland heathland and has to its northwest two areas of ancient woodland (Holt Forest and Holt Wood); the National Trust owns the area and manages it in association with Natural England.

The reserve is particularly fine in July and August when wildflowers are prolific. The heath is home to large populations of Dartford warbler, stonechat and nightjar and it is Dorset's only site for breeding curlew. All six British species of reptile (adder, grass snake, smooth snake, slow worm, sand lizard and common lizard) are present. The reserve offers a quiet retreat from the busy East Dorset coast, and the chance of a leisurely walk or ride.

INDEX

Entries in **bold** refer to major entries; those in *italics* indicate maps.

INDEX OF ADVERTISERS

ALEX STONE

Psychological Thrillers set in Dorset

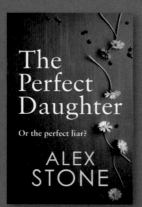

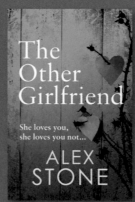

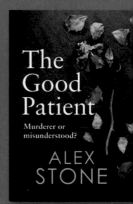

"A brilliant book. I loved it!"
- Bestselling author B.A Paris.

www.AlexStoneAuthor.com
@AlexStoneAuthor

Sign up to my newsletter for
my latest books & events